IN THE SHADE OF THE QUR'ĀN

In the name of God, the Compassionate, the Merciful

Sayyid Quṭb

IN THE SHADE OF THE QUR'ĀN

Fī Ẓilāl al-Qur'ān

VOLUME XVIII

SŪRAHS 78–114 [JUZ' 'AMMA]

Al-Naba' – Al-Nās

Translated and Edited by
Adil Salahi

THE ISLAMIC FOUNDATION
AND
ISLAMONLINE.NET

Published by

THE ISLAMIC FOUNDATION,

Markfield Conference Centre,
Ratby Lane, Markfield, Leicestershire LE67 9SY, United Kingdom
Tel: (01530) 244944, Fax: (01530) 244946
E-mail: i.foundation@islamic-foundation.org.uk
Website: www.islamic-foundation.org.uk

Quran House, PO Box 30611, Nairobi, Kenya

PMB 3193, Kano, Nigeria

ISLAMONLINE.NET,
PO Box 22212, Doha, Qatar
E-mail: webmaster@islam-online.net
Website: www.islamonline.net

British Library Cataloguing-in-Publication Data
Qutb, Sayyid, 1903–1966
In the shade of the Qur'an: Fi zilal al-Qur'an,
Vol. 18: Surahs 78–114: Al-Naba' – Al-Nas
1. Koran – Commentaries
I. Title II. Salahi, M.A. III. Islamic Foundation
IV. Fi zilal al-Qur'an
297.1'227

ISBN 0 86037 374 6
ISBN 0 86037 369 X pbk

Typeset by: N.A.Qaddoura
Cover design by: Imtiaze A. Manjra

Printed and bound in Great Britain by
Antony Rowe Ltd, Chippenham, Wiltshire

بسم الله الرحمن الرحيم

Contents

Transliteration Table

Consonants. Arabic

initial: unexpressed medial and final:

ء	’	د	d	ض	ḍ	ك	k
ب	b	ذ	dh	ط	ṭ	ل	l
ت	t	ر	r	ظ	ẓ	م	m
ث	th	ز	z	ع	‘	ن	n
ج	j	س	s	غ	gh	هـ	h
ح	ḥ	ش	sh	ف	f	و	w
خ	kh	ص	ṣ	ق	q	ي	y

Vowels, diphthongs, etc.

Short:	ـَ	a	ـِ	i	ـُ	u
long:	ـَا	ā	ـِي	ī	ـُو	ū
diphthongs:			ـَوْ	aw		
			ـَىْ	ay		

On the Translation of the Qur'ānic Text

Introduction by Adil Salahi

This volume represents the final part of the work undertaken by Sayyid Quṭb during the 1950s and 60s to explain the meaning of the Qur'ān. It was the first to be published in English and that by the Muslim Welfare House, London, 1979. Since then that edition has been reproduced many times, including several pirate editions. In its original form, this volume was assigned number 30, as it appears in the Arabic edition. This is in line with the original Arabic edition which conformed to the division of the Qur'ān into 30 equal parts, with little consideration given as to where the dividing lines occur. The idea being to enable the reader to recite the Qur'ān once a month, without much difficulty.

When the Islamic Foundation undertook the task of publishing the complete work in English, the decision was taken to dispense with the Arabic arrangement, and instead make the units of the Qur'ānic text, i.e. its *sūrahs*, the basis for arrangement. The Qur'ān contains 114 *sūrahs*, some of which are very short, with no more than one or two lines, while others are very long. Each one though is a complete unit, focusing on a central idea. The first eight volumes of this series contain one *sūrah* each, with the exception of Vol. I, which included the first *sūrah*, which is very short, together with the second, which is the longest in the Qur'ān. Thereafter, we incorporated a number of *sūrahs* into each volume, trying to make them all of similar length. Hence, the change in the number that appears on this volume, making it number XVIII.

But this is not the only change the present volume makes. A thorough revision has been undertaken, with numerous modifications introduced into the English version, including the rendering of Qur'ānic textual meanings. We trust that this has improved the quality of the work presented.

Translating such a work is not an easy task. Most people might appreciate such difficulty if they realized that it also involves rendering the meaning of the Qur'ān into English. The Qur'ān has been translated into English no less than 20 times. George Sale's translation, the first in English, appeared in 1734, followed by J.M. Rodwell's in 1861, then Palmer's in 1880. The twentieth century saw a rapid rise in Qur'ānic translations, with a large number of new versions, many of which were put together by Muslim translators.

It is not our aim to discuss the merits and faults of these translations, nor to make any judgement in favour of any particular one. We only want to say that while most of these translations have considerable merit, an Arabic reader familiar with the language of the Qur'ān finds them inadequate, unable to convey the full meaning of the original text. Indeed, many of the translators have expressed the feeling that their rendering remains short of expressing the full sense of the text. Many resort to adding in parenthesis words and phrases that are not in the original text. They feel that only in this way can they make the English version closer to the Arabic original.

Perhaps this gives us a glimpse of the difficulty of the task of translating the Qur'ān into a European language. It also tells us something about the reasons that have motivated this long line of translators to attempt the same. There is no doubt that each one of them felt that he would be adding something that earlier translations had missed. Otherwise, he would consider himself to be undertaking a needless task. Nonetheless, the process continues, and today and in the future there will be no shortage of Qur'ānic translators who want to bring the art of Qur'ānic translation to a higher level of excellence.

Had the Qur'ān been an ordinary book, written by a human being, and had it been the subject of the efforts of such a long line of translators, we would have had a perfect translation a long time ago. But the fact that both its translators and discerning readers remain unsatisfied with the outcome of these efforts, individually and collectively, poses some questions that are very difficult to answer. Before publishing the first part of his translation, entitled *The Message of the Qur'ān,* the late Muhammad Asad published a pamphlet under the title "Can the Qur'ān Be Translated?" This has now been incorporated as the Foreword to his full translation which he describes as "an attempt – perhaps the first attempt – at a really idiomatic, explanatory rendition of the Qur'ānic message into a European language."

Asad dwells at length on the Qur'ānic characteristic of *ījāz*, or brevity and word economy in Qur'ānic expression. It is this particular characteristic which presents the translator with the greatest difficulty. It is this that compels Asad to add numerous words and phrases in parenthesis in order to make the meaning clear. But word economy in the original text accounts for only one aspect of the difficulties encountered in translating the Qur'ān. If we were to compare the task to that of translating poetry, we can imagine the numerous difficulties the translator has to overcome in rendering the images and associations a poet deliberately brings together when selecting his words. While translating poetry into prose has to deal with this difficulty, the translator may overcome some of his problems by making his rendering somewhat explanatory, occasionally using a phrase in place of a word, or borrowing the occasional image in order to make the product closer to the meanings intended by the poet. But if poetry is to be translated into poetry, the difficulties are multiplied. The translator feels that he has no option but to depart from the form used in the original and focus on the ideas conveyed so as to express them in a different form, tapping the images and associations of the target language.

Although no translator of the Qur'ān has tried to emulate the Qur'ānic style in his rendering of its text into a new language, the difficulties encountered by Qur'ānic translators are akin to those encountered when translating poetry into poetry. The problem here is that the Qur'ān often uses the connotations of its words to the full, intending its statements to have all the associations that may be derived from a thorough examination and analysis. To give a simple example, we may cite verse 53 of *Sūrah* 20, which speaks of God as having made the earth man's cradle. The sentence is phrased in such a way that it also means that God has made the earth level for man's benefit.

What would a translator do in a situation like this, where he is unable to make a choice one way or the other? If he is lucky, he will find in his target language one word which conveys both meanings, even though it may not be the first choice for either sense. But this is hardly likely; certainly not in English. So his only option is to make a preference and discard the other sense. This is what all translators do, but it means that we may find that in some translations the verse is rendered in one sense and in the other sense in others. Whichever sense is used, discerning readers who are familiar with the original verse will consider the rendering inadequate.

Yet this is a simple case where the choice made by the translator or the commentator has no legal implications. Sometimes different connotations may have such implications, and the translator will face criticism if his choice of meaning does not take these implications into account.

Related to this is a whole range of stylistic characteristics that writers and translators use. When dealing with an ordinary text, a translator may allow himself the liberty to change the order of some words or phrases separated by conjunctions, or to add or omit some functional words that do not change the overall meaning of the translated text. While literary writing uses such conjunctions and functional words in a deliberately selective manner, many writers use them in a casual way. This accounts for the liberality of translators' approach to such stylistic features. A translator aims to make his final product better suited to the idiomatic usage in his target language, while expressing the ideas in the original text as fully as possible. The Qur'ān, however, uses such words and features very deliberately. Muslims believe that every particle, let alone a verb or adjective, is specifically selected, purposely employed. A translator is bound to have difficulty in this area, because stylistic features and functional words differ greatly from one language to another, particularly in discerning usage. When he is bound by usage in the source language, this may sound rather arbitrary in the target language. The use of 'and' at the beginning of verses is very frequent in the Qur'ān. Some translators retain it in every instance, while others choose to omit it, because they feel that it does not add to the meaning in the English version.

Qur'ānic translators have always agonized over their task. For example, should they make their translation literal or adopt an idiomatic style? Literal translation tries to be faithful not only to the meaning of the text in hand, but also to the construction of its sentences. There are certain merits achieved by literal translation, particularly when we are translating important documents. Hence, many international organizations insist on this type of translation, sacrificing easier readability in the interest of avoiding problems that may arise from different language usage. But in translating the Qur'ānic text, literal translation has led many an intelligent reader to formulate a grossly mistaken view of the language and style of the Qur'ān. Idiomatic usage, on the other hand, may sacrifice some important connotations in the interest of readability. The dilemma is not an easy one to resolve.

When the Qur'ān was revealed the Arabs who were the first to listen to it wondered a great deal about its style. They realized that it was unique in its beauty. They could not compare it to any type of literary expression known to them. But when eventually they wished to make such a comparison, they always tended to compare it to poetry. Yet the Qur'ān has nothing of the apparent features of poetry.

Translators of the Qur'ān have also faced a similar problem. Do they introduce a poetic element in their rendering of the meaning of the Qur'ān, or do they confine themselves to prose? N.J. Dawood, a non-Muslim who has continuously endeavoured to improve his highly readable translation of the Qur'ān, has also sought to maintain some rhythm in his text. A.J. Arberry, on the other hand, has tried to produce a work which varies its rhythm where the Qur'ān changes rhythm to heighten its effect. The translations of Dawood and Arberry are miles apart in their approach, with Dawood adopting a highly idiomatic style.

Another dilemma that has faced Qur'ānic translators has been whether to confine themselves to the text in hand or to add explanatory words or phrases. Pickthall chose the former while Asad preferred the latter. No two translations of the same text could differ more widely. What we have to realize here is that the Qur'ān often deletes words and phrases that can be easily understood, leaving some indications to clearly retain the full meaning, while limiting the deletion to words only. With such brevity of style, the translator is bound to encounter enormous difficulties. Should he add words to express the full meaning, including that of the deleted words, he would be accused of adding what is not in the Qur'ān. If he confines himself to rendering only the words and expressions of the text, the outcome is often poorly constructed, losing clear and concise meaning.

In his masterly work, *The Qur'ān: An Eternal Challenge,* Muhammad Abdullah Draz discusses at length the unique characteristics of the Qur'ānic style. When we examine these, we are bound to conclude that the task of translating it will always defy even the most accomplished of literary translators. Moreover, he shows in a highly scrupulous manner how each *sūrah* manifests a remarkable unity of theme. This is an aspect that has defied Orientalists who often accuse the Qur'ān of lacking coherence or of being too disjointed. A translator is supposed to be the most discerning of readers. Yet this aspect of the Qur'ānic style has presented some translators with an additional difficulty. But not so those, like Yusuf Ali, Asad and Dawood, who have been able to relate all verses in a *sūrah* to its central theme.

The very idea of translating the Qur'ān has been subject to controversy right from the early days of Islam, when God's last message to mankind started to win new believers who belonged to non-Arabic speaking communities. The question whether such people may offer their obligatory prayers in their own languages was raised and discussed. The unanimous view of scholars throughout history has been that this is not possible. All worshippers must read from the Qur'ān in its original form, i.e. in Arabic, because that is God's word as He revealed it. A new Muslim who does not speak Arabic must learn a small portion of the Qur'ān to offer his prayers.

Yet the question does not stop there. A non-Arab Muslim needs to know more about his faith, and to learn the divine message. He may be able to learn how to read Arabic, but not everyone can learn the language up to a standard that enables him to understand the meaning of the Qur'ān. Translation was felt to be a necessity, particularly with the spread of Islam among non-Arabs. For many centuries, the Arabs have represented only a minority among Muslims. Today, Arabs form less than 15 percent of all Muslim peoples. Hence, the need to understand God's message is particularly acute.

In the early generations when the Muslim state was one of the world's major powers, and Islamic civilization was setting the pace in all branches of science, Arabic was learnt in all new Muslim areas. Indeed, Arabic was the second language of all Muslim peoples. Every schoolchild learnt Arabic. But this could not be maintained for two reasons: the great and rapid increase in non-Arabic Muslim populations, and, later, the gradual weakening of the position of Muslims on the world stage. Thus, translations of the Qur'ān into the languages of other Muslim communities began to appear. But these took different approaches. Even today we have copies of the Qur'ān in Arabic with the meanings of individual words written under them in such languages as Urdu and Turkish. Needless to say, this is not a translation of the text but a sort of a dictionary arranged in the particular order of the Qur'ān.

Scholars' opposition to a complete, translated copy of the Qur'ān arose from their fear that such a translation could supplant the Arabic original and facilitate non-Arabic speaking Muslims' satisfaction with such a translation, feeling no need to learn God's word as He revealed it. They felt that the Qur'ān, God's word, is expressed only in the Arabic tongue, while any rendering of its meaning into another language is the translator's version expressing his own understanding of it. The difficulties to which we have referred, combined with a translator's misunderstanding of some statements in the Qur'ān, make the presence of serious errors in a Qur'ānic translation a distinct possibility. No one wants to be party to such errors in conveying God's message. Hence, scholars have always been reluctant to sanction translations of the Qur'ān.

Are such fears justified? By way of an answer, I quote from the introduction written by Pickthall to his own translation of the Qur'ān: "The Koran cannot be translated. That is the belief of old-fashioned Sheykhs and the view of the present writer. The Book is here rendered almost literally and every effort has been made to choose befitting language. But the result is not the Glorious Koran, that inimitable symphony, the very sounds of which move men to tears and ecstasy. It is only an attempt to present the meaning of the Koran – and peradventure something of the charm – in English. It can never take the place of the Koran in Arabic, nor is it meant to do so."

Pickthall had recourse to considerable help from some Egyptian scholars and he presented the result of his efforts to Al-Azhar, the great seat of Islamic learning. The Rector, however, would not sanction publication until Pickthall said that he intended to call it: "A translation of the meanings of the Qur'ān". The same has been done with later editions of Yusuf Ali's version, which is perhaps the most frequently published translation, particularly by Islamic authorities.

While fully agreeing with Pickthall's view, expressed above, the present writer does not see the significance achieved by describing an effort as 'a translation of the meanings of the Qur'ān' rather than 'a translation of the Qur'ān'. Every translation is an expression in another language of the meaning of a text or a statement. Moreover, a text is an expression of an idea, or its translation into words and sentences according to rules of grammar and syntax. So, when we say 'a translation of the meanings of the Qur'ān,' the words, 'the meanings of', are redundant and rather confusing. They may quieten the worries of devout scholars and believers who wish to preserve the position of the Qur'ān, but they are otherwise needless. When we translate the Qur'ān, we simply try to express the meaning of its text to the best of our ability and understanding. If we make a mistake, we acknowledge our human frailty and pray to God for forgiveness.

Qur'ānic study in English has moved on with the rapidly increasing needs of English-speaking Muslim communities. There is definitely a need for a thorough interpretation of God's message in an easy to read style. This cannot come about through a translation of the text of the Qur'ān, excellent as this may be. Rather, it requires a commentary on the Qur'ān, taking into account the Prophet's explanation of God's words and the way he and his Companions put them into practice. It must also benefit by the long tradition of Qur'ānic study which makes the full meanings of the Qur'ān as understood by the Arabs in whose language it was revealed.

Rarely has a generation passed since the revelation of the Qur'ān without new commentaries being published by scholars of high standing. Later commentaries have always benefited by earlier works and by what might have been acquired by human knowledge. Our present generation is no exception. The present commentary is one of the best that have been written for several centuries. It benefits from its author's resourceful literary talent. And it steers away from controversy. Hence, its translation could be of immense value to new generations of English-speaking Muslims.

In translating this book our aim is to render into English a work that seeks to make the meanings of the Qur'ān readily available and accessible to the ordinary reader. The author's aim was to make these meanings available today in the same way as the Arabs addressed by the Qur'ān for the first time understood them. In this endeavour, he was especially successful. If we can do something similar in English, we contribute to a proper understanding of the message of Islam, free from the distortions of those who carry it to opposite extremes of stringency or indiscipline.

In our rendering of the Qur'ānic text, we have not 'adopted' a single translation of the many that are available. Nor have we tried to produce our own without recourse to the efforts of those who have trodden this path before us. Instead, we have mainly relied on three translations that combine merits of style and understanding. These are the translations produced by Muhammad Asad, Yusuf Ali and N.J. Dawood. The choice is based on merit. Asad wanted his translation to be both idiomatic and explanatory, and he relied heavily on Yusuf Ali's translation, adding numerous improvements, while making every effort to be very faithful to the text and to capture the finer nuances of the words and phrases used. Dawood was largely successful in his aim to present a flowing, readable text reflecting the meaning of the Qur'ān. To all three we are much indebted, as we are to other translations of the Qur'ān which we often consulted. In a few instances, our rendering differs not only with all three translations, but also with all others. These are instances where we felt that a certain aspect of the meaning of the text had been missed out, or where Sayyid Quṭb highlights a particular meaning that further demonstrates his profound understanding of the Qur'ān.

London **Adil Salahi**
Al-Muḥarram 1425
February 2004

SŪRAH 78

Al-Naba'

(The Tiding)

Al-Naba' (The Tiding)

سُورَةُ النَّبَإِ

In the name of God, the Merciful, the Beneficent.

بِسْمِ اللَّهِ الرَّحْمَٰنِ الرَّحِيمِ

About what are they asking? (1)

عَمَّ يَتَسَاءَلُونَ ﴿١﴾

About the fateful tiding (2)

عَنِ النَّبَإِ الْعَظِيمِ ﴿٢﴾

on which they dispute. (3)

الَّذِي هُمْ فِيهِ مُخْتَلِفُونَ ﴿٣﴾

No indeed; they shall certainly know! (4)

كَلَّا سَيَعْلَمُونَ ﴿٤﴾

Again, no indeed; they shall certainly know! (5)

ثُمَّ كَلَّا سَيَعْلَمُونَ ﴿٥﴾

Have We not spread and levelled the earth, (6)

أَلَمْ نَجْعَلِ الْأَرْضَ مِهَادًا ﴿٦﴾

and made the mountains as pegs? (7)

وَٱلْجِبَالَ أَوْتَادًا ﴿٧﴾

We created you in pairs, (8)

وَخَلَقْنَـٰكُمْ أَزْوَٰجًا ﴿٨﴾

and made your sleep a cessation of activity. (9)

وَجَعَلْنَا نَوْمَكُمْ سُبَاتًا ﴿٩﴾

We made the night a mantle, (10)

وَجَعَلْنَا ٱلَّيْلَ لِبَاسًا ﴿١٠﴾

and appointed the day for gaining a livelihood. (11)

وَجَعَلْنَا ٱلنَّهَارَ مَعَاشًا ﴿١١﴾

We built above you seven mighty ones, (12)

وَبَنَيْنَا فَوْقَكُمْ سَبْعًا شِدَادًا ﴿١٢﴾

and placed therein a blazing lamp. (13)

وَجَعَلْنَا سِرَاجًا وَهَّاجًا ﴿١٣﴾

We send down out of the rain-clouds water in abundance, (14)

وَأَنزَلْنَا مِنَ ٱلْمُعْصِرَٰتِ مَآءً ثَجَّاجًا ﴿١٤﴾

by which We bring forth grain and varied plants, (15)

لِّنُخْرِجَ بِهِۦ حَبًّا وَنَبَاتًا ﴿١٥﴾

and gardens thick with trees. (16)

وَجَنَّـٰتٍ أَلْفَافًا ﴿١٦﴾

Fixed is the Day of Decision. (17)

إِنَّ يَوْمَ ٱلْفَصْلِ كَانَ مِيقَـٰتًا ﴿١٧﴾

On that day the Trumpet is blown and you shall come in crowds, (18)

يَوْمَ يُنفَخُ فِى ٱلصُّورِ فَتَأْتُونَ أَفْوَاجًا ﴿١٨﴾

and heaven is opened, and becomes gates, (19)

وَفُتِحَتِ ٱلسَّمَآءُ فَكَانَتۡ أَبۡوَٰبٗا ١٩

and the mountains are made to move away, and seem to have been a mirage. (20)

وَسُيِّرَتِ ٱلۡجِبَالُ فَكَانَتۡ سَرَابًا ٢٠

Hell stands as a vigilant watch guard, (21)

إِنَّ جَهَنَّمَ كَانَتۡ مِرۡصَادٗا ٢١

a home for the tyrants and the transgressors. (22)

لِّلطَّٰغِينَ مَـَٔابٗا ٢٢

Therein they shall abide for ages, (23)

لَّٰبِثِينَ فِيهَآ أَحۡقَابٗا ٢٣

tasting neither coolness nor any drink, (24)

لَّا يَذُوقُونَ فِيهَا بَرۡدٗا وَلَا شَرَابًا ٢٤

except boiling fluid and decaying filth: (25)

إِلَّا حَمِيمٗا وَغَسَّاقٗا ٢٥

a fitting recompense. (26)

جَزَآءٗ وِفَاقًا ٢٦

They did not expect to be faced with a reckoning, (27)

إِنَّهُمۡ كَانُواْ لَا يَرۡجُونَ حِسَابٗا ٢٧

and roundly denied Our revelations. (28)

وَكَذَّبُواْ بِـَٔايَٰتِنَا كِذَّابٗا ٢٨

But We have placed on record every single thing, (29)

وَكُلَّ شَيۡءٍ أَحۡصَيۡنَٰهُ كِتَٰبٗا ٢٩

[and We shall say]: 'Taste this, then; the only increase you shall have is increase of torment.' (30)

فَذُوقُواْ فَلَن نَّزِيدَكُمْ إِلَّا عَذَابًا ﴿٣٠﴾

The God-fearing shall have a place of security, (31)

إِنَّ لِلْمُتَّقِينَ مَفَازًا ﴿٣١﴾

gardens and vineyards, (32)

حَدَآئِقَ وَأَعْنَٰبًا ﴿٣٢﴾

and high-bosomed maidens, of equal age, for companions, (33)

وَكَوَاعِبَ أَتْرَابًا ﴿٣٣﴾

and a cup overflowing. (34)

وَكَأْسًا دِهَاقًا ﴿٣٤﴾

There they shall hear no idle talk, nor any falsehood. (35)

لَّا يَسْمَعُونَ فِيهَا لَغْوًا وَلَا كِذَّٰبًا ﴿٣٥﴾

Such is the recompense of your Lord, a truly sufficient gift. (36)

جَزَآءً مِّن رَّبِّكَ عَطَآءً حِسَابًا ﴿٣٦﴾

Lord of the heavens and earth and all that lies between them, the Most Gracious, with whom they have no power to speak. (37)

رَّبِّ ٱلسَّمَٰوَٰتِ وَٱلْأَرْضِ وَمَا بَيْنَهُمَا
ٱلرَّحْمَٰنِ لَا يَمْلِكُونَ مِنْهُ خِطَابًا ﴿٣٧﴾

On the day when the Spirit and the angels stand in ranks, they shall not speak, except those to whom the Most Gracious has given leave, and who shall say what is right. (38)

يَوْمَ يَقُومُ ٱلرُّوحُ وَٱلْمَلَٰٓئِكَةُ صَفًّا
لَّا يَتَكَلَّمُونَ إِلَّا مَنْ أَذِنَ لَهُ
ٱلرَّحْمَٰنُ وَقَالَ صَوَابًا ﴿٣٨﴾

That day is a certainty. Let him who will seek a way back to his Lord. (39)	ذَٰلِكَ ٱلْيَوْمُ ٱلْحَقُّ فَمَن شَآءَ ٱتَّخَذَ إِلَىٰ رَبِّهِۦ مَـَٔابًا ﴿٣٩﴾
We have forewarned you of an imminent scourge, on the day when man will look on what his hands have forwarded and the unbeliever will cry: 'Would that I were dust!' (40)	إِنَّآ أَنذَرْنَٰكُمْ عَذَابًا قَرِيبًا يَوْمَ يَنظُرُ ٱلْمَرْءُ مَا قَدَّمَتْ يَدَاهُ وَيَقُولُ ٱلْكَافِرُ يَٰلَيْتَنِى كُنتُ تُرَٰبًۢا ﴿٤٠﴾

Overview

This volume contains 37 *sūrahs* forming what is traditionally known as the thirtieth part of the Qur'ān, on the basis that divides the Qur'ān into 30 parts of equal length, so as to make it easy to read the whole book once a month. Yet this part has a special, distinctive colour. All the *sūrahs* it includes are Makkan, except two, The Clear Proof and Divine Help, which take numbers 98 and 110 respectively. Although they vary in length, they are all short. More significant, however, is the fact that they form a single group with more or less the same theme. They enjoy the same characteristics of rhythm, images, connotations and overall style. They are, indeed, like a persistent and strong knocking on a door, or a series of loud shouts seeking to awaken those who are fast asleep, or those who are drunk and have lost consciousness, or are in a night club, completely absorbed in their dancing or entertainment. The knocks and the shouts come one after the other: Wake up! Look around you! Think! Reflect! There is a God! There is planning, trial, liability, reckoning, reward, severe punishment and lasting bliss. The same warning is repeated time after time. A strong hand shakes them violently. They seem to open their eyes, look around for a second and return to unconsciousness. The strong hand shakes them again. The shouts and knocks are repeated even more loudly. They may wake up once or twice to say obstinately, "No!" They may stone the person warning them or insult him and then resume their position of inattention. He shakes them anew.

This is how I feel when I read this part of the Qur'ān. It places much emphasis on a small number of significant facts and strikes certain notes which touch people's hearts. It concentrates on certain scenes in the universe and in the world of the human soul, as well as certain events which take place on the Day of Decision. I note how they are repeated in different ways, which suggests that the repetition is intended.

This is how one feels when one reads: "*Let man reflect on the food he eats.*" (80: 24) Or: "*Let man then reflect of what he is created.*" (86: 5) Or: "*Let them reflect on the camels, how they were created; and heaven, how it is raised aloft; and the mountains, how they are hoisted; and the earth, how it is spread out.*" (88: 17–20) Or: "*Which is stronger in constitution: you or the heaven He has built? He raised it high and gave it its perfect shape, and gave darkness to its night, and brought out its daylight. After that He spread out the earth. He brought out water from it, and brought forth its pastures; and the mountains He set firm, for you and your cattle to delight in.*" (79: 27–33) Or: "*Have We not spread and levelled the earth, and made the mountains as pegs? We created you in pairs, and made your sleep a cessation of activity. We made the night a mantle, and appointed the day for gaining a livelihood. We built above you seven mighty ones, and placed therein a blazing lamp. We send down out of the rain-clouds water in abundance, by which We bring forth grain and varied plants, and gardens thick with trees.*" (78: 6–16)

We entertain similar feelings when we read: "*Let man reflect on the food he eats: how We pour down the rain in torrents, and cleave the earth in fissures; how We bring forth the corn, the grapes and the fresh vegetation, the olive and the palm, the dense-treed gardens, the fruit-trees and the green pastures, for you and your cattle to delight in.*" (80: 24–32) Or: "*O man, what has lured you away from your gracious Lord, who created and moulded you and gave you an upright form. He can give you whatever shape He wills.*" (82: 6–8) Or: "*Extol the limitless glory of the name of your Lord, the Most High, who creates and proportions well, who determines and guides, who brings forth the pasturage, then turns it to withered grass.*" (87: 1–5) Or: "*We indeed have created man in the finest form, then We brought him down to the lowest of the low, except for those who believe and do good deeds; for theirs shall be an unfailing recompense. Who, then, can henceforth cause you to deny the Last Judgement? Is not God the most just of judges?*" (95: 4–8) Or: "*When the sun is darkened, when the stars fall and disperse, when the mountains are made to move away, when the camels, ten months pregnant, are left untended, when the wild beasts are brought together, when the seas are set alight, when people's souls are paired (like with like), when the infant girl, buried alive, is asked for what crime she was slain, when the records are laid open, when the sky is stripped bare; when hell is made to burn fiercely, when paradise is brought near, every soul shall know what it has put forward.*" (81: 1–14) Or: "*When the sky is cleft asunder, when the stars are scattered, when the oceans are made to explode, when the graves are hurled about, each soul shall know its earlier actions and its later ones.*" (82: 1–5) Or: "*When the sky is rent asunder, obeying her Lord in true submission; when the earth is stretched out and casts forth all that is within her and becomes empty, obeying her Lord in true submission.*" (84: 1–5) Or: "*When the earth is rocked by her [final] earthquake, when the earth shakes off her burdens, and man asks: 'What is the matter with her?' On that day she will tell her news, for your Lord will have inspired her.*" (99: 1–5)

We experience the same feeling as we meditate on the scenes of the universe portrayed at the beginning or in the middle of some of the *sūrahs* in this part of the Qur'ān: "*I swear by the turning stars, which move swiftly and hide themselves away, and by the night as it comes darkening on, and by the dawn as it starts to breathe.*" (81: 15–18) Or: "*I swear by the twilight, and by the night and what it envelops, and by the moon in her full perfection.*" (84: 16–18) Or: "*By the dawn, by the ten nights, by that which is even and that which is odd, by the night as it journeys on!*" (89: 1–4) Or: "*By the sun and his morning brightness, by the moon as she follows him, by the day, which reveals his splendour, by the night, which veils him. By the heaven and its construction, by the earth and its spreading, by the soul and its moulding and inspiration with knowledge of wickedness and righteousness.*" (91: 1–8) Or: "*By the night when she lets fall her darkness, by the day in full splendour, by Him who created the male and the female.*" (92: 1–3) Or: "*By the bright morning hours, and the night when it grows still and dark.*" (93: 1–2)

Strong emphasis is laid, throughout this part of the Qur'ān, on the origin of man as well as on the origin of life, in both its vegetable and animal forms. Emphasis is also given to various scenes in the universe, such as the Day of Resurrection, which is described in different places as the Greatest Catastrophe, the Stunning Blast, the Enveloper, etc. Scenes of the reckoning, fine reward and severe retribution are also given prominence. They are drawn with images which leave a stunning effect. All these are given as a proof of the reality of creation and the elaborate planning of the universe by God, as well as evidence confirming the reality of the life to come, and its decisive reckoning. These scenes are, at times, combined with scenes of the fate of some of the communities which rejected the divine messages. The whole of this part exemplifies all this. We will make, however, a brief reference in this introduction to some examples.

The present *sūrah*, The Tiding, lays its emphasis on the realities of creation and resurrection, and on scenes of the universe and the hereafter. The same applies to the next *sūrah*, The Pluckers. The third *sūrah* in this part, The Frowning, begins with a reference to a certain incident during the early days of Islam. The rest of the *sūrah* is devoted to a discussion of the origins of man and plants before it tackles what it terms the 'Stunning Blast':

> *On that day everyone will forsake his brother, his mother and his father, his wife and his children: for each one of them will on that day have enough preoccupations of his own. Some faces on that day shall be beaming, smiling and joyful. Some other faces on that day shall be covered with dust, veiled with darkness.* (80: 34–41)

Sūrah 81, The Darkening, portrays scenes of the great upheaval which envelops the whole universe on the Day of Resurrection. It also draws some fine and inspiring scenes of the universe in the context of affirming the reality of revelation and the Prophet's honesty. The next *sūrah*, Cleaving Asunder, also contains scenes of universal upheaval, coupled with scenes of perfect happiness and eternal suffering in the hereafter. As it portrays these it aims to shake and awaken people's hearts: "*O man, what has lured you away from your gracious Lord?*" (82: 6) Scenes of both types are also portrayed in *Sūrah* 84, The Rending. *Sūrah* 85, The Constellations, touches very briefly on aspects of the universe and the hereafter by way of introduction to its main theme. The *sūrah* then tackles the history of a group of believers who were subjected to extreme fire torture by the unbelievers. It also states how God will inflict greater and more severe torture with fire on those unbelievers.

The next *sūrah*, The Night Visitor, draws some scenes of the universe and speaks of the origins of man and plants prior to an oath, by all these, affirming that "*This is surely a decisive word; it is no idle talk.*" (86: 13–14) *Sūrah* 87, The Most High, speaks of creation, planning, divine guidance and the various stages of the growth of pastures. All this is given by way of introduction to the theme of the hereafter, reckoning, reward and retribution. The next *sūrah*, The Enveloper, provides some images of the believers' happiness in the hereafter, and the unbelievers' misery. It also draws attention to the creation of camels, heaven, earth and the mountains. The same applies right through to the end of this part, with the exception of a few *sūrahs* which are devoted to the exposition of the fundamental principles of faith, such as those *sūrahs* entitled Purity of Faith, The Unbelievers, Small Kindness, The Declining Day, Power, and Divine Help. Also excepted are a few *sūrahs* which give encouragement and solace to the Prophet and direct him to seek refuge with his Lord against all evil, such as those entitled, The Morning Hours, Solace, Abundance, The Daybreak, and Mankind.

Another aspect of this part is its artistic use of fine expressions, images, rhythm, meter and rhyme to touch upon areas of exceptional beauty in the human soul and in the universe at large. It does this in order to achieve better results as it addresses those who have lost sight of the truth, trying to attract their attention and awaken their feelings. This is clearly evident, for example, in its portrait of the stars as they turn in their orbits, rise and set, in the image of deer disappearing in their dens then appearing again, its image of the night as a living being walking quietly in the dark, and the dawn breathing with the first rays of light: "*I swear by the turning stars, which move swiftly and hide themselves away, and by the night as it comes darkening on, and by the dawn as it starts to breathe.*" (81: 15–18)

It is also clear in the description of sunset, the night and the moon: "*I swear by the twilight, and by the night and what it envelops, and by the moon in her full perfection.*" (84: 16–18) And in the scenes of dawn and the travelling night: "*By the dawn, by the ten nights, by that which is even and that which is odd, by the night as it journeys on!*" (89: 1–4) Or: "*By the bright morning hours, and the night when it grows still and dark.*" (93: 1–2)

Again it is markedly evident in the inspiring address to the human heart: "*O man, what has lured you away from your gracious Lord, Who created and moulded you and gave you an upright form? He can give you whatever shape He wills.*" (82: 6–8) The same applies to scenes from heaven: "*Other faces on that day are jocund, well-pleased with their striving, in a sublime garden, where they hear no babble.*" (88: 8–11) And in a similar fashion it applies to scenes from hell: "*But he whose weight is light in the balance, shall have the abyss for his home. Would that you knew what that is like! It is a scorching fire.*" (101: 8–11)

Allegory is often employed and an unusual derivation is sometimes preferred in order to obtain the intended musical effect. All this shows the artistry which so entirely pervades this part of the Qur'ān.

The present *sūrah* is a good example of the general bent of this part, its themes, the fundamental principles it seeks to establish, the scenes and images it portrays, its inferences, its music and its fine touches, as well as its artistic selection and manipulation of terms and expressions to enhance its effect. It opens with a form of question imparting a sense of gravity to the matter in dispute, yet it is something that admits of no dispute. This is followed by an immediate warning of what will happen on the day when they will realize its nature: "*About what are they asking? About the fateful tiding on which they dispute. No indeed; they shall certainly know! Again, no indeed; they shall certainly know!*" (Verses 1–5) Discussion of this fateful tiding is then temporarily dropped. The *sūrah* draws attention to what we see around us in the universe and what we feel in our souls which give an unmistakable indication of what will follow: "*Have We not spread and levelled the earth, and made the mountains as pegs? We created you in pairs, and made your sleep a cessation of activity. We made the night a mantle, and appointed the day for gaining a livelihood. We built above you seven mighty ones, and placed therein a blazing lamp. We send down out of the rain-clouds water in abundance, by which We bring forth grain and varied plants, and gardens thick with trees.*" (Verses 6–16)

After this multitude of images taken from actual life the *sūrah* takes up the issue of the event of which they have been warned. It explains to them its nature and how it takes place: "*Fixed is the Day of Decision. On that day the Trumpet is blown and you shall come in crowds, and heaven is opened, and becomes gates, and the mountains are made to move away, and seem to have been a mirage.*" (Verses 17–20)

Then follows a scene of misery, that is at once both violent and infinitely powerful: "*Hell stands as a vigilant watch guard, a home for the tyrants and the transgressors. Therein they shall abide for ages, tasting neither coolness nor any drink, except boiling fluid and decaying filth, a fitting recompense. They did not expect to be faced with a reckoning, and roundly denied Our revelations. But We have placed on record every single thing, [and We shall say]: 'Taste this, then; the only increase you shall have is increase of torment.'*" (Verses 21–30) The scene of happiness, on the other hand, overflows with beauty: "*The God-fearing shall have a place of security, gardens and vineyards and high-bosomed maidens, of equal age, for companions, and a cup overflowing. There they shall hear no idle talk, nor any falsehood. Such is the recompense of your Lord, a truly sufficient gift.*" (Verses 31–36)

The *sūrah* closes with a distinctive note which accompanies a majestic scene of the day when all this takes place: "*Lord of the heavens and earth and all that lies between them, the Most Gracious, with whom they have no power to speak. On the day when the Spirit and the angels stand in ranks, they shall not speak, except those to whom the Most Gracious has given leave, and who shall say what is right. That day is a certainty. Let him who will seek a way back to his Lord. We have forewarned you of an imminent scourge, on the day when man will look on what his hands have forwarded and the unbeliever will cry: 'Would that I were dust!'*" (Verses 37–40)

This is the fateful tiding about which they ask, and this is what will happen on the day when they realize the true nature of this great event.

Needless Enquiry

> *About what are they asking? About the fateful tiding on which they dispute. No indeed; they shall certainly know! Again, no indeed; they shall certainly know!* (Verses 1–5)

The *sūrah* opens by shunning the enquirers and the enquiry. It wonders that anyone should raise doubts about resurrection and judgement, which were central points of bitter controversy. For the unbelievers could hardly imagine that resurrection were possible, despite the fact that it is most logical. The *sūrah* asks what they are talking about: "*About what are they asking?*" (Verse 1) We are then given the answer. The question is not meant to solicit information but rather draws attention to the subject of their questions and stating its nature: "*About the fateful tiding on which they dispute.*" (Verses 2–3) The answer does not name the event but describes it to enhance the feeling of wonder and amazement at such people. The dispute was between those who believed in resurrection and those who denied it, but the questions were raised by the latter only.

The *sūrah* does not provide any more details about the event in question. It simply describes it as great before adding an implicit threat which is much more frightening than a direct answer. "*No indeed, they shall certainly know! Again, no indeed, they shall certainly know!*" (Verses 4–5) The phrase, '*no indeed,*' is used here as the nearest possible rendering of the Arabic term, *kallā*, which denotes strong shunning. The whole sentence is repeated to add force to the threat implied.

Around Man's World

The *sūrah* then puts aside, apparently, that great event which is at the centre of controversy, only to pick it up later on. We are then taken on a quick round of the universe in which we see a multitude of scenes, creatures and phenomena. Contemplation of which strongly shakes any human heart: "*Have We not spread and levelled the earth, and made the mountains as pegs? We created you in pairs, and made your sleep a cessation of activity. We made the night a mantle, and appointed the day for gaining a livelihood. We built above you seven mighty ones, and placed therein a blazing lamp. We send down out of the rain-clouds water in abundance, by which We bring forth grain and varied plants, and gardens thick with trees.*" (Verses 6–16)

In this round we traverse the vast universe, observing a great multitude of scenes and phenomena, which are sketched out with great economy of words. This helps make the rhythm sharp and penetrating, like an incessant hammering. The form of questioning implying a statement is also used here deliberately. It may be likened to a strong hand shaking those who are still unaware. It draws their attention to all these creatures and phenomena which provide strong evidence of the deliberate planning and designing which go into their creation, the ability to create and re-create, and the wisdom behind creation, which dictates that no creature will be left out of the great reckoning. Hence we come back to the fateful tiding, the subject of the argument.

The first leg in this round takes us across the earth and the mountains: "*Have We not spread and levelled the earth, and made the mountains as pegs?*" (Verses 6–7) Both facts mentioned here can be easily recognized and appreciated by everyone. Indeed, even primitive man can be affected by them once his attention is drawn to them.

As human knowledge advances and man acquires better insight into the nature of the universe and its varied phenomena, his appreciation of these two aspects is enhanced. He recognizes more fully God's elaborate planning of the universe, the accurate balance maintained between the individual kinds of creation and their respective needs, the preparation of the earth for human existence and man's adaptability to his environment. That the earth has been specially prepared as a comfortable home for human life in particular is irrefutable evidence of the careful designing of this existence. It is sufficient to break one relation in the conditions available on earth or in the conditions and proportions required for life and the earth would no longer be that comfortable home for mankind to tread on.

Man recognizes easily, by eyesight, that the mountains are very much like the pegs of a tent. From the Qur'ān we learn that they steady the earth and keep its balance. This may be because the height of the mountains offsets the depth of the seas and oceans. An alternative explanation is that mountains balance out the inner with the outer movements of our planet. Or probably they merely increase the weight of the earth at certain spots to prevent its violent shaking with earthquakes, volcanoes or internal tremors. There may be another explanation not yet known to man. In the Qur'ān we find numerous references to natural laws the essence of which was completely unknown to man at the time of revelation, but knowledge of which was acquired a few centuries later.

In its second leg, this round touches upon various aspects of human existence: "*We created you in pairs.*" (Verse 8) Again, this is a well established phenomenon, easily recognized by every human being. God has made the survival and continuity of mankind conditional on each of the two different sexes, male and female, playing its role in life fully. Not much knowledge is required to appreciate what this involves of comfort, pleasure and recreation. Hence the Qur'ānic statement stands to be appreciated by every generation in every society according to its abilities and knowledge.

Beyond the primitive importance of this fact there is the wider scope of contemplation as man's knowledge increases and his feelings become more refined. We may contemplate how one sperm produces a male child while another, absolutely similar to the first, produces a female one. Our contemplation, however penetrating, is bound to lead us to the inescapable conclusion that it is God's perfect planning which gives each sperm its distinctive characteristics, so that we may eventually have a male and a female, for life to continue.

"*And made your sleep a cessation of activity. We made the night a mantle, and appointed the day for gaining a livelihood.*" (Verses 9–11) God has willed that sleep should overpower man and make him lose consciousness and activity. When asleep, man is in a state which is unlike life and unlike death. It ensures rest for his body and mind and compensates both for whatever effort they have exerted during wakefulness. All this happens in a way the true nature of which man cannot conceive. His will plays no part in it and it is impossible for him to discover how it happens. When awake, man does not know his condition while he is asleep. He is also unable, when asleep, to observe his condition and how sleep affects him. It is one of the secrets of man's constitution and of all living creatures, unknown except to the Creator Who has made sleep essential for life. For there is no living creature who can stay without sleep except for a limited period. If he were forced, by external means, to stay awake, he would certainly die.

Sleep does not merely satisfy some of man's physical and mental needs. It is, indeed, a truce for the human soul from the fierce struggle of life. It is a respite which allows man to lay down his armour, willingly or unwillingly, and enjoy a period of perfect peace which he needs no less than he needs food and drink. Sometimes, when one is low-spirited, mentally exhausted, possessed by fear and alarm, sleep may overpower one, for a few minutes perhaps, and bring about a total change in one's condition. Sleep does not merely renew one's strength, but it may revive one in such a way as to wake up a new person altogether. This is miraculous, yet very true. It happened on a large scale to the early Muslims who fought in the Battles of Badr and Uḥud. God mentions both occasions in the Qur'ān, reminding the Muslims of His favours. "*He made slumber fall upon you, as an assurance from Him.*" (8: 11) "*Then, after sorrow, He let peace fall upon you, in the shape of a slumber which overtook some of you.*" (3: 154) Many other people have had the same experience in similar conditions.

Cessation of activity and consciousness through sleep is a prerequisite for the continuity of life. Yet it can be given only by God. It is mentioned here by way of inviting man to contemplate his own creation and constitution.

God's perfection of creation has provided a correspondence between the movement of the universe and that of living creatures. As man requires sleep after his day's work, so God has provided the night as a covering mantle for man to enjoy his slumber. Day is also provided as a period of activity for man to pursue his livelihood. Thus perfect harmony is established. The world is perfectly suited to the creatures who live in it, and God's creation is endowed with those characteristics which fit in easily and gently with the universe. What perfect planning by a scrupulous Designer!

The final leg of this round touches on the creation of heaven: "*We built above you seven mighty ones, and placed therein a blazing lamp. We send down out of the rain-clouds water in abundance, by which We bring forth grain and varied plants, and gardens thick with trees.*" (Verses 12–16) The seven mighty ones God has built above the earth are the seven heavens or skies, the precise nature of which is known only to God. They may be seven galaxies which have a bearing on our planet or on our solar system. The phrase may also refer to something else that is unknown to us. What we know for certain, however, is that these seven have a strong constitution and do not easily disintegrate. This much we know about the stars and we observe in what we call 'the sky'. The *sūrah* also points out that the construction of the seven mighty ones is in perfect harmony with the creation of the earth and the world of man. This is implied in the following verses: "*And placed therein a blazing lamp.*" (Verse 13) This is a reference to the sun which shines and gives the heat necessary for the earth and its living creatures. It also plays an important part in forming the clouds by evaporating sea water: "*We send down out of the rain-clouds water in abundance.*" (Verse 14) The Arabic text refers to these clouds as something squeezable. But who squeezes them to extract their juice? The winds, maybe, or perhaps some kind of electric charge in the atmosphere! Beyond both types, however, there is the hand of the Designer, who has assigned to everything in the universe its respective qualities.

The use of the word '*lamp*' to refer to the sun is very apt, for a lamp gives heat and light. It also shines as if it is ablaze. The heat and the light provided by the sun combine with the water flowing in abundance, time after time, from the 'squeezable' clouds to help the seeds send out their shoots. This is how grains, vegetables, bushes and wide-branching trees grow. This consonance in the design of the universe could not have been achieved without God's careful planning. Any man can appreciate this if his attention is drawn to it. If he acquires advanced knowledge, he finds even more consonance and congruity in the universe, which leaves him wondering in complete amazement. He then finds completely insupportable the argument that all this is the result of coincidence. He considers those who evade admitting the fact of elaborate and conscious planning pig-headed and unworthy of respect.

Reckoning and Reward

All this has been for work and pleasure, but there are reckoning and reward to follow, on the appointed day: "*Fixed is the Day of Decision. On that day the Trumpet is blown and you shall come in crowds, and heaven is opened and becomes gates, and the mountains are made to move away, and seem to have been a mirage.*" (Verses 17–20) Creation is not without purpose. The Creator, who has accurately measured human life and carefully provided perfect harmony between it and the universe, will not let people just live and die in vain. Reason cannot accept that those who do good and the evildoers should both end in dust. The rightly-guided and the straying folk, the just and the tyrants cannot all share the same fate. There must be a day when everything is judged and evaluated. The day is appointed by God: "*Fixed is the Day of Decision.*" (Verse 17)

It is a day when upheaval overtakes the universe and destroys its systems. "*On that day the Trumpet is blown and you shall come in crowds, and heaven is opened and becomes gates, and the mountains are made to move away, and seem to have been a mirage.*" (Verses 18–20) The '*Trumpet*' is a kind of horn of which we know nothing except its name and that it will be blown. We need not waste our time trying to discover how, for such discovery will not strengthen our faith.

God has revealed to us what we need to know of the secrets of the universe so that we may not waste our energy in the futile pursuit of useless knowledge. We can imagine, however, a blast on a Trumpet which people answer by arriving in droves. We can visualize the scene whereby all the generations of mankind rise up, walking in their multitudes, from all directions, to attend the great reckoning. We can imagine the fearful sight of people rising from their graves and the great, huge, endless crowd they form. We can feel the horror of the day, people's helplessness and fear. We do not know where all this will happen, nor when, for the universe is full of great events: "*And heaven is opened and becomes gates, and the mountains are made to move away, and seem to have been a mirage.*" (Verses 19–20)

Heaven, the mighty heaven, is opened up so that it becomes gates. It is, as described elsewhere in the Qur'ān, rent asunder. So, it will look very unfamiliar to us. The firmly dug-in pegs, i.e. the mountains, are made to move away. They are hammered, scattered, turned into dust, blown by the wind, as other Qur'ānic verses describe. Hence, they become non-existent, like a mirage which has no reality. Or, probably, different rays are reflected against them after they have been turned into dust and they look like a mirage.

All in all, horror is apparent in the upheaval which envelops the universe as well as in men's resurrection after the Trumpet is blown. Such is the Day of Decision carefully and wisely fixed.

The Fateful Day

The *sūrah* takes another step, beyond resurrection, to describe the fate of the tyrant unbelievers and also that of the righteous. It begins with the former group who raise doubts about the fateful tiding: "*Hell stands as a vigilant watch guard, a home for the tyrants and the transgressors. Therein they shall abide for ages, tasting neither coolness nor any drink, except boiling fluid and decaying filth: a fitting recompense. They did not expect to be faced with a reckoning, and roundly denied Our revelations. But We have placed on record every single thing, [and We shall say]: 'Taste this, then; the only increase you shall have is increase of torment.*'" (Verses 21–30)

Hell has been created so that it may watch the tyrants and transgressors and await their arrival. They find it well prepared to receive them, as if they are returning to their natural home after having sojourned on earth a while. It is a home in which they stay endlessly. But they taste "*neither coolness nor any drink.*" (Verse 24) The next verse provides an exception to this, but the exception is even worse: "*except boiling fluid and decaying filth.*" (Verse 25) Their throats and stomachs burn as they drink the boiling fluid, which is the only '*coolness*' they have, while their other drink is the filth of the burning bodies, decaying in the enormous heat. The Qur'ān comments that this is 'a fitting recompense'. It is in keeping with what they have done in their lives. For they thought they would never return to God: "*They did not expect to be faced with a reckoning, and roundly denied Our revelations.*" (Verses 27–28) Their denial, as the Arabic verse suggests, is strongly emphatic and stubbornly upheld. But God keeps a meticulous record which does not leave out anything they do or say: "*But We have placed on record every single thing.*" (Verse 29) Then follows a reproach coupled with the tiding that they can hope for no change in their condition and no abatement of its intensity: "*Taste this, then; the only increase you shall have is increase of torment.*" (Verse 30)

We then have the corresponding scene of the righteous in complete bliss. "*The God-fearing shall have a place of security, gardens and vineyards, and high-bosomed maidens, of equal age, for companions, and a cup overflowing. There they shall hear no idle talk, nor any falsehood. Such is the recompense of your Lord, a truly sufficient gift.*" (Verses 31–36) If hell is a vigilant watch guard which the tyrants cannot escape, the righteous, the God-fearing will end in a place of security. What a place it is: "*gardens and vineyards.*" (Verse 32) The vine tree is specifically mentioned because it is well known to the addressees. The God-fearing will also have companions who are described here as high-bosomed and of equal age. They also drink from a cup overflowing with refreshing beverage.

These luxuries are given a physical description so that we may better appreciate them. The precise nature of these luxuries and how they may be enjoyed remain unknown to us as our understanding is restricted by our limited world. But the enjoyment provided to the righteous is not purely physical. "*There they shall hear no idle talk, nor any falsehood.*" (Verse 35) So it is a pure life there, free of the idle chatting and falsehood which give rise to controversy. The reality is known to everyone, which means that there is no room for futile argument. It is a sublime state of affairs suitable for eternal life. Then follows the Qur'ānic comment: "*Such is the recompense of your Lord, a truly sufficient gift.*" (Verse 36)

In God's Presence

The *sūrah* closes with the final scene of the day when all this happens. It is a scene in which we see the angel Gabriel, who is the Holy Spirit, and all the angels standing in ranks before God, their Most Merciful Lord. They stand in awe of Him; no one dares utter a word without prior permission from Him. "*Lord of the heavens and earth and all that lies between them, the Most Gracious, with whom they have no power to speak. On the day when the*

Spirit and the angels stand in ranks, they shall not speak, except those to whom the Most Gracious has given leave, and who shall say what is right." (Verses 37–38)

The recompense given to the righteous and to the tyrant transgressors, which was detailed in the previous section, is from your Lord. "*Lord of the heavens and earth and all that lies between them, the Most Gracious.*" (Verse 37) What a befitting context to reaffirm the eternal truth of Godhead. God is the Supreme Lord of man, the heavens and earth, this life and the next, who metes out reward for righteousness and punishment for transgression and tyranny. But above all He is the Most Gracious. The reward He assigns to each group is a manifestation of His mercy. Even the torment endured by the transgressors originates from God's mercy. For it is indeed part of mercy that evil should be punished and that it should not have the same end as good.

The other divine attribute implied here is majesty: "*with whom they have no power to speak.*" (Verse 37) In this awesome situation neither man nor angel can speak without permission from the Most Gracious. Whatever is said will be right because He does not permit anyone to speak whom He knows will not be saying what is right.

When we think that the angels, who are favoured by God, and absolutely pure from sin, stand silent in front of God and dare not speak without His permission, we are bound to feel how awesome the atmosphere is. Having motivated such a feeling, the *sūrah* delivers a warning to those who have chosen not to hear or see: "*That day is a certainty. Let him who will seek a way back to his Lord. We have forewarned you of an imminent scourge, on the day when man will look on what his hands have forwarded and the unbeliever will cry: 'Would that I were dust!'*" (Verses 39–40)

Those who raise doubts and question the reality of the Day of Resurrection are here shaken violently: "*That day is a certainty.*" (Verse 39) There is no room left for doubt and controversy. Yet there is time for mending one's erring ways before the fearful watch guard, i.e. hell, becomes a permanent home: "*Let him who will seek a way back to his Lord.*" (Verse 39) The warning is stern enough to make the drunken awake: "*We have forewarned you of an imminent scourge.*" (Verse 40) It will not be long coming, for man's life is but a short period. The scourge is so fearful that the unbelievers, when faced with it, will send up that great cry expressing the wish that they had never lived: "*On the day when man will look on what his hands have forwarded and the unbeliever will cry: 'Would that I were dust!*'" (Verse 40)

This is the cry of one who is in great distress, who feels ashamed for what he has been and what he has done. He feels that it is better not to be, or to be something as worthless as dust, than to witness such a fearful occasion. The terrible position of the unbelievers is the subject of the questions and doubts they raise concerning that fateful tiding.

SŪRAH 79

Al-Nāzi ʿāt

(The Pluckers)

Al-Nāzi ʿāt (The Pluckers)

سُورَةُ النَّازِعَاتِ

In the name of God, the Beneficent, the Merciful.

بِسْمِ اللَّهِ الرَّحْمَٰنِ الرَّحِيمِ

By those that pluck out vehemently, (1)

وَالنَّازِعَاتِ غَرْقًا ١

and those that move forward rapidly; (2)

وَالنَّاشِطَاتِ نَشْطًا ٢

by those that float along at ease, (3)

وَالسَّابِحَاتِ سَبْحًا ٣

and those that outstrip swiftly, (4)

فَالسَّابِقَاتِ سَبْقًا ٤

and those that conduct matters. (5)

فَالْمُدَبِّرَاتِ أَمْرًا ٥

On the day when a violent convulsion will [be overwhelming], (6)

يَوْمَ تَرْجُفُ ٱلرَّاجِفَةُ ٦

to be soon followed by a further [convulsion], (7)

تَتْبَعُهَا ٱلرَّادِفَةُ ٧

all hearts shall be filled with terror, (8)

قُلُوبٌ يَوْمَئِذٍ وَاجِفَةٌ ٨

and all eyes shall be downcast. (9)

أَبْصَٰرُهَا خَٰشِعَةٌ ٩

They say, 'What! Are we being restored to our former state, (10)

يَقُولُونَ أَءِنَّا لَمَرْدُودُونَ فِى ٱلْحَافِرَةِ ١٠

even though we have become [no more than] hollow bones?' (11)

أَءِذَا كُنَّا عِظَٰمًا نَّخِرَةً ١١

They say, 'That will be a return with loss.' (12)

قَالُوا۟ تِلْكَ إِذًا كَرَّةٌ خَاسِرَةٌ ١٢

But with just one blast (13)

فَإِنَّمَا هِىَ زَجْرَةٌ وَٰحِدَةٌ ١٣

they shall be alive on earth. (14)

فَإِذَا هُم بِٱلسَّاهِرَةِ ١٤

Have you heard the story of Moses? (15)

هَلْ أَتَىٰكَ حَدِيثُ مُوسَىٰٓ ١٥

His Lord called out to him in the sacred valley of Ṭuwā, (16)

إِذْ نَادَىٰهُ رَبُّهُۥ بِٱلْوَادِ ٱلْمُقَدَّسِ طُوًى ١٦

saying: 'Go to Pharaoh: he has transgressed all bounds, (17)

ٱذْهَبْ إِلَىٰ فِرْعَوْنَ إِنَّهُۥ طَغَىٰ ١٧

and say to him: "Would you like to reform yourself? (18)

فَقُلْ هَل لَّكَ إِلَىٰٓ أَن تَزَكَّىٰ ﴿١٨﴾

I will guide you to your Lord, so that you may be in awe of Him." (19)

وَأَهْدِيَكَ إِلَىٰ رَبِّكَ فَتَخْشَىٰ ﴿١٩﴾

He showed Pharaoh the mightiest miracle, (20)

فَأَرَىٰهُ ٱلْـَٔايَةَ ٱلْكُبْرَىٰ ﴿٢٠﴾

but Pharaoh cried lies and rebelled. (21)

فَكَذَّبَ وَعَصَىٰ ﴿٢١﴾

He then turned away hastily. (22)

ثُمَّ أَدْبَرَ يَسْعَىٰ ﴿٢٢﴾

He summoned all his men and made a proclamation to them: (23)

فَحَشَرَ فَنَادَىٰ ﴿٢٣﴾

'I am your supreme Lord', he said. (24)

فَقَالَ أَنَا۠ رَبُّكُمُ ٱلْأَعْلَىٰ ﴿٢٤﴾

God smote him with the scourge of both the life to come and this life. (25)

فَأَخَذَهُ ٱللَّهُ نَكَالَ ٱلْـَٔاخِرَةِ وَٱلْأُولَىٰٓ ﴿٢٥﴾

Surely in this there is a lesson for the God-fearing. (26)

إِنَّ فِى ذَٰلِكَ لَعِبْرَةً لِّمَن يَخْشَىٰٓ ﴿٢٦﴾

Which is stronger in constitution: you or the heaven He has built? (27)

ءَأَنتُمْ أَشَدُّ خَلْقًا أَمِ ٱلسَّمَآءُ ۚ بَنَىٰهَا ﴿٢٧﴾

He raised it high and gave it its perfect shape, (28)

رَفَعَ سَمْكَهَا فَسَوَّىٰهَا ﴿٢٨﴾

and gave darkness to its night, and brought out its daylight. (29)

وَأَغْطَشَ لَيْلَهَا وَأَخْرَجَ ضُحَىٰهَا ﴿٢٩﴾

After that He spread out the earth. (30)

وَٱلْأَرْضَ بَعْدَ ذَٰلِكَ دَحَىٰهَآ ﴿٣٠﴾

He brought out water from it, and brought forth its pastures; (31)

أَخْرَجَ مِنْهَا مَآءَهَا وَمَرْعَىٰهَا ﴿٣١﴾

and the mountains He set firm, (32)

وَٱلْجِبَالَ أَرْسَىٰهَا ﴿٣٢﴾

for you and your cattle to delight in. (33)

مَتَٰعًا لَّكُمْ وَلِأَنْعَٰمِكُمْ ﴿٣٣﴾

Then, when the great, overwhelming event comes to pass – (34)

فَإِذَا جَآءَتِ ٱلطَّآمَّةُ ٱلْكُبْرَىٰ ﴿٣٤﴾

on that day man will clearly remember what he has done, (35)

يَوْمَ يَتَذَكَّرُ ٱلْإِنسَٰنُ مَا سَعَىٰ ﴿٣٥﴾

when hell is brought in sight of all who are looking on; (36)

وَبُرِّزَتِ ٱلْجَحِيمُ لِمَن يَرَىٰ ﴿٣٦﴾

then, he who transgressed the bounds of what is right, (37)

فَأَمَّا مَن طَغَىٰ ﴿٣٧﴾

and chose this present life (38)

وَءَاثَرَ ٱلْحَيَوٰةَ ٱلدُّنْيَا ﴿٣٨﴾

will have hell for his dwelling place. (39)	فَإِنَّ ٱلْجَحِيمَ هِىَ ٱلْمَأْوَىٰ ٣٩
But he who feared that he will stand before his Lord and forbade his soul its base desire (40)	وَأَمَّا مَنْ خَافَ مَقَامَ رَبِّهِۦ وَنَهَى ٱلنَّفْسَ عَنِ ٱلْهَوَىٰ ٤٠
will dwell in paradise. (41)	فَإِنَّ ٱلْجَنَّةَ هِىَ ٱلْمَأْوَىٰ ٤١
They question you about the Last Hour, when will it come to pass? (42)	يَسْـَٔلُونَكَ عَنِ ٱلسَّاعَةِ أَيَّانَ مُرْسَىٰهَا ٤٢
But why should you be concerned with its exact timing? (43)	فِيمَ أَنتَ مِن ذِكْرَىٰهَآ ٤٣
The final word concerning it belongs to your Lord. (44)	إِلَىٰ رَبِّكَ مُنتَهَىٰهَآ ٤٤
Your mission is merely to warn those who fear it. (45)	إِنَّمَآ أَنتَ مُنذِرُ مَن يَخْشَىٰهَا ٤٥
On the day when they see that hour, it will seem to them that their life on earth had spanned only one evening, or one morning. (46)	كَأَنَّهُمْ يَوْمَ يَرَوْنَهَا لَمْ يَلْبَثُوٓا۟ إِلَّا عَشِيَّةً أَوْ ضُحَىٰهَا ٤٦

Overview

This *sūrah* is just one example of many in this part of the Qur'ān which shares a common objective; namely, to drive home to man the reality of the hereafter, its inevitability and its awesome nature, and to stress its importance to the divine planning of man's life in this world. Such planning culminates in man's death and subsequent resurrection in a new life. As it sets out to drive this idea home to man, the *sūrah* touches upon our emotions in a variety of ways that are directly relevant to its central theme.

First we have an ambiguous opening which creates an air of fear and worried expectation. The rhythm here is quick and throbbing; it helps evoke feelings of fear, surprise and wonder: "*By those that pluck out vehemently, and those that move forward rapidly; by those that float along at ease, and those that outstrip swiftly, and those that conduct matters.*" (Verses 1–5)

This equivocal, shaking opening is followed by the first of those scenes which deal with the hereafter. The style and tempo of the opening is here maintained and thus serves as a framework for the overall scene: "*On the day when a violent convulsion will [be overwhelming], to be soon followed by a further [convulsion], all hearts shall be filled with terror, and all eyes shall be downcast. They say, "What! Are we being restored to our former state, even though we have become [no more than] hollow bones?' They say, 'That will be a return with loss.' But with just one blast they shall be alive on earth.*" (Verses 6–14)

Having cast an air of awe, the *sūrah* then provides an account of the end met by some of the unbelievers during the time of Moses and Pharaoh. Here the rhythm is quieter and more relaxed to suit the narrative style: "*Have you heard the story of Moses? His Lord called out to him in the sacred valley of Ṭuwā, saying: 'Go to Pharaoh: he has transgressed all bounds, and say to him: "Would you like to reform yourself? I will guide you to your Lord, so that you may be in awe of Him."' He showed Pharaoh the mightiest miracle, but Pharaoh cried lies and rebelled. He then turned away hastily. He summoned all his men and made a proclamation to them: 'I am your supreme Lord', he said. God smote him with the scourge of both the life to come and this life. Surely in this there is a lesson for the God-fearing.*" (Verses 15–26) This account serves as an introduction to the great principle the *sūrah* aims to establish.

Leaving history aside, the *sūrah* then takes up the open book of the universe. It paints great scenes of the universe which testify to the limitless power and careful planning of God, the Creator of the universe who controls its destiny both in this life and in the life to come. These scenes are drawn in a powerful style and contain a strong rhythm in harmony with the opening of the *sūrah* and its general cadence. "*Which is stronger in constitution: you or the heaven He has built? He raised it high and gave it its perfect shape, and gave darkness to its night, and brought out its daylight. After that He spread out the earth. He brought out water from it, and brought forth its pastures; and the mountains He set firm, for you and your cattle to delight in.*" (Verses 27–33)

Then comes a statement about the great and overwhelming event, which will be accompanied by the distribution of rewards for actions done in this life. The rewards are portrayed in such a way as to fit in harmoniously with the event itself: "*Then, when the great, overwhelming event comes to pass – on that day man will clearly remember what he has done, when hell is brought in sight of all who are looking on; then, he who transgressed the bounds of what is right, and chose this present life will have hell for his dwelling place. But he who feared that he will stand before his Lord and forbade his soul its base desire will dwell in paradise.*" (Verses 34–41)

At this point, when we are overwhelmed by the respective fates of the transgressors who prefer this life to the next, and the God-fearing who restrain themselves, the *sūrah* turns to those who deny resurrection, yet ask the Prophet to fix its time. The rhythm here is superb. It further contributes to the awe produced by the account of the Last Hour. "*They question you about the Last Hour, when will it come to pass? But why should you be concerned with its exact timing? The final word concerning it belongs to your Lord. Your mission is merely to warn those who fear it. On the day when they see that hour, it will seem to them that their life on earth had spanned only one evening, or one morning.*" (Verses 42–46) Perhaps we should note that these verses end with the sound '*āhā*', which adds length to the metre, intensifying the effect of majesty and awe.

The Pluckers and the Event

> *By those that pluck out vehemently, and those that move forward rapidly; by those that float along at ease, and those that outstrip swiftly, and those that conduct matters.* (Verses 1–5)

Some commentators say of these verses that they refer to the angels who pluck out souls vehemently, move along with ease and speed, float along as they move in the outer world, outstrip other creatures to embrace the faith and carry out God's commands and conduct whatever affairs they are charged with. Other commentators maintain that they refer to the stars which come on as they traverse their orbits, move rapidly in phases, float in space, outstrip others as they run fast and bring about certain phenomena and results which are entrusted to them by God and which affect life on earth. A third group of commentators are of the view that the pluckers, runners, floaters and outstrippers refer to the stars while the conductors of affairs are the angels. Another group believe that the first three are the stars while the outstrippers and conductors of affairs are the angels.

Whatever the referents of these terms are, their mention in this particular way produces a shock and a feeling of expectation of something fearful. Thus, they contribute, right at the outset, to preparing our minds for the frightening account of the first and second quakes and of the overwhelming event mentioned later in the *sūrah*.

Perhaps it is better not to go into great detail in trying to explain and discuss these verses. It is perhaps more fruitful to let these verses produce their effect naturally. The Qur'ān seeks to achieve its objective of awakening people's hearts in different ways. If we do this we simply follow the example of 'Umar ibn al-Khaṭṭāb. He once read *Sūrah* 80, The Frowning. When he reached the verse which reads '*wa fākihatan wa abba*', he wondered, "we know the fruit trees, *fākihatan*, but what is *abba*?" But then he reproached himself, saying: "You, Ibn al-Khaṭṭāb, are being really fussy today! What harm is there in your not knowing the meaning of a word used in God's book?" He then said to the people around: "Follow what you understand of this book; what you do not understand you may leave alone." His statement, aimed at discouraging people from trying to explain what may be equivocal to them, without the backing of perfectly sound authority, represents an attitude of veneration towards God's words. Indeed, some words and phrases may deliberately have been left equivocal so as to fulfil a certain objective.

The opening of the *sūrah* takes the form of an oath, to confirm the event related in verses that immediately follow: "*On the day when a violent convulsion will [be overwhelming], to be soon followed by a further [convulsion], all hearts shall be filled with terror, and all eyes shall be downcast. They say, "What! Are we being restored to our former state, even though we have become [no more than] hollow bones?' They say, 'That will be a return with loss." But with just one blast they shall be alive on earth.*" (Verses 6–14) It has been suggested that the convulsion refers to the earth being overwhelmed by a violent quake. This is based on what the Qur'ān says in another *sūrah*: "*On the day when the earth and the mountains will be convulsed.*" (73: 14) It has also been suggested that the convulsion that follows affects the sky, as it follows the earth in witnessing its own upheaval causing it to split and the stars to scatter. An alternative suggestion claims that the first convulsion refers to the first blast on the Trumpet which causes the earth, the mountains and all creation to quake and tremble, and makes all who are in heaven and on earth fall down fainting, except those who are spared by God. The follower, it is claimed, refers to the second blast on the Trumpet which brings all creation back to life as stated in verse 68 of *Sūrah* 39.

Whichever suggestion is correct, these verses make men's hearts feel the convulsion and shake with fear and worry. They prepare us for the terror that will fill people's hearts on the Day of Judgement: "*All hearts shall be filled with terror and all eyes shall be downcast.*" (Verses 8–9) Thus, it is a combination of worry, fear, humiliation and breakdown. This is what happens on that day, and it is this fact which the oath at the opening of the *sūrah* seeks to establish. In both sense and rhythm, the scene portrayed by these verses fits in perfectly with the opening.

The *sūrah* goes on to speak of people's surprise and wonder when they are resurrected: "*They say: 'What! Are we being restored to our former state, even though we have become [no more than] hollow bones?'*" (Verses 10–11) They wonder whether they are being returned to life again. Amazed, they ask how this can be done after they have been dead for so long that their bones are hollow. Then they realize that their awakening does not take them back to their life on earth, but to their second life. At this point they feel their great loss and cry: "*That will be a return with loss.*" (Verse 12) They have not banked on such a return, and have not prepared for it, so they have everything to lose by it. The Qur'ānic comment is to state what will actually happen: "*But with just one blast they shall be alive on earth.*" (Verses 13–14)

The '*blast*' is a shout, but it is described here as a blast to emphasize its force, and to strike a note of perfect harmony between this scene and others drawn in the *sūrah*. The term used for '*the earth*' here refers to a bright white earth which is the land of resurrection. We do not know its exact location. All we know of it is that which the Qur'ān or the authentic traditions of the Prophet relate. We have no intention of adding anything unauthoritative to their account. Other Qur'ānic statements lead us to the conclusion that this one blast is most probably the second blow on the Trumpet, i.e. the blow of resurrection. The expression used here gives a sense of speed. The blast itself is associated with speed, and the general rhythm of the *sūrah* is a rapid one. Terrified hearts also beat fast. Hence the perfect harmony between the sense, the rhythm, the scenes and the *sūrah* as a whole.

Instructions Given to Moses

The rhythm then slows down a little in order to suit the style of narration. For next we have an account of what took place between Moses and Pharaoh, and the end which Pharaoh met after he had tyrannized and transgressed all bounds: "*Have you heard the story of Moses? His Lord called out to him in the sacred valley of Ṭuwā, saying: 'Go to Pharaoh: he has transgressed all bounds, and say to him: "Would you like to reform yourself? I will guide you to your Lord, so that you may be in awe of Him."' He showed Pharaoh the mightiest miracle, but Pharaoh cried lies and rebelled. He then turned away hastily. He summoned all his men and made a proclamation to them: 'I am your supreme Lord', he said. God smote him with the scourge of both the life to come and this life. Surely in this there is a lesson for the God-fearing.*" (Verses 15–26)

The story of Moses is the most frequent and detailed of Qur'ānic historical accounts. It is mentioned in many other *sūrahs*, in different ways and with varying emphasis. At times, certain episodes are given greater prominence than others. This variation of style and emphasis aims at striking harmony between the historical account and the *sūrah* in which it occurs. Thus, the story helps to make the message of the *sūrah* clearer. This method is characteristic of the Qur'ān. Here the historical account is given in quick successive scenes which open with the call Moses receives in the sacred valley and end with the destruction of Pharaoh in this life and perdition in the life to come. Thus, it fits very well with the main theme of the *sūrah*, namely the hereafter. The part given here of Moses's history spans a long period, yet it is conveyed by only a few short verses that fit in well with the rhythm and message of the *sūrah* as whole.

They start with an introductory question addressed to the Prophet: "*Have you heard the story of Moses?*" (Verse 15) The question serves to prepare us to listen to the history and contemplate its lessons. Moses's story is described here as history to emphasize that it actually happened. It starts with Moses being called by God: "*His Lord called out to him in the sacred valley of Ṭuwā.*" (Verse 16) Ṭuwā is probably the name of the valley which lies to the right of Mount Ṭūr in Sinai, as one comes up from Madyan in North Hijaz.

The moment this call was made was an awesome one. The call from God to one of His servants is beyond description, yet it embodies a secret of divinity, and a secret of how God has made man susceptible to His call. No one can comprehend what is involved here without inspiration from God Himself.

The communication between God and Moses is discussed in more detail elsewhere in the Qur'ān. However, with the brevity and rapid rhythm that characterize this *sūrah*, it is touched upon here only very briefly, before God's command to Moses is stated: "*Go to Pharaoh: he has transgressed all bounds, and say to him: 'Would you like to reform yourself? I will guide you to your Lord, so that you may be in awe of Him.'*" (Verses 17–19)

"*Go to Pharaoh: he has transgressed all bounds.*" (Verse 17) The Arabic term for 'transgress', which is *ṭaghā*, also suggests tyranny. Neither tyranny nor transgression should be allowed to take place or be left unchecked. They lead to corruption and to what displeases God. So God [limitless is He in His glory] selects one of His noble servants and charges him with the task of trying to put an end to them. The instructions given to this noble servant require him to go to a tyrant in an attempt to turn him away from his erring ways, so that he has no excuse should God decide to exact His retribution.

"*Go to Pharaoh: he has transgressed all bounds.*" God teaches Moses how to address this tyrant in the most persuasive manner: "*Say to him: 'Would you like to reform yourself?'*" (Verse 18) The first question then is whether or not the tyrant would like to purify himself of the stains of tyranny and abominable disobedience to God. Would he like to know the path of the pious, the blessed?: "*I will guide you to your Lord, so that you may be in awe of Him.*" (Verse 19) The offer here is for Pharaoh to be shown the way acceptable to God. Once he knows it, he will feel the fear of God in his heart. Man does not transgress and tyrannize unless he loses his way and finds himself taking a road which does not lead to God. His heart hardens as a result, and he rebels and resorts to tyranny.

Moses was told all this when God called to him. He of course puts these questions to Pharaoh when he encounters him. The *sūrah*, however, does not repeat them when it describes the encounter. It skips over what happens after God's call to Moses and deletes what Moses says when he conveys his message. It is as if the curtain falls after the call to repentance. When it is lifted again, we are presented with the end of the encounter: "*He showed Pharaoh the mightiest miracle, but Pharaoh cried lies and rebelled.*" (Verses 20–21)

Unrivalled Insolence

Thus, Moses conveys the message with which he has been entrusted in the manner God has taught him. This warm, friendly attitude, however, cannot win over a heart that has been hardened by tyranny and ignorance of the Lord of the universe. So Moses shows him the great miracles of the stick turning into a snake and Moses's own hand becoming a brilliant white, as they are described in other *sūrahs*, "*but he cried lies and rebelled.*" (Verse 21) The scene ends with Pharaoh's rejection and rebellion against God.

Pharaoh then turns away to mobilize his forces and bring forward his sorcerers for an encounter between magic and the truth. Essentially, Pharaoh was determined not to accept the truth or submit to right. "*He then turned away hastily. He summoned all his men and made a proclamation to them: 'I am your supreme Lord', he said.*" (Verses 22–24) The *sūrah* does not give any details of Pharaoh's efforts to muster his magicians, sorcerers and men. It simply says that he went away to do so, and then uttered his impertinent proclamation: "*I am your supreme Lord*". (Verse 24)

Pharaoh's declaration betrays the fact that he was deceived by his people's ignorance and their submission to his authority. Nothing deceives tyrants more than the ignorance and abject submission of the masses. A tyrant is in fact an individual who has no real power or authority. The ignorant and the submissive simply bend their backs for him to ride, stretch out their necks for him to harness with reins, hang down their heads to give him a chance to show his conceit, and forego their rights to be respected and honoured. In this way they allow themselves to be tyrannized. The masses do all this because they are deceived and afraid at the same time. Their fear has no real basis except in their imagination. The tyrant, an individual, can never be stronger than thousands or millions, should they attach proper value to their humanity, dignity, self-respect and freedom. Every individual in the nation is a match for the tyrant in terms of power. No one can tyrannize a nation which is sane, or knows its true Lord, believes in Him and refuses to submit to any creature who has no power over its destiny.

Pharaoh, however, found his people so ignorant, submissive and devoid of faith that he was able to make his insolent, blasphemous declaration, "*I am your supreme Lord!*" (Verse 24) He would never have dared to make it had his nation possessed the qualities of general awareness, self-respect and faith in God.

Against such intolerable insolence, the Supreme Power moved in: "*God smote him with the scourge of both the life to come and this life.*" (Verse 25) The scourge of the life to come is mentioned first because it is much more severe and perpetual. It is indeed the real punishment for tyrants and transgressors. It is also appropriate to give it prominence since the life to come is the main theme of the *sūrah*. Besides, it fits in perfectly with the general rhythm of the *sūrah*.

Nevertheless, the scourge that engulfed Pharaoh in this life was fearful and severe, but that of the life to come will be much more so. Pharaoh had power, authority and glory, yet none of this will be of any use to him. One can only imagine what the fate that will be faced by unbelievers who do not have similar power, authority or glory but who still resist God's message and try to suppress it.

"*Surely in this there is a lesson for the God-fearing.*" (Verse 26) Only those who know their true Lord and fear Him will benefit from the lessons of Pharaoh's history. Those who do not fear God will continue in their erring ways until they reach their appointed end, when they shall suffer the scourge of both this life and the life to come.

Having mentioned the end met by tyrants who thought themselves very powerful, the *sūrah* turns to the present unbelievers who also depend on their own power. It directs their attention to some manifestations of the work of the Supreme Power in the universe. Their power holds no sway against God's: "*Which is stronger in constitution: you or the heaven He has built? He raised it high and gave it its perfect shape, and gave darkness to its night, and brought out its daylight. After that He spread out the earth. He brought out water from it, and brought forth its pastures; and the mountains He set firm, for you and your cattle to delight in.*" (Verses 27–33)

The question these verses start with, "*Which is stronger in constitution: you or the heaven He has built?*" admits of one answer only: heaven. So the question seems to infer another: 'Why should you think so highly of your own power when heaven is much stronger in constitution than you and the Lord who created it is much stronger than it?' The question may also be carried forward in a different direction: 'Why do you think resurrection is impossible, when God has created heaven, the creation of which requires more power than your own creation?' Resurrection is merely a repetition of creation. It follows that He who has built heaven will find your resurrection an easier proposition.

It is He who has 'built' heaven. The term 'build' suggests strength and firm constitution. Heaven is indeed so. Its planets are held together in perfect harmony. They neither scatter, nor fall out of their orbits.

Conducive to Life

"*He raised it high and gave it its perfect shape.*" (Verse 28) We need no more than a glance in order to recognize the perfect coherence and harmony in the building of heaven. Knowledge of the laws which govern the existence of the creatures in the sky above us and provide a perfect balance between their actions, movements and mutual effects helps us to understand the full meaning of this verse. It intensifies our feeling of the limitlessness of their very real world, of which human knowledge has uncovered only a tiny part. It overwhelms us with wonder and astonishment. We stand speechless at the infinite beauty of the universe. We can give no explanation for it except that a superhuman power has planned and governs it. This explanation is now accepted even by most of those who profess not to believe in any religion.

"*And gave darkness to its night, and brought out its daylight.*" (Verse 29) The Arabic words used in this verse add to the strength of the general tone. They also have stronger connotations than the translation suggests. They are used here because they are more fitting with the general context. The succession of darkness and light, at night and in the morning, is a phenomenon recognized by all, but it may be overlooked because we are so familiar with it. Here, the Qur'ān reminds us of its permanent novelty. For it is repeated anew every day, producing the same effects and reactions. The natural laws governing this phenomenon are so precise and miraculous that they continue to impress and astonish man as his knowledge increases.

"*After that He spread out the earth. He brought out water from it, and brought forth its pastures; and the mountains He set firm.*" (Verses 30–32) Spreading out the earth is a reference to the levelling of its surface so that it becomes easy to walk on, and to the formation of a layer of soil suitable for cultivation. Setting the mountains firm is a result of the final shaping of the surface of the earth and its cooling down to a level suitable for the emergence of living organisms. God also brought out water from the earth. This applies to springs that allow deep waters to flow out onto the surface of the earth. It also applies to rain water, since it comes originally from the earth. He also brought forth the pastures, which is, in this context, a reference to all plants upon which man and animals feed, and which directly and indirectly sustain life.

All this happened after heaven was built, the night darkened and the earth spread. Recent astronomical theories support this Qur'ānic statement, for they assume that the earth was moving in its orbit, with day and night succeeding each other for hundreds of millions of years before it was levelled and spread out, becoming suitable for vegetation, and before its surface took its final, present shape of plains, valleys, mountains and oceans.

The Qur'ān declares that all this is "*for you and your cattle to delight in.*" (Verse 33) This is a reminder to man of what God has made for him, and of His perfect and elaborate planning. It is not by chance that heaven was built in this fashion and the earth spread out to take its present shape. Man's existence, as God's vicegerent, was taken into account. Indeed, human life and progress depend on so many factors which operate in the universe generally, and in the solar system in particular, and even more particularly on the earth itself. All these factors must be made to function in absolute harmony.

Following the Qur'ānic method of delivering a short statement which embodies the basic fact, yet is rich with hints and inferences, the *sūrah* names just a few of these harmonized factors – the building of heaven, the darkening of the night, the bringing forth of daylight, the spreading of the earth, the manipulation of its waters and pastures and the setting firm of mountains – for man and his cattle to delight in. This statement ensures the elaborate planning of the universe is understood by everybody, regardless of education standard. It addresses all mankind, throughout all ages and societies, whether primitive or advanced. The reality of such meticulous and elaborate planning, however, goes far beyond the level mentioned here. The very nature of this universe rules out any possibility of its formation by chance, for no chance construct could result in such perfect and absolute harmony on such an immeasurable scale. The harmony starts with the fact that our solar system is unique among millions and millions of planetary systems, and our earth is also a unique planet with regard to its location in the solar system. It is this uniqueness that makes life on earth possible.

> Life may appear on a certain planet if certain conditions are met: the planet must be of suitable size, at a medium distance from the sun, and it has to be of a composition which mixes the elements in the right proportion to permit the emergence of life. The suitable size is necessary because the atmosphere of the planet is conditioned by the force of its gravity. The medium distance is also a necessary condition because the planets which are near to the sun are so hot that nothing can solidify on them, and those that are far from the sun are so cold that nothing on them can have any measure of elasticity. The right composition

of elements is necessary because such a composition in the right proportion is a must for the growth of vegetation which is, in turn, essential for the sustenance of life. The Earth has the ideal location to satisfy all these conditions which are conducive to the emergence of life in the only form which we now know.[1]

Establishing the fact of elaborate planning of the grand universe, and giving man a special place in it prepares man's heart and mind to receive and accept the statement about the reality of the hereafter and its final judgement. If the origins of the universe and of man are such, then the cycle must be completed, and everyone must have their reward. It is inconceivable that the final end comes with the end of man's short life in this world, or that evil and tyranny can get away without retribution, or that good, justice and right can be left to suffer whatever hardship is visited on them in this life, without there being a chance to put matters right. Such an assumption is, in its very essence, contrary to the fact of elaborate planning so apparent everywhere in the universe. Hence the reality touched upon in this part of the *sūrah* serves as an introduction to the reality of the hereafter, which is the main theme of the whole *sūrah*.

Different Dwellings

Then, when the great, overwhelming event comes to pass – on that day man will clearly remember what he has done, when hell is brought in sight of all who are looking on; then, he who transgressed the bounds of what is right, and chose this present life will have hell for his dwelling place. But he who feared that he will stand before his Lord and forbade his soul its base desire will dwell in paradise. (Verses 34–41)

This present life is a period of comfort and enjoyment which are given in precise and accurate measure. Its duration is determined

1. A.M. Al-Aqqad, *'Aqā'id al-Mufakkirīn fī al-Qarn al-'Ishrīn*, Beliefs of Twentieth Century Thinkers, Maktabat al-Anglo–al-Maiṣriyyah, Cairo, n.d., p. 36.

according to the overall planning of the universe and human life. Its comfort and enjoyment will end at the time appointed for their expiry. When the great event takes place, it ravages all and overwhelms all. The fleeting comfort of this life is extinguished. The whole universe, its built heaven, spread out earth and firm mountains are overturned and all living creatures are overwhelmed. At that moment "*man will clearly remember what he has done.*" (Verse 35) He might have been distracted by the events and comforts of this life and he might have overlooked what he has done. But he will recall it all then, when remembrance brings him nothing but sadness and grief as he realizes what a miserable end he faces. "*When hell is brought in sight of all who are looking on.*" (Verse 36) The term '*bringing in sight*' is particularly powerful. It is rich in connotations and further strengthens the rhythm. The result is an image so vivid we almost see it in front of us now.

Then, people will have different destinies and the aim of earlier planning in the first life is revealed: "*Then, he who transgressed the bounds of what is right, and chose this present life will have hell for his dwelling place.*" (Verses 37–39) The Arabic term, *ṭaghā*, rendered here as 'transgress the bounds of what is right' means literally 'tyrannize', but this term is used here, as elsewhere in the Qur'ān, in a much wider sense than the strict despotism of rulers and dictators. 'Tyranny' is used here as being synonymous with exceeding the limits of right and truth. Hence these three verses refer to all those who transgress the boundaries of right, prefer this life to the future life, taking no heed of the latter. Since consciousness of the hereafter defines the values and standards to be applied, he who prefers this present life suffers a breakdown of values and standards resulting in his adoption of faulty standards of behaviour. This puts him in the category of despots and transgressors. Thus, hell which is brought in sight of everybody on that great day will be his dwelling place.

"*But he who feared that he will stand before his Lord and forbade his soul its base desire will dwell in paradise.*" (Verses 40–41) The one who fears to stand in front of God does not indulge in sin. If he slips and commits a sin, in a moment of weakness, his fear of God will lead him to repent and pray for forgiveness. Thus, he remains within the area of obedience, the central point of which is the control of one's caprice and desires. Indulgence of desire and caprice is essentially the cause of all forms of tyranny and transgression. It is the spring of evil. Man hardly ever falls for any reason other than succumbing to caprice and desire. Ignorance is easy to cure. Desire, once ignorance has been cured, is a plague which requires a long and hard struggle to overcome. Yet fear of God is the only solid defence against violent attacks of desire. Indeed, there is hardly any other defence which can withstand such attacks. Hence, the *sūrah* mentions fear of God and control of desire together in one verse. This fact is here stressed by God, the Creator of man and the only One who knows the human soul, its weaknesses and their effective cure.

God does not ask man to suppress his desires, because He knows that it is not possible for him to do so. He simply asks man to control his desires and not to let them control him. He tells him that fear of standing before his Lord, the Almighty, should be of great assistance. He has fixed his reward for this hard struggle: paradise as a dwelling place. For God knows perfectly well the hardships involved in this struggle and the high standards to which man is elevated by the same. This struggle, self-control and elevation help man fulfil his humanity. Such fulfilment cannot be achieved by giving way to all desires, and following caprice wherever it leads, on the pretext that desire and caprice are part of human nature. God, who made man sensitive to certain urges, also gave him self discipline. He also gives him paradise as a reward when he elevates himself to a high standard of humanity.

There are two types of freedom. The first is achieved through scoring a victory over one's desires and releasing oneself from the chains of caprice. When man achieves such a victory he finds himself able to fulfil these desires and caprices in a controlled and balanced way which emphasizes his freedom of choice. This type of freedom is human, one which suits the honour God has bestowed on man. The other type is animal freedom, represented in man's defeat, his enslavement by his desires, and his loss of control over himself. This type of freedom is advocated only by those who have lost their humanity, so they try to cover their slavery with a dress of deceptive freedom.

The Timing of the Last Hour

The last part of the *sūrah* is expressed in a rhythm which evokes awe. "*They question you about the Last Hour, when will it come to pass? But why should you be concerned with its exact timing? The final word concerning it belongs to your Lord. Your mission is merely to warn those who fear it. On the day when they see that hour, it will seem to them that their life on earth had spanned only one evening, or one morning.*" (Verses 42–46)

Every time the diehards among the pagan Arabs heard a description of the fearful events of the Day of Judgement, and the reckoning which then takes place, they used to ask the Prophet (peace be upon him) to specify its time: "*When will it come to pass?*" The answer given here to such questions takes the form of a rhetorical question, "*But why should you be concerned with its exact timing*?" (Verse 43) It is an answer which suggests that the Last Hour, or the Day of Judgement, is so great and majestic that the questions put by the unbelievers concerning it sound stupid and pitiful. Moreover, such questions are only put forward by the impudent. The great Prophet himself is asked, "*Why should you be concerned with its exact timing?*" It is so great that neither you nor anyone else should ask to be informed of its exact time. This knowledge belongs to God alone, not to anybody else. "*The final word concerning it belongs to your Lord.*" (Verse 44) He is the Master of everything which relates to it. The Prophet's own duties, and the limits he should not, and need not exceed are well defined: "*Your mission is merely to warn those who fear it.*" (Verse 45) He is to warn those who will benefit by such warnings. Such people will then live according to their firm belief that it will arrive at the time appointed by God.

The majesty and awe of the Last Hour is explained through the description of its effects on men's feelings and the comparison that is drawn between its duration and the length of this present life.

"*On the day when they see that hour, it will seem to them that their life on earth had spanned only one evening, or one morning.*" (Verse 46) It so grips the soul that our present life with all its epics, events and luxuries will seem to those who lived them shorter than a single day, just one evening or one morning. So, the whole world, its centuries and generations will shrink to nothing longer than a morning or an evening in the sight of the very people who quarrel and fight for it, preferring it to their share in the life to come. Yet for such passing enjoyment they abandon the hereafter and forego the certain prospect of dwelling in paradise. This is definitely the greatest stupidity of all, which no man who has ears to hear and eyes to see can ever perpetrate.

SŪRAH 80

‘Abasa

(The Frowning)

‘**Abasa** (The Frowning)

سُورَةُ عَبَسَ

In the name of God, the Beneficent, the Merciful.

بِسْمِ ٱللَّهِ ٱلرَّحْمَٰنِ ٱلرَّحِيمِ

He frowned and turned away (1)

عَبَسَ وَتَوَلَّىٰٓ ١

when the blind man came to him. (2)

أَن جَآءَهُ ٱلْأَعْمَىٰ ٢

How could you tell? He might have sought to purify himself. (3)

وَمَا يُدْرِيكَ لَعَلَّهُۥ يَزَّكَّىٰٓ ٣

He might have been reminded and the reminder might have profited him. (4)

أَوْ يَذَّكَّرُ فَتَنفَعَهُ ٱلذِّكْرَىٰٓ ٤

But to the one who considered himself self-sufficient (5)

أَمَّا مَنِ ٱسْتَغْنَىٰ ٥

you were all attention. (6)	فَأَنتَ لَهُۥ تَصَدَّىٰ ﴿٦﴾
Yet the fault would not be yours if he remained uncleansed. (7)	وَمَا عَلَيۡكَ أَلَّا يَزَّكَّىٰ ﴿٧﴾
As to him who comes to you with zeal, (8)	وَأَمَّا مَن جَآءَكَ يَسۡعَىٰ ﴿٨﴾
and with a feeling of fear in his heart, (9)	وَهُوَ يَخۡشَىٰ ﴿٩﴾
him you ignore. (10)	فَأَنتَ عَنۡهُ تَلَهَّىٰ ﴿١٠﴾
No indeed! This is an admonition. (11)	كَلَّآ إِنَّهَا تَذۡكِرَةٞ ﴿١١﴾
Let him who will, bear it in mind. (12)	فَمَن شَآءَ ذَكَرَهُۥ ﴿١٢﴾
It is written on honoured pages, (13)	فِي صُحُفٖ مُّكَرَّمَةٖ ﴿١٣﴾
exalted, purified, (14)	مَّرۡفُوعَةٖ مُّطَهَّرَةِۭ ﴿١٤﴾
by the hands of noble and devout scribes. (15–16)	بِأَيۡدِي سَفَرَةٖ ﴿١٥﴾ كِرَامِۭ بَرَرَةٖ ﴿١٦﴾
Perish man! How ungrateful he is! (17)	قُتِلَ ٱلۡإِنسَٰنُ مَآ أَكۡفَرَهُۥ ﴿١٧﴾
Of what did God create him? (18)	مِنۡ أَيِّ شَيۡءٍ خَلَقَهُۥ ﴿١٨﴾

Of a drop of sperm. He created him and proportioned him. (19)	مِن نُّطۡفَةٍ خَلَقَهُۥ فَقَدَّرَهُۥ ١٩
He makes his path smooth for him. (20)	ثُمَّ ٱلسَّبِيلَ يَسَّرَهُۥ ٢٠
He then causes him to die and puts him in his grave. (21)	ثُمَّ أَمَاتَهُۥ فَأَقۡبَرَهُۥ ٢١
He will surely bring him back to life when He pleases. (22)	ثُمَّ إِذَا شَآءَ أَنشَرَهُۥ ٢٢
But by no means has man fulfilled His bidding. (23)	كَلَّا لَمَّا يَقۡضِ مَآ أَمَرَهُۥ ٢٣
Let man reflect on the food he eats: (24)	فَلۡيَنظُرِ ٱلۡإِنسَٰنُ إِلَىٰ طَعَامِهِۦٓ ٢٤
how We pour down the rain in torrents, (25)	أَنَّا صَبَبۡنَا ٱلۡمَآءَ صَبّٗا ٢٥
and cleave the earth in fissures; (26)	ثُمَّ شَقَقۡنَا ٱلۡأَرۡضَ شَقّٗا ٢٦
how We bring forth the corn, (27)	فَأَنۢبَتۡنَا فِيهَا حَبّٗا ٢٧
the grapes, and the fresh vegetation, (28)	وَعِنَبٗا وَقَضۡبٗا ٢٨
the olive and the palm, (29)	وَزَيۡتُونٗا وَنَخۡلٗا ٢٩
the dense-treed gardens, (30)	وَحَدَآئِقَ غُلۡبٗا ٣٠

the fruit-trees and the green pastures, (31)	وَفَٰكِهَةً وَأَبًّا ﴿٣١﴾
for you and your cattle to delight in. (32)	مَّتَٰعًا لَّكُمْ وَلِأَنْعَٰمِكُمْ ﴿٣٢﴾
But when the stunning blast is sounded, (33)	فَإِذَا جَآءَتِ ٱلصَّآخَّةُ ﴿٣٣﴾
on that day everyone will forsake his brother, (34)	يَوْمَ يَفِرُّ ٱلْمَرْءُ مِنْ أَخِيهِ ﴿٣٤﴾
his mother and his father, (35)	وَأُمِّهِۦ وَأَبِيهِ ﴿٣٥﴾
his wife and his children: (36)	وَصَٰحِبَتِهِۦ وَبَنِيهِ ﴿٣٦﴾
for each one of them will on that day have enough preoccupations of his own. (37)	لِكُلِّ ٱمْرِئٍ مِّنْهُمْ يَوْمَئِذٍ شَأْنٌ يُغْنِيهِ ﴿٣٧﴾
Some faces on that day shall be beaming, (38)	وُجُوهٌ يَوْمَئِذٍ مُّسْفِرَةٌ ﴿٣٨﴾
smiling and joyful. (39)	ضَاحِكَةٌ مُّسْتَبْشِرَةٌ ﴿٣٩﴾
Some other faces on that day shall be covered with dust, (40)	وَوُجُوهٌ يَوْمَئِذٍ عَلَيْهَا غَبَرَةٌ ﴿٤٠﴾
veiled with darkness. (41)	تَرْهَقُهَا قَتَرَةٌ ﴿٤١﴾
These shall be the faces of the unbelievers, the hardened in sin. (42)	أُوْلَٰٓئِكَ هُمُ ٱلْكَفَرَةُ ٱلْفَجَرَةُ ﴿٤٢﴾

Overview

This *sūrah* discusses certain principles of grave importance. It is unique in its images and the impressions it leaves. Furthermore, it combines its marked spiritual effect with superb musical rhythm.

Its first part treats a certain incident which took place in the early days of Islam. The Prophet (peace be upon him) was busy with a few Quraysh dignitaries, explaining to them the Islamic message, when Ibn Umm Maktūm, a poor blind man, interrupted him. Unaware that the Prophet was busy, the blind man asked him repeatedly to teach him some verses from the Qur'ān. The Prophet (peace be upon him) was not very pleased at this interruption. He frowned and turned away from Ibn Umm Maktūm. This *sūrah* opens by criticizing the Prophet's behaviour in this incident. It lays down clearly the values and principles upon which Islamic society is founded and states the true nature of the message of Islam. "*He frowned and turned away when the blind man came to him. How could you tell? He might have sought to purify himself. He might have been reminded and the reminder might have profited him. But to the one who considered himself self-sufficient you were all attention. Yet the fault would not be yours if he remained uncleansed. As to him who comes to you with zeal, and with a feeling of fear in his heart, him you ignore. No indeed! This is an admonition. Let him who will, bear it in mind. It is written on honoured pages, exalted, purified, by the hands of noble and devout scribes.*" (Verses 1–16)

Man's ungrateful attitude towards God and his denial of Him come up for discussion in the second part. Here man is reminded of his origin; how his life is made easy; how God determines his death and resurrection; and how, after all this, he fails to carry out His orders: "*Perish man! How ungrateful he is! Of what did God create him? Of a drop of sperm. He created him and proportioned him. He makes his path smooth for him. He then causes him to die and puts him in his grave. He will surely bring him to life when He pleases. But by no means has man fulfilled His bidding.*" (Verses 17–23)

The third part directs man to reflect upon things of immediate concern to him, namely, his food. Absolute perfection of creation is obvious in the provision of food for man as it is obvious in the creation, proportioning and development of man himself: "*Let man reflect on the food he eats: how We pour down the rain in torrents, and cleave the earth in fissures; how We bring forth the corn, the grapes, and the fresh vegetation, the olive and the palm, the dense-treed gardens, the fruit-trees and the green pastures, for you and your cattle to delight in.*" (Verses 24–32)

The final part touches upon "the stunning blast" and its fearful effects. The very sound of the words gives the impression of horror. It makes people unaware of anything around them. Their faces, however, provide a lucid account of what is happening to them. "*But when the stunning blast is sounded, on that day everyone will forsake his brother, his mother and his father, his wife and his children: for each one of them will on that day have enough preoccupations of his own. Some faces on that day shall be beaming, smiling and joyful. Some other faces on that day shall be covered with dust, veiled with darkness. These shall be the faces of the unbelievers, the hardened in sin.*" (Verses 33–42)

A quick preview of the *sūrah* leaves a profound effect on the reader. Its message and its implications are so powerful that no human heart can avoid being deeply touched, even by a quick perusal of it. In the following pages we will attempt to illustrate some of the far-reaching effects certain parts of the *sūrah* have and which may not be immediately apparent.

The Basis of Social Values

> *He frowned and turned away when the blind man came to him. How could you tell? He might have sought to purify himself. He might have been reminded and the reminder might have profited him. But to the one who considered himself self-sufficient you were all attention. Yet the fault would not be yours if he remained uncleansed. As to him who comes to you with zeal and with a feeling of fear in his heart, him you ignore. No indeed! This is an*

admonition. Let him who will, bear it in mind. It is written on honoured pages, exalted, purified, by the hands of noble and devout scribes. (Verses 1–16)

The divine instructions which followed this incident are much more far reaching than appears at first sight. They are indeed a miracle. These instructions, the principles they seek to establish and the change they aim to accomplish in human society are, perhaps, the most important miracle of Islam. But the instructions are made here as a direct comment on a single incident. It is part of the Qur'ānic method to make use of isolated incidents in order to lay down fundamental and permanent principles. The principles established here and their practical effects, as seen in the early Islamic society, are indeed the essence of Islam. They constitute the truth which Islam, and all divine religions that preceded it, seek to plant in human life.

The point at issue here is not merely how an individual or a class of people should be treated. This is indeed the significance of the Qur'ānic comment on the incident itself, taken in isolation. The heart of the matter is, however, something far more important. It is: how should people evaluate everything in their lives? From where should they derive the values and standards necessary for such an evaluation?

What the divine instructions contained in the opening part of the *sūrah* seek to establish is that people must base their values and standards on divine considerations, laid down by God. No social circumstances, traditions or practices, nor any concept of life derived from them should be allowed either to encumber or determine these values and standards. There is no denying the difficulties involved in conducting human life on the basis of values and standards laid down by the Divine Being, free from the pressure of all worldly considerations.

If we consider the pressure of society on the individual's feelings and attitudes, and the weight of considerations to be taken into account such as traditional values, family and social ties, as well as the values that prevail in one's own environment, we can appreciate the difficulty of carrying out these divine instructions. Our appreciation of such difficulty is even greater when we remember that in order to convey it to people, Muḥammad himself (peace be upon him) needed this special directive, or rather censure. Reference to this is sufficient to convey the gravity of the matter. For Muḥammad (peace be upon him) attained greater heights of sublimity and greatness than any man can aspire to. Yet the fact that special instructions were required for him to convey a certain principle makes that principle greater than greatness, subliminally unique.

This is, indeed, a true description of the principle established here, namely that mankind should derive their values and standards from the Divine Being, after they have freed themselves from the pressure of their social set-up with all its values and standards.

The basic standard God has, through His prophets, commanded mankind to adopt is: "*The noblest of you in God's sight is he who fears Him most.*" (49: 13) This is the standard by which all values, traditions and practices should be evaluated. It establishes a purely divine criterion which has nothing to do with any worldly considerations. But people live on earth and establish a multitude of ties, each having its own weight and gravity. They have considerations of family relations, power and wealth. The distribution or concentration of these creates certain practical and economic results which determine the position of every man, woman or class of people in relation to others. Thus some acquire a position superior to that of others, in worldly standards.

When Islam declares, "*The noblest of you in God's sight is he who fears Him most,*" it simply indicates that all these values and considerations are void, however important they seem to us. It substitutes for them a single value derived directly from God. Moreover, it is the only value acceptable to Him. The incident depicted here serves to establish this value in an actual situation. Thus the essential principle is established: the scales recognized are those of God; the supreme value which should govern human life is the divine one. Hence, the Muslim community must abandon all human values, standards, traditions and concepts.

Who Takes Priority?

Let us now consider the incident itself. Ibn Umm Maktūm, a poor blind man, comes to the Prophet (peace be upon him) at a time when he is busy with a group of the most powerful and influential personalities in Makkah, including 'Utbah and Shaybah, sons of Rabī'ah, Abū Jahl, 'Amr ibn Hishām, Umayyah ibn Khalaf, al-Walīd ibn al-Mughīrah. Also present is al-'Abbās ibn 'Abd al-Muṭṭalib, the Prophet's uncle. It is a crucial meeting. The Prophet explains the message of Islam to them and hopes for a favourable response. He feels that the cause of Islam stands to gain much by such a response. Islam is facing a hard time in Makkah. Those very people have been using all their wealth, power and influence to check its advancement, and stop people from accepting it. They have managed to freeze Islam in Makkah and hinder its progress elsewhere. Outside Makkah, the other tribes have adopted an attitude of wait and see. For they feel this to be their best stand in a society which gives paramount importance to the tribe's attitude. They are aware that against Muḥammad, the Prophet of Islam, stand his own kinsmen, who, theoretically speaking, should be his most ardent supporters.

It must be emphasized that when we say that the Prophet is busy with these people, he has no personal interest in them. He is simply working for Islam. Acceptance of Islam by these influential and powerful people means the removal of all impediments from the path of Islam in Makkah. It also ensures for Islam the freedom to progress in the rest of Arabia.

While this crucial meeting is in progress, a poor man comes and interrupts the Prophet (peace be upon him) saying: 'Messenger of God! Teach me some verses of what God has taught you.' Although he could sense that the Prophet is busy, he repeats his request several times. The Prophet dislikes this interruption. His face, which remains unseen by the blind man, expresses his aversion. He frowns and looks away from the poor man. Indeed, the Prophet's motive has been his great enthusiasm to win badly needed support for Islam.

Here, heaven intervenes to say the final word in this matter and to put landmarks along the whole length of the road the Islamic message should take. Thus we are given the scales by which to weigh our values regardless of all other considerations, including those which may appear to serve the interests of Islam, as seen by human beings, including Muḥammad, the greatest of all mankind. This is why the Prophet who has been described elsewhere in the Qur'ān as having "*great and sublime nature*", (68: 4) is strongly censured by God, the Most High. It is the only point in the Qur'ān where the Prophet, who is very dear to God, is addressed by the term *kallā*, [inadequately translated as "no indeed"]. *Kallā* is a term of censure and an order to desist. This is because the contravened principle is central to this religion.

The reproof is made in a unique style, which defies translation into ordinary language. Written language has to apply certain rules and observe some well defined norms. These would dampen the effects of the very vivid style which is characterized in this instance by its rapid touches and short phrases which are more like reflex actions and instant pictures.

"*He frowned and turned away when the blind man came to him.*" (Verses 1–2) The use of the third person here is significant. It suggests that the subject matter is so distasteful to God that He does not like to confront His beloved Messenger with it. This in itself is a gesture of mercy and kindness to the Prophet. Thus, the action which necessitated the reproof has been disguised with great subtlety. The reproof then takes the form of direct address, starting somewhat mildly: "*How could you tell? He might have sought to purify himself. He might have been reminded and the reminder might have profited him.*" (Verses 3–4) How could you tell but that a great gain might have been made? That is to say that the poor, blind man who came to you seeking light might have profited by God's reminder and set about purifying himself. His heart might have been brightened by

God's light and he might have become like a lighthouse, guiding people to safety. This is exactly what happens every time a human being genuinely accepts the faith. It is, indeed, what carries real weight on God's scales.

The reproof then takes a stronger tone. It wonders at the action in question: "*But to the one who considered himself self-sufficient you were all attention. Yet the fault would not be yours if he remained uncleansed. As to him who comes to you with zeal and with a feeling of fear in his heart, him you ignore.*" (Verses 5–10) The one who pretends that he can do without you and your religion, light, goodness and purity is the one who receives your attention! You go to him yourself when he turns away, and you are at pains to try to persuade him to accept the faith. "*Yet the fault would not be yours if he remained uncleansed.*" (Verse 7) What is it to you if he chooses to remain in filth? You are not answerable for his sins. He will not secure your victory. "*As to him who comes to you with zeal,*" out of his own free will, "*and with a feeling of fear in his heart,*" groping his way with outstretched hands, fearful of pitfalls, "*him you ignore.*" What a strong description of not paying due attention to the man who came to seek right guidance.

The tone becomes even stronger and the reproof then takes the form of outright censure: *kallā* or "no indeed", this must never be the case.

Then follows a statement affirming that Islam is an honourable and noble call. It has no need for anybody's support. It cares only for the one who accepts it on its merits, regardless of his position in human society! "*This is an admonition. Let him who will, bear it in mind. It is written on honoured pages, exalted, purified, by the hands of noble and devout scribes.*" (Verses 11–16) It is a noble and honoured message in every respect. Its pages are purified and exalted, entrusted to '*noble and devout*' angel ambassadors who convey it to those human beings selected to convey it to their people. It is also dignified. No one who pretends that he is self-sufficient need be approached about accepting this message of Islam. It is only for those who know its value and seek to be purified by it.

So this is the divine standard by which all values and considerations should be evaluated, and all people should be judged. This is also God's word, which is the final judgement in all situations.

But where and when was this laid down? The answer is in Makkah when the Muslims were few in number, and Islam was the weaker side in an unequal battle. The attempt to win a group of powerful and influential men was not motivated by any personal interest. Ignoring the poor blind man was not occasioned by any personal consideration. All was for the sake of the new message. But the message itself calls for the adoption and application of this very standard and these very values. For Islam can never acquire any real power or achieve any true victory except through the establishment of these values and standards.

As stated earlier, the essential principle involved is far greater and wider in scope than this single incident. It is that humanity should derive its values and standards from God, not from any worldly source. "*The noblest of you in God's sight is he who fears Him most.*" (49: 13) Indeed, the one whom God considers noble is the one who deserves to be attended to and looked after, even if he is completely lacking in family relations, power and wealth, assets highly valued by worldly standards. These and all other worldly values are worthless when they part ways with faith and fear of God. This is the great issue which divine instruction in this *sūrah* seeks to settle.

A Reproach and a Principle

The Prophet was deeply touched by these divine instructions and by God's reproof. Throughout his life, he worked tirelessly for the establishment of this great principle in Islamic society.

The first action he took was to announce these instructions and the reproof in public. This in itself is something very great. Taken from any point of view, no person other than a messenger from God would have announced in public that he had been censured so strongly for his slip. It would have been enough for any other great man to recognize his mistake and to avoid any repetition in the future. With God's Messenger however, things acquire different proportions. No person other than God's Messenger could have had the courage, in such circumstances as Islam was facing, to make this declaration, challenging with it the masters of the Quraysh, who were very proud of their lineage, power and wealth.

These were, at the time, the only considerations of any importance in Makkan society, where people wondered: "*Why was this Qur'ān not revealed to some great man from the two towns?*" (43: 31) They were, of course, aware of Muḥammad's lineage, and that he was a descendant of the noblest family in Arabia. His ancestors were masters of Makkah. They nonetheless asked the question because Muḥammad himself did not occupy a position of power in Makkah before his prophethood.

In such a society, at that particular time, such a great principle could never have been the product of any earthly factor, or factors. It could only have had one source: God. No power could have ensured it other than divine will. Islamic society received it directly from the Prophet. Thereafter it became well established acquiring depth and momentum, which helped it to continue its operation in the Islamic community over the centuries.

The establishment of this principle was, indeed, a rebirth of humanity. It was greater in importance than the birth of the first man. Man was able to free himself from all worldly bonds and standards, and substitute for them a set of heavenly values independent of all earthly considerations. These new values were soon understood and accepted by everybody. Soon the grave matter which had required a special directive to be issued to Muḥammad, God's Messenger, and an order to him to deliver it in detail, became the operative principle of the Islamic conscience and the basic code of Islamic society. It remained so for a very long time.

Perhaps we cannot fully appreciate the true nature of this rebirth of humanity, because we cannot conceive the practical significance of our release from the pressures of social environment, values, standards, traditions and practices. In order to appreciate the magnitude of these pressures we have only to remember that advocates of a materialistic view of history consider that the economic condition of a certain society determines its beliefs, arts, literature, laws and customs, as well as its view of life and its destiny. What a narrow and mistaken view of man's true nature! It was with this basic principle that Islam accomplished the miracle of the rebirth of man.

Instilling a New Value

Since then the values attached to this great principle have become supreme. Their ascendancy, however, was by no means easy, neither in the Arabian society, nor in the minds of the Muslims themselves. Through his actions and directives, coloured by the profound effect the divine instructions in this *sūrah* left on him, the Prophet was able to implant this basic Islamic principle into his Companions' consciences and into the life of the Islamic society he had established. He looked after his new plant with unfailing care until it had established deep roots and spread its branches wide. Hence why this principle remained for centuries the guiding principle of the Muslim community.

After this incident the Prophet always welcomed Ibn Umm Maktūm warmly. Whenever he met him, he said: "Welcome to the man for whose sake my Lord reproved me." Twice, he appointed him as his deputy governor in Madinah when he himself had to be away.

The Prophet married his own cousin Zaynab bint Jaḥsh of the Asad clan to his former slave Zayd ibn Ḥārithah. Marriage has always been a very delicate issue, and it was particularly so in the Arabian Peninsula at that time. The Prophet's motive was to deal a deadly blow to all the social values and standards based on worldly considerations .

Soon after the Makkan Muslims settled in Madinah the Prophet established a bond of brotherhood between every two Muslims. He made his own uncle, Ḥamzah, a brother to his former slave, Zayd; and Khālid ibn Ruwayḥah of the Khatham tribe and Bilāl, the former slave, were made brothers.

He appointed Zayd as Commander-in-Chief of the Muslim army which fought the Battle of Mu'tah. Zayd's first deputy was the Prophet's own cousin Ja'far ibn Abī Ṭālib. The second deputy was 'Abdullāh ibn Rawāḥah of the *Anṣār*. A number of well-known personalities from Makkah and Madinah were in that army of three thousand men, including the most famous Muslim commander of all time, Khālid ibn al-Walīd. The Prophet himself went out to bid them farewell. It is also worth mentioning that Zayd and his two deputies were killed during that battle.

The Prophet's last action was to appoint Usāmah ibn Zayd, a young man, as commander of an army he had raised to fight the Byzantines. A large number of early Muslims, from both the *Muhājirīn* (Makkans) and the *Anṣār* (Madinans), including his two most distinguished Companions and immediate successors, Abū Bakr and 'Umar, as well as his own relative Sa'd ibn Abī Waqqāṣ, one of the very earliest people to embrace Islam, were in that army. Some people, however, grumbled about the fact that Usāmah had been made commander, young as he was. 'Abdullāh ibn 'Umar takes up the story: "When some people complained about giving the army command to Usāmah, the Prophet said: 'You are deprecating his appointment as commander in the same way as you previously deprecated his father's appointment. By God, his father was a worthy commander, and one of the dearest people to me. Usāmah is also one of the dearest people to me.'" [Related by al-Bukhārī, Muslim and al-Tirmidhī.]

Some people spoke in derogatory terms about the Prophet's Companion, Salmān, the Persian. They took a narrow nationalistic view and spoke of the inferiority of the Persians in relation to the Arabs. The Prophet took a decisive step to eradicate such narrow tendencies. He declared: "Salmān belongs to the Prophet's family." [Related by al-Ṭabarānī and al-Ḥākim.] This statement transcends all lineage, tribal and national considerations, which carried immense weight in Arabia.

Furthermore a disagreement occurred between Abū Dharr and Bilāl, two of the Prophet's highly esteemed Companions. In a fit of temper,

Abū Dharr called Bilāl "the son of a black woman". The Prophet was extremely upset at this. He rebuked Abū Dharr saying: "That is too much, Abū Dharr. He who has a white mother has no advantage which makes him better than the son of a black mother." [Related by Ibn al-Mubārak with slightly different wording.] Thus the Prophet put the dispute into its proper perspective. What distinguishes people is their faith, not their colour. This is the Islamic criterion, which is so unlike the worldly criteria of *jāhiliyyah* societies. The Prophet's rebuke had a profound effect on Abū Dharr, who was very sensitive. He wanted to atone for his mistake, so he put his head on the ground swearing that he would not raise it until Bilāl had put his foot over it.

Bilāl achieved a position of great distinction in Islamic society. What made his achievement possible was the application of heaven's values. Abū Hurayrah related that the Prophet once said to Bilāl: "Tell me, which of your actions do you hope to be the most rewarding for you, for last night I heard your footsteps as you drew near to me in heaven?" Bilāl answered: "I do not think that since becoming a Muslim I have ever done anything which I hope to be more rewarding than that every time I perform ablution at any time of the day or night I pray whatever I can." [Related by al-Bukhārī and Muslim.]

Once ʿAmmār ibn Yāsir asked for permission to see the Prophet. The Prophet said: "Let him come in. Welcome to the cleansed, good man." [Related by al-Tirmidhī.] He also said of him: "ʿAmmār is full of faith to the top of his head." [Related by al-Nasā'ī.] Ḥudhayfah related that the Prophet said: "I do not know how long I shall be with you, so accept the leadership of the two who will follow me [and he pointed to Abū Bakr and ʿUmar], and follow ʿAmmār's guidance. Believe whatever Ibn Masʿūd tells you." [Related by al-Tirmidhī.]

Ibn Masʿūd was so close to the Prophet that any stranger in Madinah would have thought him a member of the Prophet's household. Abū Mūsā said: "I came to Madinah from the Yemen with my brother. For quite some time we were under the impression that Ibn Masʿūd and his mother belonged to the Prophet's household, an impression we had formed because of the frequency of their comings and goings from the Prophet's homes, and their long companionship with him." [Related by al-Bukhārī and Muslim and al-Tirmidhī.]

The Prophet himself sought the hand of an *Anṣārī* woman in marriage for Julaybib, a former slave. "Her parents were reluctant to sanction such a marriage. She, however, said to them: 'Do you mean to reject the Prophet's suit? If the Prophet thinks that this man is suitable for us, then let this marriage go through.' So they gave their consent." [Related by Aḥmad.]

Soon after his marriage, Julaybib took part in an armed expedition. After the battle, which resulted in a victory for the Muslims, the Prophet asked his Companions: "Is anybody missing?" They named a few people. He repeated the question and they named a few others. He asked the same question for the third time and they answered in the negative. He said: "I think Julaybib is missing." They looked for him and found his body next to seven enemy soldiers whom he had killed. The Prophet went over, stood near him, and said: "He killed seven before he himself was slain. This man belongs to me and I belong to him." He lifted him into his arms until a grave had been dug. He then put him in his grave. The tradition does not say whether Julaybib was given a death wash or not. [Related by Muslim.]

The Principle in Practice

With this divine instruction and the Prophet's guidance, the rebirth of humanity was accomplished in a unique manner. Thus a new society came into existence, which imported its values and standards from heaven, and lived on earth, unhampered by earthly restrictions. This is the greatest miracle of Islam; a miracle which could not have happened except by God's will, and through the Prophet's actions. This miracle is, in itself, proof that Islam is a religion revealed by God, and that the man who conveyed it to us was His Messenger.

It was divine will that leadership of the Islamic society, after the Prophet's death, should be assigned successively to Abū Bakr and 'Umar, the two who were most keenly aware of the true nature of Islam and most vividly impressed by the Prophet's guidance. Indeed, Abū Bakr and 'Umar surpassed everyone else in their love for the Prophet and determination to follow very closely in his footsteps.

Abū Bakr was well aware of the Prophet's object in assigning the army's command to Usāmah. His first action after he became Caliph was to send the army raised by the Prophet and commanded by Usāmah on its original mission. Abū Bakr, the Caliph, went along with the army to the outskirts of Madinah to bid it farewell. It was a strange scene: 'Usāmah on his horse while Abū Bakr walked. Usāmah, the young commander, felt embarrassed that he should ride while the Caliph, an old man, should walk. He begged Abū Bakr to ride, or else he would walk alongside him. Abū Bakr refused, saying: "You shall not walk and I shall not ride. It will do me no harm to walk for an hour if my walking is for God's cause."

Abū Bakr felt that he needed 'Umar to help him shoulder the responsibilities of government. 'Umar, however, was a soldier in Usāmah's army, so he had to ask Usāmah's permission to discharge him. Hence, the Caliph, the Head of State, said to his army commander: "If you think you can spare 'Umar to help me, then please do so!" What a request! It is the height of magnanimity, attainable only with God's will, by individuals well taught by God's Messenger.

A few years later 'Umar assumed the leadership of the Muslim community, as its second Caliph. One of his actions was to appoint 'Ammār ibn Yāsir, who formerly belonged to the lower classes of Makkah, as governor of the Kufah region in Iraq.

One day a number of dignitaries from the Quraysh, including Suhayl ibn 'Amr and Abū Sufyān, sought to see 'Umar. He let them wait and admitted first Ṣuhayb and Bilāl, two former slaves, on the grounds of their early acceptance of Islam and their taking part at the Battle of Badr. Abū Sufyān was angry and said: "I have never seen a day like this. These slaves are admitted and we are kept waiting!" Suhayl, who was more keenly aware of the true nature of Islam, said: "Gentlemen! I see in your faces an expression of what you feel, but I say to you that if you are angry you should be angry with yourselves. Both they and you were called upon to accept Islam at the same time. They were quick to respond but you were slow. What will you do if on the Day of Judgement you find that they are included among the chosen and you are left behind?"

ʿUmar allotted Usāmah ibn Zayd a larger share of the spoils of war than he allotted his own son ʿAbdullāh. When ʿAbdullāh queried his father's decision ʿUmar said: "Son, the Prophet used to love Zayd more than he loved your father, and he loved Usāmah more than he loved you. What I did was simply to attach to the Prophet's love higher value than I attached to my own love." As he said this ʿUmar was, of course, fully aware that the Prophet measured his love by divine standards.

ʿUmar sent ʿAmmār to question Khālid ibn al-Walīd, the victorious commander of the Muslim army who belonged to a noble family, about certain charges. ʿAmmār tied Khālid's robes round his neck. Some reports add that he tied Khālid's hands throughout the interrogation with his own turban. When the investigation proved Khālid's innocence, ʿAmmār untied him and put Khālid's turban back on his head with his own hands. Khālid did not object to this treatment. He knew that ʿAmmār was one of the Prophet's early Companions. Khālid also knew what the Prophet used to say about ʿAmmār, which we have already quoted.

It was ʿUmar himself who used to say about Abū Bakr and Bilāl: "Abū Bakr is our master and he freed our master." This refers to the days when Bilāl was Umayyah ibn Khalaf's slave, who tortured him mercilessly in order to turn him away from Islam. Abū Bakr bought Bilāl from Umayyah and set him free. This former slave, Bilāl, is described by ʿUmar, the Caliph, as "our master".

ʿUmar was the one who said, "Had Sālim, the former slave of Abū Ḥudhayfah, been alive I would have nominated him to succeed me." This statement must be taken against the background that ʿUmar did not nominate anyone to succeed him, not even 'Uthmān, 'Alī, Ṭalḥah or al-Zubayr. He only appointed a consultative committee of six, so that the next Caliph should be chosen from among them.

'Alī ibn Abī Ṭālib sent 'Ammār and al-Ḥasan, his own son, to Kūfah to seek its people's support against 'Ā'ishah [may God be pleased with her]. His message said, "I know that she is your Prophet's wife in this life and in the life to come. You are, however, faced with a test which will prove whether you follow your Prophet or his wife." [Related by al-Bukhārī.] The people of Kūfah accepted his case against 'Ā'ishah, mother of the believers and Abū Bakr's daughter, [may God be pleased with them all].

Bilāl was asked by his brother in Islam, Abū Ruwayḥah of Khatham, to speak on his behalf to the family of a Yemeni woman he wished to marry. Bilāl did so, saying: "I am Bilāl ibn Rabāḥ and this is my brother, Abū Ruwayḥah. He lacks good manners and firm belief. You may please yourselves whether you give him your daughter in marriage or not." He did not deceive them by hiding the truth, nor did he behave as a mediator, unmindful of his accountability to God. The family concerned were pleased with such honesty. They married their daughter to Abū Ruwayḥah, the noble Arab whose advocate was Bilāl, a former slave from Abyssinia.

This fundamental principle remained firmly entrenched throughout Islamic society for centuries, despite the various factors working for a setback. 'Abdullāh ibn 'Abbās was always remembered with his slave 'Ikrimah, while 'Abdullāh ibn 'Umar was remembered with his slave Nāfi'. Anas ibn Mālik was always associated with his slave Ibn Sīrīn, as was Abū Hurayrah with his slave 'Abd al-Raḥmān ibn Hurmuz.[1] In the generation that followed, the most distinguished men of learning were al-Ḥasan in Basrah, Mujāhid ibn Jabr, 'Aṭā' ibn Rabāḥ and Ṭāwūs ibn Kaysān. In Egypt, Yazīd ibn Abī Ḥabīb, a black slave from Dengla, was the grand Mufti [holder of the highest

1. All these were scholars of the highest calibre, with the four mentioned first being Companions of the Prophet. The others passed on their scholarship to the succeeding generations. – Editor's note.

position of religious authority] during the reign of 'Umar ibn 'Abd al-'Azīz.[2]

This divine standard continued to win great respect for the pious and God-fearing, even when they were deprived of all things to which worldly considerations attached great value. It is only in comparatively recent times that this divine standard has ceased to operate. For now the whole world is overwhelmed by a tide of *jāhiliyyah*, wherein there is a total disregard for divine values. In the United States, the leading Western country, a man is valued according to the size of his bank balance. In the Soviet Union,[3] where Communism, the ruling philosophy, looks at life as no more than matter, and a man is worth less than a machine. The land of Islam, on the other hand, has sunk back into *jāhiliyyah*. The creeds of *jāhiliyyah*, which Islam had rooted out, have now been revived. The divine standard has been abandoned in favour of materialistic values which are completely alien to Islam.

The only hope that remains is that the Islamic revivalist movement will rescue mankind once again from the clutches of *jāhiliyyah* and bring about humanity's second rebirth, similar to the one announced by the decisive verses at the opening of this *sūrah*.

Man's Arrogant Attitude

The second part of the *sūrah* wonders at man's conceit as he turns his back on the true faith. It wonders at how man forgets his humble origins, and how he remains totally oblivious of the care God has taken of him and His complete power over every stage of his existence, both in this life and in the hereafter. In his ingratitude man fulfils nothing of his duties towards his Lord, who has created and sustained him and who will hold him to account for his actions: "*Perish man! How ungrateful he is! Of what did God create him? Of a*

2. These details are based on information given by A.H. al-Guindi in his book *Abū Ḥanīfah*, Cairo.

3. The author is referring here to the former Soviet Union, which was one of the two superpowers in his own time. – Editor's note.

drop of sperm. He created him and proportioned him. He makes his path smooth for him. He then causes him to die and puts him in his grave. He will surely bring him back to life when He pleases. But by no means has man fulfilled His bidding." (Verses 17–23)

"*Perish man!*" He deserves to die. The mode of expression employed also adds to the sense of horror excited by this abominable attitude. "*How ungrateful he is*!" He strongly denies the claims of his creation. Had he been mindful of these claims he would have been humbly grateful to his Lord who created him. He would not have shown such conceit and he would have remembered the end he is certain to meet.

Indeed, how can man be so arrogant and conceited? What are his origins: "*Of what did God create him?*" (Verse 18) His is a very humble origin, worthless indeed except for God's grace. "*Of a drop of sperm. He created him and proportioned him.*" (Verse 19) A drop of sperm of no significance; that is man's beginning. God, the Creator, then proportioned him. The Arabic verb used here *qaddara* denotes precise and meticulous proportioning. It also denotes bestowing weight and value This is how man has been created, honoured and raised from his humble origins to a high position in which the whole world has been put at his disposal.

"*He makes his path smooth for him.*" (Verse 20) The path of life has been smoothed for him. He has also been given the ability to recognize and follow the right path.

When the journey of life is over, when every living being meets its inevitable end, "*He then causes him to die and puts him in his grave.*" (Verse 21) So in the end the case is just the same as in the beginning: man submits to his Lord who brings him to life when He wills and ends his life when He wills. He honours him by making the earth his last abode, rather than leaving him as food for wild animals. He has made it part of human nature to bury the dead. When the time He has appointed arrives, He brings him back to life for the reckoning: "*He will surely bring him back to life when He pleases.*" (Verse 22) So man will not be left without reward or retribution.

But has man prepared himself for this reckoning? It would seem that "*by no means has man fulfilled His bidding.*" (Verse 23) Mankind as a whole, from the very first to the very last, will not have fulfilled God's bidding. This is the inference of the Arabic expression used here, *lammā Yaqḍi mā amarah*. Man will always remain negligent of his duties. He will never remember his origins and creation as he should, nor will he thank and praise his Creator who has guided and looked after him as He should be thanked and praised. Man does not prepare himself in this life for the day of reward and retribution. This applies to humanity as a whole. In addition, the great majority of people arrogantly turn their backs on divine guidance.

Useful Reflection

Next, the *sūrah* invites man to reflect upon his food and that of his cattle, which is one of the great many things God has provided for him: "*Let man reflect on the food he eats: how We pour down the rain in torrents, and cleave the earth in fissures; how We bring forth the corn, the grapes, and the fresh vegetation, the olive and the palm, the dense-treed gardens, the fruit trees and the green pastures, for you and your cattle to delight in.*" (Verses 24–32)

This is the full story of man's food, related here stage by stage. Let man reflect: does he play any significant role in it? Can he determine or change its course? Indeed, the same hand which has brought him to life has brought forth the food which sustains him.

"*Let man reflect on the food he eats.*" (Verse 24) Food, the first necessity of human life, deserves a few thoughts. It is made readily available day after day. But behind all this is a simple and wonderful story. Yet such simplicity makes man forget its wonder. Nevertheless, it is as miraculous as man's own creation. Every step is determined by the Supreme Will that creates man.

"*How we pour down the rain in torrents.*" (Verse 25) The pouring rain is a fact known to every human being, wherever he lives, regardless of his level of experience or knowledge. It is, therefore, taken up in this address to all human beings. As man's knowledge has increased, he is now able to appreciate the meaning of this verse more fully. He knows that something happened a long time before the daily phenomenon of rain came to be established. Perhaps the theory closest to the truth concerning the formation of the oceans, whose water evaporates and then returns as rain, claims that they were formed somewhere above the earth and were then poured down in torrents. A contemporary scientist says on this subject:

> If it is true that the temperature of the earth at the time of its separation from the sun was about 12,000 degrees, or that of the surface of the sun, then all the elements were free and, therefore, no chemical combination of importance could exist. Gradually, as the earth, or the earth-forming fragments, cooled, combinations would take place and a nucleus of the world as we know it is formed. Oxygen and hydrogen could not combine until the temperature was reduced to 4,000 degrees Fahrenheit. At this point these elements would rush together and form water. What we know as the atmosphere must have been enormous at that time. All the oceans were in the sky and all those elements not combined were in the air as gases. Water, having formed in the outer atmosphere, fell towards the earth but could not reach it, as the temperature near the earth was higher than it was thousands of miles out. Of course, the time came when the deluge would reach the earth only to fly up again as steam. With whole oceans in the air, floods that would result as cooling progressed are beyond calculation.[4]

Although we do not claim any definite link between this theory and this particular Qur'ānic statement, we acknowledge that the theory gives us a better understanding of what it means and the period of history it refers to, i.e., the period of water pouring down in torrents. The theory may be proved right. On the other hand, other theories

4. A. Cressy Morrison, *Man Does Not Stand Alone*, London, 1962, pp. 25–26.

may be put forward to explain the origins of water. The Qur'ānic statement, however, remains valid for all ages and societies.

This is how the production of food starts: "*We pour down the rain in torrents.*" (Verse 25) No one can claim either to have produced water, at any stage of its formation, or to have caused it to be poured, so that the process of food production could be set in motion.

"*And cleave the earth in fissures.*" (Verse 26) Primitive man sees the rain falling and realizes that he has no power over it. He sees the water splitting the earth and penetrating the soil. He also sees the plants cleaving the earth with the Creator's will and growing over its surface. He notices that the plants are thin and the earth heavy yet the Creator's hand enables the plants to split the earth and move through it. Anyone who contemplates how plants grow can recognize the miracle involved here.

As human knowledge expands, a new understanding of this statement may be developed. The cleaving of the earth so that it became suitable for vegetation may have taken place a long time ago. The Qur'ānic statement may refer to the multiple break up of the earth's surface rocks caused by the great floods and by the various climatic factors which, according to modern scientists, contributed to the formation of a soil layer where vegetation could grow. This interpretation fits more closely with the sequence of events as it is reported here.

In either case, the third stage is that of the growth of all kinds of vegetation. The kind mentioned here is the best known to the people immediately addressed by the Qur'ān. "*How We bring forth the corn.*" (Verse 27) '*The corn*' refers to all cereals and grains used for human or animal food. "*The grapes, and the fresh vegetation.*" (Verse 28) The reference here is to the well-known vine fruits and to all vegetables which can be eaten raw and picked time after time. "*The olive and the palm, the dense-treed gardens, the fruit trees and the green pastures.*" (Verses 29–31) The olive and the palm fruits are well-known to all Arabs. '*The gardens*' refer to the fenced fields of fruit trees. They are described here as being dense with trees. The Arabic term '*abb*', translated here as green pastures, refers in all probability to the herbage used for cattle. As mentioned in the commentary on the preceding *sūrah*, 'Umar asked what '*abb*' meant and then blamed himself for asking. So we follow 'Umar's suit and add nothing to what has already been mentioned.

This is the story of food, the provision of which is carefully planned by the hand which created man. Man plays no role in any of its stages. Even the seeds and grains he casts on the earth are not of his making. The miraculous aspect here lies in the original production of these seeds and grains, which is beyond man's comprehension. Various seeds may be planted on the same piece of land, irrigated by one kind of water; yet each produces its own fruit. It is the hand of the Creator which makes this infinite collection of plants and their fruits, and preserves in the little seed the characteristics of its mother plant so that they may reappear in the plant which issues from it. Man remains ignorant of the secrets of this process. He has no power over it. It is God's own production: "*For you and your cattle to delight in.*" (Verse 32) This delight is, however, for a limited period. There follows something totally different which needs to be carefully considered by man before it actually arrives.

A Signal for Resurrection

> *But when the stunning blast is sounded, on that day everyone will forsake his brother, his mother and his father, his wife and his children: for each one of them will on that day have enough pre-occupations of his own. Some faces on that day shall be beaming, smiling and joyful. Some other faces on that day shall be covered with dust, veiled with darkness. These shall be the faces of the unbelievers, the hardened in sin.* (Verses 33–42)

This is the end of all delight and enjoyment. It fits perfectly with the planning and designing which included every stage of man's development. The end portrayed here fits perfectly with the scene at the beginning of the *sūrah* which shows someone coming forward with zeal and with a feeling of fear in his heart, and another considers himself self-sufficient and turns away from divine guidance. Here we have an exposition of their standing in God's view.

'*The stunning blast*' is the nearest translation of an Arabic term, *al-ṣākhkhah*, which carries a very sharp tone; it almost pierces the ears. This effect simply prepares us for the following scene in which we see "*everyone will forsake his brother, his mother and his father, his wife and his children.*" (Verses 34–36) Such ties between a person and his nearest relations cannot be severed in the normal course of events. Yet *the stunning blast* destroys these very links and throws them up into the air.

The fearfulness depicted in this scene is purely psychological. It strikes the soul, isolates it and holds it in its grip. The result is that each of us will think only of ourselves. None shall have any time or power to think of others: "*For each one of them will on that day have enough preoccupations of his own.*" (Verse 37) The description is vivid; yet there can be no shorter and yet more comprehensive statement to describe the general condition of worried minds and souls.

When *the stunning blast* takes place the condition is universal. Then follows a description of the conditions of the believers and the unbelievers after the two groups have been assigned their values by divine standards and given their respective positions: "*Some faces on that day shall be beaming, smiling and joyful.*" (Verses 38–39) These faces beam with a happiness overflowing with delight. They are hopeful and reassured because they feel that their Lord is pleased with them. These people are spared the terror of *the stunning blast*, so they can afford to smile and demonstrate their joy. Or probably the smiles and manifestations of happiness are seen after these people have realized the good end awaiting them.

"*Some other faces on that day shall be covered with dust, veiled with darkness. These shall be the faces of the unbelievers, the hardened in sin.*" (Verses 40–42) Such faces are covered with the dust of sadness and misery, darkened with humiliation and depression. They know what they have done in this life and they await their inevitable punishment. "*These shall be the faces of the unbelievers, the hardened in sin.*" (Verse 42) These people are devoid of faith. They do not believe in God or in the divine message. Moreover, they are hardened in their erring and sinful ways. They persistently violate divine commandments.

The destiny of each group is portrayed in their faces. It is a vivid portrait drawn with words and expressions – a fact which testifies to the immense power characteristic of the Qur'ānic style. The opening and the close of the *sūrah* are in perfect harmony. The opening lays down a fundamental principle and a general standard, and the close shows us the results of applying this standard. The *sūrah* is a short one; yet it states a number of major facts and principles, portraying a large number of scenes, utilizing different rhythms. Furthermore the style brings out these images in full relief.

SŪRAH 81

Al-Takwīr

(The Darkening)

Al-Takwīr (The Darkening)

سُورَةُ التَّكْوِيرِ

In the name of God, the Beneficent, the Merciful.

بِسْمِ ٱللَّهِ ٱلرَّحْمَٰنِ ٱلرَّحِيمِ

When the sun is darkened, (1)

إِذَا ٱلشَّمْسُ كُوِّرَتْ ﴿١﴾

when the stars fall and disperse, (2)

وَإِذَا ٱلنُّجُومُ ٱنكَدَرَتْ ﴿٢﴾

when the mountains are made to move away, (3)

وَإِذَا ٱلْجِبَالُ سُيِّرَتْ ﴿٣﴾

when the camels, ten months pregnant, are left untended, (4)

وَإِذَا ٱلْعِشَارُ عُطِّلَتْ ﴿٤﴾

when the wild beasts are brought together, (5)

وَإِذَا ٱلْوُحُوشُ حُشِرَتْ ﴿٥﴾

when the seas are set alight, (6)

وَإِذَا ٱلْبِحَارُ سُجِّرَتْ ﴿٦﴾

when people's souls are paired [like with like], (7)	وَإِذَا ٱلنُّفُوسُ زُوِّجَتْ ٧
when the infant girl, buried alive, is asked (8)	وَإِذَا ٱلْمَوْءُۥدَةُ سُئِلَتْ ٨
for what crime she was slain, (9)	بِأَىِّ ذَنۢبٍ قُتِلَتْ ٩
when the records are laid open, (10)	وَإِذَا ٱلصُّحُفُ نُشِرَتْ ١٠
when the sky is stripped bare, (11)	وَإِذَا ٱلسَّمَآءُ كُشِطَتْ ١١
when hell is made to burn fiercely, (12)	وَإِذَا ٱلْجَحِيمُ سُعِّرَتْ ١٢
when paradise is brought near, (13)	وَإِذَا ٱلْجَنَّةُ أُزْلِفَتْ ١٣
every soul shall know what it has put forward. (14)	عَلِمَتْ نَفْسٌ مَّآ أَحْضَرَتْ ١٤
I swear by the turning stars, (15)	فَلَآ أُقْسِمُ بِٱلْخُنَّسِ ١٥
which move swiftly and hide themselves away, (16)	ٱلْجَوَارِ ٱلْكُنَّسِ ١٦
and by the night as it comes darkening on, (17)	وَٱلَّيْلِ إِذَا عَسْعَسَ ١٧
and by the dawn as it starts to breathe, (18)	وَٱلصُّبْحِ إِذَا تَنَفَّسَ ١٨

this is truly the word of a noble and mighty messenger, (19)

إِنَّهُۥ لَقَوۡلُ رَسُولٖ كَرِيمٖ ١٩

who enjoys a secure position with the Lord of the Throne. (20)

ذِي قُوَّةٍ عِندَ ذِي ٱلۡعَرۡشِ مَكِينٖ ٢٠

He is obeyed in heaven, faithful to his trust. (21)

مُّطَاعٖ ثَمَّ أَمِينٖ ٢١

Your old friend is not mad. (22)

وَمَا صَاحِبُكُم بِمَجۡنُونٖ ٢٢

He saw him on the clear horizon. (23)

وَلَقَدۡ رَءَاهُ بِٱلۡأُفُقِ ٱلۡمُبِينِ ٢٣

He does not grudge the secrets of the unseen. (24)

وَمَا هُوَ عَلَى ٱلۡغَيۡبِ بِضَنِينٖ ٢٤

It is not the word of an accursed devil. (25)

وَمَا هُوَ بِقَوۡلِ شَيۡطَٰنٖ رَّجِيمٖ ٢٥

Whither then are you going? (26)

فَأَيۡنَ تَذۡهَبُونَ ٢٦

This is only a reminder to all mankind, (27)

إِنۡ هُوَ إِلَّا ذِكۡرٞ لِّلۡعَٰلَمِينَ ٢٧

to those of you whose will is to be upright. (28)

لِمَن شَآءَ مِنكُمۡ أَن يَسۡتَقِيمَ ٢٨

Yet, you cannot will except by the will of God, Lord of all the worlds. (29)

وَمَا تَشَآءُونَ إِلَّآ أَن يَشَآءَ ٱللَّهُ رَبُّ
ٱلۡعَٰلَمِينَ ٢٩

Overview

This *sūrah* may be divided into two parts, each of them treating one major principle of faith. The first is the principle of resurrection accompanied by a great upheaval in the universe, which affects the sun and the stars, the mountains and seas, heaven and earth, wild and domestic animals, as well as man. The second principle is that of revelation. The *sūrah* has something to say about the angel carrying the divine revelation, the Prophet receiving it, the people addressed by it, and the Supreme Will which has shaped their nature and bestowed this revelation.

The rhythm of the *sūrah* is one of violent movement which leaves nothing in its place. Everything is thrown away, smashed or scattered. The movement is so violent that it excites and frightens. It alters every familiar situation and shakes people's hearts violently so that they feel deprived of both shelter and reassurance. In such a violent destructive storm the human heart is no more than a little feather, blown in every direction. No protection and, indeed, no safety can be found except what is granted by God, the Eternal. Thus, the rhythm of the *sūrah* has, on its own, the effect of pulling man's heart and soul away from everything associated with safety and security, in order to seek peace, safety and protection with God.

The *sūrah* is also a gem of striking images drawn from the universe in both its present beautiful condition, which is familiar to us, and its condition on the Day of Resurrection when every familiar thing is changed beyond recognition. The *sūrah* is, moreover, rich in fine expressions which add colour to the images portrayed. As the *sūrah* is so short, the rhythm, images and expressions combine together to produce a very strong and lasting effect. Had it not been for the fact that the *sūrah* contains some words which are no longer familiar to us today, I would have preferred not to comment on it. Its rhythm and images leave a far stronger effect than any human interpretation can aspire to achieve.

Upheaval in the Universe

When the sun is darkened, when the stars fall and disperse, when the mountains are made to move away, when the camels, ten months pregnant, are left untended, when the wild beasts are brought together, when the seas are set alight, when people's souls are paired [like with like], when the infant girl, buried alive, is asked for what crime she was slain, when the records are laid open, when the sky is stripped bare, when hell is made to burn fiercely, when paradise is brought near, every soul shall know what it has put forward. (Verses 1–14)

These verses sketch a scene of great upheaval which envelops the whole universe. It is an event which reveals every guarded secret and leaves nothing hidden away. Every human being faces what he has put forward for the day of reckoning and judgement. The great events mentioned indicate that the present familiar state of the universe, with its perfect harmony, measured movement, controlled relations, perfected by the Maker whose work is flawless, will suffer a complete break down. Its role will be finished. Along with all creation, it will move into a new predetermined phase of life, unlike anything known to us in this world.

The *sūrah* aims to get this idea of the inevitable upheaval well established in people's hearts and minds so that they may attach little or no importance to the values and riches of this world, though these may seem to be of lasting consequence. People should establish a firm bond with the everlasting truth, i.e. the truth of God, the Eternal, who never changes when everything else changes and disappears. They should break the chains of what is familiar in this life in order to recognize the absolute truth which admits no restrictions of time, place, finite faculties or temporal standards.

As one goes through the events of this universal upheaval, one cannot fail to observe an inner feeling for this affirmation.

As to what exactly happens to all these creations during the resurrection we can only say that it is known to God alone. We can only comprehend what we have experienced. When we think of a great upheaval in the world, our imagination cannot stretch beyond a violent earthquake or volcano, or, perhaps, the fall of a comet or a small celestial body. Floods are perhaps the most destructive manifestation of the power of water known to us. The most powerful events in the universe we have monitored were some limited explosions in the sun, which is millions of miles away from us. All these events, great as they may be, seem so small when they are compared to the universal upheaval which will take place on the Day of Resurrection that they may be considered akin to child's play. If we really want to know what will happen then, we can do no more than attempt to draw some sort of comparison with what we have experienced in this life.

The darkening of the sun probably means that it will cool down and its flames which stretch out for thousands of miles in space will dwindle and die. As the sun is now in gaseous form because of its intense heat, which reaches a maximum of 12,000 degrees, its darkening probably means its transformation by freezing to a form similar to that of the surface of the earth. It may adopt a circular shape without becoming stretched out. This is probably the meaning of the opening verse, but it could also mean something different. As to how it will happen, or its causes, we can only say that this is known only to God.

The falling of the stars probably means that they will break away from the system which holds them together and lose their light and brightness. Only God knows which stars will be affected by this event: will it affect only a small group of stars, say, our own solar system, or our galaxy, which comprises hundreds of millions of stars, or will it affect all the stars in their millions of millions? The universe, as everyone knows, comprises an almost infinite number of galaxies, each with its own space.

Forcing the mountains to move away probably means that they will be crushed and blown away as indicated in other *sūrahs*: "*They ask you about the mountains. Say: 'My Lord will crush them to fine dust and leave them a desolate waste.'*" (20: 105) "*When the mountains crumble away and scatter into fine dust.*" (56: 5) "*And the mountains are made to move away, and seem to have been a mirage.*" (78: 20) All these verses refer to a certain event which will affect the mountains and do away with their firm foundations and stability. This may be the beginning of the quake which will shake the earth violently, and which is mentioned in *Sūrah* 99, The Earthquake: "*When the earth is rocked with her final earthquake, when the earth shakes off her burdens.*" (99: 1–2) All these events will take place on that very long day.

"*When the camels, ten months pregnant, are left untended.*" (Verse 4) The Arabic description of the camel here specifies that she is in her tenth month of pregnancy. When in this state, she is to the Arab his most valuable possession because she is about to add to his wealth a highly valued young camel, and to give him a lot of milk which he and his family will share with the new-born animal. However, on that day, which will witness such overwhelming events, such priceless camels will be left without care, completely untended. The Arabs who were the first to be addressed by this verse never left such camels untended, except for the gravest of dangers.

"*When the wild beasts are brought together.*" (Verse 5) The great terror which overwhelms the wild beasts in their jungles is the cause of their coming together. They forget their mutual enmities, and move together, unaware of their direction. They neither seek their homes nor chase their prey as they usually do. The overwhelming terror changes the character of even the wildest of beasts. What then will it do to man?

"*When the seas are set alight.*" (Verse 6) The Arabic term, *sujjirat*, used here may mean that the seas will be overfilled with water, from floods similar to those which characterized the early stages of life on earth. On the other hand, earthquakes and volcanoes may remove the barriers now separating the seas so that the water of one will flow into the other. The Arabic expression may also mean that the seas will experience explosions which set them ablaze, as mentioned elsewhere in the Qur'ān: "*When the oceans are made to explode.*" (82: 3) Such explosions may result from separating oxygen and hydrogen which make sea water. They could also be atomic explosions of some sort. If the explosion of a limited number of atoms in a hydrogen or atom bomb produces such dreadful consequences as we have seen, then the atomic explosion of the waters of the oceans, in whatever manner it may occur, will produce something much too fearful for our minds to visualize. Similarly, we cannot conceive the reality of hell, which stands beyond these vast oceans.

"*When people's souls are paired.*" (Verse 7) The pairing of souls may mean the reunion of body and soul at the time of resurrection. It may also mean their grouping, like with like, as mentioned elsewhere in the Qur'ān: "*You will be divided into three groups.*" (56: 7) These are the chosen élite, the people of the right, and the people of the left. It may also mean some other way of grouping.

Girls Buried Alive

"*When the infant girl, buried alive, is asked for what crime she was slain.*" (Verses 8–9) The value of human life must have sunk very low in pre-Islamic Arabian society. There existed a convention of burying young girls alive, for fear of shame or poverty. The Qur'ān describes this practice in order to portray its horror and denounce it as a practice of ignorance or *jāhiliyyah*. Its condemnation fits in perfectly with the declared aim of Islam, to destroy *jāhiliyyah* and save mankind from sinking to its depths. In *Sūrah* 16, The Bee, we read in translation: "*When the birth of a girl is announced to one of them, his face grows dark and he is filled with rage and inward gloom. Because of the bad news he hides himself from everybody: should he keep her with disgrace or bury her under the dust? How ill they judge.*" (16: 58–9) And in *Sūrah* 17, The Night Journey: "*You shall not kill your children for fear of want. We will provide for them and for you.*" (17: 31)

Girls were killed in an extremely cruel way. They were buried alive! The Arabs used different ways of doing so. Some would leave the girl until she was six years of age. The father would then say to his wife to dress the girl in her best clothes and make her presentable because she would be visiting her prospective in-laws. He would have already dug a hole for her in the desert. When the girl got there, he would tell her that the hole is a well and then tell her to look down it. As she stood at the edge, he would push her into the hole and as she fell, he would throw sand over her and bury her. In certain tribes when a pregnant woman was about to give birth, she would sit over a hole in the ground. When the baby was born she would first establish its sex. If it was a boy, she would take him home, and if it was a girl, she would throw her in the hole and bury her. If a father decided not to bury his daughter alive, he would bring her up in a condition of deprivation until she was old enough to tend sheep or cattle, giving her only an overall made of rough wool to dress and making her do this type of work.

Those Arabs who did not kill their young daughters or send them to mind cattle, had different methods of ill-treating women. If a man died, the head of the clan would throw his gown over the widow. This was a gesture of acquisition which meant that the widow could not marry anyone except the owner of the gown. If he was attracted to her, he would marry her, paying absolutely no regard to her feelings. If he did not marry her, he would keep her until she died so as to inherit any money or property she might leave behind.

Such was the attitude of *jāhiliyyah* society in Arabia to women. Islam condemns this attitude and spurns all these practices. It forbids the murder of young girls and shows its abhorrent and horrifying nature. It is listed as one of the subjects of reckoning on the Day of Judgement. Here, the *sūrah* mentions it as one of the great events which overwhelms the universe in total upheaval. We are told that the murdered girl will be questioned about her murder. The *sūrah* leaves us to imagine how the murderer will be brought to account.

The *jāhiliyyah* social order of the pre-Islamic period would never have helped women to gain a respectable, dignified position. That had to be decreed by God. The way of life God has chosen for mankind secures a dignified position for both men and women who share the honour of having a measure of the divine spirit breathed into them. Women owe their respectable position to Islam, not to any environmental factor or social set-up.

When the new man with heavenly values came into being, women became respected and honoured. The woman's weakness of being a financial burden to her family was no longer of any consequence in determining her position and the respect she enjoyed. Such considerations have no weight on the scales of heaven. Real weight belongs to the noble human soul when it maintains its relationship with God. In this men and women are equal.

When one puts forward arguments in support of the fact that Islam is a divine religion, and that it has been conveyed to us by God's Messenger who received His revelations, one should state the change made by Islam in the social status of women as being irrefutable. Nothing in the social set-up of Arabia at the time pointed to such elevation for women. No social or economic consideration made it necessary or desirable. It was a deliberate move made by Islam for reasons which are totally different from those of this world and from those of *jāhiliyyah* society in particular.

"*When the records are laid open.*" (Verse 10) This is a reference to the records of people's deeds. They are laid open in order that they may be known to everybody. This, in itself, is hard to bear. Many a breast has a closely hidden secret, the remembrance of which brings shame and a shudder to its owner. Yet all secrets are made public on that eventful day. This publicity, representative of the great upheaval which envelops the whole universe, is part of the fearful events which fill men's hearts with horror on the day.

"*When the sky is stripped bare.*" (Verse 11) This image corresponds closely to throwing open people's secrets. When the word 'sky' is used, our first thoughts reach to the blue cover hoisted over our heads. Its stripping means the removal of that cover. How this happens remains a matter of conjecture. It is enough to say that when we look up we will no longer see our familiar blue dome.

The last scene of that fearful day is portrayed by the next two verses: "*When hell is made to burn fiercely, when paradise is brought near.*" (Verses 12–13) Where is hell? How does it burn? What fuel is used in lighting and feeding its fire? The only thing we know of it is that it "*has the fuel of men and stones.*" (66: 6) This is, of course, after they have been thrown in it. Its true nature and its fuel prior to that is part of God's knowledge. Heaven, on the other hand, is brought near to those who have been promised admission. They see it to be of easy access. Indeed, the expression here shows it ready to receive its dwellers.

When all these great events take place throughout the universe, changing the status of all life, no one can entertain any doubt about what they have done in this present life, or what they have carried with them to the next life: "*Every soul shall know what it has put forward.*" (Verse 14) In the midst of all these overwhelming events, every soul shall know for certain what sort of deeds it has brought and that it cannot change, omit from or add to what it has done.

People will find themselves completely separated from all that has been familiar to them, and from their world as a whole. Everything will have undergone a total change except God. If man turns to God, he will find that His support is forthcoming when the whole universe is overwhelmed by change. Thus ends the first part of this *sūrah*, leaving us with a vivid impression of the universal upheaval on the Day of Resurrection.

A Splendid Universal Scene

The second part of the *sūrah* opens with a form of oath using some very beautiful scenes of the universe. Essentially, this oath is made to assert the nature of revelation, the angel carrying it, and the Messenger receiving and delivering it to us, as well as people's attitudes to it, all in accordance with God's will: "*I swear by the turning stars, which move swiftly and hide themselves away, and by the night as it comes darkening on, and by the dawn as it starts to breathe, this is truly the word of a noble and mighty messenger, who enjoys a secure position with the Lord of the Throne. He is obeyed in heaven, faithful to his trust. Your old friend is not mad. He saw him on the clear horizon.*

He does not grudge the secrets of the unseen. It is not the word of an accursed devil. Whither then are you going? This is only a reminder to all mankind, to those of you whose will is to be upright. Yet, you cannot will except by the will of God, Lord of all the worlds." (Verses 15–29)

The stars referred to here are those which turn in their orbit, and are characterized by their swift movement and temporary disappearance. In translating the text we have to forego the metaphor used in Arabic which draws an analogy between these stars and the deer as they run at great speed towards their homes, disappear for a while and then reappear at a different point. This metaphor adds considerable liveliness and beauty to the description of the movement of the stars, which echoes the fine rhythm of the expression.

Again, the rhythm of the Arabic verse translated as "*and by the night as it comes darkening on*" gives a feeling of life, depicting the night as a living being. The beauty of the Arabic expression is of surpassing excellence. The same applies to the next verse: "*and by the dawn as it starts to breathe*". This verse is indeed more effective in portraying dawn as alive, breathing. Its breath is the spreading light and the life that begins to stir in everything. I doubt whether the Arabic language, with its inexhaustible wealth of imagery and vivid expression, can produce an image portraying dawn which can be considered equal to this Qur'ānic image in aesthetic effect. After a fine night, one can almost feel that dawn is breathing.

Any aesthete will readily perceive that the divine words of the first four verses of this second part of the *sūrah* constitute a gem of expression and description: "*I swear by the turning stars, which move swiftly and hide themselves away, and by the night as it comes darkening on, and by the dawn as it starts to breathe.*" (Verses 15–18) This descriptive wealth adds power to man's feelings as he responds to the natural phenomena to which the verses refer.

The Two Messengers

As the Qur'ān makes this brief, full-of-life description of these phenomena it establishes a spiritual link between them and man, with the result that, as we read, we feel the power which created these phenomena, and the truth which we are called upon to believe. This truth is then stated in a manner which fits in superbly with the general theme of the *sūrah*: "*This is truly the word of a noble and mighty messenger, who enjoys a secure position with the Lord of the Throne. He is obeyed in heaven, faithful to his trust.*" (Verses 19–21) This Qur'ān with its description of the Day of Judgement is the word of a noble and mighty messenger, i.e. Jibrīl or Gabriel, the angel who carried and delivered it to Muḥammad (peace be upon him).

The *sūrah* then gives a description of this chosen messenger. He is 'noble', honoured by God who says that he is 'mighty', which suggests that considerable strength is required to carry and convey the Qur'ān. "*Who enjoys a secure position with the Lord of the Throne.*" (Verse 20) What a great honour for Jibrīl to enjoy such a position with the Lord of the universe. "*He is obeyed in heaven*", i.e. by the other angels. He is also "*faithful to his trust*", carrying and discharging the message.

These qualities add up to a definite conclusion: that the Qur'ān is a noble, mighty and exalted message and that God takes special care of man. It is a manifestation of this care that He has chosen an angel of Jibrīl's calibre to bring His revelations to the man He has chosen as His Messenger. As man reflects on this divine care he should feel humble. For he himself is worth very little in the kingdom of God, were it not for the care God takes of him and the honour He bestows on him.

There follows a description of the Prophet who conveys this revelation to mankind. The *sūrah* seems to say to them: You have known Muḥammad very well over a considerable length of time. He is your old, honest, trusted friend. Why, then, are you fabricating tales about him, when he has been telling you the simple truth which he has been entrusted to deliver to you: "*Your old friend is not mad. He saw him on the clear horizon. He does not grudge the secrets of the unseen. It is not the word of an accursed devil. Whither then are you going? This is only a reminder to all mankind.*" (Verses 22–27)

They knew the Prophet perfectly well. They knew that he was a man of steady character, great sagacity and complete honesty. But in spite of all this they claimed that he was mad, and that he received his revelations from the devil. Some of them took this view as the basis for their sustained attack on the Prophet and his Islamic message. Others did so out of amazement and wonder at the words revealed to him, which are unlike anything said or written by man. Their claim confirmed the traditional belief that each poet had a devil writing his poems, and each monk had a devil uncovering for him the secrets of the unknown world. They also believed that the devil might come into contact with people causing them to say some very strange things. They ignored the only valid explanation, that the Qur'ān was revealed by God, the Lord of all the worlds.

The *sūrah* counters this attitude by a reference to the surpassing beauty of God's creation, noticeable everywhere in the universe, and by portraying some universal scenes, as they appear, full of life. This method of reply suggests that the Qur'ān comes from the same creative power which has endowed the universe with matchless beauty. It also tells them about the two messengers entrusted with the Qur'ān, the one who brought it down and the one who delivered it to them, i.e. their own friend whom they knew to be sane, not mad. The *sūrah* tells them that he has indeed seen the other noble and mighty messenger, Gabriel, with his own eyes, on a clear horizon where no confusion is possible. He is faithful to his trust and cannot be suspected of telling anything but the truth. After all, they have never associated him with anything dishonest. "*It is not the word of an accursed devil*". (Verse 25) Devils, by nature, cannot provide such a straightforward and consistent code of conduct. Hence the *sūrah* asks disapprovingly: "*Whither then are you going*?" (Verse 26) How far can you err in your judgement. And where can you go away from the truth which stares you in the face wherever you go?

"*This is only a reminder to all mankind.*" (Verse 27) It reminds them of the nature of their existence, their origin and the nature of the universe around them. The reminder is to all men and women.

Islam here declares the universal nature of its call right from the start, in Makkah, where it was subjected to sustained and unabating persecution.

Free Choice

The *sūrah* then reminds us that it is up to every individual to choose whether to follow the right path or not. Since God has granted everyone his or her free will, then every human being is responsible for himself: "*To those of you whose will is to be upright*", (Verse 28) that is to say, to follow God's guidance. All doubts have been dispelled, all excuses answered by this clear statement of all the relevant facts. The right path has been indicated for everyone who wishes to be upright. Anyone who follows a different path shall, therefore, bear the responsibility for his actions.

There are, in the human soul and in the universe at large, numerous signs which beckon every man and woman to follow the path of faith. These are so clearly visible and so powerful in their effect that one needs to make a determined effort to turn one's back on them, especially when one's attention is drawn to them in the stirring, persuasive manner of the Qur'ān. It is, therefore, man's own will which leads him away from God's guidance. He has no other excuse or justification.

The *sūrah* concludes by stating that the operative will behind everything is the will of God: "*You cannot will except by the will of God, Lord of all the worlds.*" (Verse 29) We notice that the Qur'ān makes statements of this type whenever the will of human beings or creatures generally is mentioned. The reason for this is that the Qur'ān wants to keep the fundamental concepts of faith absolutely clear. These include the fact that everything in the universe is subject to God's will. No one has a will which is independent from that of God. That He grants man free will is part of His own divine will, like everything else. The same applies to His granting the angels the ability to show complete and absolute obedience to Him and to carry out all His commandments.

This fundamental fact must be clearly understood by believers, so that they have a clear concept of absolute truth. When they acquire this concept they will turn to divine will for guidance and support, and regulate their affairs according to this will.

SŪRAH 82

Al-Infiṭār

(Cleaving Asunder)

Al-Infiṭār (Cleaving Asunder)

سُورَةُ الانفِطَارِ

In the name of God, the Beneficent, the Merciful.

بِسۡمِ ٱللَّهِ ٱلرَّحۡمَٰنِ ٱلرَّحِيمِ

When the sky is cleft asunder, (1)

إِذَا ٱلسَّمَآءُ ٱنفَطَرَتۡ ١

when the stars are scattered, (2)

وَإِذَا ٱلۡكَوَاكِبُ ٱنتَثَرَتۡ ٢

when the oceans are made to explode, (3)

وَإِذَا ٱلۡبِحَارُ فُجِّرَتۡ ٣

when the graves are hurled about, (4)

وَإِذَا ٱلۡقُبُورُ بُعۡثِرَتۡ ٤

each soul shall know its earlier actions and its later ones. (5)

عَلِمَتۡ نَفۡسٞ مَّا قَدَّمَتۡ وَأَخَّرَتۡ ٥

O man, what has lured you away from your gracious Lord, (6)

يَٰٓأَيُّهَا ٱلْإِنسَٰنُ مَا غَرَّكَ بِرَبِّكَ ٱلْكَرِيمِ ﴿٦﴾

who created and moulded you and gave you an upright form? (7)

ٱلَّذِى خَلَقَكَ فَسَوَّىٰكَ فَعَدَلَكَ ﴿٧﴾

He can give you whatever shape He wills. (8)

فِىٓ أَىِّ صُورَةٍ مَّا شَآءَ رَكَّبَكَ ﴿٨﴾

Shun it! But you deny the Last Judgement. (9)

كَلَّا بَلْ تُكَذِّبُونَ بِٱلدِّينِ ﴿٩﴾

Yet there are guardians watching over you, (10)

وَإِنَّ عَلَيْكُمْ لَحَٰفِظِينَ ﴿١٠﴾

noble recorders, (11)

كِرَامًا كَٰتِبِينَ ﴿١١﴾

who know all that you do. (12)

يَعْلَمُونَ مَا تَفْعَلُونَ ﴿١٢﴾

Surely the righteous shall be in bliss, (13)

إِنَّ ٱلْأَبْرَارَ لَفِى نَعِيمٍ ﴿١٣﴾

while the wicked shall be in a blazing fire, (14)

وَإِنَّ ٱلْفُجَّارَ لَفِى جَحِيمٍ ﴿١٤﴾

which they shall enter on the Day of Judgement; (15)

يَصْلَوْنَهَا يَوْمَ ٱلدِّينِ ﴿١٥﴾

nor shall they ever be absent from it. (16)

وَمَا هُمْ عَنْهَا بِغَآئِبِينَ ﴿١٦﴾

Would that you knew what the Day of Judgement is! (17)	وَمَآ أَدۡرَىٰكَ مَا يَوۡمُ ٱلدِّينِ ١٧
Oh, would that you knew what the Day of Judgement is! (18)	ثُمَّ مَآ أَدۡرَىٰكَ مَا يَوۡمُ ٱلدِّينِ ١٨
It is the day when no soul can be of any help to any other soul; for on that day all sovereignty is God's alone. (19)	يَوۡمَ لَا تَمۡلِكُ نَفۡسٞ لِّنَفۡسٖ شَيۡـٔٗاۖ وَٱلۡأَمۡرُ يَوۡمَئِذٖ لِّلَّهِ ١٩

Overview

This short *sūrah* refers to the great upheaval discussed in the previous *sūrah* The Darkening, but gives it a special colour. It has a different rhythm, deep and calm. It adds a touch of expostulation coupled with an implicit threat. Hence, it does not detail the scenes of the great upheaval as in the previous *sūrah*, where these scenes predominate. Instead the scenes here are shorter, in order to suit its quieter atmosphere and slower rhythm.

At the opening the *sūrah* mentions the cleaving of the sky, the scattering of the stars, the bursting of the oceans and the hurling of the graves as simultaneous with every soul's knowledge of its earlier and later actions, on that momentous day.

The second part starts with a remonstration combined with an implicit threat to man who is the recipient of abundant grace but who shows no gratitude for it. "*O man, what has lured you away from your gracious Lord, who created and moulded you and gave you an upright form? He can give you whatever shape He wills.*" (Verses 6–8)

The third part provides the reason for man's ungrateful attitude. Denial of reckoning and judgement, the *sūrah* tells us, is the source of every evil. The reality of meting out reward and punishment at the Last Judgement is re-emphasized; "*Shun it! But you deny the Last Judgement. Yet there are guardians watching over you, noble recorders, who know all that you do. Surely the righteous shall be in bliss, while the wicked shall be in a blazing fire, which they shall enter on the Day of Judgement, nor shall they ever be absent from it.*" (Verses 9–16)

The final part gives an idea of how fearful the Day of Judgement is, how everyone is absolutely helpless and how all power belongs to God: "*Would that you knew what the Day of Judgement is! Oh, would that you knew what the Day of Judgement is! It is the day when no soul can be of any help to any other soul; for on that day all sovereignty is God's alone.*" (Verses 17–19) Thus, the *sūrah* represents yet another way of portraying the same basic principles stressed in this thirtieth part of the Qur'ān in various methods and styles.

The Great Upheaval

> *When the sky is cleft asunder, when the stars are scattered, when the oceans are made to explode, when the graves are hurled about, each soul shall know its earlier actions and its later ones.* (Verses 1–5)

In the commentary on the previous *sūrah* we described the feelings generated in people when they visualize the universe undergoing a change so violent that it leaves nothing in its familiar shape and condition. We also said that such feelings tend to pull man away from anything which gives him a sense of security, with the exception of God, the Creator of the universe, the One who lives on after everything has died and withered away. Man's heart is thus made to turn to the only true being who neither changes nor dies, to seek His support and security in the face of the general upheaval which destroys everything that might once have seemed so permanent. For nothing lives forever except the Creator who is the only one worthy of worship.

The first aspect mentioned here of the universal upheaval is the cleaving or rending of the sky, which is mentioned in other *sūrahs*: "*When the sky is split asunder and becomes rose red, like freshly tanned leather.*" (55: 37) "*When the sky will be rent asunder, for on that day it is frail and tottering.*" (69: 16) "*When the sky is rent asunder.*" (84: 1) That the sky will be split or rent asunder on that hectic day is certain. What is meant exactly by such rending, and how the sky will look after it has been rent are difficult to say. All that we are left with is a feeling of violent change which overwhelms the universe, as we see it, and a realization that its perfect system will no longer be in operation.

The violent upheaval in the universe causes the stars to scatter after they have been held together by a system which makes every star stick to its orbit, even though its movement is exceedingly fast. If this system is broken, as will happen when the life of the stars comes to its end, they will just disappear in the wide space, as does a particle of dust running loose.

The explosion of the oceans may refer to their being overfull to the extent that they swallow all dry land and rivers. It may, alternatively, mean an explosion which separates oxygen from hydrogen, the two gases which form water. Thus water returns to its original gas condition. The verse may also be taken to refer to a nuclear explosion of the atoms of the two gases. If this is the case, then the explosion would be so fearful that our nuclear devices of today would seem, in comparison, like child's toys. The explosion may also take a different form, totally unknown to us. One thing, however, we know for certain is that there will be a horror far greater than any man could ever have experienced.

The hurling about of the graves may be a result of one of the events mentioned above. It may also be a separate event which occurs on that eventful day. As these graves are hurled about people are resurrected so as to face the reckoning and receive their reward or punishment. This is complemented by the verse which follows: "*Each soul shall know its earlier actions and its later ones.*" (Verse 5) That is, each soul shall come face to face with what it has done and what it has left behind of the consequences of its actions; or, what it has enjoyed in this present life and what it has saved for the hereafter. Such knowledge, however, will accompany these horrific events. It will indeed be part of them, for it terrifies the soul no less than any of the other events.

The Arabic expression used here, *ʿalimat nafsun*, may be translated literally as "a soul shall know..." It is, however, in Arabic a neater and more effective denotation of "*each soul shall know...*" Furthermore, such knowledge by every soul is not the end of the matter. It has consequences which are as violent as the scenes portrayed here of the great upheaval. These consequences are merely implied, not stated, and this is even more effective.

Grace Without Limits

After this opening which alerts men's senses and consciences, the *sūrah*, by means of gentle remonstrance coupled with an implicit threat, touches the hearts of men who busy themselves with trivialities. It reminds man of God's very first act of grace towards him, namely, his moulding in such an upright, perfectly proportioned form. God could have easily given him any form He wished. Yet man is ungrateful: "*O man, what has lured you away from your gracious Lord, who created and moulded you and gave you an upright form? He can give you whatever shape He wills.*" (Verses 6–8) The address appeals to man's most noble quality, his humanity, which distinguishes him from all other creatures and assigns to him the highest position among them. This quality represents God's gracious blessing to man and His abundant generosity.

This appeal is immediately followed by a gentle remonstrance: "*What has lured you away from your gracious Lord?*" (Verse 6) What makes you neglect your duties to your Lord and behave impudently towards Him when He has given you your humanity which raises you above all His creation and provides you with the ability to distinguish between right and wrong. A few details of God's generosity are then added: "*O man, what has lured you away from your gracious Lord, who created and moulded you and gave you an upright form.*" (Verses 6–7) It is an address which appeals straight to man's heart. He listens to God's remonstrance as He reminds him of His grace while he continues with his erring ways and impudent behaviour towards Him.

Indeed, man should reflect deeply over his creation, and the fact that he has been given a physically and physiologically perfect constitution. Reflection should prompt him to show his real love, deep respect and genuine gratitude towards God, his gracious Lord, who has blessed him with such constitution: perfect, upright and handsome. The miraculous aspects of man's constitution are far greater than what he sees all around him and what he can imagine. Perfection and right balance are easily evident in man's physical, mental and spiritual constitution. Full volumes have been written on the perfection of creation as evidenced by man. It is perhaps useful to include here one or two quotations from such works.

The human body is composed of a number of specialized systems: the skeleton, muscular system, skin, digestive system, blood circulation, respiratory system, procreative system, lymphatic system, nervous system, the urinal system and the senses of taste, smell, hearing and sight. Every one of these systems is miraculous and far more wonderful than any scientific achievement. Yet man tends to overlook the wonders of his own constitution! A contributor to the British Scientific Journal writes:[1]

> Man's hand is one of the most remarkable wonders of nature. It is extremely difficult, indeed impossible, to invent a device which can match the human hand for simplicity, efficiency, ability and instant adaptability. When you read a book you take it in your hand, then you hold it in the position most suitable for your reading. The same hand will automatically correct the position of your book whenever a correction of position is necessary. When you turn a page you place your finger underneath the

1. The original passages of this journal could not be traced by the translators, so a re-translation is given to put back into English the two passages quoted here. The author quotes them from ʻAbd al-Razzāq Nawfal, *Allah wal-ʻIlm al-Ḥadīth*, or ʻGod and Modern Science', Cairo, 1957. Nawfal, however, does not specify the name and number of the Journal he quotes from. – Editor's note.

paper and apply the amount of pressure needed for turning the page. When the page is turned no more pressure is applied. You also use your hand to hold a pen and to write. With your hand you use all the tools you need such as a spoon, a knife or a pen. You use it to open or close the window and to carry anything you wish to carry. Each hand has 27 pieces of bone in addition to 19 groups of muscles.[2]

A part of the human ear is a series of some four thousand minute but complex arches graduated with exquisite regularity in size and shape. These may be said to resemble a musical instrument, and they seem adjusted to catch, and transmit in some manner to the brain, every cadence of sound or noise, from the thunderclap to the whisper of the pines and the exquisite blending of the tones and harmonies of every instrument in the orchestra. If in forming the ear the cells were impelled to evolve strict efficiency only that man might survive, why did they not extend the range and develop a superacutness? Perhaps the power behind these cells' activities anticipated man's coming need of intellectual enjoyment, or did they by accident build better than they knew?[3]

The visual functions are carried out mainly by the eye with its 130 million retinal light receptors. The eyelids with the eyelashes at their tips protect the eyes day and night. Their movement, which is involuntary, keeps out dust particles and other alien bodies. The eyelashes throw their shades over the eye to lessen the intensity of light. Furthermore, by their movement the eyelids prevent the eyes from becoming dry. The fluid around the eye, which we call tears, is a highly effective, most powerful disinfectant ...

In human beings, the taste function is carried out by the tongue, through groups of the taste cells which are located in the taste buds of the mucosal surface of the tongue. These buds are of

2. Ibid.
3. A.C. Morrison, *Man Does Not Stand Alone*, London, 1962, pp. 63–64.

different shapes: some are filamentary, some mushroom-shaped and others are lenticular. They are supplied by fine branches of the glosso-pharangeal nerve as well as the nerve which carries the taste sense. When we eat, these fine branches of the taste nerve are stimulated and convey the impulses of the taste sensation to the brain. This system is located at the front of the tongue, so that we may reject what we sense to be harmful. It is this system which helps us sense whether what we eat is bitter or sweet, hot or cold, sour or salty, etc. The tongue contains nine thousand of these fine taste buds, each of which is linked with the brain by more than one nerve. Hence we may wonder: How many nerves have we? What are their sizes? How do they function individually and how do they combine to give the brain their various types of sensation?

The nervous system, which effectively controls the body, is composed of fine neurons which cover every part of the body. The neurons are linked to larger nerves which are, in turn, linked to the central nervous system. Whenever any part of the body feels any sensation, even the slightest change of temperature, the neurons convey this sensation to the peripheral nerves which, in turn, convey it to the brain so that it may order the necessary action. The signals are carried through the nerves at the speed of 100 metres per second.[4]

If we think of digestion as a process in a chemical laboratory and of the food that we eat as raw materials, we immediately discover that it is a wonderful process which will digest anything edible except the stomach itself.

First into this laboratory we put a variety of food as a raw material without the slightest regard for the laboratory or how the chemistry of digestion will handle it. We eat steak, cabbage, corn and fried fish, wash it down with any quantity of water, and

4. A. Nawfal, op. cit.

top it off with alcohol, bread, and beans. We may add sulfur and molasses as spring medicine. Out of this mixture the stomach selects those things which are useful by breaking down into its chemical molecules every item of food, discarding the waste, and reconstructs the residue into new proteins, which become the food of the various cells. The digestive tract selects calcium, sulphur, iodine, iron and any other substances which are necessary, takes care that the essential molecules are not lost, that the hormones can be produced and that all of the valid necessities of life are on hand in regulated quantities, ready to meet every necessity. It stores fat and other reserves to meet such an emergency as starvation, and does all this in spite of human thought or reason. We pour this infinite variety of substances into this chemical laboratory with almost total disregard of what we take in, depending on what we consider the automatic process to keep us alive. When these foods have been broken down and are again prepared, they are delivered constantly to each of our billions of cells, a greater number than all the human beings on earth. The delivery to each individual cell must be constant, and only those substances which the particular cell needs to transform them into bones, nails, flesh, hair, eyes, and teeth are taken up by the proper cell. Here is a chemical laboratory producing more substances than any laboratory which human ingenuity has devised. Here is a delivery system greater than any method of transportation or distribution the world has ever known, all being conducted in perfect order.[5]

Man's Unique Qualities

A lot may be said about every other system of the human body. But wonderful as these systems are, man may have them in common with animals. He, however, is privileged to possess his unique mental and spiritual qualities, regarded in this *sūrah* as a special favour from

5. A.C. Morrison, op. cit., pp. 88–89.

God. After the *sūrah* has dealt with man's humanity, it mentions the perfection of his creation and the right proportioning of his mould: "*O man, what has lured you away from your gracious Lord, who created and moulded you and gave you an upright form.*" (Verses 6–7)

Let us reflect on our powers of comprehension, the nature of which is unknown to us. The mind is the medium of comprehension but the working of our minds and how they function remain to us incomprehensible. If we suppose that what we grasp is transmitted to the brain through the nerves, where and how does the brain store its information? If we compare the brain to a magnetic recording tape, every man needs in his average lifetime of sixty years[6] a great many billion metres on which to record such a huge multitude of pictures, words, meanings, feelings and responses so that he may, as he actually does, remember them several decades later. Furthermore, how does man sort out individual words, meanings, events and pictures to mould them together in a sort of coherent education? How does he transform information and experiences into knowledge?

Yet this is by no means the most significant of man's distinctive qualities. There is that wonderful ray of God's spirit which provides a link between man and the beauty of the universe and its Creator. As this link is established, man can experience at clear, bright moments a sense of communion with the infinite, the absolute, which prepares him for a blissful eternal life in God's paradise. Yet man has no power to comprehend the nature of his spirit, which is God's greatest favour to him and which makes him a man. Hence God addresses him by this quality *"O man!"* He then remonstrates with him directly: "*What has lured you away from your gracious Lord?*" Thus man is reminded of God's greatest favour, but he stands impudent, negligent of his duties, unashamed and ungrateful. But man does not need more than to realize the source of this

---

6. Average life expectancy has considerably risen since the author's time, but the idea is still correct. If anything the tape required for storing all what human memory stores would today be far greater in length, and its efficiency much more enhanced. – Editor's note.

remonstrance and what attitude he adopts when he stands before his Lord to be absolutely overwhelmed by shame: *"O man, what has lured you away from your gracious Lord, who created and moulded you and gave you an upright form? He can give you whatever shape He wills."* (Verses 6–8)

The *sūrah* moves on to explain the reason for man's impudence and negligence, namely, denial of the Last Judgement. It emphatically confirms the reality of reckoning, reward and punishment: "*Shun it! But you deny the Last Judgement. Yet there are guardians watching over you, noble recorders, who know all that you do. Surely the righteous shall be in bliss, while the wicked shall be in a blazing fire, which they shall enter on the Day of Judgement; nor shall they ever be absent from it.*" (Verses 9–16) The English expression, 'shun it', is used here to render the meaning of the Arabic word, *kallā*, which is a command to desist and an indication of a change of subject and style. Hence the following verses are in the form of a statement.

"*Shun it! But you deny the Last Judgement.*" (Verse 9) You think that reckoning and accountability are falsehoods, and this is precisely the cause of your impudence and negligence of duties. How can any person disbelieve in the judgement and still lead a life based on goodness and right guidance? Some people may achieve a higher degree of faith: they worship God because they love Him, neither out of fear of punishment nor in hope of reward. But these people continue to believe in the Last Judgement. They fear it and look forward to it at the same time, because they hope to be with their beloved Lord. When man, however, flatly rejects the Day of Judgement he will be devoid of politeness and light; his heart and conscience are dead.

You deny the Day of Judgement when you will certainly face it. Everything you do in this life will be counted for or against you. Nothing is lost, nothing forgotten: "*Yet there are guardians watching over you, noble recorders, who know all that you do.*" (Verses 10–12) These recorders are the angels charged with accompanying people, watching them and recording all what they do and say. We do not know, and are not required to know, how this takes place. God knows that we are neither given the ability to understand it nor are we going to benefit by understanding it because it does not affect the purpose of our existence. Hence it is useless to attempt to explain by our means what God has chosen not to reveal to us of the world of imperceptibles. It is sufficient for us to feel that we do not live in vain and that there are noble recorders who note what we do, in order to be so that we are always alert and prudent.

Since the atmosphere of the *sūrah* is one of benevolence and nobility, the description of those recorders is that they are "*noble*", so that we are shy and polite in their presence. It is only natural for people to exercise extra care not to say or do anything impolite or disgraceful when they are in the presence of people whose character reflects nobility. How careful would they be if they realized they were always in the presence of angels? The *sūrah* then arouses the most noble feelings of our upright nature by portraying this fact in such a familiar way.

Different Destinies

We are then told of the destinies of the righteous and the wicked, which are determined by the reckoning based on the recordings of the noble angels: "*Surely the righteous shall be in bliss, while the wicked shall be in a blazing fire, which they shall enter on the Day of Judgement; nor shall they ever be absent from it.*" (Verses 13–16) The end is certain. That the righteous shall dwell in blissful happiness and the wicked shall end in hell is already determined. A righteous person is the one who consistently does right actions, i.e. good deeds, until doing them becomes his intrinsic quality. The adjective 'righteous' has connotations which fit in well with nobility and humanity. The contrasting quality, 'wickedness', carries connotations of insolence and impudence as the wicked indulge in sinful actions. Hell is a proper recompense for wickedness. The *sūrah* emphasizes the certainty of this punishment: "*which they shall enter on the Day of Judgement.*" Then it re-emphasizes it: "*nor shall they ever be absent from it.*" They cannot escape it in the first place, nor will they be allowed to leave it, not even for a short while

Having stated what happens on the Day of Judgement, the *sūrah* emphasizes again the certainty of that day, since it is denied by some. The emphasis provided here is in the form of a rhetorical question which enhances the mystery surrounding the object of the question. The *sūrah* then states the complete helplessness of everyone, the absolute impossibility of giving or receiving support and that God is the absolute sovereign on that awesome day: "*Would that you knew what the Day of Judgement is! Oh, would that you knew what the Day of Judgement is! It is the day when no soul can be of any help to any other soul; for on that day all sovereignty is God's alone.*" (Verses 17–19)

The form "*would that you knew...*" is a form of rhetorical question often used in the Qur'ān. It suggests that the matter under discussion is far beyond our imagining and understanding. This is stressed here by repetition of the question before details about conditions on the day concerned are given: "*It is the day when no soul can be of any help to any other soul.*" (Verse 19) It is a state of total helplessness when everyone stands alone, busy with their own problems, unable to think of anyone else, relative or friend. "*For on that day all sovereignty is God's alone.*" (Verse 19) He indeed reigns supreme in this life and the next. This fact, however, becomes so clear on that day that no one can overlook it, as the ignorant and the conceited do in this life.

The *sūrah* closes with an air of fear and speechless expectation which contrasts with the opening air of violent horror. In between the two man is addressed with that remonstrance which overwhelms him with shame.

SŪRAH 83

Al-Muṭaffifīn

(The Stinters)

Al-Muṭaffifīn (The Stinters)

سُورَةُ المُطَفِّفِين

In the name of God, the Beneficent, the Merciful.

بِسۡمِ ٱللَّهِ ٱلرَّحۡمَٰنِ ٱلرَّحِيمِ

Woe to the stinters (1)

وَيۡلٞ لِّلۡمُطَفِّفِينَ ١

who, when others measure for them, exact in full, (2)

ٱلَّذِينَ إِذَا ٱكۡتَالُواْ عَلَى ٱلنَّاسِ يَسۡتَوۡفُونَ ٢

but who, when they measure or weigh for others, defraud them. (3)

وَإِذَا كَالُوهُمۡ أَو وَّزَنُوهُمۡ يُخۡسِرُونَ ٣

Do such people not think that they will be raised to life (4)

أَلَا يَظُنُّ أُوْلَٰٓئِكَ أَنَّهُم مَّبۡعُوثُونَ ٤

on a great day, (5)

لِيَوۡمٍ عَظِيمٖ ٥

the day when all mankind shall stand before the Lord of all the worlds? (6)

يَوْمَ يَقُومُ ٱلنَّاسُ لِرَبِّ ٱلْعَـٰلَمِينَ ﴿٦﴾

No indeed! The record of the transgressors is in *Sijjīn*. (7)

كَلَّآ إِنَّ كِتَـٰبَ ٱلْفُجَّارِ لَفِى سِجِّينٍ ﴿٧﴾

Would that you knew what *Sijjīn* is! (8)

وَمَآ أَدْرَىٰكَ مَا سِجِّينٌ ﴿٨﴾

It is a record inscribed. (9)

كِتَـٰبٌ مَّرْقُومٌ ﴿٩﴾

Woe on that day to the unbelievers (10)

وَيْلٌ يَوْمَئِذٍ لِّلْمُكَذِّبِينَ ﴿١٠﴾

who deny the Day of Judgement. (11)

ٱلَّذِينَ يُكَذِّبُونَ بِيَوْمِ ٱلدِّينِ ﴿١١﴾

None denies it but the guilty aggressors, the evildoers, (12)

وَمَا يُكَذِّبُ بِهِۦٓ إِلَّا كُلُّ مُعْتَدٍ أَثِيمٍ ﴿١٢﴾

who, when Our revelations are recited to them, cry: 'Fables of the ancients!' (13)

إِذَا تُتْلَىٰ عَلَيْهِ ءَايَـٰتُنَا قَالَ أَسَـٰطِيرُ ٱلْأَوَّلِينَ ﴿١٣﴾

No indeed! Their own deeds have cast a layer of rust over their hearts. (14)

كَلَّا ۖ بَلْ ۜ رَانَ عَلَىٰ قُلُوبِهِم مَّا كَانُوا۟ يَكْسِبُونَ ﴿١٤﴾

No indeed! On that day they shall be shut out from their Lord. (15)

كَلَّآ إِنَّهُمْ عَن رَّبِّهِمْ يَوْمَئِذٍ لَّمَحْجُوبُونَ ﴿١٥﴾

They shall enter the blazing fire, (16)

ثُمَّ إِنَّهُمْ لَصَالُوا۟ ٱلْجَحِيمِ ﴿١٦﴾

and will be told: 'This is [the reality] which you denied!' (17)

ثُمَّ يُقَالُ هَٰذَا ٱلَّذِى كُنتُم بِهِۦ تُكَذِّبُونَ ١٧

But the record of the righteous is in *'Illiyūn*. (18)

كَلَّآ إِنَّ كِتَٰبَ ٱلْأَبْرَارِ لَفِى عِلِّيِّينَ ١٨

Would that you knew what *'Illiyūn* is! (19)

وَمَآ أَدْرَىٰكَ مَا عِلِّيُّونَ ١٩

It is a record inscribed, (20)

كِتَٰبٌ مَّرْقُومٌ ٢٠

witnessed by those who are closest to God. (21)

يَشْهَدُهُ ٱلْمُقَرَّبُونَ ٢١

The righteous will surely be in bliss. (22)

إِنَّ ٱلْأَبْرَارَ لَفِى نَعِيمٍ ٢٢

[Reclining] on couches, they will look around them. (23)

عَلَى ٱلْأَرَآئِكِ يَنظُرُونَ ٢٣

In their faces you shall mark the glow of bliss. (24)

تَعْرِفُ فِى وُجُوهِهِمْ نَضْرَةَ ٱلنَّعِيمِ ٢٤

They will be given to drink of a pure-drink, securely sealed, (25)

يُسْقَوْنَ مِن رَّحِيقٍ مَّخْتُومٍ ٢٥

with a seal of musk, for this let the strivers emulously strive. (26)

خِتَٰمُهُۥ مِسْكٌ وَفِى ذَٰلِكَ فَلْيَتَنَافَسِ
ٱلْمُتَنَٰفِسُونَ ٢٦

It is a drink mixed with the waters of *Tasnīm*, (27)

وَمِزَاجُهُۥ مِن تَسْنِيمٍ ٢٧

عَيْنًا يَشْرَبُ بِهَا ٱلْمُقَرَّبُونَ ﴿٢٨﴾

a fountain at which those who are closest to God will drink. (28)

إِنَّ ٱلَّذِينَ أَجْرَمُوا۟ كَانُوا۟ مِنَ ٱلَّذِينَ
ءَامَنُوا۟ يَضْحَكُونَ ﴿٢٩﴾

Those who are given to sinful practices scoff at the faithful (29)

وَإِذَا مَرُّوا۟ بِهِمْ يَتَغَامَزُونَ ﴿٣٠﴾

and wink at one another as they pass by them. (30)

وَإِذَا ٱنقَلَبُوٓا۟ إِلَىٰٓ أَهْلِهِمُ ٱنقَلَبُوا۟
فَكِهِينَ ﴿٣١﴾

When they go back to their folk they speak of them with jests, (31)

وَإِذَا رَأَوْهُمْ قَالُوٓا۟ إِنَّ هَٰٓؤُلَآءِ
لَضَآلُّونَ ﴿٣٢﴾

and when they see them they say: 'These have indeed gone astray!' (32)

وَمَآ أُرْسِلُوا۟ عَلَيْهِمْ حَٰفِظِينَ ﴿٣٣﴾

Yet they have not been assigned the mission of being their guardians. (33)

فَٱلْيَوْمَ ٱلَّذِينَ ءَامَنُوا۟ مِنَ ٱلْكُفَّارِ
يَضْحَكُونَ ﴿٣٤﴾

So on this Day [of Judgement] the faithful will laugh at the unbelievers, (34)

عَلَى ٱلْأَرَآئِكِ يَنظُرُونَ ﴿٣٥﴾

as they recline upon their couches and look around them. (35)

هَلْ ثُوِّبَ ٱلْكُفَّارُ مَا كَانُوا۟ يَفْعَلُونَ ﴿٣٦﴾

Shall the unbelievers be requited for what they were wont to do? (36)

Overview

The *sūrah* describes the conditions the Islamic message faced in Makkah. Its other objective is to awaken people's hearts and draw their attention to the new event which would help the Arabs, and mankind in general, to take a new turn in their lives. The event in question is the arrival of the divine message to earth.

A particular aspect of Arabian society is portrayed at the outset, as the *sūrah* threatens the stinters with what will befall them on the great day, "*the day when all mankind shall stand before the Lord of all the worlds.*" (Verse 6) The reason for such a threat is revealed at the end, when the *sūrah* sketches the manners of the evildoers, their attitude towards the believers, their scoffing at them, winking to one another as they pass by and their assertion that the believers have gone astray. Moreover, the *sūrah* shows the reality of the righteous on the one hand and the transgressors on the other.

The *sūrah* can be divided into four parts The first opens with a declaration of war against the stinters: "*Woe to the stinters who, when others measure for them, exact in full, but who, when they measure or weigh for others, defraud them. Do such people not think that they will be raised to life on a great day, the day when all mankind shall stand before the Lord of all worlds?*" (Verses 1–6)

The second part warns the transgressors and denounces them in strong terms. It threatens them with woe and ruin and establishes their guilt and aggression. It explains the reasons for their blindness and describes the punishment awaiting them on the Day of Judgement. "*No indeed! The record of the transgressors is in* Sijjīn. *Would that you knew what* Sijjīn *is! It is a record inscribed. Woe on that day to the unbelievers who deny the Day of Judgement. None denies it but the guilty aggressors, the evildoers, who, when Our revelations are recited to them, cry: 'Fables of the ancients! No indeed! Their own deeds have cast a layer of rust over their hearts. No indeed! On that day they shall be shut out from their Lord. They shall enter the blazing fire, and will be told: 'This is [the reality] which you denied!'*" (Verses 7–17)

The third part gives an account of the righteous. It describes their high rank, the bliss they will enjoy, the delight on their faces, and the pure drink they will have while they recline on soft couches, and look all around them. It is an image of happiness: "*But the record of the righteous is in* 'Illiyūn. *Would that you knew what* 'Illiyūn *is! It is a record inscribed, witnessed by those who are closest to God. The righteous will surely be in bliss. [Reclining] on couches, they will look around them. In their faces you shall mark the glow of bliss. They will be given to drink of a pure-drink, securely sealed, with a seal of musk, for this let the strivers emulously strive. It is a drink mixed with the waters of* Tasnīm, *a fountain at which those who are closest to God will drink.*" (Verses 18–28)

The last part of the *sūrah* describes what the transgressors mete out to the righteous in this world of conceit and hollow vanity, harsh treatment, ridicule and bad manners. Juxtaposed are descriptions of the ultimate situation of each group, the transgressors and the righteous, in the world of truth and immortality: "*Those who are given to sinful practices scoff at the faithful and wink at one another as they pass by them. When they go back to their folk they speak of them with jests, and when they see them they say: 'These have indeed gone astray!' Yet they have not been assigned the mission of being their guardians. So on this Day [of Judgement] the faithful will laugh at the unbelievers, as they recline upon their couches and look around them. Shall the unbelievers be requited for what they were wont to do?*" (Verses 29–36)

The *sūrah* depicts a social environment. It also provides an account of the Islamic way of dealing with the world as it exists and with the human mind. This is what we shall attempt to explain as we consider the *sūrah* in detail.

Giving a Raw Deal

> *Woe to the stinters who, when others measure for them, exact in full, but who, when they measure or weigh for others, defraud them. Do such people not think that they will be raised to life*

on a great day, the day when all mankind shall stand before the Lord of all the worlds? (Verses 1–6)

The *sūrah* opens with God's declaration of war against the stinters: "*Woe to the stinters*". The Arabic term, *wayl*, used for 'woe' implies destruction and ruin. The implication is the same whether we consider this verse as a statement of a future eventuality or a curse, for a curse made by God has the same effect as that of a statement about what is going to happen. The next two verses explain the meaning of the 'stinters' or defrauders as intended in the *sūrah*. They are those "*who, when others measure for them, exact in full, but who, when they measure or weigh for others, defraud them.*" (Verses 2–3) They are those who want their merchandise complete and intact when they buy, but who do not give the right amount when they sell. The following three verses wonder at the defrauders, who behave as if they will not have to account for what they gain in this life. "*Do such people not think that they will be raised to life on a great day, the day when all mankind shall stand before the Lord of all the worlds?*"

The fact that the defrauders' behaviour is tackled in this manner in a Makkan revelation is very interesting. Makkan *sūrahs* generally concentrate on the fundamentals, such as the assertion of God's unity, the supremacy of His will and His dominion over the universe and mankind, and with assertions about the truth of revelation and prophethood, the truth of the Day of Judgement, reckoning and reward. The Makkan revelations also endeavour to form and develop the moral sense and relate it to the fundamentals of faith. The tackling of a specific issue of morality, such as the stinting of weights and measures, or business dealings in general, is a later concern; it is more characteristic of Madinan revelations, which regulate the life of the community in an Islamic state. The fact that this Makkan *sūrah* makes the issue of stinting its focal point therefore deserves careful consideration.

The first point to note is that in Makkah the nobility were very rich, but totally unscrupulous. They exercised a complete monopoly of trade in their business concerns. They organized the export and import trade using caravans which travelled to Yemen in winter and to Syria in summer. They had their seasonal trade fairs such as the 'Ukāẓ fair which was held during the pilgrimage season. The fairs were for business dealings as well as literary activities.

The text suggests that the defrauders against whom war was declared belonged to the nobility and wielded much power and influence, enabling them to force others to succumb to their wishes. Several features of the Arabic wording used here connote that for some unspecified reason they were able to impose their will and exact in full. The meaning implied is not that they exacted their full due; for this would not justify a declaration of war against them. What is meant is that they obtained by sheer force what they had no right to demand. But when it was their turn to weigh or measure for others, they exercised their power by giving less than what was due.

Indeed this warning, coming so early in the Makkan period, gives an idea of the nature of the religion of Islam. It demonstrates that Islam embraces all sides of life and aims to establish a firm moral code which accords with the basic principles of divine teachings. At the time when this *sūrah* was revealed the Muslim community was still weak. The followers of Islam had not yet won power in order to organize society and the life of the community according to Islamic principles. Yet Islam demonstrated its opposition to those acts of flagrant injustice and unethical dealings. It declared war against stinters and threatened them with woe and destruction at a time when they were the powerful rulers of Makkah. It declared its uncompromising stand against the injustices suffered by the masses whom it has never sought to lull into a state of lethargy and apathy.

This gives us an insight into the real motives behind the stubborn opposition to Islam by the masters of Makkah. They were undoubtedly keenly aware that what Muḥammad (peace be upon him) was calling for was not merely a matter of personal conviction which demanded no more than a verbal assertion of God's oneness and Muḥammad's prophethood, and a form of prayer addressed to

God and not idols. They realized that the new faith would establish a way of life which would cause the very basis of their positions and interests to crumble. They were fully aware that the new religion, by its very nature, did not admit any partnership or compromise with any worldly concepts alien to its divine basis, and that it posed a mighty threat to all *jāhiliyyah* values. This is why they launched their offensive, which continued in full force both before and after the Muslims' migration to Madinah. It was an offensive launched to defend their way of life in its entirety, not only a set of concepts which have no effect beyond individual acceptance and personal conviction.

Those, in any age or land, who attempt to prevent Islam from organizing and ruling human life also recognize these essential facts. They know very well that the pure and straightforward Islamic way of life endangers their unjust order, interests, hollow structure and deviant practices. Indeed the tyrannical stinters – whatever form their stinting takes and wherever it is, in money and finance, or in rights and duties – are those who fear most the ascendancy of Islam and the implementation of its just methods.

The representatives of the two Arabian tribes of Madinah, the Aws and the Khazraj, who pledged their support and loyalty to the Prophet were also aware of all this. Ibn Isḥāq, the Prophet's biographer, wrote: 'Āṣim ibn 'Umar ibn Qatādah told me that when the Madinan Muslims came to give their pledge to the Prophet, al-'Abbās ibn 'Ubadah al-Anṣārī, who belonged to the clan of Sālim ibn 'Awf, said to them: "You Khazraj! Do you know what your pledge to this man really means?" They answered "Yes, we do." His rejoinder was: "You are pledging to fight the rest of mankind, white and black alike! So it would be better to leave him alone now if you think you would give him up to his enemies in the event of your sustaining material losses or losing your leaders. If you do such a thing you will bring upon yourselves great humiliation both in this life and in the life hereafter. But if you feel that you will honour your pledges despite any sacrifice in money and men, then go ahead, because this will be best for you here and in the hereafter!" They said: "We offer our loyalty and support and declare our readiness to sustain any sacrifice, material or personal!" Turning to the Prophet, they asked him: "What will be our reward if we honour our pledges?" He said: "Heaven." They said: "Stretch out your hand." He did and they gave him their pledges of support.

These supporters, like the Makkan tyrants, were keenly aware of the nature of Islam. They realized that it stands for absolute justice and fairness in the social order it seeks to create. It accepts no tyranny, oppression, conceit, injustice or exploitation. Hence it faces the combined forces of all forms of despotism, arrogance and exploitation.

"*Do such people not think that they will be raised to life on a great day, the day when all mankind shall stand before the Lord of all the worlds?*" (Verses 4–6) Their attitude is singularly strange. The mere idea of being raised to life again on that great day, when all mankind shall stand as ordinary individuals in front of the Lord of the universe, awaiting His just judgement, without support from any quarter, should be enough to make them change course. But they persist, as if the thought of being raised to life after death has never crossed their minds.

The Inevitable Reckoning

They are called stinters in the first part of the *sūrah*; but in the second they are described as transgressors. The *sūrah* proceeds to describe the standing of this group with God, their situation in this life, and what awaits them on the great day. "*No indeed! The record of the transgressors is in* Sijjīn. *Would that you knew what* Sijjīn *is! It is a record inscribed. Woe on that day to the unbelievers who deny the Day of Judgement. None denies it but the guilty aggressors, the evildoers, who, when Our revelations are recited to them, cry: 'Fables of the ancients!' No indeed! Their own deeds have cast a layer of rust over their hearts. No indeed! On that day they shall be shut out from their Lord. They shall enter the blazing fire, and will be told: 'This is [the reality] which you denied!'"* (Verses 7–17) They think they will not be raised to life after death, so the Qur'ān rebukes them and affirms that a record of their actions is kept. The location of that record is specified as an additional confirmation of the fact, albeit a location unknown to man. They are threatened with woe and ruin on that day when their record shall be reviewed: "*No indeed! The record of the transgressors is in* Sijjīn. *Would that you knew what* Sijjīn *is! It is a record inscribed. Woe on that day to the unbelievers.*" (Verses 7–10)

The transgressors, as the Arabic term, *fujjār*, here connotes, are those who indulge excessively in sin. Their book is the record of their deeds. We do not know the nature of this book and nor are we required to know. The whole matter belongs to that realm of which we know nothing except what we are told by God. The statement that there is a record in *Sijjīn* of the transgressors' deeds, is followed by the familiar Qur'ānic form of expression associated with connotations of greatness: "*Would that you knew what* Sijjīn *is!*" (Verse 8) Thus, the addressee is made to feel that the whole matter is too great to be fully understood.

The *sūrah* then gives a further account of the transgressors' book: "*It is a record inscribed.*" (Verse 9) There is no possibility of addition or omission until it is thrown open on that great day. When this takes place, "*woe on that day to the unbelievers.*" (Verse 10) Then we are given information about the subject of unbelief, and the true character of the unbelievers who deny the Day of Judgement. "*None denies it but the guilty aggressors, the evildoers, who, when Our revelations are recited to them, cry: 'Fables of the ancients!'*" (Verses 12–13) So, aggression and bad deeds lead the perpetrators to deny the Day of Judgement and to take a rude and ill-mannered attitude towards the Qur'ān, describing it as "*Fables of the ancients!*" This description by the unbelievers is, of course, based on the fact that the Qur'ān contains some historical accounts of former nations. These accounts are related as a lesson for later generations as they demonstrate with much clarity the working of the divine rules to which all nations and generations are subject.

They are strongly rebuked and reprobated for their rudeness and rejection of the truth. These connotations, carried by the Arabic term *kallā*, translated here as '*No indeed*', are coupled with an assertion that their allegations are unfounded. We are then given an insight into the motives of their insolent disbelief and the reasons for their inability to see the obvious truth or respond to it: "*Their own deeds have cast a layer of rust over their hearts.*" (Verse 14) Indeed the hearts of those who indulge in sin become dull, as if they are veiled by a thick curtain which keeps them in total darkness, unable to see the light. Thus they gradually lose their sensitivity and become lifeless.

The Prophet says: "When a man commits a sin, it throws a black spot over his heart. If he repents, his heart is polished; but if he persists in his practice, the stains increase." [Related by Ibn Jarīr, al-Tirmidhī, al-Nasā'ī and Ibn Mājah.] Al-Tirmidhī describes this *ḥadīth* as authentic. Al-Nasā'ī's version differs in wording but not in import. His version may be translated as follows: "When a man commits a sin, a black spot is formed on his heart. If he desists, prays for forgiveness and repents, his heart will be polished; but if he persists, the spot grows bigger until it has covered his whole heart. This is what God refers to when He says: '*No indeed! Their own deeds have cast a layer of rust over their hearts.*'" (Verse 14) Explaining this verse, Imām al-Ḥasan al-Baṣrī said: "It is a case of one sin on top of another until the heart is blinded and dies."

Thus we have learnt the situation of transgressing unbelievers, as well as their motives for transgression and rejection of the truth. Then we are told what will happen to them on that great day, a destiny which befits their evil deeds and denial of the truth: "*On that day they shall be shut out from their Lord. They shall enter the blazing fire, and will be told: 'This is [the reality] which you denied!'*" (Verses 15–17) Because their sins have cast a thick veil over their hearts, they are unable in this life to feel God's presence, and it is only appropriate that they not be allowed to see His glorious face. They will be deprived of this great happiness, which is bestowed only on those whose hearts and souls are so clean and transparent that they deserve to be with their Lord, without any form of separation or isolation. Such people are described in *Sūrah* 75, The Resurrection: "*On that day there shall be joyous faces, looking towards their Lord.*" (75: 22–23)

This separation from their Lord is the greatest and most agonizing punishment and deprivation. It is a miserable end of a man whose very humanity is derived from only one source, namely his contact with God, his benevolent Lord. When man is torn away from this source of nobleness he loses all his humanity and sinks to a level which ensures hell is his just reward: "*They shall enter the blazing fire.*" (Verse 16) On top of this, there is something much worse and much more agonizing, namely, rebuke. "*And will be told: 'This is [the reality] which you denied!*'" (Verse 17)

Faces Radiant with Joy

Then follows an account of the other group, the righteous. This is given in the customary Qur'ānic manner of providing two elaborately contrasting images, so that a detailed comparison may be drawn: "*But the record of the righteous is in* 'Illiyūn. *Would that you knew what* 'Illiyūn *is! It is a record inscribed, witnessed by those who are closest to God. The righteous will surely be in bliss. [Reclining] on couches, they will look around them. In their faces you shall mark the glow of bliss. They will be given to drink of a pure-drink, securely sealed, with a seal of musk, for this let the strivers emulously strive. It is a drink mixed with the waters of* Tasnīm, *a fountain at which those who are closest to God will drink.*" (Verses 18–28)

This section of the *sūrah* starts with the Arabic term, *kallā,* which connotes strong reproach and a firm command to the transgressors to desist from their rejection of the truth. It then proceeds to speak about the righteous. Since the record of the transgressors is in *Sijjīn*, that of the righteous is in *'Illiyūn*. The term 'righteous' refers to the obedient who do good. They are the exact opposite of the transgressors, who indulge in every excess. The name *'Illiyūn* connotes elevation and sublimity, which suggests that *Sijjīn* is associated with baseness and ignominy. The name is followed by the form of exclamation often used in the Qur'ān to cast notions of mystery and grandeur: "*Would that you knew what* 'Illiyūn *is*!" (Verse 19)

The *sūrah* then states that the book of the righteous is "*a record inscribed, witnessed by those who are closest to God.*" (Verses 20–21) We have already stated what is meant by '*a record inscribed.*' We are told here that the angels closest to God see this book and witness it. This statement gives the feeling that the record of the righteous is associated with nobility, purity and sublimity. The angels closest to God look at it and enjoy its description of noble deeds and glorious characteristics. The whole image provides evidence of the honour the righteous receive.

There follows an account of the situation in which the righteous find themselves. We are told of the bliss they enjoy on that great day: "*The righteous will surely be in bliss.*" (Verse 22) This contrasts with hell, in which the transgressors dwell. "*[Reclining] on couches they will look around them.*" (Verse 23) This means that they are given a place of honour. They look wherever they wish. They do not have to look down, out of humility; and they suffer nothing which distracts their attention. The description here represents to the Arabs, who were the first to be addressed by the Qur'ān, the highest form of comfort and luxury.

In their bliss, the righteous live in mental and physical comfort. Their faces are radiant with unmistakable joy: "*In their faces you shall mark the glow of bliss. They will be given to drink of a pure-drink, securely sealed, with a seal of musk.*" (Verses 24–26) Their drink is absolutely pure without any unwanted additions or particles of dust. Describing it as securely sealed with musk indicates, perhaps, that it is ready made in secured containers to be opened when refreshment is needed. All this adds to the impression of meticulous care being taken. The fact that the seal is of musk also adds an element of elegance and luxury. The whole picture, however, is understood only within the limits of human experience in this world.

In the life to come people will have different concepts, tastes and standards which will be free from all the bonds of this limited world.

The description is carried further in the following two verses: "*It is a drink mixed with the waters of* Tasnīm, *a fountain at which those who are closest to God will drink.*" (Verses 27–28) So, this pure, securely sealed drink is opened and mixed with a measure of the water from a fountain called *Tasnīm* and described as the one from which the favoured who are close to God drink. Before this last part of the description is given we are also given a significant instruction: "*For this let the strivers emulously strive.*" (Verse 26)

Those stinters who defraud their fellow men pay no regard to the Day of Judgement, and, worse still, deny that such a Day of Reckoning will come. Hardened by their sins and excesses, they strive endlessly for the petty riches of this world. Each of them tries to outdo the others and gain as much as possible. Hence, he indulges in all types of injustice and vice for the sake of ephemeral luxuries. It is the other type of luxury and honour which deserves emulous striving: "*For this let the strivers emulously strive.*" (Verse 26)

Those who strive for an object of this world, no matter how superb, grand or honourable it is, are in reality striving for something hollow, cheap and temporary. This world, in its totality, is not worth, in God's view, one mosquito's wing. It is the hereafter which carries real weight with Him. So, it should be the goal for strenuous competition and zealous striving.

It is remarkable that striving for the hereafter elevates the souls of all strivers, while competition for worldly objects sinks the competitors' souls to the lowest depths. As man works continuously to achieve the happiness of the hereafter, his work makes this world a happy and pure one for everybody. On the other hand, efforts made for the achievement of worldly ends turn this world into a filthy marsh, where animals devour one another and insects bite the flesh of the righteous.

Striving for the hereafter does not turn the earth into a barren desert, as some transgressors imagine. Islam considers this world a farm, and the hereafter its fruits. It defines the role of the true believer as the building of this world while following the path of piety and righteousness. Islam stipulates that man must look on his task as an act of worship which fulfils the purpose of his existence as defined by God: "*I have not created the* jinn *and mankind to any end other than that they may worship Me.*" (51: 56) The statement, "*For this let the strivers emulously strive,*" inspires man to look far beyond this finite, little world, as he sets out to fulfil his mission as God's vicegerent on earth. Thus as they work on purifying the filthy marsh of this world their souls are elevated to new heights.

Man's life on earth is limited while his future life is of limitless duration. The luxuries of this world are also limited while the happiness of paradise is much too great for us to conceive. The elements of happiness in this life are well known to everyone, but in the next world they are on a level befitting a life everlasting.

What comparison can then hold between the two spheres of competition or the two goals, even when we apply the human method of balancing losses against profits? It is, indeed, one race and a single competition: "*For this let the strivers emulously strive.*" (Verse 26)

Stark Contrast

The beatitude enjoyed by the righteous is discussed at length in order to give a detailed account of the hardships, humiliation and insolence they are made to suffer at the hands of the transgressors. The final comment of the *sūrah* taunts the unbelievers as they behold the righteous enjoying heavenly bliss: "*Those who are given to sinful practices scoff at the faithful and wink at one another as they pass by them. When they go back to their folk they speak of them with jests, and when they see them they say: 'These have indeed gone astray!' Yet they have not been assigned the mission of being their guardians. So on this Day [of Judgement] the faithful will laugh at the unbelievers, as they recline upon their couches and look around them. Shall the unbelievers be requited for what they were wont to do*?" (Verses 29–36)

The images portrayed by the Qur'ān of the evildoers' derision of the faithful, their rudeness and insolence, and their description of the faithful, as having '*gone astray*' are taken directly from Makkan life at the time. But the same actions happen over and over again in all ages and places. Many people in our own age have witnessed similar actions, and it is as if the *sūrah* was revealed to describe what they see with their own eyes. This proves that the attitude of the transgressors and the evildoers to the believers hardly ever changes from one country to another or from one period of time to another.

"*Those who are given to sinful practices scoff at the faithful.*" (Verse 29) In the Arabic original, the past tense is used here so as to take us away from this world to the hereafter to see the righteous in their bliss while we also hear what happened to them in this world. The believers were made to suffer ridicule and derision by the transgressors, either because they were poor or weak or because their self-respect would not allow them to return the abuse of base evildoers. What a contrast: the evildoers persecute the believers and laugh at them shamelessly while the believers stick to dignified self respect and perseverance.

"*And wink at one another as they pass by them.*" (Verse 30) They wink at one another or make certain actions intended as mockery and derision. Such behaviour betrays their baseness and bad manners. They try to make the believers feel embarrassed and helpless. "*When they go back to their folk they speak of them with jests.*" When they have nourished their evil, little minds with such mockery and injurious actions they go back to their own folk to continue their laughter and derision. They are satisfied with what they have done. Although they have sunk to the lowest depths, they cannot imagine how contemptible they are.

"*And when they see them they say: 'These have indeed gone astray!'*" (Verse 32) This is even more singular! Nothing is more absurd than that those transgressors should speak about right and error, or that they should say that the believers have gone astray. Transgression knows no limits. The transgressors never feel ashamed of what they do or say. Their description of the believers as having gone astray is a clear manifestation of this fact. The Qur'ān does not try to defend the believers or refute the evil accusation levelled at them, because it is not worth refuting. It laughs loudly, however, at those who involve themselves impudently in something which does not concern them, "*Yet they have not been assigned the mission of being their guardians!*" (Verse 33) No one has asked them to look after the believers, or to watch over them, or to assess their situation. So why do they give their unsolicited opinion?

This sarcasm concludes the narration of what the transgressors do in this life. The *sūrah* relates it as if it is something of the past, and gives an image of the present, i.e. in the hereafter, when the believers rejoice in their heavenly bliss: "*So on this Day [of Judgement] the faithful will laugh at the unbelievers, as they recline upon their couches and look around them.*" (Verses 34–35) On that day the unbelievers will be shut out from their Lord, suffering isolation combined with the torture of hell when they are told: "*This is [the reality] which you denied!*" (Verse 17) At the other end of the scale, the believers recline on couches, in total beatitude, partaking of a pure drink which is secured with a seal of musk and mixed with the waters of *Tasnīm*. As the *sūrah* draws the two images, it shows how the tables are turned; for then it is the believers who laugh at the unbelievers.

The *sūrah* concludes with another loud, ironic question: "*Shall the unbelievers be requited for what they were wont to do.*" (Verse 36) Their requital is not a good one, as the term used here connotes. For we have just been given an image of their doom, which is described here sarcastically, as their reward.

Who Laughs at Whom?

The scene of the evildoers' ridicule of the believers merits further discussion. It is portrayed in considerable detail, in the same way as the earlier scene of the righteous in heavenly bliss. This detailed description is highly artistic. It also has a marked psychological effect which is at once soothing, comforting and reassuring. The Muslim minority in Makkah was facing a sustained, demoralizing onslaught by the unbelievers, but God did not leave the Muslims on their own: He comforted them and urged them to persevere.

They are comforted by the very fact that their sufferings are outlined by God in detail. He sees what the believers suffer and does not ignore what He sees, although He may let the unbelievers do as they wish, if only for a while. He also sees how the transgressors laugh unrepentantly at the sufferings of the faithful. Since He describes all this in the Qur'ān then He must take it into account. This, in itself, is enough consolation for the believers.

There are also those scornful remarks about the evildoers. They may go unnoticed by the unbelievers because their indulgence in their sinful practices have made them insensitive. The highly sensitive hearts of the believers, however, are touched and comforted by them.

It must be noted that the only consolation offered by God to the believers who were subjected to harsh treatment and painful ridicule was heaven for the believers and hell for the unbelievers. This, again, was the only promise the Prophet (peace be upon him) made to the believers when they pledged all their property as well as their lives for the cause of Islam. Victory in this life was never mentioned in the Makkan Qur'ānic revelations as a consolation or as an incentive to persevere. The Qur'ān was instead cultivating the hearts of the believers, and preparing them to fulfil the task with which they were entrusted. It was necessary that such hearts attain a high standard of strength and self-denial so that they would give everything and suffer all hardship without looking for anything in this life. They were to seek only the reward of the hereafter and to win God's pleasure. They were prepared to go through life suffering all sorts of hardship and deprivation with no promise of reward in this life, not even victory for the cause of Islam.

Such a group of people must be first established. When this happens and God knows that they are sincere and determined in what they have pledged themselves to do, then He will give them victory in this life. Victory will not be theirs as a personal reward. They will be given power as trustees appointed for the implementation of the Islamic way of life. They will be worthy trustees because neither were they promised nor did they look for any worldly gain. They pledged themselves truly to God at a time when they were unaware of any worldly benefit that may befall them except that they would win God's pleasure.

All the Qur'ānic verses which speak of victory were revealed later in Madinah when this was no longer an issue. Victory was given because God willed that successive human generations should have an actual, definite and practical example of the Islamic way of life. It was not a reward for sacrifices made or hardships suffered.

SŪRAH 84

Al-Inshiqāq

(The Rending)

Al-Inshiqāq (The Rending)

سُورَةُ الانشِقَاقِ

In the name of God, the Beneficent, the Merciful.

بِسْمِ اللَّهِ الرَّحْمَٰنِ الرَّحِيمِ

When the sky is rent asunder, (1)

إِذَا السَّمَاءُ انشَقَّتْ ١

obeying her Lord in true submission; (2)

وَأَذِنَتْ لِرَبِّهَا وَحُقَّتْ ٢

when the earth is stretched out (3)

وَإِذَا الْأَرْضُ مُدَّتْ ٣

and casts forth all that is within her and becomes empty, (4)

وَأَلْقَتْ مَا فِيهَا وَتَخَلَّتْ ٤

obeying her Lord in true submission! (5)

وَأَذِنَتْ لِرَبِّهَا وَحُقَّتْ ٥

O man! You have been toiling towards your Lord, and you shall meet Him. (6)

يَٰٓأَيُّهَا ٱلْإِنسَٰنُ إِنَّكَ كَادِحٌ إِلَىٰ رَبِّكَ
كَدْحًا فَمُلَٰقِيهِ ﴿٦﴾

He who is given his record in his right hand (7)

فَأَمَّا مَنْ أُوتِىَ كِتَٰبَهُۥ بِيَمِينِهِۦ ﴿٧﴾

will in time have a lenient reckoning, (8)

فَسَوْفَ يُحَاسَبُ حِسَابًا يَسِيرًا ﴿٨﴾

and return rejoicing to his people. (9)

وَيَنقَلِبُ إِلَىٰٓ أَهْلِهِۦ مَسْرُورًا ﴿٩﴾

But he who is given his record behind his back (10)

وَأَمَّا مَنْ أُوتِىَ كِتَٰبَهُۥ وَرَآءَ ظَهْرِهِۦ ﴿١٠﴾

will in time call down destruction upon himself (11)

فَسَوْفَ يَدْعُوا۟ ثُبُورًا ﴿١١﴾

and will enter the fire of hell. (12)

وَيَصْلَىٰ سَعِيرًا ﴿١٢﴾

He lived joyfully among his people. (13)

إِنَّهُۥ كَانَ فِىٓ أَهْلِهِۦ مَسْرُورًا ﴿١٣﴾

He surely thought he would never return. (14)

إِنَّهُۥ ظَنَّ أَن لَّن يَحُورَ ﴿١٤﴾

Yes, indeed; his Lord was watching over him. (15)

بَلَىٰٓ إِنَّ رَبَّهُۥ كَانَ بِهِۦ بَصِيرًا ﴿١٥﴾

I swear by the twilight, (16)

فَلَآ أُقْسِمُ بِٱلشَّفَقِ ﴿١٦﴾

and by the night and what it envelops, (17)

وَٱلَّيۡلِ وَمَا وَسَقَ ﴿١٧﴾

and by the moon in her full perfection, (18)

وَٱلۡقَمَرِ إِذَا ٱتَّسَقَ ﴿١٨﴾

that you shall certainly move onward, stage after stage. (19)

لَتَرۡكَبُنَّ طَبَقًا عَن طَبَقٖ ﴿١٩﴾

Why then do they not accept the faith? (20)

فَمَا لَهُمۡ لَا يُؤۡمِنُونَ ﴿٢٠﴾

Or, when the Qur'ān is read to them, they do not fall down in prostration? (21)

وَإِذَا قُرِئَ عَلَيۡهِمُ ٱلۡقُرۡءَانُ
لَا يَسۡجُدُونَ ۩ ﴿٢١﴾

But the unbelievers persist in rejecting [the truth], (22)

بَلِ ٱلَّذِينَ كَفَرُواْ يُكَذِّبُونَ ﴿٢٢﴾

yet God knows very well what they are hiding. (23)

وَٱللَّهُ أَعۡلَمُ بِمَا يُوعُونَ ﴿٢٣﴾

So give them the tidings of a grievous suffering, (24)

فَبَشِّرۡهُم بِعَذَابٍ أَلِيمٍ ﴿٢٤﴾

except for those who believe and do good deeds; for theirs is an unfailing reward. (25)

إِلَّا ٱلَّذِينَ ءَامَنُواْ وَعَمِلُواْ ٱلصَّٰلِحَٰتِ
لَهُمۡ أَجۡرٌ غَيۡرُ مَمۡنُونِۭ ﴿٢٥﴾

Overview

The *sūrah* opens by sketching a few images of the universal upheaval portrayed in greater detail in *Sūrahs* 81, 82 and earlier in *Sūrah* 78, The Darkening, Cleaving Asunder and The Tiding, respectively. These scenes, however, are now given a special tone by means of the emphasis placed on the complete submission to God by both heaven and earth: "*When the sky is rent asunder, obeying her Lord in true submission; when the earth is stretched out and casts forth all that is within her and becomes empty, obeying her Lord in true submission.*" (Verses 1–5)

This powerful opening, with its emphasis on submission to God, is a foreword to the subsequent address encouraging man towards humbleness before his Lord. Man is reminded of his position and his ultimate destiny when he returns to God: "*O man! You have been toiling towards your Lord, and you shall meet Him. He who is given his record in his right hand will in time have a lenient reckoning, and return rejoicing to his people. But he who is given his record behind his back will in time call down destruction upon himself and will enter the fire of hell. He lived joyfully among his people. He surely thought he would never return. Yes, indeed; his Lord was watching over him.*" (Verses 6–15)

The third part of the *sūrah* paints a picture of life on earth which is well known to man. Such images point to God's planning, which is both elaborate and faultless. An oath is made to assert that men must live through deliberately planned stages which they cannot escape from: "*I swear by the twilight, and by the night and what it envelops, and by the moon in her full perfection, that you shall certainly move onward, stage after stage.*" (Verses 16–19)

The last part of the *sūrah* wonders at those who deny the faith when their position is as described in the previous two parts, and the end of their world is as described at the beginning of the *sūrah*: "*Why then do they not accept the faith? Or, when the Qur'ān is read to them, they do not fall down in prostration? But the unbelievers persist in rejecting [the truth], yet God knows very well what they are hiding. So give them the tidings of a grievous suffering, except for those who believe and do good deeds; for theirs is an unfailing reward.*" (Verses 20–25)

Two main qualities are evident in this *sūrah*: its quiet rhythm and its earnest message. Both are clearly felt, even in the images of universal upheaval the *sūrah* sketches. Scenes of this upheaval are portrayed with much more violence elsewhere, as in *Sūrah* 81, The Darkening. Here an attitude of sympathetic and compassionate cautioning is adopted. The cautioning is gradual, presented in a quiet, inspiring statement beginning with the words "*O man*". This awakens people's consciences.

The various parts of the *sūrah* are ordered according to a special plan. This carries the reader through a variety of scenes, some relating to the universe, others to man himself. The scenes are sketched one after the other in a thoughtful order starting with universal submission to God, which leaves a gentle but real impression on the reader's heart. Then we are given an image of the reckoning, reward and retribution, followed by a contemporary scene of life on earth and its phenomena. Then follows a statement of wonder at those who, after all this, still refuse to accept the faith. This statement combines with a warning of severe punishment, and a promise of unfailing reward to the believers.

All this is embodied in the few lines which compose this short *sūrah*. Such succinctness is just one aspect of the unique nature of the Qur'ān . The ideas the *sūrah* sets out to explain could not normally be tackled with such power and to such effect, even if entire books were devoted to the task. But the Qur'ān achieves its purpose because it addresses our hearts directly. No wonder! It is the word of God.

Complete Universal Submission

"*When the sky is rent asunder, obeying her Lord in true submission; when the earth is stretched out and casts forth all that is within her and becomes empty, obeying her Lord in true submission.*" (Verses 1–5) The splitting of the sky has been dwelt upon in the commentary on other *sūrahs*. One new element here is the submission and complete obedience of the sky to her Lord: "*obeying her Lord in true submission.*" (Verse 2) Another new element is the stretching of the earth: "*When the earth is stretched out.*" (Verse 3) This means perhaps an expansion of her size or shape as a result of a disruption of the laws of nature which govern her and preserve her in her present shape. The statement, made in the passive, suggests that this will be carried out through the intervention of an outside force. "*And casts forth all that is within her and becomes empty.*" (Verse 4) This image portrays the earth as a living entity casting out what is within her and getting rid of it.

There are indeed a great many things within the earth, countless types of creation that have lived, died and been buried over a long period of time, the span of which is known to no one but God. It also includes an abundant resource of metals, water and other secrets unknown except to the Creator. The earth carries all this load one generation after another until that final day when it casts forth all that is within her. "*Obeying her Lord in true submission,*" she follows the sky's suit and declares total obedience and complete submission to God.

These short verses vividly demonstrate how both the living sky and earth receive their orders and instantly comply with them. Their obedience is a manifestation of their conscious and dutiful submission. The image drawn here has shades of humility, solemnity and tranquillity that are brought out in full relief. The impression it leaves is one of humble and obedient submission to God.

Man's Hard Labour

In such an atmosphere of conscious obedience, man is addressed from on high: "*O man! You have been toiling towards your Lord, and you shall meet Him.*" (Verse 6) "O man!" your Lord has made you in a perfect way. He has given you your humanity which distinguishes you from the rest of creation. Your humanity endows you with certain characteristics which should have made you more conscious of your Lord, and more obedient and submissive to Him than both the sky and the earth. He has given man of His own spirit and endowed him with the ability to communicate with Him, receive His light, ennoble himself with God's grace in order to achieve the highest degree of perfection attainable by man. This is no little distinction.

"*O man! You have been toiling towards your Lord and you shall meet Him.*" (Verse 6) Man certainly labours hard in this life, shouldering his responsibilities and exerting himself. All this he does in order to return, in the end, like all the rest of creation, to God. Man labours even for what he enjoys! Nothing in this life comes easily or without effort: if sometimes no physical labour is needed, then surely some mental and emotional effort is required. In this the rich and poor are alike, although the labour exerted may differ in kind and form. This address reminds man that labouring hard is the lot of all in this life on earth. But when we meet our Lord, we will fall into two groups: one will suffer hardship incomparable to that suffered on earth; and the other, consisting of those who have demonstrated their obedience and true submission, will enjoy a rest in which the suffering of this life will be forgotten.

"*He who is given his record in his right hand will in time have a lenient reckoning, and return rejoicing to his people.*" (Verses 7–9) He who is given his book in his right hand is the happy one who was true to his faith. God is pleased with him and rewards him well. He will have a lenient reckoning, that is to say that he will not be called to account for what he did in this life. This is abundantly clear in the traditions of the Prophet. 'Ā'ishah, the Prophet's wife, quotes him as saying: "He who is called to account will suffer affliction." Continuing her report, she pointed out that God says, 'He... shall have a lenient reckoning.' God's Messenger answered: 'That is not what is meant by reckoning and accountability. Lenient reckoning signifies no more than showing him his record. He who is called to account on the Day of Judgement will suffer affliction.'" [Related by al-Bukhārī, Muslim, al-Tirmidhī and al-Nasā'ī.]

'Ā'ishah also related: "I heard God's Messenger (peace be upon him) saying in his prayers 'My Lord, make my reckoning a lenient one'. When he had finished his prayers I asked him, 'What is the lenient reckoning?' He answered: 'He who receives lenient reckoning will have his record looked into and will be forgiven, but he who is called to account on that day will perish." [Related by Aḥmad.]

This is, then, the lenient reckoning accorded to him who receives his record in his right hand. He shall win "*and return rejoicing to his people*," who will also have won and arrived in heaven ahead of him. We deduce from this statement that those who accept the faith in this life and adhere to the right path will gather together in heaven. Everyone ends up with those whom he loves. We also have an image of the winner's all-important test: he returns with his face overflowing with happiness.

This image is the opposite of what happens to the afflicted one who has to account for his evil deeds and receives his record with reluctance. "*But he who is given his record behind his back will in time call down destruction upon himself and will enter the fire of hell.*" (Verses 10–12)

The Qur'ān usually makes a distinction between receiving one's record with one's right or left hand. Here we have a new image: the record is given from behind one's back. There is no reason to prevent anyone being given his record in his left hand and from behind his back at the same time. It is an image of one who feels great shame and hates to be confronted with what he has done. We have no real knowledge of the nature of this record or how it is given in one's right or left hand or behind one's back. But we can comprehend from the first expression the reality of being a winner, and from the second the reality of doom. This is indeed what we are meant to appreciate. These various forms of expression are used mainly to drive the point home to us and to enhance its effects. For exact knowledge of what will happen and how it will happen belongs only to God.

So, the unfortunate one who lived his life on earth labouring hard but disobeying God and indulging in what is forbidden will know his destiny. He realizes that what lies in front of him is more suffering and hard labour with the only difference being that this time the suffering is greater, uninterrupted and endless. So, he calls destruction upon himself, for he sees his own destruction as the only means of salvation from what will befall him. When man seeks refuge in his own destruction, then he is certainly in a helpless position. His own non-existence becomes his strongest desire. His hopelessness is beyond description. This is the meaning implied by the Arab poet al-Mutanabbī in his poem which starts with what may be rendered in English as: "Suffice it a malady that you should think death a cure. It says much that doom should be eagerly desired." It is certainly a case of indescribable distress and misery. "*And [he] will enter the fire of hell.*" (Verse 12) This is the end from which he wishes to escape by means of his own destruction; but there is no way out.

Having portrayed this miserable scene, the *sūrah* gives us a glimpse of the sufferer's past which led him to this endless misery: "*He lived joyfully among his people. He surely thought he would never return.*" (Verses 13–14) The past tense is used here because we feel that the Day of Judgement has arrived, after this life has ended. The indulgence and the joy had taken place in this life. "*He lived joyfully among his people.*" He cared for nothing beyond the moment he was in, and made no preparation for the hereafter. "*He surely thought he would never return,*" to his Lord. Had he thought about the return at the end of his journey through life, he would have carried provisions to sustain him. "*Yes, indeed; his Lord was watching over him.*" (Verse 15) Indeed God has always been aware of man's thoughts, actions and feelings. God knows that, contrary to what man may think, there will be a return to Him to receive the reward merited by actions on earth. This is indeed what happens when all return to God to meet their appointed destiny, when what God has ordained will take place.

He lived joyfully among his people. He surely thought he would never return. Yes, indeed; his Lord was watching over him." (Verses 13–15) This image of the misery of the one who was joyful among his people during his short life on earth has a counterpart in the image of the happy one who returns rejoicing to his people to live with them an eternal happy life, free from hardship: "*He who is given his record in his right hand will in time have a lenient reckoning and return rejoicing to his people.*" (Verses 7–9)

Suffering Through Life

The *sūrah* then refers briefly to some worldly scenes. People, however, continue to overlook the evidence such scenes provide of the deliberate planning that has gone into the making of this world. Indeed, this planning includes the creation of man himself, and his phases and transitions through life: "*I swear by the twilight, and by the night and what it envelops, and by the moon in her full perfection, that you shall certainly move onward, stage after stage.*" (Verses 16–19) The oath, which is indirect in the Arabic text, serves to draw man's attention to these universal scenes. The connotations here are in perfect harmony with those of the opening of the *sūrah* and the scenes portrayed there. The twilight refers to that period of stillness after sunset when the soul is overwhelmed by a deep feeling of awe. The heart feels, at such a time, the significance of parting with a beloved companion, and the quiet sadness and deep melancholy this involves. It also experiences fear of the approaching darkness.

"*And by the night and what it envelops.*" (Verse 17) What the night envelops is left unspecified to enhance the effect. Imagination can travel far and wide as one thinks of what the night may conceal of events and feelings. But the travels of the imagination cannot capture all the images generated by the short Qur'ānic verse, "*And by the night and what it envelops.*" We are left with an overwhelming feeling of reverence which is in perfect harmony with the stillness and awe associated with the twilight.

"*And by the moon in her full perfection.*" (Verse 18) This is another quiet and splendid scene, describing the full moon as her light descends over the earth. The full moon is always associated with tranquillity. The general impression formed here is closely associated with twilight, and the dark night as it conceals everything. The feeling is one of a complementary stillness and reverence.

"*That you shall certainly move onward, stage after stage.*" (Verse 19) This means, you will pass from one stage of suffering to another, as has been charted for you. The Qur'ān uses the term 'ride', although we use the expression 'move onward', to denote the undergoing of various stages of suffering. 'Ride' is frequently used in Arabic to signify the passage through risk and difficulty. This usage suggests that difficulties and risks are like horses or mules to be ridden. Each one will take the rider to the stage determined for them. Thus each one will deliver the rider to a new, predetermined stage, in the same way as twilight, the night and perfect moon are predetermined. They eventually end with their meeting with God, which was mentioned in the preceding part. This coherent ordering of the parts of the *sūrah* and the smooth movement from one point to another is characteristic of the superb Qur'ānic style.

Unfailing Reward

There then follows an expression of wonder at those who persist in their denial of the faith when they have all these signs and all this abundant evidence within themselves and in the world at large which indicates the truth: "*Why then do they not accept the faith? Or, when the Qur'ān is read to them, they do not fall down in prostration?*" (Verses 20–21) Indeed, why do they not accept the faith? There are numerous indications in the universe and within the soul which point out that the path of faith is the right path. They are at once numerous, profound and powerful, so they besiege the heart if it tries to run away from them. But if someone listens to them, then they address him in a friendly and affectionate way.

The Qur'ān addresses them in the language of pure human nature. It opens the heart to the truth and points out its evidence both within themselves and over the horizon. It kindles in people's hearts God-consciousness, humbleness, obedience and submission to the Creator of the universe. The expression, "*fall down in prostration,*" refers to these feelings. The universe is splendid and inspiring: it offers a multitude of signs, mental stimuli and moments of purity which combine to arouse in us a ready response and a willing submission. The Qur'ān is also superb and inspiring; it links the human heart with the splendid universe and, consequently, with the Creator who made it. It gives us a feeling of truth about the universe which also demonstrates the truth of creation and the Creator. Hence the wonder: "*Why then do they not accept the faith? Or, when the Qur'ān is read to them, they do not fall down in prostration?*" (Verses 20–21)

It is indeed amazing, but the Qur'ān does not dwell on this for long. It proceeds to describe the behaviour of the unbelievers and the end which awaits them. "*But the unbelievers persist in rejecting [the truth], yet God knows very well what they are hiding. So give them the tidings of a grievous suffering.*" (Verses 22–24) The unbelievers shout, 'lies', but the object of their denunciation as lies is unspecified. In Arabic, omission of the object serves to widen the scope of reference for the verb. Thus, here we understand that the denunciation as lies is an entrenched habit and a characteristic of unbelievers. But God is fully aware of the evil they conceal in their hearts and He knows perfectly well their motives for denouncing the truth.

The *sūrah* then halts its discussion of their state and addresses God's Messenger: "*So give them the tidings of a grievous suffering,*" an unpleasant tiding for anyone who is awaiting news of his future.

At the same time the *sūrah* describes what awaits the believers who prepare for their future by good deeds. This description is made in the form of an exception from what awaits the unbelievers: "*except for those who believe and do good deeds; for theirs is an unfailing reward.*" (Verse 25) This type of exception is known in Arabic linguistics as "unrelated exception". The believers, not originally among the recipients of the gloomy news, are then excepted from it. This form of expression serves to draw attention to what follows. The unfailing recompense is one which is continuous and unceasing, and will be given in the hereafter, when people will be immortal.

On this decisive note the *sūrah* ends. It is a *sūrah* of short yet immensely powerful verses.

SŪRAH 85

Al-Burūj

(The Constellations)

Al-Burūj (The Constellations)

سُورَةُ البُرُوجِ

In the name of God, the Beneficent, the Merciful.

بِسْمِ ٱللَّهِ ٱلرَّحْمَٰنِ ٱلرَّحِيمِ

By the heaven with its constellations, (1)

وَٱلسَّمَآءِ ذَاتِ ٱلْبُرُوجِ ﴿١﴾

by the promised day, (2)

وَٱلْيَوْمِ ٱلْمَوْعُودِ ﴿٢﴾

by the witness and that which is witnessed, (3)

وَشَاهِدٍ وَمَشْهُودٍ ﴿٣﴾

slain be the people of the pit (4)

قُتِلَ أَصْحَٰبُ ٱلْأُخْدُودِ ﴿٤﴾

of the fire abounding in fuel, (5)

ٱلنَّارِ ذَاتِ ٱلْوَقُودِ ﴿٥﴾

when they sat around it, (6)

إِذْ هُمْ عَلَيْهَا قُعُودٌ ﴿٦﴾

وَهُمْ عَلَىٰ مَا يَفْعَلُونَ بِٱلْمُؤْمِنِينَ شُهُودٌ ﴿٧﴾

watching what they did to the believers. (7)

وَمَا نَقَمُوا۟ مِنْهُمْ إِلَّآ أَن يُؤْمِنُوا۟ بِٱللَّهِ
ٱلْعَزِيزِ ٱلْحَمِيدِ ﴿٨﴾

They took vengeance on them for no reason other than that they believed in God, the Almighty, to whom all praise is due, (8)

ٱلَّذِى لَهُۥ مُلْكُ ٱلسَّمَٰوَٰتِ وَٱلْأَرْضِ ۚ
وَٱللَّهُ عَلَىٰ كُلِّ شَىْءٍ شَهِيدٌ ﴿٩﴾

to whom the dominion of the heavens and the earth belongs. But God is witness of all things. (9)

إِنَّ ٱلَّذِينَ فَتَنُوا۟ ٱلْمُؤْمِنِينَ وَٱلْمُؤْمِنَٰتِ
ثُمَّ لَمْ يَتُوبُوا۟ فَلَهُمْ عَذَابُ جَهَنَّمَ وَلَهُمْ
عَذَابُ ٱلْحَرِيقِ ﴿١٠﴾

Those who persecute the believers, men and women, and do not repent shall suffer the punishment of hell, and suffer the punishment of burning. (10)

إِنَّ ٱلَّذِينَ ءَامَنُوا۟ وَعَمِلُوا۟ ٱلصَّٰلِحَٰتِ
لَهُمْ جَنَّٰتٌ تَجْرِى مِن تَحْتِهَا ٱلْأَنْهَٰرُ ۚ
ذَٰلِكَ ٱلْفَوْزُ ٱلْكَبِيرُ ﴿١١﴾

But those who believe and do righteous deeds shall have gardens through which running waters flow; that is the supreme triumph. (11)

إِنَّ بَطْشَ رَبِّكَ لَشَدِيدٌ ﴿١٢﴾

Stern indeed is your Lord's vengeance. (12)

إِنَّهُۥ هُوَ يُبْدِئُ وَيُعِيدُ ﴿١٣﴾

It is He who brings into being, and then restores to life. (13)

وَهُوَ ٱلْغَفُورُ ٱلْوَدُودُ ﴿١٤﴾

He is All-Forgiving, Compassionate, (14)

Lord of the Throne, Glorious, (15)	ذُو ٱلۡعَرۡشِ ٱلۡمَجِيدُ ﴿١٥﴾
He does whatever He wills. (16)	فَعَّالٞ لِّمَا يُرِيدُ ﴿١٦﴾
Have you heard the story of the hosts, (17)	هَلۡ أَتَىٰكَ حَدِيثُ ٱلۡجُنُودِ ﴿١٧﴾
of Pharaoh and Thamūd? (18)	فِرۡعَوۡنَ وَثَمُودَ ﴿١٨﴾
Yet the unbelievers persist in their denial [of the truth]. (19)	بَلِ ٱلَّذِينَ كَفَرُواْ فِي تَكۡذِيبٖ ﴿١٩﴾
But God surrounds them all. (20)	وَٱللَّهُ مِن وَرَآئِهِم مُّحِيطُۢ ﴿٢٠﴾
This is indeed a glorious Qur'ān, (21)	بَلۡ هُوَ قُرۡءَانٞ مَّجِيدٞ ﴿٢١﴾
inscribed on an imperishable tablet. (22)	فِي لَوۡحٖ مَّحۡفُوظِۭ ﴿٢٢﴾

Overview

This short *sūrah* outlines the essentials of faith and the basics of belief as matters of great importance. It sheds a powerful and searching light over these essentials in order to reveal what lies beyond the elementary facts expressed in the text. Every verse, and sometimes every word, in this *sūrah* virtually opens a window overlooking a limitless world of truth.

The immediate theme of the *sūrah* is the pit incident, when a community of believers who lived before the advent of Islam, said to be unitarian Christians, were faced by ruthless and tyrannical enemies who sought to force them away from their faith. The believers refused. The tyrants then lit a great fire in a pit they had dug, and threw them into it. The believers were thus burnt to death in front of large crowds that had gathered to witness this ghastly act of extermination. The tyrants sat by, amused by the believers' sufferings: "*They took vengeance on them for no reason other than that they believed in God, the Almighty, to whom all praise is due.*" (Verse 8)

The *sūrah* starts with an oath: "*By the heaven with its constellations, by the promised day, by the witness and that which is witnessed, slain be the people of the pit.*" (Verses 1–4) In this way the *sūrah* links heaven and its magnificent constellations, the promised Day of Judgement and its great events, the multitudes which witness that day and the events they witness with the pit incident and God's anger with the aggressors responsible for it. The *sūrah* then proceeds to portray the tragic scene in a few, quick flashes which demonstrate the horror without dwelling on detail.

It includes a reference to the greatness of faith which exalted itself over the tyrants' atrocious cruelty and triumphed over the fire, attaining a level of sublimity which is an honour to all mankind. It also refers to the heinous crime and the evil and injustice it involves in comparison with the sublimity, innocence and purity of the believers: "*Slain be the people of the pit of the fire abounding in fuel, when they sat around it, watching what they did to the believers.*" (Verses 4–7)

Then follows a series of short comments stating a number of principles which are highly important to the Islamic faith, its outlook and advocacy. We have firstly a reference to the fact that all the heavens and earth are part of God's kingdom and to His witnessing of all that takes place in them. He is the Sovereign of the heavens and the earth, who witnesses all.

Secondly, we have a reference to the burning in hell which awaits the tyrants, and a reference to the perfect heavenly bliss which awaits the believers who choose faith over life and exalt themselves despite their persecution. The believers' action is referred to as the great triumph: "*Those who persecute the believers, men and women, and do not repent shall suffer the punishment of hell, and suffer the punishment of burning. But those who believe and do righteous deeds shall have gardens through which running waters flow; that is the supreme triumph.*" (Verses 10–11)

A further reference is made to the power with which God smites His enemies and to the fact that He creates and brings back to life after death: "*Stern indeed is your Lord's vengeance. It is He who brings into being, and then restores to life.*" (Verses 12–13) This relates directly to the lives blotted out in the pit incident.

The *sūrah* then mentions some of the divine attributes, each of which has a specific relevance to the subject matter of the *sūrah*: "*He is All-Forgiving, Compassionate.*" (Verse 14) He forgives those who repent regardless of the enormity and horror of their sins. He also loves His servants who choose Him. His love is the soothing balsam which heals whatever injuries they may have suffered. "*Lord of the Throne, Glorious, He does whatever He wills.*" (Verses 15–16) These attributes portray God's absolute will, dominance and power, all of which are relevant to the event discussed in the *sūrah*.

Then follows a reference to examples of God's punishment of tyrants even though they were heavily armed. "*Have you heard the story of the hosts, of Pharaoh and Thamūd?*" (Verses 17–18) These were two very different instances of God's punishment with widely different effects. Along with the pit horror, they carry numerous implications.

Finally, the *sūrah* explains the situation of the unbelievers and that God surrounds them though they may be unaware of the fact. "*Yet the unbelievers persist in their denial [of the truth]. But God surrounds them all.*" (Verses 19–20) It concludes with a statement of the truth of the Qur'ān and its blessed origin: "*This is indeed a glorious Qur'ān, inscribed on an imperishable tablet.*" (Verses 21–22)

The Horrendous Event

"*By the heaven with its constellations, by the promised day, by the witness and that which is witnessed.*" (Verses 1–3) Before making any reference to the pit event, the *sūrah* opens with an oath by a heaven full of constellations. The Arabic term, *burūj*, used for 'constellations' may be taken to mean the huge mass of planets which resemble great towers or palaces built in the sky. In this sense the verse can be related to two other verses: "*We built heaven with Our might, and gave it a wide expanse.*" (51: 47) and, "*Which is stronger in constitution: you or the heaven He has built?*" (79: 27) The Arabic term may, alternatively, be interpreted as meaning the positions between which these planets move as they go round in orbit. These constitute the spheres within which the planets remain as they move. This reference to the constellations however, gives an impression of a huge creation. This is, indeed, the connotation intended at the outset.

"*By the promised day.*" (Verse 2) That is the day when judgement is passed on all the events of this life and when the accounts of this world are settled. It is a day God has promised will come, and is a great day awaited by all creation. "*By the witness and that which is witnessed.*" (Verse 3) On that day all deeds and creatures are exposed and witnessed. Everybody becomes a witness. Everything becomes known as there is no cover to hide anything from beholding eyes.

References to the heaven and the constellations, the promised day, the witness and what is witnessed all combine to impart an aura of seriousness, concern, attention and momentum to the manner in which the pit event is related. They also provide the framework in which the event is viewed, judged and settled on the basis of its true nature. It is a framework stretching far beyond the limits of this short life.

Having thus provided the desired atmosphere, the *sūrah* then refers to the event in just a few brief strokes. "*Slain be the people of the pit of the fire abounding in fuel, when they sat around it, watching what they did to the believers. They took vengeance on them for no reason other than that they believed in God, the Almighty, to whom all praise is due, to whom the dominion of the heavens and the earth belongs. But God is witness of all things.*" (Verses 4–9)

Reference to the event starts with a declaration of anger with the tyrants: "*Slain be the people of the pit.*" (Verse 4) It also gives an impression of the enormity of the crime which has invoked the displeasure and anger of God, the All-Clement, and which makes Him threaten the perpetrators. We then have a description of the pit: "*The fire abounding in fuel.*" (Verse 5) The literal meaning of 'pit' is a hole in the ground, but the *sūrah* defines it as 'the fire' instead of using the term 'trench' or 'hole' in order to give an impression that the whole pit was turned into a blazing furnace.

The perpetrators aroused God's wrath for the evil crime they committed: "*When they sat around it, watching what they did to the believers.*" (Verses 6–7) They sat over the fire, in the actual vicinity of the horror, watching the various stages of torture, and madly enjoying the burning of human flesh in order to perpetuate in their minds this ghastly scene.

The believers had not committed any crime or evil deed against them: "*They took vengeance on them for no reason other than that they believed in God, the Almighty, to whom all praise is due, to whom the dominion of the heavens and the earth belongs. But God is witness of all things.*" (Verses 8–9) That was their only crime: they believed in God Almighty who deserves praise for every situation even though ignorant people do not do so. He is the Lord who deserves to be worshipped, the sole sovereign of the kingdoms of the heavens and the earth. As He witnesses all things He has witnessed what the tyrants did to the believers. This verse reassures the believers and delivers a powerful threat to the tyrants. God has been a witness and He suffices for a witness.

The narration of the event is completed in a few short verses which charge our hearts with a feeling of repugnance towards the terrible crime and its evil perpetrators. They also invite us to contemplate what lies beyond the event, its importance in the sight of God and what it has aroused of God's wrath. It is a matter which is not yet completed. Its conclusion lies with God.

As the narration of the event concludes we feel overwhelmed by the magnificence of faith as it exalts the believers and attains its triumph over all hardships, and indeed over life itself. We feel the elevation of the believers as they rid themselves of the handicaps of human desire and worldly temptation. The believers could easily have saved their lives by accepting the tyrants' terms. But what a loss humanity as a whole would have incurred! How great the loss would have been had they killed that sublime concept of the worthlessness of life without faith, its ugliness without freedom and its baseness when tyrants are left free to exercise their tyranny over people's souls after they have exercised it over their bodies. But they have won a very noble and sublime concept while the fire burned their flesh. Their noble concept has triumphed as it was purified by the fire. They will, later on, have their reward from God and their tyrannical enemies will have their retribution. The *sūrah* then goes on to explain both.

Different Destinies

"*Those who persecute the believers, men and women, and do not repent shall suffer the punishment of hell, and suffer the punishment of burning. But those who believe and do righteous deeds shall have gardens through which running waters flow; that is the supreme triumph.*" (Verses 10–11) What happens on earth in this first life is not the end of the story. There remains an inevitable part which will follow later. There remains the allocation of awards, which will restore the balance of justice and provide the final settlement of what took place between the believers and the tyrants.

That it will come is certain and confirmed by God: "*Those who persecute the believers, men and women*" and persist with their evil ways, careless, unrepentant, "*and do not repent shall suffer the punishment of hell, and suffer the punishment of burning.*" Burning is specified although it is also implied by the very mention of hell.

It earns its specific mention in order to serve as a counterpart to the burning in the pit. Although the same word signifying the action is used, the two types of burning are dissimilar in intensity and duration. The burning here is by fire lit by human beings while the burning in the hereafter is by fire lit by the Creator. In this present world, the burning is over in a few minutes while in the hereafter it goes on for ages unknown except to God. The believers who suffer the burning here earn with it God's pleasure, and ensure the triumph of that noble human concept referred to earlier. In the hereafter the burning is attended by God's anger and man's abject degradation.

Paradise symbolizes God's pleasure with righteous believers and His reward to them. "*But those who believe and do righteous deeds shall have gardens through which running waters flow; that is the supreme triumph.*" (Verse 11) The Arabic term, *fawz*, used here for triumph also connotes escape and success. To escape the punishment of the hereafter is to achieve success. How to describe, then, the reward of gardens with running waters!

With this conclusion justice is restored and the whole question is finally resolved. What has taken place on earth is no more than one part; the matter remains unfinished here. This is the fact emphasized by this initial comment on the pit event, so that it may be fully comprehended by the few believers who have accepted the faith in Makkah, and by every group of believers subjected to trial and tyranny during any period of history.

God's Unique Attributes

Further comments follow: "*Stern indeed is your Lord's vengeance.*" (Verse 12) This comment suitably contrasts God's punishment with the petty and trifling vengeance exacted by tyrants, and thought by them and by people generally to be very powerful. The real power is that levelled by the Almighty, to whom belongs the heavens and the earth, not that levelled by insignificant people who impose their rule over a limited piece of land for a limited period of time.

The statement also emphasizes the relationship between the addressee, namely, God's Messenger (peace be upon him) and the speaker, who is God Almighty. He says to him, "*stern indeed is your Lord's vengeance.*" He is your Lord, in whose Godhead you believe, and on whose assistance you rely. This relationship is very significant in situations where believers are afflicted by tyrants.

"*It is He who brings into being, and then restores to life.*" (Verse 13) In their wider connotations, origination and restoration refer to the first and second processes of bringing into life. The two terms, however, signify two events which constantly take place. In every moment there is origination as well as restoration of what has died and decayed. The whole universe is in a state of continuous renovation, and constant decay. Within the context of this ever-repeated cycle of origination and re-origination the whole affair of the pit and its apparent results seem to be, in reality, no more than a beginning of what can be created anew, or a re-creation of what has already been originated. It is part of a continuous process.

"*He is All-Forgiving, Compassionate.*" (Verse 14) Forgiveness relates to the earlier statement: "*and do not repent*". Forgiveness is part of God's mercy and grace which have no limits or restrictions. It is an open door which is never closed in the face of anyone who repents, no matter how grave his sins are. Compassion, however, relates to the believers' attitude who choose their Lord in preference to all things. It is a generous touch of divine benevolence. God elevates His servants who love and choose Him to a grade which one would hesitate to describe except for the fact that God, out of His blessing, bestows it. It is the grade of friendship between Lord and servant. It is a tie of love which exists between God and His favoured servants. How insignificant the transitory life they have sacrificed and the momentary affliction they have suffered appear when compared to only a small part of this splendid and tender love. Some of those who live in servitude to another human being take fatal risks in order to win a word of encouragement or receive a sign of pleasure from their master. They do this although both master and servant are God's slaves. What, then, should be the attitude of God's servants who receive that compassionate love and benevolence from the "*Lord of the Throne, the Glorious*", the All-Powerful, the Sublime. So petty becomes life, so paltry becomes all suffering, and so trifling becomes every treasured object when the pleasure of the loving Lord of the Throne is at stake.

"*He does whatever He wills.*" (Verse 16) This is His constantly realized, never failing attribute. His will is absolute. He may choose, on a certain occasion, that believers should, by His grace, win victory for a specific purpose He wants to accomplish. He may choose, on other occasions, that faith should triumph over persecution and trial. This may be manifested, at times, through the physical elimination of believers from this transitory life, again to accomplish a specific purpose. He may decide to smite tyrants in this life, or to delay their punishment to the promised day. Either course of action fulfils a certain purpose behind which divine wisdom lies. Any action He performs is part of His well-defined scheme and His ability to do what He wills. All this fits very well with the account of the pit and with what comes later of reference to the fates of Pharaoh and Thamūd and their respective hosts. Beyond all these events and beyond life and the universe there exist the free will and absolute power of God.

Examples of this are given: "*Have you heard the story of the hosts, of Pharaoh and Thamūd?*" (Verses 17–18) This is a reference to two long stories well known to the addressees as they have been mentioned several times in the Qur'ān. The two nations concerned are described here by the term "the hosts" in reference to their might and equipment. Have you heard their stories and how God did with them as He pleased? Theirs were two stories, different in nature and consequence. Pharaoh and his army were eliminated when the Children of Israel were saved by God. He gave them power to rule for a certain period in order to accomplish a certain scheme. As for the Thamūd, God exterminated them and saved His prophet, Ṣāliḥ, along with his few followers. The believers in this instance did not establish a state of their own; they were merely saved from corrupt enemies.

Both stories are manifestations of the divine will and its performance. They provide two examples of what may befall advocates of the Islamic faith. They are mentioned along with a third possibility which distinguishes the pit event. The Qur'ān explains all three eventualities to the believers in Makkah and to all generations of believers.

The *sūrah* concludes with two statements characterized by their sharp and decisive rhythm. Each is a statement of fact and a final verdict. "*Yet the unbelievers persist in their denial [of the truth]. But God surrounds them all.*" (Verses 19–20) The truth about the unbelievers is that they are in a constant state of disbelief, crying "lies" morning and evening "*But God surrounds them all.*" They are unaware that God's might and His knowledge engulf them, making them even more powerless than mice stranded in a great flood.

"*This is indeed a glorious Qur'ān, inscribed on an imperishable tablet.*" (Verses 21–22) The term 'glorious' signifies nobility and sublimity. Indeed, there is nothing more noble or more sublime or more glorious than God's word. It is inscribed on an imperishable tablet, the nature of which we cannot comprehend because it is part of the knowledge God has reserved for Himself. We benefit, however, from the connotations of the statement and the impression it leaves that the Qur'ān is well preserved and well-guarded. It is the final word in every matter it deals with.

The Qur'ān states its judgement in the pit event and what lies behind it. This judgement is final.

SŪRAH 86

Al-Ṭāriq

(The Night Visitor)

Al-Ṭāriq (The Night Visitor)

سُورَةُ الطَّارِقِ

In the name of God, the Beneficent, the Merciful.

بِسْمِ اللَّهِ الرَّحْمَٰنِ الرَّحِيمِ

By the heaven and by the night visitor. (1)

وَالسَّمَاءِ وَالطَّارِقِ ﴿١﴾

Would that you knew what the night visitor is! (2)

وَمَا أَدْرَاكَ مَا الطَّارِقُ ﴿٢﴾

It is the star that pierces through darkness. (3)

النَّجْمُ الثَّاقِبُ ﴿٣﴾

For every soul there is a guardian who watches over it. (4)

إِن كُلُّ نَفْسٍ لَّمَّا عَلَيْهَا حَافِظٌ ﴿٤﴾

Let man then reflect: of what he is created. (5)

فَلْيَنظُرِ الْإِنسَانُ مِمَّ خُلِقَ ﴿٥﴾

He is created of gushing water; (6)	خُلِقَ مِن مَّآءٍ دَافِقٍ ﴿٦﴾
he issues from between the loins and the chest bones. (7)	يَخْرُجُ مِنۢ بَيْنِ ٱلصُّلْبِ وَٱلتَّرَآئِبِ ﴿٧﴾
God is well able to bring him back [to life]. (8)	إِنَّهُۥ عَلَىٰ رَجْعِهِۦ لَقَادِرٌ ﴿٨﴾
On the day when consciences are tried, (9)	يَوْمَ تُبْلَى ٱلسَّرَآئِرُ ﴿٩﴾
man shall be helpless, with no supporter. (10)	فَمَا لَهُۥ مِن قُوَّةٍ وَلَا نَاصِرٍ ﴿١٠﴾
By the heaven with its returning rain, (11)	وَٱلسَّمَآءِ ذَاتِ ٱلرَّجْعِ ﴿١١﴾
by the earth ever splitting with verdure, (12)	وَٱلْأَرْضِ ذَاتِ ٱلصَّدْعِ ﴿١٢﴾
this is surely a decisive word; (13)	إِنَّهُۥ لَقَوْلٌ فَصْلٌ ﴿١٣﴾
it is no idle talk. (14)	وَمَا هُوَ بِٱلْهَزْلِ ﴿١٤﴾
They devise many an artful scheme, (15)	إِنَّهُمْ يَكِيدُونَ كَيْدًا ﴿١٥﴾
but I too have My schemes. (16)	وَأَكِيدُ كَيْدًا ﴿١٦﴾
So give respite to the unbelievers; leave them alone for a while. (17)	فَمَهِّلِ ٱلْكَٰفِرِينَ أَمْهِلْهُمْ رُوَيْدًۢا ﴿١٧﴾

Overview

It is stated in the introduction to the first *sūrah* in this volume, which forms the thirtieth part of the Qur'ān, that its *sūrahs* are "like a persistent and strong knocking on a door, or a series of loud shouts seeking to awaken those who are fast asleep, or those who are drunk and have lost consciousness, or are in a night club, completely absorbed in their dancing or entertainment. The knocks and the shouts come one after the other: Wake up! Look around you! Think! Reflect! There is a God! There is planning, trial, liability, reckoning, reward, severe punishment and lasting bliss."

The present *sūrah* is a typical example of these qualities. Its tone is sharp. The scenes portrayed, the rhythm chosen, the sounds of the individual words and their meanings – all contribute to this sharpness of tone. The scenes include the night visitor, the star piercing with brightness, the gushing water, the returning rain and the splitting earth. The meanings include watching over souls: "*For every soul there is a guardian who watches over it*"; the lack of strength and help: "*On the day when consciences are tried, man shall be helpless, with no supporter*"; the complete seriousness: "*This is surely a decisive word; it is no idle talk.*" The same characteristics apply to the warnings given in this *sūrah*: "*They devise many an artful scheme, but I too have My schemes. So give respite to the unbelievers; leave them alone for a while.*"

There is complete harmony between the scenes of the universe portrayed in the *sūrah* and the facts it states. This harmony becomes abundantly clear when the *sūrah* is carefully considered.

A Special Type of Visitor

"*By the heaven and by the night visitor. Would that you knew what the night visitor is! It is the star that pierces through darkness. For every soul there is a guardian who watches over it.*" (Verses 1–4) This oath includes a scene of the universe and a fact of faith. It opens by mentioning heaven and the night visitor and follows with a form of exclamation made familiar in the Qur'ān; "*Would that you knew what the night visitor is!*" (Verse 2) This exclamation gives the impression that it is mysterious, beyond explanation.

The Qur'ān then states its nature and form: "*It is the star that pierces through darkness.*" (Verse 3) Its powerful, penetrating rays travel at speed through the surrounding darkness. The description applies to all stars. There is no need to attach it to a particular one. Generality is more useful in this kind of context. Thus, the meaning sounds as follows: By heaven and its stars which pierce darkness and penetrate through that veil covering all things. Thus, this reference sheds its own light on the facts outlined in this *sūrah* and the scenes it portrays.

God swears by heaven and its piercing stars that every soul has an observer appointed by Him to watch over it: "*For every soul there is a guardian who watches over it.*" (Verse 4) This implies a strong assertion that there is an agent appointed by God to watch over every soul and keep a record of its actions and thoughts. The watch is over the soul because it is there that thoughts and secrets which are responsible for action and reward lie. Thus, people are not left to roam about the earth as they wish. On the contrary, an accurate and immediate record is kept, on the basis of which reckoning is made.

This awesome inference becomes clear as the soul feels that it is never alone even when without company. There is always the watcher who remains nearby even when one hides from all and is secure against any visitor or intruder. There is still the watcher who penetrates all covers and has access to all things concealed, in the same way as the piercing star tears through the night cover. For God's method of creation is the same with regard to human souls and the wide horizons.

Man's Humble Origin

This opening touch, which unites the human soul with the universe, is followed by another which emphasizes the truth of organized creation and deliberate planning to which God has sworn by the heaven and the night visitor. The early stages of man's creation constitute a proof of this fact and suggest that man is not forgotten as something insignificant: "*Let man then reflect: of what he is created. He is created of gushing water; he issues from between the loins and the chest bones.*" (Verses 5–7)

Let man consider his origins and what has become of him. It is a very wide gulf which divides the origins from the final product, the gushing water from man the intelligent, rational being with his highly sophisticated organic, neurological, mental and psychological systems. The reference to this great gulf which the gushing water crosses in order to be made into a communicating being suggests that there is a power beyond the province of man which moves that shapeless and powerless fluid along its remarkable and impressive journey until it is shaped into its magnificent ultimate form. It implies that there is a guardian appointed by God to look after that moist germ, and to guide it through its remarkable journey.

This one fertilizing cell, of which there are millions in every gush, is hardly visible under the microscope. It is a creature without support, reason or will. But as soon as it settles in the womb it proceeds to search for food. The guarding hand of God equips it with a quality which enables it to convert the lining of the womb around it into a pool of blood, thus supplying it with fresh nourishment. Once it is sure of the availability of food it starts another process of continuous division to produce new cells. This shapeless and powerless creature which has no reason or will, knows exactly what it is doing and what it wants. The guarding hand watching over it provides it with guidance, knowledge, power and will to enable it to know its way. It is charged with the task of making every group of newly produced cells specialize in building a part of the magnificent structure of the human body. One group proceeds to produce the skeleton; another group forms the muscles; a third the nervous system; a fourth the lymphatic system. The same applies to every major part of the human structure. But the matter is not as simple as that: it involves a higher degree of specialization; for every bone, every muscle and every nerve is unique and dissimilar to every other. The structure is accurately planned, and has a wide range of functions. Hence, as every group of cells proceeds to fulfil its appointed task in building this structure, it learns to break up into specialized subdivisions, each having its particular function in the general set up. Every little cell proceeds knowing its way, destination and function. Those cells entrusted with the task of forming the eye know that the eye must be in the face, and that it cannot be situated in the abdomen or the foot or the arm, despite the fact that any of these localities is a suitable place for forming an eye. If the first cell charged with making the eye was taken off course and planted in any of these localities, it would have fulfilled its mission and made an eye there. But when it sets out on its mission it simply goes to the exact spot specified for the eye. Who then has told this cell that this structure needs its eye to be in that particular spot? It is God the watching Guardian who guides it, looks after it and shows it its way.

All the cells work individually and collectively within a framework set for them by certain elements functioning inside the cells. These elements are known as the genes which preserve the general characteristics of the species and the distinctive traits of the parents and forefathers. When the eye cell divides and proliferates in order to form the eye, it endeavours at the same time to preserve its shape and particular features so that it turns out to be a human eye and not the eye of an animal. Furthermore, it endeavours to make it an eye of a human whose forefathers had certain features and characteristics distinguishing their eyes. The slightest error in designing that eye, whether in shape or qualities, forces the forming cell out of its set course. So who has endowed power, ability and knowledge to this insignificant cell which has no reason, will or power of its own? It is God who taught it to design and produce what all mankind can never design or produce. For man cannot design an eye or a part of it, even if charged with this task, while an insignificant cell or group of cells in the body can accomplish this great mission.

This is merely a quick glance at parts of the remarkable journey which transforms the gushing water into the communicative human being. But there is indeed a great multitude of wonders in the physiological functions of the various organs and systems. It is beyond the scope of this work to trace these wonders but they all constitute evidence of elaborate planning and organization and bear the stamp of God's guarding, helping and guiding hand. They emphasize the first fact in the *sūrah* sworn to by the heaven and the night visitor, and prepare for the next fact, namely, the resurrection, which was denied by the idolaters who were among the first to be addressed by the Qur'ān.

"*God is well able to bring him back [to life]. On the day when consciences are tried, man shall be helpless, with no supporter.*" (Verses 8–10) God, who has created him and looked after him, is well able to bring him back to life after death. The first creation is evidence of His ability as well as His elaborate planning and organization. Unless there is a return in order to accord everyone his or her fair reward then this highly sophisticated and wise creation would be in vain. "*On the day when consciences are tried.*" (Verse 9) The Arabic terms, *tublā* and *sarā'ir* used by the Qur'ān have much wider connotations than conscience and trial. They suggest that that part of the human soul where secrets are safely deposited will be thrown open, searched and exposed in the same way as the night visitor penetrates the covering darkness of the night. As the guarding watcher penetrates through the soul hidden under multiple covers, secrets are examined and man finds himself powerless and without support: "*Man shall be helpless, with no supporter.*" (Verse 10) Standing bare without cover and strength adds to the strains and hardships of the situation. This has a deep effect on the reader's perception, as it moves from talking of the universe and the human soul to man's creation and his remarkable journey, until he reaches the end when his secrets are exposed and he stands alone, powerless, without support.

A Powerful Discourse

There may be some lingering doubts within some people's minds that this could happen. Therefore, the *sūrah* gives an oath to its seriousness. It adds a link between this assertion and the universe at large, as we saw at the opening of the *sūrah*: "*By the heaven with its returning rain, by the earth ever splitting with verdure, this is surely a decisive word; it is no idle talk.*" (Verses 11–14)

The rain which comes from the sky again and again and the vegetation which splits the earth and springs forth are two images describing one of the many manifestations of life, the life of plants and their origins. Water which pours down from heaven and verdure which springs out from the earth, are akin to the infant coming into the world, passing between the loins springing out from the darkness of the womb. It is the same life, the same scene, the same movement. It is one system pointing to the Maker who has no competitors.

The image of rain and verdure is not dissimilar to that of the night visitor, the piercing star as it splits covers and curtains. It is also similar to the scene depicting consciences being searched and all that is concealed being thrown open. It is again the same sort of structure which tells of the Maker. God swears by these two creations and their two events, the heaven of returning rains and the earth splitting with verdure. The impact of the scene portrayed combines with the rhythm to strike a strong note of finality and decisiveness. The oath is that this word, or the Qur'ān generally, which states that people will return to life so as to face a trial, is the decisive word which admits of no frivolity. It puts an end to all argument, doubts and uncertainties. It is a true and final word, to which both the heaven of the returning rain and the earth splitting with verdure are witnesses

When this final statement of return and trial is made, there follows an address to God's Messenger. At the time of revelation he had only a few believers who supported him in Makkah. They were suffering the brunt of the idolaters' hostility and their plots against the Islamic message. The idolaters were tirelessly trying to smother the call. The address is made to the Prophet so as to encourage and reassure him, and to disparage what the schemers devise. It states that their scheming is only temporary; the battle is in God's hands and under His command. So, let the Prophet persevere and be patient, and let him and the believers be reassured: "*They devise many an artful scheme, but I too have My schemes. So give respite to the unbelievers; leave them alone for a while.*" (Verses 15–17)

Those who were created from gushing water, then issued between the loins, brought forth without any strength, ability or will of their own, guided along their long journey by divine power and destined to that return when secrets are searched and tried and where they have no strength or support – are devising a scheme against the Prophet and the Muslims! I, the Creator who guides, preserves, directs, brings back to life and puts to trial; the Almighty; the Victor who has made the sky, the night visitor, the gushing water and man; the Maker of the heaven with its returning rain and the earth splitting with verdure; I, God, am devising a scheme of My own. So, there are the two schemes and the battle. It is, in truth, a one-sided battle but described as being between two sides for the sake of sarcasm.

"*So give respite to the unbelievers; leave them alone for a while.*" (Verse 17) Do not be impatient. Do not precipitate the end of the battle when you have seen its true nature. There is wisdom behind this respite and delay which is short even though it may take up the whole length of this first life; for how short this life appears when compared with a life of limitless duration.

God's benevolent and compassionate attitude to His Messenger is noticeable in the final verse: "*So give respite to the unbelievers; leave them alone for a while.*" He is addressed here as if he were the final authority, or as if he were the one who decides or approves that they may take a short respite. But the Prophet has no such authority; it is merely an expression of kind and benevolent tenderness which bestows compassion on his heart. It is divine kindness which suggests that God's Messenger has a say in the whole matter as if he had a share or interest in it. It lifts all barriers between the Prophet and the divine domain, where all matters are judged and settled.

SŪRAH 87

Al-Aʿlā

(The Most High)

Al-Aʿlā (The Most High)

سُورَةُ الأَعْلَى

In the name of God, the Beneficent, the Merciful.

بِسۡمِ ٱللَّهِ ٱلرَّحۡمَٰنِ ٱلرَّحِيمِ

Extol the limitless glory of the name of your Lord, the Most High, (1)

سَبِّحِ ٱسۡمَ رَبِّكَ ٱلۡأَعۡلَى ١

who creates and proportions well, (2)

ٱلَّذِي خَلَقَ فَسَوَّىٰ ٢

who determines and guides, (3)

وَٱلَّذِي قَدَّرَ فَهَدَىٰ ٣

who brings forth the pasturage, (4)

وَٱلَّذِيٓ أَخۡرَجَ ٱلۡمَرۡعَىٰ ٤

then turns it to withered grass. (5)

فَجَعَلَهُۥ غُثَآءً أَحۡوَىٰ ٥

We shall teach you and you shall not forget, (6)

سَنُقْرِئُكَ فَلَا تَنسَىٰٓ ٦

except what God wills. He knows what is manifest and what is kept hidden. (7)

إِلَّا مَا شَآءَ ٱللَّهُ إِنَّهُۥ يَعْلَمُ ٱلْجَهْرَ وَمَا يَخْفَىٰ ٧

And We shall smooth your way to perfect ease. (8)

وَنُيَسِّرُكَ لِلْيُسْرَىٰ ٨

Give warning, therefore, [regardless of] whether such warning is of use. (9)

فَذَكِّرْ إِن نَّفَعَتِ ٱلذِّكْرَىٰ ٩

He who fears God will heed it, (10)

سَيَذَّكَّرُ مَن يَخْشَىٰ ١٠

but the most hapless wretch will turn aside from it, (11)

وَيَتَجَنَّبُهَا ٱلْأَشْقَى ١١

who shall be cast into the great fire, (12)

ٱلَّذِى يَصْلَى ٱلنَّارَ ٱلْكُبْرَىٰ ١٢

in which he shall neither die nor remain alive. (13)

ثُمَّ لَا يَمُوتُ فِيهَا وَلَا يَحْيَىٰ ١٣

Successful will be he who purifies himself, (14)

قَدْ أَفْلَحَ مَن تَزَكَّىٰ ١٤

and glorifies the name of his Lord and prays. (15)

وَذَكَرَ ٱسْمَ رَبِّهِۦ فَصَلَّىٰ ١٥

Yet you prefer this present life, (16)

بَلْ تُؤْثِرُونَ ٱلْحَيَوٰةَ ٱلدُّنْيَا ١٦

while the life to come is better and longer lasting. (17)	وَٱلۡأٓخِرَةُ خَيۡرٞ وَأَبۡقَىٰٓ ﴿١٧﴾
All this has indeed been stated in the earlier revelations; (18)	إِنَّ هَٰذَا لَفِي ٱلصُّحُفِ ٱلۡأُولَىٰ ﴿١٨﴾
the scriptures of Abraham and Moses. (19)	صُحُفِ إِبۡرَٰهِيمَ وَمُوسَىٰ ﴿١٩﴾

Overview

Imam Aḥmad ibn Ḥanbal relates on the authority of 'Alī, the Prophet's cousin and Companion, that the Prophet loved this *sūrah*. The famous *Ḥadīth* anthologist, Muslim, also relates that the Prophet used to read this *sūrah* and *Sūrah* 88, The Enveloper, in 'Īd prayers and also in Friday prayers. If one of the festivals fell on a Friday, the Prophet would be sure to read these two *sūrahs* in the prayers.

The Prophet is right to love this *sūrah* as it turns the whole universe into a temple whose four corners echo the praises and glorification of God, the Sublime. "*Extol the limitless glory of the name of your Lord, the Most High, who creates and proportions well, who determines and guides, who brings forth the pasturage, then turns it to withered grass.*" (Verses 1–5) The rhythm of the *sūrah*, characterized by the long vowels with which each of its verses ends, imparts a feeling of the praises echoed everywhere in the universe.

The Prophet is also right to love this *sūrah* as it brings him good news. As God charges him with the double task of delivering His message and warning people, He promises him: "*We shall teach you and you shall not forget, except what God wills. He knows what is manifest and what is kept hidden. And We shall smooth your way to perfect ease. Give warning, therefore, [regardless of] whether such warning is of use.*" (Verses 6–9) So God takes upon Himself the responsibility of making His Messenger not forget anything of the Qur'ān. He also promises that his path will be smoothed in all his affairs, whether they are personal or concerned with his message. This is certainly a great favour.

Again, the Prophet is right to love this *sūrah* as it includes the basic ingredients of the Islamic concept of life and existence: the oneness of the Creator; the reality of divine revelation; and the certainty of the life to come with the reward and punishment it involves. The *sūrah* also affirms that these basic principles have well-established roots in earlier divine messages. "*All this has indeed been stated in the earlier revelations; the scriptures of Abraham and Moses.*" (Verses 18–19) All this is in addition to the impression it imparts of the easy nature of the Islamic ideology, the Messenger who conveys it, and the nation it builds.

Glorifying the Creator

"*Extol the limitless glory of the name of your Lord, the Most High, who creates and proportions well, who determines and guides, who brings forth the pasturage, then turns it to withered grass.*" (Verses 1–5) The *sūrah* opens with an order to praise the Lord, which means to glorify Him, recognize His supremacy and infallibility in everything, and remember His divine attributes. It is much more than verbal repetition of the phrase '*Subhan Allah*', which we normally translate as 'limitless is God in His glory.' It is a genuine feeling of the sublimity of His attributes.

As the *sūrah* inspires us with the splendour of a life based on constant appreciation of divine attributes, we experience a feeling which is very real and very difficult to describe at the same time.

The two immediately presented attributes are Lordship and Highness. The "Lord" or the Arabic equivalent, *Rabb*, is the one who tends and nurtures. The connotations of this attribute fit in very well with the general atmosphere of the *sūrah*, the happy news it brings and its easy rhythm. The 'Highness' attribute prompts one to look up to endless horizons. Having a genuinely vivid feeling of this attribute is indeed the essential purpose of praising God and glorifying Him.

The *sūrah* opens with an order addressed by God to the Prophet in the first instance: "*Extol the limitless glory of the name of your Lord, the Most High.*" (Verse 1) The order is given with an air of friendliness and compassion almost beyond description.

Whenever the Prophet read this *sūrah* he used to fulfil this order promptly by stopping after the first verse to say: "Limitless in his glory is my Lord, the Most High". Thus, he would receive the order, carry it out promptly and read on. When this *sūrah* was revealed the Prophet told the Muslims to fulfil the divine order as they prostrated themselves in their daily prayers. Similarly he told them to carry out the other order to '*Extol the limitless glory of the name of your Lord, the Most Great,*' (56: 96) as they bowed in prayer. These praises, warm with life, have been included in the prayers as a direct response to a direct order, or more precisely to a direct permission. For God's permission to His servants to praise Him is one of the favours He has bestowed on them. It is a permission to them to be in contact with Him in a way, given their limited abilities, they can appreciate. He, out of His grace, has permitted them to do this so that they may know Him and His attributes as best they can.

"*Extol the limitless glory of the name of your Lord, the Most High, who creates and proportions well, who determines and guides.*" (Verses 1–3) Everything God has created is well proportioned and perfected. Every creature is assigned its own role and given guidance so that it may know its role and play it. It is told the purpose of its creation, given what it needs for sustenance and guided to it. This is clearly visible in everything around us, large or small, important or trivial. For everything is well perfected and guided to fulfil the purpose of its creation. Furthermore, all things are also collectively perfected so that they may fulfil their role together.

The Perfection of God's Creation

A single atom is well balanced between its electrons and protons, to the same degree as the solar system, its sun, planets and satellites are well balanced. Each of the two knows the way it is assigned to travel and fulfils its role. A single living cell is also perfect and well equipped to do everything it is asked to do, in the same measure as the most advanced and complex species. This perfect balance, in the individual and collective sense, is easily noticed in every one of the countless types of creation that fill the gap between the single atom and the solar system or between the single cell and the most advanced living creature.

This basic fact, evidenced by everything in the universe, is well recognized by the human heart as it contemplates what is in the universe. This sort of inspiration and recognition is within the reach of every man in every age, regardless of his standard of education. All that is required is an open mind which contemplates and responds. Increased knowledge then endorses and emphasizes, with numerous examples, what inspiration has already proven at first glance. The results of study and research endorse, within their limited scope, this basic truth which applies to everything in the universe.

The American scientist, A. Cressy Morrison, Head of the Science Academy in New York, says in his book *Man Does Not Stand Alone*:

> Birds have the homing instinct. The robin that nested at your door may go south in the autumn, but will come back to his old nest the next spring. In September, flocks of many of our birds fly south, often over a thousand miles of open sea, but they do not lose their way. The homing pigeon, confused by new sounds on a long journey in a closed box, circles for a moment then heads almost unerringly for home. The bee finds its hive while the wind waving the grasses and trees blots out every visible guide to its whereabouts. This homing sense is

slightly developed in man, but he supplements his meagre equipment with instruments of navigation. We need this instinct and our brain provides the answer. The tiny insects must have microscopic eyes, how perfect we do not know, and the hawks, the eagle and the condor must have telescopic vision. Here again man surpasses them with his mechanical instruments. With his telescope he can see a nebula so faint that it requires two million times his vision, and with the electron microscope he can see hitherto invisible bacteria and, so to speak, the little bugs that bite them.

If you let old Dobbin alone he will keep to the road in the blackest night. He can see, dimly perhaps, but he notes the difference in temperature of the road and the sides with eyes that are slightly affected by the infra-red rays of the road. The owl can see the nice warm mouse as he runs in the cooler grass in the blackest night. We turn night into day by creating radiation in that short octave we call light.[1]

The honey-bee workers make chambers of different sizes in the comb used for breeding. Small chambers are constructed for the workers, larger ones for the drones, and special chambers for the prospective queens. The queen bee lays unfertilized eggs in the cells designed for males, but lays fertilized eggs in the proper chambers for the female workers and the possible queens. The workers, who are the modified females, having long since anticipated the coming of the new generation, are also prepared to furnish food for the young bees by chewing and predigesting honey and pollen. They discontinue the process of chewing, including the predigesting, at a certain stage of the development of the males and females, and feed only honey and pollen. The females so treated become the workers.

---

1. A. Cressy Morrison, *Man Does Not Stand Alone,* Morrison & Gibb Ltd., London, 1962, pp. 58–59.

For the females in the queen chambers the diet of chewed and predigested food is continued. These specially treated females develop into queen bees, which alone produce fertile eggs. This process of reproduction involves special chambers, special eggs, and the marvellous effect of a change of diet. This means anticipation, discretion, and the application of a discovery of the effect of diet. These changes apply particularly to a community life and seem necessary to its existence. The knowledge and skills required must have been evolved after the beginnings of this community life, and are not necessarily inherent in the structure or the survival of the honey bee as such. The bee, therefore, seems to have outstripped man in knowledge of the effects of diet under certain conditions.

The dog with an inquiring nose can sense the animal that has passed. No instrument of human invention has added to our inferior sense of smell, and we hardly know where to begin to investigate its extension. Yet even our sense of smell is so highly developed that it can detect ultra-microscopic particles. How do we know that we all get the same reaction from any single odour? The fact is that we do not. Taste also gives a very different sensation to each of us. How strange that these differences in perception are hereditary.

All animals hear sounds, many of which are outside our range of vibration, with an acuteness that far surpasses our limited sense of hearing. Man by his devices can now hear a fly walking miles away as though it was on his eardrums, and with like instruments record the impact of a cosmic ray.[2]

One of the water spiders fashions a balloon-shaped nest of cobweb filaments and attaches it to some object under water. Then she ingeniously entangles an air bubble in the hairs of her under-body, carries it into the water, and releases it under

2. Ibid., pp. 61–63.

the nest. This performance is repeated until the nest is inflated, when she proceeds to bring forth and raise her young safe from attack by air. Here we have a synthesis of the web, engineering, construction, and aeronautics. Chance perhaps, but that still leaves the spider unexplained.

The young salmon spends years at sea, then comes back to his own river, and, what is more, he travels up the side of the river into which flows the tributary in which he was born. The laws of the States on one side of the dividing stream may be strict and the other side not, but these laws affect only the fish which may be said to belong to each side. What brings them back so definitely? If a salmon going up a river is transferred to another tributary he will at once realize he is not in the right tributary and will fight his way down to the main stream and then turn up against the current to finish his destiny. There is, however, a much more difficult reverse problem to solve in the case of the eel. These amazing creatures migrate at maturity from all the ponds and rivers everywhere, those from Europe across thousands of miles of ocean, all go to the abysmal deeps south of Bermuda. There they breed and die. The little ones, with no apparent means of knowing anything except that they are in a wilderness of water, start back and find their way to the shore from which their parents came and thence to every river, lake and little pond, so that each body of water is always populated with eels. They have braved the mighty currents, storms and tides, and have conquered the beating waves on every shore. They can now grow and when they are mature, they will, by some mysterious law, go back through it all to complete the cycle. Where does the directing impulse originate? No American eel has ever been caught in European waters and no European eel has ever been caught in American waters. Nature has also delayed the maturity of the European eel by a year or more to make up for its much greater journey. Do atoms and molecules when combined in an eel have a sense of direction and willpower to exercise it?[3]

A female moth placed in your attic by the open window will send out some subtle signal. Over an unbelievable area, the male moths of the same species will catch the message and respond in spite of your attempts to produce laboratory odours to disconcert them. Has the little creature a broadcasting station, and has the male moth a mental radio set beside his antennae? Does she shake the ether and does he catch the vibration? The cricket rubs its legs or wings together, and on a still night can be heard half a mile away. It shakes six hundred tons of air and calls its mate. Miss Moth, working in a different realm of physics and, in apparent silence, calls quite as effectively. Before the radio was discovered, scientists decided it was odour that attracted the male moth. It was a miracle either way, because the odour would have to travel in all directions, with or without the wind. The male moth would have to be able to detect a molecule and sense the direction from whence it came. By a vast mechanism, we are developing the same ability to communicate, and the day will come when a young man may call his loved one from a distance and without mechanical medium and she will answer. No lock or bars will stop them. Our telephone and radio are instrumental wonders and give us means of almost instant communication, but we are tied to a wire and a place. The moth is still ahead of us, and we can only envy her until our brain evolves an individual radio. Then, in a sense, we will have telepathy.

Vegetation makes subtle use of involuntary agents to carry on its existence – insects to carry pollen from flower to flower and the winds and everything that flies or walks to distribute seed. At last, vegetation has trapped masterful man. He has improved nature, and she generously rewards him. But he has

3. Ibid., pp. 64–65.

multiplied so prodigiously that he is now chained to the plough. He must sow, reap, and store; breed and cross-breed; prune and graft. Should he neglect these tasks starvation would be his lot, civilization would crumble, and earth return to her pristine state.[4]

Many animals are like a lobster, which, having lost a claw, will by some restimulation of the cells and the reactivation of the genes discover that a part of the body is missing and restore it. When the work is complete, the cells stop work, for in some way they know it is quitting time. A fresh-water polyp divided into halves can reform itself out of one of these halves. Cut off an angle worm's head and he will soon create a new one. We can stimulate healing but when will our surgeons, if ever, know how to stimulate the cells to produce a new arm, flesh, bones, nails, and activating nerves?[5] An extraordinary fact throws some light on this mystery of recreation. If cells in the early stages of development are separated each has the ability to create a complete animal. Therefore, if the original cell divides into two and they are separated, two individuals will be developed. This may account for identical twins but it means much more – each cell at first is in detail potentially a complete individual. There can be no doubt then, that you are you in every cell and fibre.[6]

An acorn falls to the ground – its tough brown shell holds it safe. It rolls into some earthy crevice. In the spring the germ awakes, the shell bursts, food is provided by the egg-like kernel in which the genes were hidden. They send roots into the earth, and behold a sprout, a sapling, and in years a tree. The germ

---

4. Ibid., pp. 66–67.
5. At the time when this book was published, such tasks seemed a long time coming. However, most of them now seem possible. Still, the argument is correct and the more advancements science makes the more amazing God's creation appears to be. – Editor's note.
6. A.C. Morrison, op. cit., p. 68.

with its genes has multiplied by trillions and made the trunk, bark and every leaf and acorn identical with that of the oak which gave it birth. For hundreds of years in each of the countless acorns is preserved the exact arrangement of atoms that produced the first oak tree millions of years ago.[7]

The author says in another chapter:

Every cell that is produced in any living creature must adapt itself to be part of the flesh, to sacrifice itself as a part of the skin, which will soon be worn off. It must deposit the enamel of teeth, produce the transparent liquid in an eye, or become a nose or an ear. Each cell must then adapt itself in shape and every other characteristic necessary to fulfil its function. It is hard to think of a cell as right-handed or left-handed, but one becomes part of a right ear, the other becomes part of the left ear. Some crystals that are chemically identical turn the rays of light to the left, others to the right. There seems to be such a tendency in the cells. In the exact place where they belong, they become a part of the right ear or the left ear and your two ears are opposite each other on your head, and not as in the case of a cricket, on your elbows. Their curves are opposite, and when complete, they are so much alike you cannot tell them apart. Hundreds of thousands of cells seem impelled to do the right thing at the right time in the right place.[8]

Elsewhere in his book Morrison says:

In the mêlée of creation many creatures have come to exhibit a high degree of certain forms of instinct, intelligence, or what not. The wasp catches the grasshopper, digs a hole in the earth, stings the grasshopper in exactly the right place so that he becomes

7. Ibid., pp. 86–87.
8. Ibid., pp. 52–53.

> unconscious but lives as a form of preserved meat. The wasp lays her eggs exactly in the right place, perhaps not knowing that when they hatch, her children can eat without killing the insect on which they feed, which would be fatal to them. The wasp must have done all this right the first and every time, or there would be no wasps of this species. Science cannot explain this mystery, and yet it cannot be attributed to chance. The wasp covers a hole in the earth, departs cheerfully, and dies. Neither she nor her ancestors have reasoned out the process, nor does she know what happens to her offspring. She doesn't even know that she has worked and lived her life for the preservation of the race.[9]

In the same book we also read:

> In some species, the workers bring in little seeds to feed the other ants through the winter. The ants establish what is known as the grinding room, in which those which have developed gigantic jaws especially built for grinding, prepare the food for the colony. This is their sole occupation. When the autumn comes and the seeds are all ground, 'the greatest good for the greatest number' requires that the food supply be conserved and as there will be plenty of grinders in the new generation, the soldier ants kill off the grinders, satisfying their entomological conscience by believing perhaps that the grinders had had reward enough in having had first chance at the food while they ground.
>
> Certain ants, by means of instinct or reasoning (choose which you prefer), cultivate mushrooms for food in what may be called mushroom gardens, and capture certain caterpillars and aphids (plant lice). These creatures are the ants' cows and goats, from which they take certain exudations of a honey-like nature

9. Ibid., pp. 71–72.

> for food. Ants capture and keep slaves. Some ants, when they make their nests, cut the leaves to size, and while certain workers hold the edges in place, use their babies, which in the larval stage are capable of spinning silk, as shuttles to sew them together. The poor baby may be bereft of the opportunity of making a cocoon for himself, but he has served his community.
>
> How do the inanimate atoms and molecules of matter composing an ant set these complicated processes in motion? There must be Intelligence somewhere.[10]

True, there must be a Creator who guides these and other creatures, large and small. He is the One "*who creates and proportions well, who determines and guides.*" (Verses 2–3)

The examples we have quoted above are but a few of the large number of remarkable aspects science has recorded in the worlds of plants, insects, birds and animals. But all these aspects reflect only a part of the import of the two verses: "*who creates and proportions well, who determines and guides.*" (Verses 2–3) For our knowledge covers only a scanty part of what is in the visible universe, beyond which extends a whole world of which we know nothing apart from the few hints God has chosen to drop us, as befits our limited abilities.

Having fired such a great volley of praises to God, resounding in even the remotest corners of the universe, the *sūrah* complements this with an inspiring insight from the realm of plants: "*who brings forth the pasturage, then turns it to withered grass.*" (Verses 4–5) The pasturage, as used here, refers to all plants. Every plant is suitable for one sort of species or another. The term then has a much wider sense than the familiar pastures where cattle feed. God has created this planet and provided on it enough food to nourish every single living creature which walks, swims, flies or hides itself underground.

10. Ibid., pp. 72–73.

The pasturage is green when it first shoots forth, but it withers away and blackens. It may be used for feeding when green, after it blackens and withers, or in between. Thus, it is useful in every condition, and it serves a purpose according to the elaborate planning of the One who creates, proportions, determines and guides.

The reference here to the life of plants carries also an implicit connotation that all plants are reaped and harvested. Similarly, every living being will come to its appointed end. This connotation fits in well with the reference to the two worlds of man: "*Yet you prefer this present life, while the life to come is better and longer lasting.*" (Verses 16–17) This life is a pasture which comes to its end when it withers away and blackens, while the life to come is the one which lasts.

Happy News for the Prophet

As the beginning of the *sūrah* opens up this limitless horizon, it provides a framework for the fundamental facts tackled in this *sūrah* to be related to the whole universe. This framework is especially suitable, for it is in perfect harmony with the atmosphere of the *sūrah*, its rhythm and shades of meaning.

The *sūrah* then gives the Prophet, and the Muslim nation in general, a very welcome tiding: "*We shall teach you and you shall not forget, except what God wills. He knows what is manifest and what is kept hidden. And We shall smooth your way to perfect ease. Give warning, therefore, [regardless of] whether such warning is of use.*" (Verses 6–9) The happy news starts with sparing the Prophet the trouble of memorizing the Qur'ān. All he needs to do is to read as he is taught and God will ensure that he will never forget any part of it. "*We shall teach you and you shall not forget.*" (Verse 6) So keen to keep the Qur'ān in his memory, the Prophet used to repeat it after Gabriel, the angel, delivered it to him. He felt that it was part of his responsibility to keep it registered in his mind. But God decided that He would look after this task. The promise is also a happy one for the Islamic community, since it is a reassurance that the faith the Prophet preaches is authentic. It is from God and He looks after it. This is part of God's grace. It shows how weighty the question of purity of faith is in His scales.

Every time the Qur'ān states a definite promise or constant law, it follows it with a statement implying that divine will is free of all limitations and restrictions, even those based on a promise or law from God. For His will is absolute. Here, the *sūrah* emphasizes this principle after the promise is made to the Prophet that he will never forget any part of the Qur'ān: "*except what God wills.*" (Verse 7) The two are complementary in the sense that the promise is within divine will. So we look forward to God's fulfilment of what He has willed to promise.

"*He knows what is manifest and what is kept hidden.*" (Verse 7) This is stated here by way of giving a reason for all that has passed: teaching to read, freedom from forgetfulness and the exception made to it. Everything is decided according to the wisdom of the One who knows the secret and the manifest. He views everything from all angles and makes His decisions on the basis of His unfailing knowledge.

Then follows another promise, happy and all-embracing: "*And We shall smooth your way to perfect ease.*" (Verse 8) This is again happy news for the Prophet personally and for the Muslim community at large. It is furthermore a statement of the nature of Islam, its role in human life and in the universe. This verse, which is rendered in Arabic in no more than two words, states one of the most fundamental principles of faith and existence. It provides a link between the nature of the Prophet and the nature of Islam on the one hand and the nature of the whole universe on the other. It is a universe created by God with ease; it follows its appointed way with ease and draws nearer its final objective with ease. Thus it is an inspiration lighting limitless horizons.

If God smooths a certain person's path, he finds ease in everything in his life. For he will move along his way to God with the universe, which is characterized by its harmony of construction, movement and direction. Hence he does not clash with those who digress, for these are of no importance, compared with the vast universe. Ease will pervade his whole life. It will be evident in his hand, tongue, movement, work, concepts, way of thinking and in the way he conducts all affairs and tackles all matters. Ease will be the main feature of how he carries himself and how he deals with others as well.

A Life Characterized by Ease

Such was the Prophet in all affairs. His wife, 'Ā'ishah, reports that "whenever faced with a choice, the Prophet would always choose the easier of the two alternatives." [Related by al-Bukhārī and Muslim.] She also reports: "Whenever the Prophet was alone with his family at home, he was the easiest of men, always smiling and laughing." Al-Bukhārī also relates: "Any woman would take the Prophet by the hand to take him wherever she wished." His guidance in matters of clothing, food, household furniture and other matters of day to day life pointed to a preference for what is easy.

Imām Ibn Qayyim al-Jawziyyah speaks in his book, *Zād al-Ma'ād*, of the Prophet's guidance concerning what to wear:

> He had a turban which he gave to 'Alī as a gift, but he used to wear it over a cap. But he also wore either the turban or the cap separately. When he wore the turban, however, he used to leave the end part of it hanging between his shoulders. This is related by Muslim in his Ṣaḥīḥ anthology of authentic aḥādīth, on the authority of 'Umar ibn Ḥarīth, who said, 'I saw the Prophet speaking on the platform of the mosque, wearing a black turban with its end hanging between his shoulders'. Muslim also relates on the authority of Jābir ibn 'Abdullāh that the Prophet entered Makkah wearing a black turban, but nothing is mentioned here about his leaving its end part hanging. This

> signifies that the Prophet did not always leave the tail of his turban hanging between his shoulders. It is also said that the Prophet entered Makkah wearing his fighting attire, with a helmet on his head, which suggests that he used to wear what suited the occasion.[11]
>
> The best method, it is true, is that followed by the Prophet and which he encouraged his Companions to adopt. His guidance regarding clothes is, in short, that he used to wear whatever was available, whether woollen, cotton, linen or other types of material. He used Yemeni gowns and had a green gown. He also used different types of dress such as overcoat, long robe, shirts, trousers, top gown, sandals and shoes. He left the end of his turban hanging between his shoulders on occasions, and not on other occasions.[12]

On food, the Prophet's guidance gives a similar message:

> The Prophet never refused what was available at home, nor did he ever go out of his way to get what was not. He would eat whatever was served of good food and he never slighted any sort of food whatsoever. If he did not like something he would simply not eat it, but would not forbid it. An example of his attitude is the case of lizard, which he would not eat without forbidding others to eat it. On the contrary, he was present when others ate it at his own table.
>
> He liked sweets and honey, used to eat dates, fresh and preserved... drank milk, pure and mixed, added water to ice and honey and drank a drink made from dates. He also ate *khazīrah*, which is a thick soup made of milk and flour. He ate cucumber with fresh dates, butter, dates with bread, bread with vinegar, bread with meat, dried meat, a dish called dubbā'

---

11. Ibn al-Qayyim, *Zād al-Ma'ād*, Mu'assasat al-Risalah, and Maktabat al-Manar, Beirut and Kuwait, 1994, Vol. 1, pp. 135–136.
12. Ibid., Vol. 1, p. 143.

> (which was one of his favourites), boiled meat, rice and meat cooked with fat, cheese, bread with oil, water melon with fresh dates, and he used to like dates cooked with butter. In short, he never refused good food, nor did he go to any trouble to get it. His guidance was to eat what was available. If he did not have anything to eat, he would simply go hungry, etc.[13]

As for the Prophet's example regarding sleep:

> He used to sleep sometimes on a mattress, sometimes on a simple animal skin. Occasionally he would sleep on a rough mat, or on the cold earth with nothing under him. He sometimes used a bed; a plain one at times and covered with a black bedspread at other times.[14]

The Prophet's traditions urging the adoption of an easy, gentle and tolerant attitude in all matters, especially those which concern religious duties are numerous. By way of example we may quote: "This religion is of an easy nature. Anyone who pulls hard against it shall be the loser." [Related by al-Bukhārī.] "Do not be hard on yourselves lest it should be made hard for you. A former community chose to be hard and it was made harder for them." [Related by Abū Dāwūd.] "A rider driving hard neither reaches his destination nor keeps his transport." [Related by al-Bukhārī.] "Make it easy, not difficult, for others." [Related by al-Bukhārī and Muslim.] Concerning social dealings, the Prophet says: "May God have mercy on any person who is tolerant when he buys, sells and asks for his rights." [Related by al-Bukhārī.] "A believer is gentle and friendly." [Related by al-Bayhaqī.] "A believer gets on well with others and is easy to get on well with." [Related by al-Dāraquṭnī.] "The type of man God dislikes most is the quarrelsome one who does not budge." [Related by al-Bukhārī and Muslim.]

13. Ibid., Vol. 1, pp. 147–148.
14. Ibid., Vol. 1, p. 155.

A highly significant feature of his character is that he hated hardness even in names and physical features. This shows how God moulded his nature and smoothed even his temperament. Sa'īd ibn al-Musayyib reports that the Prophet asked his father what his name was, since al-Musayyib was his nickname. He answered, Ḥazn, [which means rough and difficult]. The Prophet said, "No, you are Sahl [i.e. plain and easy]."[15] The man said, "I will never change a name given to me by my father." Sa'īd comments, "As a result, we have always had a trace of hardness in our characters." [Related by al-Bukhārī.] Ibn 'Umar reports that the Prophet changed the name of a woman from 'Āṣiyah [meaning disobedient] to Jamīlah [meaning pretty]." [Related by Muslim.] He also said: "It is part of kindness to receive your brother with a smiling face." [Related by al-Tirmidhī.] Thus we realize how refined and gentle the Prophet was, disliking even names and features which smacked of roughness and trying to substitute for them what related to gentility and kindness.

Ease in Practice

The Prophet's life story is composed of pages of gentility, ease, tolerance and understanding in all affairs. Let us quote here an incident which reveals his method of dealing with people of difficult temperament: "Once a bedouin came to the Prophet asking something. The Prophet granted his request then said, 'Have I treated you well?' The bedouin said, 'No, and you have not been kind either!' The Prophet's Companions present felt very angry and wanted to punish the man. The Prophet, however, motioned them to leave him alone. He then went into his house, sent for the man and gave him something over and above his original request. He then asked him: 'Have I treated you well?' The man said: 'Yes, indeed. May God reward you well for you are a good kinsman and a good

15. This was the Prophet's way of changing a name which he did not approve of. – Editor's note.

tribesman.' The Prophet then said to him: 'When you said what you said you made my Companions feel angry with you. Would you now like to tell them what you have just told me so that they hold nothing against you.' The man said: 'I will.' The following day he came and the Prophet said: 'This bedouin said yesterday what you heard. We gave him more and he claimed that he was satisfied. Is that so?' The bedouin said: 'Yes indeed! May God reward you well, for you are a good kinsman and a good tribesman.' The Prophet then said to his Companions: 'My affair with this bedouin is similar to that of a man who had a she-camel which ran loose. Other people rushed to try to catch her but they managed only to make her run wild. The owner then appealed to them to let him alone with his she-camel as he was gentler to her and knew her temperament. The owner then went towards her, having picked something to feed her with. He approached her gently until she responded and sat down. He then saddled her and mounted her back. Had I left you alone when the man said what he said, you would probably have killed him and he would have gone to hell."

So gentle, simple and compassionate was the Prophet's attitude towards any person of rough nature. Examples of this attitude abound in the records of his life. These examples are practical manifestations of how his path was smoothed for him to achieve perfect ease in every aspect of life. He was given a tolerant, understanding nature so that he might carry out his mission as God's Messenger to mankind. In this way his nature and the nature of Islam, the message he carried and delivered, are alike. He was able, with God's grace, to fulfil the great task with which he was entrusted. For when his path was smoothed, the heavy burden of his mission became an enjoyable sport.

The Qur'ān carries descriptions of Muḥammad, God's Messenger, and the role assigned to him: "*We have sent you forth only as a mercy to mankind.*" (21: 107) "*Those who follow the Messenger, the unlettered Prophet whom they shall find described in the Torah and the Gospel that are with them. He commands them to do what is right and forbids them to do what is wrong, and makes lawful to them the good things of life and forbids them all that is foul. He lifts from them their burdens and the shackles that weigh upon them.*" (7: 157) As the Qur'ān states, Muḥammad (peace be upon him) was a messenger bringing mercy to mankind, lifting their burdens which were imposed on them when they sought to make things hard.

The Qur'ān also describes the message the Prophet delivered in statements of like import: "*We have made the Qur'ān easy for warning: but will any take heed?*" (54: 22) "*He has laid on you no hardships in the observance of your religion.*" (22: 78) "*God does not charge a soul with more than it can bear.*" (2: 286) "*God does not want to impose any hardship on you, but He wants to purify you.*" (5: 6) The message of Islam is made easy for people to follow since it takes into consideration the limitations of human abilities. It imposes no burdens which are too heavy. This easy nature of Islam is readily identifiable in its spirit as well as in its commandments: "*Follow the upright nature God has endowed mankind with.*" (30: 30)

When we look carefully through this religion we find that care has been taken to make it easy for people to follow, without overstraining themselves. It takes into consideration the different situations man finds himself in, and the conditions he faces in different environments. The faith itself is based on concepts which are easy to grasp: a single deity; none like Him; He has created everything; He has guided everything to realize the purpose of its existence; He has also sent messengers to remind people of their role in life and to call them back to their Lord who created them. All obligations imposed by this faith fit perfectly together: there are no conflicts, no contradictions. People have to fulfil these obligations according to their abilities. There need be no overstraining, no heavy burdens. The Prophet teaches us: "When I give you an order, fulfil it as much as you can; but leave off what I forbid you." [Related by al-Bukhārī and Muslim.] Prohibition may also be relaxed "*He has clearly spelled out to you what He has forbidden you [to eat] unless you are driven to do so by sheer necessity.*" (6: 119) These basic principles provide the limits within which the Islamic commandments and principles operate.

Hence the Messenger and the message have in common this basic feature of easy nature. So does the Muslim community which is brought into being by Islam, the easy message: it is a 'middle' community, merciful, the recipient of divine mercy, easy natured, enjoying a life which is perfectly harmonious with the wider universe. The universe itself with its perfect harmony provides a true picture of how God's creation moves easily and smoothly, without clash or crash. Millions and millions of stars move in their orbits in the great space God has provided, each with its own gravity, yet none moves out of step and none crashes into another. There are countless millions of living creatures, each moving through life to its appointed aim, near or distant, according to a perfect plan. Each is given the abilities which make its aim easy to achieve. Endless millions of movements, events and conditions come together then go their separate ways; yet they are much the same as the sounds of the different instruments in an orchestra: so different but which combine together to produce beautiful harmonies.

In short, perfect harmony exists between the nature of the universe, the message, the Messenger and the Muslim community. They are all the creation of God, the One, the Most Wise.

The Prophet's Great Task

"*Give warning, therefore, [regardless of] whether such warning is of use.*" (Verse 9) God has taught the Prophet so as not to forget, smoothed his way to perfect ease so that he may be able to discharge his great task of warning mankind. For this he has been the subject of careful preparation. Hence, he is asked to warn whenever he has a chance to address people and to convey to them God's message.

"*Regardless of whether such warning is of use.*" Warning is always useful. There will always be, in every land and every generation, those who will listen to the reminders and warnings and will benefit by them, no matter how corrupt their society is and how hardened their people are.

If we ponder a little over the verses in this *sūrah* and their sequence, we realize how great the message entrusted to the Prophet is. To deliver it, and to give the warnings he is asked to give, he needs special equipment: a smooth way to perfect ease in everything, to be taught what to say, and God's preservation of the message intact.

Once the Prophet has delivered his message, his task is fulfilled. Everyone is left to choose his way. Destinies differ according to the choice of ways people follow: "*He who fears God will heed it, but the most hapless wretch will turn aside from it, who shall be cast into the great fire, in which he shall neither die nor remain alive. Successful will be he who purifies himself, and glorifies the name of his Lord and prays.*" (Verses 10–15) The Prophet is told here that his warnings will benefit those who fear God and dread to incur His displeasure. Any intelligent person will shudder when he learns that there is a Creator who proportions well, determines and guides. For he realizes that such a Creator must hold everyone responsible for their actions, good or evil, and will reward them accordingly. Hence they fear Him and heed the warnings they are given.

"*But the most hapless wretch will turn aside from it.*" (Verse 11) If a man does not listen to the warning given, then he is absolutely "*the most hapless wretch.*" He lives in a void, uninspired by the facts surrounding him, turning a deaf ear and a senseless mind to the evidence they give. Such a person lives in constant worry, striving hard to attain the paltry pleasures of this world. Hence he is the most wretched in this life. But he is also the most wretched in the hereafter as he will there suffer endless torment: He "*shall be cast into the great fire, in which he shall neither die nor remain alive.*" (Verses 12–13) The great fire is that of hell. It is indeed the greatest of all fires in intensity, duration and size. He who suffers it finds it endless. He neither dies to rest from its torment, nor does he live in it a life of rest and security. It is an unending agony which makes the sufferer yearn for death as his greatest hope.

At the other end we find prosperity accompanied with self-purification and a heeding of warnings: "*Successful will be he who purifies himself, and glorifies the name of his Lord and prays.*" (Verses 14–15) Purification is used here in the widest sense of the word: purification from everything filthy or sinful. The person who seeks to purify himself, glorifies his Lord, feels His power and majesty in his inmost soul and prays, [whether praying is taken in its general sense or its specific Islamic sense] will definitely be successful, as God states here. He will achieve success here in this life as he enjoys his relationship with God and the perfect bliss that results from his glorification of God. He will achieve even greater success in the hereafter as he escapes hell and is rewarded with perfect happiness in heaven. How different the two destinies are.

Having sketched the two different ends of the most wretched and the God-fearing, the *sūrah* points out to the addressees the real reason for their great wretchedness, the failure which drives them headlong into the great fire: "*Yet you prefer this present life, while the life to come is better and longer lasting.*" (Verses 16–17) This short-sighted preference is the real reason for every misery which befalls man. It is indeed the cause of man's taking no heed of the warnings given to him. The Qur'ān calls the present life *dunia* which connotes both contempt and easy access. The life to come is better in kind and duration. Only the foolish who are deprived of sound judgement would, in the circumstances, prefer the present life to the next.

In conclusion, the *sūrah* points out that the message of Islam is not new; its roots go back far deep in time. "*All this has indeed been stated in the earlier revelations; the scriptures of Abraham and*

Moses." (Verses 18–19) The basics of the grand faith contained in this *sūrah* are the same old basic facts outlined in the ancient scriptures of Abraham and Moses.

The truth is one and the faith is one. This results from the fact that their origin is one, God, whose will it was to send messengers to mankind. The messengers deliver basically the same message, the same simple truth. Details of the messages may differ according to local or temporal needs, but the basics are the same. They have one origin: God, the Most High, who creates, proportions well, determines and guides.

SŪRAH 88

Al-Ghāshiyah

(The Enveloper)

Al-Ghāshiyah (The Enveloper)

سُورَةُ الغَاشِيَةِ

In the name of God, the Beneficent, the Merciful.

بِسْمِ اللَّهِ الرَّحْمَٰنِ الرَّحِيمِ

Have you heard the story of the Enveloper? (1)

هَلْ أَتَىٰكَ حَدِيثُ ٱلْغَٰشِيَةِ ﴿١﴾

Some faces on that day are downcast, (2)

وُجُوهٌ يَوْمَئِذٍ خَٰشِعَةٌ ﴿٢﴾

labour weary, worn out, (3)

عَامِلَةٌ نَّاصِبَةٌ ﴿٣﴾

about to enter a scorching fire, (4)

تَصْلَىٰ نَارًا حَامِيَةً ﴿٤﴾

made to drink from a boiling fountain. (5)

تُسْقَىٰ مِنْ عَيْنٍ ءَانِيَةٍ ﴿٥﴾

Their only food shall be nothing but dry thorns, (6)	لَّيۡسَ لَهُمۡ طَعَامٌ إِلَّا مِن ضَرِيعٖ ٦
which will neither nourish nor satisfy their hunger. (7)	لَّا يُسۡمِنُ وَلَا يُغۡنِي مِن جُوعٖ ٧
Other faces on that day are jocund, (8)	وُجُوهٞ يَوۡمَئِذٖ نَّاعِمَةٞ ٨
well-pleased with their striving, (9)	لِّسَعۡيِهَا رَاضِيَةٞ ٩
in a sublime garden, (10)	فِي جَنَّةٍ عَالِيَةٖ ١٠
where they hear no babble. (11)	لَّا تَسۡمَعُ فِيهَا لَٰغِيَةٗ ١١
A running fountain shall be there, (12)	فِيهَا عَيۡنٞ جَارِيَةٞ ١٢
and raised couches, (13)	فِيهَا سُرُرٞ مَّرۡفُوعَةٞ ١٣
and goblets placed ready, (14)	وَأَكۡوَابٞ مَّوۡضُوعَةٞ ١٤
and cushions laid in order, (15)	وَنَمَارِقُ مَصۡفُوفَةٞ ١٥
and carpets spread out. (16)	وَزَرَابِيُّ مَبۡثُوثَةٌ ١٦
Let them reflect on the camels, how they were created; (17)	أَفَلَا يَنظُرُونَ إِلَى ٱلۡإِبِلِ كَيۡفَ خُلِقَتۡ ١٧

and heaven, how it is raised aloft; (18)	وَإِلَى ٱلسَّمَآءِ كَيۡفَ رُفِعَتۡ ١٨
and the mountains, how they are hoisted; (19)	وَإِلَى ٱلۡجِبَالِ كَيۡفَ نُصِبَتۡ ١٩
and the earth, how it is spread out. (20)	وَإِلَى ٱلۡأَرۡضِ كَيۡفَ سُطِحَتۡ ٢٠
Therefore exhort them; your task is only to exhort. (21)	فَذَكِّرۡ إِنَّمَآ أَنتَ مُذَكِّرٞ ٢١
You are not their overseer. (22)	لَّسۡتَ عَلَيۡهِم بِمُصَيۡطِرٍ ٢٢
But he who turns his back and disbelieves, (23)	إِلَّا مَن تَوَلَّىٰ وَكَفَرَ ٢٣
God shall inflict on him the greatest suffering. (24)	فَيُعَذِّبُهُ ٱللَّهُ ٱلۡعَذَابَ ٱلۡأَكۡبَرَ ٢٤
To Us they shall surely return, (25)	إِنَّ إِلَيۡنَآ إِيَابَهُمۡ ٢٥
when We shall bring them to account. (26)	ثُمَّ إِنَّ عَلَيۡنَا حِسَابَهُم ٢٦

Overview

This *sūrah* is a deep and calm melody which invites meditation, hope and fear. It warns man to be ready for the day of reckoning. It carries man's heart into two vast spheres: the life hereafter with its limitless world and moving scenes; and the visible sphere of existence, with the signs God has spread in all the creatures sharing this existence held out for everyone to see. After these two great scenarios, the *sūrah* reminds man of the reckoning on the Day of Judgement, of God's power, and of the inevitable return to Him. Throughout, the style is characterized by its depth of tone: it is calm but highly effective, powerful and awesome.

"*Have you heard the story of the Enveloper?*" (Verse 1) With this introduction, the *sūrah* wants to make hearts turn back to God, to remind men of His signs in the universe, His reckoning on the Day of Judgement, and His certain reward. It starts with this inquiry, which implies greatness and indicates a positive statement. It points out that the question of the hereafter had already been affirmed and earlier reminders had been given. The Day of Resurrection is here given a new name, "the Enveloper", which suggests that a calamity will befall mankind and envelop them with its horrors. It is one of the many evocative names mentioned in the *sūrahs* included in this volume. Others are: The Overwhelming, The Deafening, The Stunning Event. They all suit the general tone and nature of these *sūrahs*.

Whenever the Prophet (peace be upon him) listened to this *sūrah*, he felt that the address "*Have you heard...*" was directed to him personally, as if he was receiving it from his Lord directly for the first time. He was extremely moved by this. The reality of this divine address was always present in his mind. A tradition related by 'Umar ibn Maymūn says that the Prophet once passed by a woman who was reading this *sūrah*. When she read "*Have you heard the story of the Enveloper...?*" he stopped to listen and said "Yes, I have heard it."

The address is nevertheless a general one, directed at everyone who hears the Qur'ān. The story of the Enveloper is an oft-repeated theme in the Qur'ān, reminding men of the hereafter, warning them of its punishment, and promising its rewards. It is a story which aims to awaken people's consciences, to arouse their fear and apprehension as well as their hope and expectancy.

The Story in Brief

The *sūrah* opens with a question: "*Have you heard the story of the Enveloper?*" (Verse 1) It follows this by relating part of its story: "*Some faces on that day are downcast, labour weary, worn out, about to enter a scorching fire, made to drink from a boiling fountain. Their only food shall be nothing but dry thorns, which will neither nourish nor satisfy their hunger.*" (Verses 2–7) The scene of suffering and torture is given before the scene of joy, because the former is closer to the connotations of the name given to the event, the Enveloper, and the impressions it generates.

Thus we are told that there are on that day faces which look humble, downcast and worn out. They belong to people who have laboured and toiled without satisfactory results. Indeed the results they get are a total loss, which increases their disappointment, and causes looks of humiliation and exhaustion on their faces. Hence they are described as "*labour weary, worn out*". (Verse 3) They had laboured and toiled for something other than God's cause. Their work was totally for themselves and their families, for their own ambitions in the life of this world. Then they come to reap the fruits of their toil, not having made any provision for their future life. Hence they face the end with a mixture of humiliation, exhaustion, misery and hopelessness. In addition to all this they roast "*at a scorching fire.*" (Verse 4)

They are "*made to drink from a boiling fountain. Their only food shall be nothing but dry thorns, which will neither nourish nor satisfy their hunger.*" (Verses 5–7) The Arabic text uses the term *ḍarīʿ*, which is translated here as 'dry thorns'. However, some commentators say that it refers to a tree of fire in hell. This explanation is based on what has been revealed about the tree of *zayqūm* which grows at the centre of hell. It is also said to be a kind of cactus thorn, which when green is called *shabraq* and is eaten by camels. However, when it is fully grown it becomes poisonous and cannot be eaten. Whatever it is in reality, it is a kind of food like *ghislīn* and *ghassāq* [names given in the Qur'ān to refer to the food available in hell] which neither nourishes nor appeases hunger.

It is obvious that we, in this world, cannot fully comprehend the nature of such suffering in the hereafter. The description is made in order to give our perceptions the feeling of the greatest possible pain, which is produced by a combination of humiliation, weakness, failure, the scorching fire, drinking and bathing in boiling water, and eating food unacceptable even to camels, which are used to eating thorns when they travel in desert areas. This type of thorn, however, is dry and gives no nourishment. From all these aspects we get a sense of the ultimate affliction. But the affliction of the hereafter is, nevertheless, greater. Its true nature is incomprehensible except to those who will actually experience it. May God never count us among them.

On the other hand we find "*other faces on that day are jocund, well-pleased with their striving, in a sublime garden, where they hear no babble. A running fountain shall be there, and raised couches, and goblets placed ready, and cushions laid in order, and carpets spread out.*" (Verses 8–16) Here are faces bright with joy, animated with pleasure. They are well pleased with what they are given. They enjoy that splendid, spiritual feeling of satisfaction with what they have done, as they sense God's pleasure with them. There is no better feeling for man than to be reassured of his own actions, and to see the results reflected in God being pleased with him. The Qur'ān gives precedence to this kind of happiness over the joys of heaven. Then it describes heaven and the joys it affords to its happy dwellers: "*in a sublime garden.*" (Verse 10) It is glorious and sublime, with lofty positions and elevated gardens.

The description of height and elevation gives us a special feeling. "*Where they hear no babble.*" (Verse 11) This expression creates a sense of calmness, peace, reassurance, love, satisfaction and pleasant discourse between friends. It also provides a feeling of raising oneself above any vain conversation. This is in itself a kind of joy and happiness, which is better felt when one remembers the first life and its increasing polemics, disputes, contentions, quarrels, sin and uproar. When one remembers all this, one relaxes into complete calmness, total peace of mind and a pleasant happiness generated by the Qur'ānic expression "*where they hear no babble*". The very words are endowed with a pleasant fragrance. They flow with gratifying rhythm. It also implies that, as the believers turn away in this life from polemics and vain discourse, their way of life acquires a heavenly element.

As has been said earlier, of all the descriptions of heaven, God emphasizes first this sublime and brilliant element, before He mentions the joys which satisfy the senses. These are given in a form comprehensible to man, but in heaven they take the form which is suited for the elevated standards of the people there. Thus they remain unknown except to those who actually experience them.

"*A running fountain shall be there.*" (Verse 12) The description combines a sense of quenching thirst, with beauty of movement and flow. Running water gives a sense of liveliness and youth. It is pleasant to the eye and the mind, and touches the depths of human feeling.

"*And raised couches.*" (Verse 13) The adjective, raised, gives an impression of cleanliness and purity. "*And goblets placed ready,*" (Verse 14) so they are ready for drinking – there is no need to order or prepare them. "*And cushions laid in order.*" (Verse 15) These are prepared for dwellers to recline and relax. "*And carpets spread out.*" They serve the dual purpose of decoration and comfort. All these luxuries are similar to the luxuries enjoyed in this life, but these are mentioned merely to make them comprehensible to us. Their true nature, and the nature of their enjoyment, are left for the experience of those whom God has rewarded.

It is useless to make comparisons or enquiries concerning the nature of the joys of the hereafter, or the nature of its afflictions. People gain their understanding by means that are limited to this world, and the nature of life in it. When they are in the next life all veils will be lifted and barriers removed. Souls and senses will be free from all restrictions, and the connotations of the very words will alter as a result of the change in the feelings to which they refer. These Qur'ānic descriptions help us to imagine the ultimate of sweetness and joy. This is all that we can do while we live on earth, but when God honours us with His grace and pleasure, as we pray He will, we will know the reality to which the Qur'ān refers.

Reflection on God's Creation

When this account of the hereafter comes to its close, the *sūrah* refers to the present world, which is in itself a manifestation of the power and perfect planning of God, the Almighty: "*Let them reflect on the camels, how they were created; and heaven, how it is raised aloft; and the mountains, how they are hoisted; and the earth, how it is spread out.*" (Verses 17–20) These four short verses join together the boundaries of the world of the Arabs – the first people to be addressed by the Qur'ān. They also group together the prominent ends of creation in the universe as they speak of the sky, earth, mountains and camels. The last of these stands for all animals, although the camel has its own distinctive features and a special value for Arabs.

All these aspects of creation – the sky, earth, mountains and animals – are always in front of man wherever he is. Whatever man's level of civilization and scientific advancement, they remain within his world and within his sphere of consciousness. When he considers their roles, they suggest to him something of what lies beyond. In each of them there is a miracle of creation. The distinctive, incomparable work of the Creator is clear in them all, and this alone is sufficient to indicate the true faith. Hence the Qur'ān directs to them the attention of every human being.

"*Let them reflect on the camels, how they were created.*" (Verse 17) The camel was the most important animal for the Arab. It was his means of transport which also carried his belongings. It gave him food and drink. From its hair and skin he made his clothes and dwellings. Besides, the camel is unique among all animals. Despite its strength, size and firm build, it is tame: a young boy can manage it. It gives man great service and, at the same time, it is inexpensive to keep and its food is easy to find. Moreover, it is the only animal to endure hunger, thirst, hard work and poor conditions. Its shape has also a special characteristic which is in perfect harmony with the portrait drawn here, and this will be discussed later on.

So, the Qur'ān asks of its first audience to ponder on how the camel is made. This does not require them to undertake any difficult task or to discover any obscure field of science. "*Let them reflect on the camels, how they were created.*" (Verse 17) Camels were a part of their world, and they only needed to look and consider how they were made most suitable for their role; how their shape and build fitted perfectly with their environment and function. Man did not create camels, nor did camels create themselves. So, they must have been made by the Supreme Maker whose work reflects His limitless ability and perfect planning, and testifies to His existence.

"*And heaven, how it is raised aloft.*" (Verse 18) The Qur'ān repeatedly directs man's reflective faculties to the skies. The desert people should be the first to undertake this, because in the desert the sky is much richer and more inspiring – as if it has a unique existence. In the middle of the day, the sky is brilliant and beaming; at late afternoon, it is captivating and fascinating; at sunset, most charming and inspiring. Then as the night spreads its wings the sky shows its sparkling stars and makes its friendly whispers. At sunrise, the sky comes alive again and becomes animating. All this is certainly worth a good deal of reflection and contemplation. They should consider how it was raised up. Who placed it so high without pillars to support it? Who scattered those innumerable stars? Who endowed it with its beauty and inspiration? They certainly did not lift it up, and it could not have been lifted by itself. A power is responsible for its creation and erection, and intelligent thought is enough to indicate Him.

"*And the mountains, how they are hoisted.*" (Verse 19) For the Arab in particular, a mountain is a refuge and a friend. In general, it always looks majestic and awesome. Next to a mountain, a man appears small and humble. It is natural for a man on a mountain to think of God, and feel himself nearer to Him. He feels a distinct detachment from the petty concerns of his worldly life. It was neither a vain whim nor a coincidence that Muḥammad (peace be upon him) should go to the cave on Mount Ḥirā' for periods of worship and contemplation before he was given God's message. It is also not surprising that those who want to spend a period in self-purification should seek to do so on a mountain. The reference here to the mountains speaks of them being 'hoisted', because this fits in perfectly with the image portrayed, which we will discuss presently.

"*And the earth, how it is spread out.*" (Verse 20) The earth is obviously outstretched and made suitable for human life and its full and varied range of activities. Man could not have made it so, as its creation was completed long before his existence. So should not man consider who spread out the earth and made life feasible on it? Intelligent reflection on all these aspects will always inspire minds and excite souls into recognition of God, the Creator.

Perhaps we should pause a little to consider the perfection with which this image of the universe is portrayed. The Qur'ān addresses man's religious conscience in a language of artistic beauty, and both coalesce in the believer's perception to bring the whole image into full relief. The scene portrayed here includes the elevated heaven and the spread out earth. Across such a boundless horizon stand the mountains. They are not described as firmly-rooted, but rather they are 'hoisted'. The camels also stand with their upright humps. It is a majestic scene, vast and infinite, with merely two horizontal lines and two vertical ones. This manipulation of graphic description for the expression of ideas is a distinct characteristic of the Qur'ānic style.

The Prophet's Mission

Having dealt first with the hereafter, and pointed out some apparent aspects of the universe, the *sūrah* now addresses the Prophet, (peace be upon him), laying down the nature of his mission and limits of his role. It then concludes with a final reminder to mankind: "*Therefore exhort them; your task is only to exhort. You are not their overseer. But he who turns his back and disbelieves, God shall inflict on him the greatest suffering. To Us they shall surely return, when We shall bring them to account.*" (Verses 21–26)

Remind them, then, of the hereafter and the universe, and all there is in each of them. Your specific task is to remind people, and you have no other role. This is indeed your mission for which you have been suitably equipped.

"*You are not their overseer.*" (Verse 22) You have no control over their hearts and you cannot compel them to adopt the faith. Men's hearts are in the hands of God, the Merciful. *Jihād*, which means striving for God's cause and which was later made a duty of the Prophet and all Muslims, did not aim at converting people to Islam by force. Its only aim was to remove all hindrances in the way of the Islamic message, so that it could be delivered freely, and people would not be prevented from listening to it or be persecuted for doing so. This is the role the Prophet can fulfil: to remove the obstacles which prevent him from delivering his message.

The notion that the Prophet's mission is confined to reminding people and delivering God's message is often repeated and stressed in the Qur'ān. There are several reasons for this emphasis, the first of which is to relieve the Prophet of the heavy burden of directing the course of the Islamic message once he has conveyed it. He must leave it to God to decide its course. The urgency of the human yearning to win victory for the truth and to get people to benefit from its absolute goodness is so keen that such repetition is required to make the advocates of this message distinguish their own desires and ambitions from their mission. When this distinction is clear, they proceed in fulfilment of their duty, regardless of the response and consequence. Thus advocates of Islam do not worry themselves over who has accepted the faith and who has not. They are not charged with this burden, which becomes particularly heavy at times of adversity, when a favourable response becomes a rarity and enemies abound.

But the delivery of the message, which is the limit of the Prophet's task, is not the end of the matter. The unbelievers are not to be left alone. They cannot deny God and be safe. "*But he who turns his back and disbelieves, God shall inflict on him the greatest suffering.*" (Verses 23–24) They will no doubt return to God, and He will inevitably administer their retribution. Such is the final and decisive note on which the *sūrah* ends: "*To Us they shall surely return, when We shall bring them to account.*" (Verses 25–26)

The definition of the Prophet's role and the role of every subsequent advocate of Islam is thus completed. They have only to remind and the reckoning will be made by God. It must be stressed, however, that the process of reminding includes the removal of hindrances so that people are free to listen to the divine message. This is the aim of *jihād* as it is understood from the Qur'ān and the Prophet's history. It is a process which neither admits negligence nor permits aggression.

SŪRAH 89

Al-Fajr

(The Dawn)

Al-Fajr (The Dawn)	سُورَةُ الفَجْرِ
In the name of God, the Beneficent, the Merciful.	بِسْمِ ٱللَّهِ ٱلرَّحْمَٰنِ ٱلرَّحِيمِ
By the dawn, (1)	وَٱلْفَجْرِ ١
by the ten nights, (2)	وَلَيَالٍ عَشْرٍ ٢
by that which is even and that which is odd, (3)	وَٱلشَّفْعِ وَٱلْوَتْرِ ٣
by the night as it journeys on! (4)	وَٱلَّيْلِ إِذَا يَسْرِ ٤
Is there not in that an oath for a man of sense? (5)	هَلْ فِي ذَٰلِكَ قَسَمٌ لِّذِي حِجْرٍ ٥
Have you not heard how your Lord dealt with the ʿĀd, (6)	أَلَمْ تَرَ كَيْفَ فَعَلَ رَبُّكَ بِعَادٍ ٦

the people of Iram, the many-pillared [city], (7)

إِرَمَ ذَاتِ ٱلْعِمَادِ ٧

the like of whom has never been created in the whole land? (8)

ٱلَّتِى لَمْ يُخْلَقْ مِثْلُهَا فِى ٱلْبِلَٰدِ ٨

And with the Thamūd, who hollowed out rocks in the valley? (9)

وَثَمُودَ ٱلَّذِينَ جَابُوا۟ ٱلصَّخْرَ بِٱلْوَادِ ٩

And with Pharaoh, of the tent-pegs? (10)

وَفِرْعَوْنَ ذِى ٱلْأَوْتَادِ ١٠

They were all transgressors throughout their lands, (11)

ٱلَّذِينَ طَغَوْا۟ فِى ٱلْبِلَٰدِ ١١

bringing about much corruption there. (12)

فَأَكْثَرُوا۟ فِيهَا ٱلْفَسَادَ ١٢

Therefore, your Lord let loose on them the scourge of suffering. (13)

فَصَبَّ عَلَيْهِمْ رَبُّكَ سَوْطَ عَذَابٍ ١٣

Your Lord surely observes all. (14)

إِنَّ رَبَّكَ لَبِٱلْمِرْصَادِ ١٤

As for man, whenever his Lord tries him by His generosity and with a life of ease, he says, 'My Lord is bountiful to me.' (15)

فَأَمَّا ٱلْإِنسَٰنُ إِذَا مَا ٱبْتَلَىٰهُ رَبُّهُۥ فَأَكْرَمَهُۥ
وَنَعَّمَهُۥ فَيَقُولُ رَبِّىٓ أَكْرَمَنِ ١٥

But whenever He tries him by stinting his means, he says, 'My Lord has disgraced me.' (16)

وَأَمَّآ إِذَا مَا ٱبْتَلَىٰهُ فَقَدَرَ عَلَيْهِ رِزْقَهُۥ
فَيَقُولُ رَبِّىٓ أَهَٰنَنِ ١٦

No indeed; but you are not generous towards the orphan, (17)

كَلَّا ۖ بَل لَّا تُكْرِمُونَ الْيَتِيمَ ﴿١٧﴾

nor do you urge one another to feed the needy. (18)

وَلَا تَحَاضُّونَ عَلَىٰ طَعَامِ الْمِسْكِينِ ﴿١٨﴾

You devour the inheritance [of others] greedily, (19)

وَتَأْكُلُونَ التُّرَاثَ أَكْلًا لَّمًّا ﴿١٩﴾

and you love wealth passionately. (20)

وَتُحِبُّونَ الْمَالَ حُبًّا جَمًّا ﴿٢٠﴾

No indeed! When the earth is systematically levelled down, (21)

كَلَّا إِذَا دُكَّتِ الْأَرْضُ دَكًّا دَكًّا ﴿٢١﴾

and your Lord comes, with the angels rank on rank, (22)

وَجَاءَ رَبُّكَ وَالْمَلَكُ صَفًّا صَفًّا ﴿٢٢﴾

and on that day, hell is brought near, then man will remember, but how will that remembrance avail him? (23)

وَجِيءَ يَوْمَئِذٍ بِجَهَنَّمَ ۚ يَوْمَئِذٍ يَتَذَكَّرُ
الْإِنسَانُ وَأَنَّىٰ لَهُ الذِّكْرَىٰ ﴿٢٣﴾

He shall say, 'Oh, would that I had prepared for my life!' (24)

يَقُولُ يَا لَيْتَنِي قَدَّمْتُ لِحَيَاتِي ﴿٢٤﴾

On that day, none will punish as He punishes, (25)

فَيَوْمَئِذٍ لَّا يُعَذِّبُ عَذَابَهُ أَحَدٌ ﴿٢٥﴾

and none will bind with chains as He binds. (26)

وَلَا يُوثِقُ وَثَاقَهُ أَحَدٌ ﴿٢٦﴾

'Oh soul at peace! (27)	يَٰٓأَيَّتُهَا ٱلنَّفْسُ ٱلْمُطْمَئِنَّةُ ﴿٢٧﴾
Return to your Lord, well pleased and well pleasing. (28)	ٱرْجِعِىٓ إِلَىٰ رَبِّكِ رَاضِيَةً مَّرْضِيَّةً ﴿٢٨﴾
Enter, then, together with My servants! (29)	فَٱدْخُلِى فِى عِبَٰدِى ﴿٢٩﴾
Enter My paradise!' (30)	وَٱدْخُلِى جَنَّتِى ﴿٣٠﴾

Overview

The present *sūrah* follows, in general, the line of this part of the Qur'ān, inviting the human heart to faith, urging man to awake, meditate and follow the path of righteousness. It uses different kinds of emphasis, connotation and rhythm, but constitutes, nevertheless, a single harmonious piece of music, varying in tones but maintaining the same cadence. Some of its scenes impart a touch of quiet beauty and a light, pleasant rhythm. This is particularly evident in its opening, which describes certain charming aspects of the universe and provides at the same time an aura of worship and prayer: "*By the dawn, by the ten nights, by that which is even and that which is odd, by the night as it journeys on!*" (Verses 1–4) Other scenes are tense and dramatic in both what they describe and in their music, like this violent, frightening picture: "*No indeed! When the earth is systematically levelled down, and your Lord comes, with the angels rank on rank, and on that day, hell is brought near, then man will remember, but how will that remembrance avail him? He shall say, 'Oh, would that I had prepared for my life!' On that day, none will punish as He punishes, And none will bind with chains as He binds.*" (Verses 21–26)

Some of the portraits drawn in the *sūrah* are pleasing, gentle and reassuring, striking perfect harmony between subject matter and rhythm. This is especially true of its ending: "*Oh soul at peace! Return to your Lord, well pleased and well pleasing. Enter, then, together with My servants! Enter My paradise!*" (Verses 27–30)

The *sūrah* also includes references to the destruction that befell insolent peoples of the past. The rhythm here falls somewhere between that of easy narration and that of violent destruction: "*Have you not heard how your Lord dealt with the 'Ād, the people of Iram, the many-pillared [city], the like of whom has never been created in the whole land? And with the Thamūd, who hollowed out rocks in the valley? And with Pharaoh, of the tent-pegs? They were all transgressors throughout their lands, bringing about much corruption there. Therefore, your Lord let loose on them the scourge of suffering. Your Lord surely observes all.*" (Verses 6–14)

We also have an outline of some human concepts and values which are at variance with faith. This part has its own style and rhythm: "*As for man, whenever his Lord tries him by His generosity and with a life of ease, he says, 'My Lord is bountiful to me.' But whenever He tries him by stinting his means, he says, 'My Lord has disgraced me.'*" (Verses 15–16)

A refutation of these erroneous concepts and values is provided through an exposition of the human conditions which give rise to them. Here we have two kinds of style and rhythm: "*No indeed; but you are not generous towards the orphan, nor do you urge one another to feed the needy. You devour the inheritance [of others] greedily, and you love wealth passionately.*" (Verses 17–20)

It is clear that the latter style and rhythm serves as a bridge between the statement of erroneous human ways and that which explains their inevitable attendant fate. These verses are immediately followed by a picture of the earth as it is levelled.

This brief overview reveals to us the numerous colours of the scenes described and explains the change of metre and rhyme according to the change of scenes. The *sūrah* is indeed an excellent example of an exceptionally beautiful style which is varied and harmonious at the same time.

A Serene Opening

"*By the dawn, by the ten nights, by that which is even and that which is odd, by the night as it journeys on! Is there not in that an oath for a man of sense?*" (Verses 1–5) This opening groups together a few scenes and creatures who have familiar, pleasant, and transparent souls. "*By the dawn,*" refers to the time when life starts to breathe with ease and happiness, a time of fresh, friendly companionship. This dormant world gradually wakes up in a prayer-like process.

"*By the ten nights.*" (Verse 2) The Qur'ān does not specify which these ten nights are. Several explanations, however, have been advanced. Some say they are the first of the month of Dhu'l-Ḥijjah; some say they are in al-Muḥarram; and others state that they are the last ten nights of Ramaḍān. As it leaves them undefined, the Arabic reference acquires an added yet amiable effect. They are merely ten nights known to God but the expression connotes that they have special character, as if they were living creatures with souls and there was mutual sympathy between them and us, transmitted through this Qur'ānic verse.

"*By that which is even and that which is odd.*" (Verse 3) This verse adds an atmosphere of worship to that of the dawn and the ten nights. According to al-Tirmidhī, the Prophet says: "Some prayers are of even number and some are odd." This is the most appropriate import to be attached to this verse, in the general context of the *sūrah*. It suggests a mutual response between the souls of the worshippers and those of the selected nights and the brightening dawn.

"*By the night as it journeys on.*" (Verse 4) The night here is personified as if it were a traveller journeying in the universe. Its portrait is like that of an insomniac walking on and on in the darkness, or a wayfarer who prefers to start his long journey at night. What a beautiful expression, one enhanced by its superb rhythm! The harmony between this verse and the dawn, the ten nights, the even and the odd is perfect. These are not mere words and expressions: they provide a feeling of the breeze at dawn, and of the morning dew diffusing the fragrance of flowers.

This is the effect of a gentle, inspiring whisper on our hearts, souls and consciences. The beauty of this loving address is far superior to any poetic expression because it combines the beauty of originality with the statement of certain fact. Hence it concludes with a rhetorical question: "*Is there not in that an oath for a man of sense?*" (Verse 5) The oath and the conviction are certainly there for anyone with a meditative mind. Although the positive meaning is intended, the interrogative form is used because it is gentler. Thus harmony with the preceding address is maintained.

Swift Punishment of Tyranny

The subject of the oath is omitted, but it is explained by the discussion that follows on tyranny and corruption. The punishment inflicted by God on the insolent, tyrannical and corrupt communities is a law of nature asserted by this oath. The assertion takes the form of a hint befitting the generally light tone of this *sūrah*: "*Have you not heard how your Lord dealt with the ʿĀd, the people of Iram, the many-pillared [city], the like of whom has never been created in the whole land? And with the Thamūd, who hollowed out rocks in the valley? And with Pharaoh, of the tent-pegs? They were all transgressors throughout their lands, bringing about much corruption there. Therefore, your Lord let loose on them the scourge of suffering. Your Lord surely observes all.*" (Verses 6–14)

The interrogative form in such a context is more effective in drawing the attention of the addressee, who is, in the first instance, the Prophet (peace be upon him) and then all those who may ponder over the fates of those past communities. The people of the Prophet's generation, who were the first to be addressed by the Qur'ān, were aware of what happened to these nations. Their fates were also explained in reports and stories conveyed by one generation to another. The description of these outcomes as the deeds of God is comforting and reassuring for the believers. It was particularly so to those believers in Makkah who, at the time when this *sūrah* was revealed, were subjected to relentless persecution and hardship by the unbelievers.

These short verses refer to the fates of the most powerful and despotic nations in ancient history. They speak of the earlier tribe of 'Ād of Iram, a branch of extinct Arabs. They used to dwell in al-Aḥqāf, a sandy piece of land in southern Arabia, midway between Yemen and Ḥaḍramowt. The 'Ād were nomadic, using posts and pillars to erect their tents. They are described elsewhere in the Qur'ān as being extremely powerful and aggressive. Indeed they were the most powerful and prestigious of all contemporary Arabian tribes: "*The like of whom has never been created in the whole land.*" (Verse 8) The distinction here is restricted to that particular age.

"*And with the Thamūd, who hollowed out rocks in the valley?*" (Verse 9) The Thamūd used to live at Al-Ḥijr, a rocky tract in northern Arabia, on the road from Madinah to Syria. They excelled in using rocks to build their palaces and homes. They also dug shelters and caves into the mountains.

"*And with Pharaoh, of the tent-pegs.*" (Verse 10) The term, '*tent-pegs*', refers to the pyramids which are as firm in their construction as pegs well dug into the ground. The Pharaoh referred to here is the despot who was Moses's contemporary.

These people "*were all transgressors throughout their lands, bringing about much corruption there.*" (Verses 11–12) Corruption is an inevitable result of tyranny, and it affects the tyrant and his subjects alike. Indeed, tyranny ruins all human relations. It forces human life out of its healthy, constructive and straight path and diverts it into a line which does not lead to the fulfilment of man's role as God's vicegerent on earth. Tyranny makes the tyrant captive of his own desires because he is uncommitted to any principle or standard and unrestrained within any reasonable limit. Thus the tyrant is always the first to be corrupted by his own tyranny. He assumes for himself a role other than that of a servant of God, entrusted with a specific mission. This is evident in Pharaoh's boastful claim: "*I am your supreme Lord.*" (79: 24)

Here we have an example of the corrupting influence, indeed insolence, of despotism in Pharaoh's aspiring to a status greater than that of an obedient creature. Tyranny also corrupts the masses, as it humiliates them and compels them to suppress their discontent and hatred. It kills all human dignity and wastes all creative talents, which cannot flourish except in an atmosphere of freedom. A humiliated soul inevitably rots away and becomes a breeding ground for sickly desires. Hence, digression from the right path becomes the order of the day as clear vision becomes an impossibility. In such conditions no aspiration to a higher human standard can be entertained. The net result of all this is the spread of corruption.

Tyranny also destroys all healthy standards and concepts because they constitute a threat to its existence. Hence, values are falsified and standards are distorted so that the repulsive idea of despotism becomes acceptable as natural. This, in itself, is great corruption.

When these aforementioned peoples caused such corruption, the remedy was, inevitably, a complete purge: "*Therefore, your Lord let loose on them the scourge of suffering. Your Lord surely observes all.*" (Verses 13–14) God is certainly aware of their deeds and He records them all. So, when corruption increased, He severely punished the corrupt. The text connotes that the punishment was very painful as it uses the term '*scourge*', or 'whip' as the Arabic term literally means, and that it was in large supply as indicated by use of the phrase '*let loose*'. Thus these tyrants were made to suffer a plentiful and painful retribution.

As the believer faces tyranny in any age or place, he feels great reassurance emanating from far beyond the fates of all those communities. He also feels a particular comfort as he reads the verse: "*Your Lord surely observes all.*" (Verse 14) Nothing passes unnoticed and nothing is forgotten. So let the believers be always reassured that God will deal, in time, with all corruption and tyranny.

Thus the *sūrah* provides some examples of what God may do about the cause of faith, which are totally different from the example of the people of the pit outlined in *Sūrah* 85, The Constellations. All these stories are related for a definite purpose, namely, the education of the believers and their preparation to face whichever course God chooses for them. They will, then, be ready for all eventualities and equipped with God's reassurance as they submit themselves to Him and let His will be done.

Human Short-Sightedness

"*Your Lord surely observes all.*" (Verse 14) He sees, records, holds to account and rewards according to a strict and accurate measure which neither errs nor exceeds the limits of justice. It is never deceived by appearances because it judges the essence of things. Human measures and standards are liable to all sorts of errors. Man sees nothing beyond appearances unless he adopts the divine measure.

"*As for man, whenever his Lord tries him by His generosity and with a life of ease, he says, 'My Lord is bountiful to me.' But whenever He tries him by stinting his means, he says, 'My Lord has disgraced me.'*" (Verses 15–16) Such is man's thinking about the various forms of trial God may set for him, be it comfort or hardship, abundance or scarcity. God may test him with comfort, honour, wealth or position but he does not realize the probationary nature of what he is given. Rather he considers the gesture as proof that he deserves to be honoured by God and as evidence that He has chosen him for a special honour. It is a line of thinking which mistakes trial for reward and test for result. It imagines honour in the sight of God to be measured by worldly comforts. God may also try man by stinting his means, and man again mistakes trial for reward and imagines the test to be a retribution. He feels that God has made him poor in order to humiliate him.

In both situations the human concept is faulty. Wealth and poverty are two forms of a test which God sets for His servants. A test with abundance reveals whether a man is humble and thankful to his Lord or arrogant and haughty, while a trial of the opposite kind reveals his patient acceptance or his irritability and fretfulness. A man's reward is given according to what he proves himself to be. What he is given or denied of worldly comforts is not his reward, and a man's standing in the sight of God is in no way related to his possessions, for He gives and denies worldly comforts regardless of whether a man is good or bad. A man devoid of faith cannot comprehend the wisdom behind God's action of giving or denying worldly comforts. However, when his mind is enlightened with faith and truth becomes apparent to him, he realizes the triviality of worldly riches and the value of the reward after the test. So he works for this reward whether he is tried with worldly abundance or scarcity. As he disregards the hollow considerations of wealth and poverty, he is reassured about his fate and his position in God's sight.

At the time of revelation, the Qur'ān addressed a kind of people common to all *jāhiliyyah* societies, one who had lost all relation with a world beyond our present life. Such people adopt this mistaken view about God's granting or denial of wealth, and apply a set of values which reserve all honour to money and social standing. Hence, their craving for wealth is irresistible. It makes them covetous, greedy and stingy. The Qur'ān reveals their true feelings. It states that their greed and stinginess are responsible for their inability to understand the true significance of divine trial, whether by granting or denying wealth. "*No indeed; but you are not generous towards the orphan, nor do you urge one another to feed the needy. You devour the inheritance [of others] greedily, and you love wealth passionately.*" (Verses 17–20)

The real issue is that when people are given wealth they do not fulfil the duties demanded of the wealthy. They do not look after the young orphan who has lost his father and become, therefore, in need of protection and support. They do not urge one another to contribute to general welfare. Such mutual encouragement is indeed an important feature of the Islamic way of life. Since such people do not comprehend the significance of the trial, they do not even try to come out of it successfully by looking after the orphans and urging one another to feed the needy. On the contrary, they greedily devour the orphans' inheritance, and unrestrainedly crave for wealth. It is a craving which kills all their nobility.

In Makkah, Islam faced this common urge to accumulate wealth by every possible means. The weak position of orphans, and orphan girls in particular, tempted many to deprive them of their inheritance in different ways. The ardent love of wealth, the craving to accumulate it through usury and other means, was a distinctive feature of Makkan society as it is a distinctive feature of all *jāhiliyyah* societies at all times.

These few verses do not merely expose the true nature of such an attitude. They also condemn it and urge its discontinuation. Condemnation is evident in the repetition noted in these verses, their rhythm and metre: "*You devour the inheritance [of others] greedily, and you love wealth passionately.*" (Verses 19–20)

The Fateful Day

Once their erroneous concept of the trial with wealth and poverty is outlined, and their vile attitude is exposed there follows a stern warning about the Day of Judgement which comes after the result of the test is known. Here the rhythm is very powerful: "*No indeed! When the earth is systematically levelled down, and your Lord comes, with the angels rank on rank, and on that day, hell is brought near, then man will remember, but how will that remembrance avail him! He shall say, 'Oh, would that I had prepared for my life!' On that day, none will punish as He punishes, and none will bind with chains as He binds.*" (Verses 21–26)

The total destruction of all that is on earth and its systematic levelling is one of the upheavals that overwhelm the universe on the Day of Resurrection. God's coming with the angels is unexplained but the expression overflows with reverence, awe and fear. The same applies to bringing hell closer. We take it to mean that hell on that day will be very close to its prospective dwellers. What actually happens and how it happens is part of the divine knowledge God has chosen to withhold until that day. These verses, with their captivating rhythm and sharp notes, portray nevertheless a scene which strikes fear into people's hearts, and makes it apparent in their eyes. The earth is being systematically levelled; God Almighty judges everyone; the angels stand there rank on rank, while hell is brought near and set in readiness.

At that moment "*man will remember.*" Man, who lived unaware of the wisdom behind the trial with worldly riches or with deprivation; who devoured the inheritance of orphans greedily; who craved for money and did not care for the orphans or the needy; who tyrannized, spread corruption and turned away from divine guidance, will then remember the truth and take account of what he beholds. But alas! It is too late: "*But how will that remembrance avail him?*" (Verse 23) The time for remembrance is over, so remembrance on the Day of Judgement and reward will not profit anybody. It serves merely as an act of grief for a chance given but not taken in this present life.

When man is fully aware of the true nature of his situation he says despairingly, "*Oh, would that I had prepared for my life!*" (Verse 24) For the true life, the only one that deserves the name, is indeed the life hereafter. It is the one which is worth preparing for. *"Oh, would that I had..."* It is a sigh of evident regret and grief, but it is the most a man can do for himself then.

The *sūrah* goes on to portray man's fate after his desperate sighing and useless wishing: "*On that day, none will punish as He punishes, and none will bind with chains as He binds.*" (Verses 25–26) It is God Almighty who inflicts His incomparable punishment, and who binds as no one can bind. This divine punishment and binding are explained in detail in other parts of the Qur'ān, but the reference here is very brief, stressing mainly their incomparability to human action.

The reference to divine punishment here brings to mind the earlier reference to human tyranny in the given examples of the 'Ād, Thamūd and Pharaoh. Those tyrants are stated to have spread much corruption in their lands, including physically torturing people and binding them with chains and ropes. These last verses serve as an address to the Prophet and the believers, reminding them that their Lord will punish and chain those who tortured and chained others. But the two kinds of punishment are entirely different. Meagre is the torture that any creature can administer, but great is that inflicted by the Creator. Let the tyrants continue with their punishment and persecution; they will have their turn and be the sufferers of a punishment which is beyond all imagination.

Amidst all this unimaginable horror comes an address from on high to the believers: "*Oh soul at peace! Return to your Lord, well pleased and well pleasing. Enter, then, together with My servants! Enter My paradise!*" (Verses 27–30)

It is a tender, compassionate and reassuring address: "*Oh soul at peace!*" (Verse 27) It speaks of freedom and ease, after the earlier reference to chains and affliction: "*Return to your Lord.*" (Verse 28) After your alienation on earth and your separation from the one you belong to. Return now to your Lord with whom you have strong ties: "*well pleased and well pleasing.*" (Verse 28) It is a gentle address which spreads compassion and satisfaction. "*Enter, then, together with My servants,*" among those servants chosen to enjoy this divine grace. "*Enter My paradise,*" to receive God's mercy and protection.

As it opens, this address generates an aura of heaven: "*Oh soul at peace!*" The believer's is a soul at peace with its Lord, certain of its way, confident of its fate. It is a soul satisfied in all eventualities, happiness or affliction, wealth or poverty. It entertains no doubts; it is free from transgressions. The gentle music adds a feeling of intimacy and peace. The majestic face of God, the Compassionate, the Merciful, with all His splendour looks on from above.

SŪRAH 90

Al-Balad

(The City)

Al-Balad (The City)

سُورَةُ البَلَدِ

In the name of God, the Beneficent, the Merciful.

بِسْمِ ٱللَّهِ ٱلرَّحْمَٰنِ ٱلرَّحِيمِ

I swear by this city, (1)

لَآ أُقْسِمُ بِهَٰذَا ٱلْبَلَدِ ﴿١﴾

this city in which you are a dweller, (2)

وَأَنتَ حِلٌّۢ بِهَٰذَا ٱلْبَلَدِ ﴿٢﴾

by parent and offspring: (3)

وَوَالِدٍ وَمَا وَلَدَ ﴿٣﴾

indeed, We have created man in affliction. (4)

لَقَدْ خَلَقْنَا ٱلْإِنسَٰنَ فِى كَبَدٍ ﴿٤﴾

Does he think that no one has power over him? (5)

أَيَحْسَبُ أَن لَّن يَقْدِرَ عَلَيْهِ أَحَدٌ ﴿٥﴾

He says: 'I have spent abundant wealth.' (6)

يَقُولُ أَهْلَكْتُ مَالًا لُّبَدًا ﴿٦﴾

أَيَحۡسَبُ أَن لَّمۡ يَرَهُۥٓ أَحَدٌ ﴿٧﴾

Does he think that none observes him? (7)

أَلَمۡ نَجۡعَل لَّهُۥ عَيۡنَيۡنِ ﴿٨﴾

Have We not given him two eyes, (8)

وَلِسَانٗا وَشَفَتَيۡنِ ﴿٩﴾

a tongue, and two lips, (9)

وَهَدَيۡنَٰهُ ٱلنَّجۡدَيۡنِ ﴿١٠﴾

and shown him the two paths? (10)

فَلَا ٱقۡتَحَمَ ٱلۡعَقَبَةَ ﴿١١﴾

Yet he would not scale the Ascent. (11)

وَمَآ أَدۡرَىٰكَ مَا ٱلۡعَقَبَةُ ﴿١٢﴾

Would that you knew what the Ascent is. (12)

فَكُّ رَقَبَةٍ ﴿١٣﴾

It is the freeing of a slave, (13)

أَوۡ إِطۡعَٰمٞ فِي يَوۡمٖ ذِي مَسۡغَبَةٖ ﴿١٤﴾

or the feeding, on a day of famine, (14)

يَتِيمٗا ذَا مَقۡرَبَةٍ ﴿١٥﴾

of an orphaned near of kin, (15)

أَوۡ مِسۡكِينٗا ذَا مَتۡرَبَةٖ ﴿١٦﴾

or a needy man in distress, (16)

ثُمَّ كَانَ مِنَ ٱلَّذِينَ ءَامَنُواْ وَتَوَاصَوۡاْ
بِٱلصَّبۡرِ وَتَوَاصَوۡاْ بِٱلۡمَرۡحَمَةِ ﴿١٧﴾

and to be of those who believe and enjoin on one another to be patient in adversity, and enjoin mercy on one another. (17)

Those who do this shall be on the right hand. (18)	أُوْلَٰٓئِكَ أَصۡحَٰبُ ٱلۡمَيۡمَنَةِ ١٨
And those who deny Our revelations shall be on the left hand, (19)	وَٱلَّذِينَ كَفَرُواْ بِـَٔايَٰتِنَا هُمۡ أَصۡحَٰبُ ٱلۡمَشۡـَٔمَةِ ١٩
with fire closing in upon them. (20)	عَلَيۡهِمۡ نَارٞ مُّؤۡصَدَةُۢ ٢٠

Overview

This short *sūrah* touches on a great many facts which are of central importance to human life. Its style is characterized by powerful allusions. Numerous facts of this nature are not easily combined in any form of concise writing except that of the Qur'ān, with its unique ability to hit the right chords with such swift and penetrating strokes.

Affliction in Human Life

The *sūrah* opens with an emphatic oath asserting an inherent fact of human life: "*I swear by this city, this city in which you are a dweller, by parent and offspring: indeed, We have created man in affliction.*" (Verses 1–4) The city is Makkah, which houses the Ka'bah, the sacred house of God that was the first temple ever to be erected on this earth as a place of peace where people put down their weapons and forget their quarrels. They meet there in peace; each is sacred to all. Even the plants, the birds and all creatures that happen to be in this city enjoy full and complete security. It is the House built by Abraham, the father of Ishmael, who is the grandfather of all Arabs and Muslims.

God then honours His Prophet, Muḥammad, by mentioning him and his residence in Makkah, a fact which adds to the sanctity of the city, its honour and glory. This is a point of great significance in this context; for the unbelievers were violating the sanctity of the House by harassing the Prophet and the Muslims in it. But the House is sacred and the Prophet's dwelling in its neighbourhood makes it even more so. God's oath by this city and by the Prophet's residence in it adds even more to its sacredness and glory, which consequently makes the the unbelievers' attitude grossly impertinent and objectionable. Their attitude becomes even more singular, considering their claims to be the custodians of the House, Ishmael's descendants and Abraham's followers.

This last reference supports the inclination to take the next verse, "*by parent and offspring,*" to refer to Abraham and Ishmael in particular. This reading includes in the oath the Prophet, the city where he lives, the founder of the House and his offspring. However, it does not preclude that the statement can also be a general one, referring to the phenomenon of reproduction which preserves the human race. This reference may be taken as an introduction to the discussion about man's nature, which is indeed the theme of the *sūrah*.

In his commentary on this *sūrah* in *Tafsīr Juz' 'Amma*, the late Shaikh Muḥammad 'Abdūh, makes a fine remark which is useful to quote here:

> God then swears by parent and children to draw our attention to the great importance of this stage of reproduction in life, and to the infinite wisdom and perfection which this stage involves. It also emphasizes the great suffering encountered by parent and offspring during the process from its inception up to its conclusion, when the newcomer achieves a certain degree of development.
>
> Think of plants and the tough opposition met by a seed of a plant in the process of growth, until it adapts to the various factors of climate. Think of its attempts to absorb the food necessary for its survival from its surroundings, till it develops branches and leaves. It then prepares for the production of a

> similar seed or seeds that will repeat its function and add to the beauty of the world around it. Think of all this then consider the more advanced forms of animal and human life and you will see something much greater and far more wonderful concerning reproduction. You will have a feeling of the hardship and suffering met by all parents and offspring for the sake of preserving the species and the beauty of this world.

The oath reaffirms an intrinsic fact in human life: "*Indeed, We have created man in affliction.*" (Verse 4) Indeed, man's life is a process of continued hardship that never ends, as stated in *Sūrah* 84, The Rending: "*O man! You have been toiling towards your Lord, and you shall meet Him.*" (84: 6)

No sooner does the first living cell settle in the mother's womb than it starts to encounter affliction and has to work hard in order to prepare for itself the right conditions for its survival, with the permission of its Lord. It continues to do so until it is ready for the process of birth, which is a great ordeal for both mother and baby. Before the baby finally sees the light it undergoes a great deal of pushing and squeezing to the point of near suffocation in its passage out of the womb.

A stage of harder endurance and greater suffering follows. The new-born baby begins to breathe the air, which is a new experience. It opens its mouth and inflates its lungs for the first time with a cry which tells of the harsh start. The digestive system then starts to function in a manner which is totally unfamiliar, as does blood circulation. Then it starts to empty its bowels, encountering great difficulty in adapting its system to this new function. Indeed, every new step or movement is attended by suffering. If one watches this baby when it begins to crawl and walk, one sees the kind of effort required to execute such minor and elementary movements. Such affliction continues with teething, and learning to stand, walk, learn and think. Indeed, in every new experience much affliction is involved.

Then the roads diverge and the struggle takes different forms. One person struggles with his muscles, another with his mind and a third with his soul. One toils for a mouthful of food or a rag to dress himself with, another to double or treble his wealth. One person strives to achieve a position of power or influence and another for the sake of God. One struggles for the sake of satisfying lusts and desires, and another for the sake of his faith or ideology. One strives but achieves no more than hell and another strives for paradise. Everyone is carrying his own burden and climbing his own hill to arrive finally at the meeting place appointed by God, where the wretched shall endure their worst suffering while the blessed enjoy their endless happiness.

Affliction, life's foremost characteristic, takes various forms and shapes but it is always judged by its eventual results. The loser is the one who ends up suffering more affliction in the hereafter, and the prosperous is the one whose striving qualifies him to be released from affliction and ensures him the ultimate repose under his Lord's shelter. Yet there is some reward in this present life for the different kinds of struggle which people endure. The one who labours for a great cause differs from the one who labours for a trivial one, in the amount and the quality of gratification each of them gains from his labour and sacrifice.

Great Blessings

Having established this fact concerning human nature and human life, the *sūrah* goes on to discuss some of the claims that man makes and some of the concepts underlying his behaviour. "*Does he think that no one has power over him? He says: 'I have spent abundant wealth.' Does he think that none observes him?*" (Verses 5–7)

This creature, man, whose suffering and struggling never come to an end, forgets his real nature and becomes so conceited with what God has given him of power, ability, skill and prosperity that he behaves as if he is not accountable for what he does. He indulges in oppression, tyranny, victimization and exploitation, trying to acquire enormous wealth. He corrupts himself and others in total disregard of anything of value. Such is the character of a man whose heart is stripped of faith. When he is called upon to spend for good causes, he says, "*I have spent abundant wealth,*" and given more than enough. "*Does he think that none observes him?*" (Verse 7) Has he forgotten that God is watching over him? He sees what he has spent and for what purposes. But man still ignores this, thinking that God is unaware of what he has done.

In view of man's arrogance, which makes him believe that he is invincible, and in view of his meanness and claims of having spent abundantly, the Qur'ān puts before him the bounties God has bestowed on him which are manifested in his inherent abilities, although he has depreciated them: "*Have We not given him two eyes, a tongue and two lips, and shown him the two paths?*" (Verses 8–10)

Man is conceited because he feels himself powerful, but he is granted his power by God. He is mean with his wealth while God is the One who provided him with it. He neither follows right guidance nor shows gratitude, although God has given him the means to do so. He has given him eyes which are marvellous, precise and powerful. He has also granted him speech and the means of expression, "*a tongue, and two lips.*" He has equipped him with the ability to distinguish good from evil, and right from wrong: "*and shown him the two paths,*" so that he can choose between them. Inherent in his make-up is the ability to take either way. It is God's will that man should be given such ability and such freedom of choice, to perfect His scheme of creation which assigns to every creature its role in life and equips it with the means necessary for its fulfilment.

This verse explains the essence of human nature. In fact, the basis of the Islamic viewpoint of human psychology is contained in this verse and four verses in the next *sūrah*, The Sun: "*By the soul and its moulding and inspiration with knowledge of wickedness and righteousness. Successful is the one who keeps it pure, and ruined is the one who corrupts it.*" (91: 7–10)

Scaling the Ascent

These are the favours bestowed on man to help him follow right guidance: his eyes with which he recognizes the evidence of God's might and the signs throughout the universe which should prompt him to adopt the faith, and his tongue and lips which are his means of speech and expression. One word sometimes does the job of a sword or a shotgun and can be even more effective than either. It may, on the other hand, plunge a man into the fire of hell. Mu'ādh ibn Jabal said: "I was with the Prophet on a journey. One day I was walking beside him when I said, 'Messenger of God! Point out to me something I may do to take me to paradise and keep me away from hell.' He said, 'You have indeed asked about something great, yet it is quite attainable by those for whom God has made it easy. Worship God alone, assigning to Him no partner, offer your prayers regularly, pay out your *zakāt* [i.e. what is due to the poor of one's money], fast in the month of Ramaḍān and offer the pilgrimage.' The Prophet then said, 'Shall I point out to you the gates of goodness?' I said, 'Yes, Messenger of God, please do.' He said, 'Fasting is a safeguard and a means of protecting yourself; charity erases your errors just as water extinguishes a burning fire; and your praying in the late hours of the night is the sign of piety.' He then recited the verse, *'[those] who forsake their beds as they call on their Lord in fear and in hope; and who give in charity of what We have bestowed on them. No soul knows what bliss and comfort is in store for these as reward for their labours.*" (32: 16–17) The Prophet then added: 'Shall I tell you what the heart of the matter is, its backbone and its highest grade?' I said, 'Yes, Messenger of God, please do.' He said, 'The heart is Islam, i.e. submission to God, the backbone is prayers, and the highest grade is *jihād*, i.e. struggle for the cause of God.' He then said, 'Shall I tell you what commands all these?' I said, 'Yes, Messenger of God, please do.' He said, 'Control this,' pointing to his tongue. I said, 'Are we, Prophet of God, really accountable for what we say?' He said 'Watch what you are saying.

For what else are people dragged on their faces in hell apart from what their tongues produce?'" [Related by Aḥmad, al-Tirmidhī, al-Nasā'ī and Ibn Mājah.]"

All these bounties have not motivated man to attempt the Ascent that stands between him and heaven. God explains the nature of the Ascent in the following verses: "*Yet he would not scale the Ascent. Would that you knew what the Ascent is. It is the freeing of a slave, or the feeding, on a day of famine, of an orphaned near of kin, or a needy man in distress, and to be of those who believe and enjoin on one another to be patient in adversity, and enjoin mercy on one another. Those who do this shall be on the right hand.*" (Verses 11–18)

This is the ascent which man, except those who equip themselves with faith, refrains from attempting, and which separates him from paradise. If he crosses it he will arrive! Putting it in such a way serves as a powerful incentive and stimulus to take up the challenge. For the ascent has been clearly marked as the obstacle depriving man of such an enormous fortune. The importance of scaling the ascent in God's sight is then emphasized to encourage man to scale it no matter what the effort. For struggle he must, in any case. But if he attempts it, his struggle will not be wasted but will bring him favourable results.

Then follows an explanation of this ascent and its nature by means of, first, pointing out some actions which were totally lacking in the particular surroundings that the message of Islam was facing at the time: the freeing of slaves and the feeding of the poor who were subjected to the cruelty of an ungracious and greedy society. It then adds what is applicable to all ages and societies and needed by all who wish to attempt the ascent: "*To be of those who believe and enjoin on one another to be patient in adversity, and enjoin mercy on one another.*" (Verse 17) There are reports which comment on the particular usage of freeing slaves in this *sūrah*, explaining that it includes even sharing in an effort to free a slave, not merely bearing all the expense involved. Even then the outcome is the same.

Setting Practical Examples

This *sūrah* was revealed in Makkah when Islam was surrounded by powerful enemies and the state that would implement its laws was non-existent. Slavery was widespread in Arabia and the world at large. The treatment meted out to slaves was brutal. When some of the slaves or former slaves, like 'Ammār ibn Yāsir and his family, Bilāl ibn Rabāḥ, and others, accepted Islam their plight became worse, and their cruel masters subjected them to unbearable torture. It then became clear that the only way to save them was to buy them from their masters. Abū Bakr, the Prophet's Companion, was, as usual, the first to rise to the occasion, with all the boldness and gallantry it required.

Ibn Isḥāq relates:

> Bilāl, Abū Bakr's servant, was owned by some individual of the clan of Jumaḥ as he was born a slave. He was, however, a genuine Muslim and clean-hearted. Umayyah ibn Khalaf, the Jumaḥ master, used to take Bilāl out when it became unbearably hot and order him to be laid down on his back on the hot sand of Makkah and cause a massive rock to be placed on his chest. Then, he would say to Bilāl that he was to stay like that until he died or renounced Muḥammad and accepted as deities the idols called al-Lāt and al-'Uzzā, the goddesses of the pagan Arabs. Under all such pressure, Bilāl would simply say, 'One, One,' meaning that there is only one God.
>
> One day, Abū Bakr passed by and saw Bilāl in that condition. He said to Umayyah: 'Do you not fear God as you torture this helpless soul? How long can you go on doing this?' Umayyah replied, 'You spoiled him, so you save him.' Abū Bakr said, 'I will. I have a black boy who follows your religion but he is stronger and more vigorous than Bilāl. What do you say to an exchange deal?' Umayyah said, 'I accept.' Abū Bakr said, 'Then he is yours.' Then Abū Bakr took Bilāl and set him free.

While in Makkah, before the migration to Madinah, Abū Bakr freed a total of seven people: ʿĀmir ibn Fahīrah, who fought in the Battle of Badr and was killed in the Battle of Bi'r Maʿūnah, was the only other man freed by Abū Bakr. The other five were women. The first two were Umm ʿUbays and Zanīrah, who lost her eyesight when she was freed. Some of the Quraysh claimed that the two idols al-Lāt and al-ʿUzzā caused the loss of her eyesight. Zanīrah said, 'What rubbish! Al-Lāt and al-ʿUzzā are absolutely powerless.' God then willed that she should recover her sight.

Abū Bakr also freed a woman called al-Nahdiyyah and her daughter, who belonged to a woman of the clan of ʿAbd al-Dār. One day he passed by the two women as their mistress was sending them on an errand to prepare some flour. As she gave them her instructions, she declared: 'By God, I will never set you free.' Abū Bakr said to her, 'Release yourself of your oath.' She rejoined, 'It was you who spoilt them. Why don't you set them free?' He said, 'How much do you want for them?' She named her price. He said, 'It is a deal, and they are free.' He turned to the two women and told them to give the woman her flour back. They suggested that they should finish preparing it for her first and he agreed.

The fifth woman was a Muslim slave of the clan of Mu'ammal. She was being tortured by ʿUmar ibn al-Khaṭṭāb, who was then still an unbeliever. He beat her until he was tired and said to her, 'I apologize to you. I have only stopped beating you because I am bored,' to which she replied, 'And so God shall thwart you.' Abū Bakr bought her and set her free.

Abū Quḥāfah, Abū Bakr's father, said to him, 'I see you, son, freeing some weak slaves. Why don't you free some strong men who can defend and protect you?' Abū Bakr replied, 'I am only doing this for the sake of God, father.' Thus Abū Bakr scaled the ascent by freeing those helpless souls, for the sake of God. The attendant circumstances in that particular society make such an action one of the most important steps towards scaling the ascent.[1]

"*Or the feeding, on a day of famine, of an orphaned near of kin, or a needy man in distress.*" (Verses 14–16) A time of famine and hunger, when food becomes scarce, is a time when the reality of faith is tested. For orphans in that greedy, miserly and ungracious society were oppressed and mistreated even by their relatives. The Qur'ān is full of verses which urge people to treat orphans well. This, in itself, is a measure of the cruelty of the orphans' surroundings. Good treatment for orphans is also urged in the *sūrahs* revealed in Madinah, as they outline the rules of inheritance, custody and marriage, especially in *Sūrahs* 2, The Cow, and 4, Women. The same can be said of feeding the needy on a day of famine, which is portrayed here as another step for scaling the ascent. For this is again a test which reveals the characteristics of the believer, such as mercy, sympathy, co-operation and lack of selfishness. It also reveals the extent of one's fear of God.

These two steps, freeing slaves and feeding the needy, are mentioned in the *sūrah* as necessary in the existing situation at the time of revelation. However, their implication is general, which accounts for their being mentioned first. They are followed by the widest and most important step of all: "*And to be of those who believe and enjoin on one another to be patient in adversity, and enjoin mercy on one another.*" (Verse 17) The conjunction in the Arabic text is 'then', but it does not signify here any time ordering; it is used simply as an introduction to the statement about the most important and valuable step of all towards scaling the ascent. For what would be the value of freeing slaves or feeding the hungry without faith? It is faith which gives such actions their value and their weight in God's sight, because it relates them to a profound and consistent system. Thus good deeds are no longer

1. Ibn Hishām, *Al-Sīrah al-Nabawiyyah*, Dār al-Qalam, Beirut, Vol. 1, n.d., pp. 339–41.

the result of a momentary impulse. Their aim is not any social reputation or self-interest.

Patience in adversity is an important element in the general context of faith as well as in the particular context of attempting the ascent. That people should counsel each other to be patient in adversity is to attain a higher level than that of having such a quality themselves. It is a practical demonstration of the solidarity of the believers as they co-operate closely to carry out their duties as believers in God. The society formed by the believers is an integrated structure whose elements share the same feelings and the same awareness about the need to exert themselves in establishing the divine system on earth and to carry out its duties fully. Hence, they counsel each other to persevere as they shoulder their common responsibilities. They rally to support one another in order to achieve their common objective. This is something more than perseverance by individuals, although it builds on it. For it indicates the individual's role in the believers' society, namely, that he must be an element of strength and a source of hope and comfort to the whole society.

The same applies to enjoining each other to be merciful, which is a grade higher than simply being merciful themselves. Thus the spirit of mercy spreads among the believers as they consider such mutual counselling an individual and communal duty in the fulfilment of which all co-operate. Hence, the idea of 'community' is evident in this injunction, as it is emphasized elsewhere in the Qur'ān and in the traditions of the Prophet. This idea is central to the concept of Islam which is a religion and a way of life. Nevertheless, the responsibility and accountability of the individual are clearly defined and strongly emphasized. Those who scale the ascent, as defined here in the Qur'ān, shall have their dwelling place on the right hand, which indicates that they will enjoy a happy recompense for what they do in this life.

"*And those who deny Our revelations shall be on the left hand, with fire closing in upon them.*" (Verses 19–20) There is no need here to identify this group with more than '*those who deny Our revelations*,' as this is enough to settle the issue. Nothing can be good if coupled with unbelief. All evil is contained and encompassed by the denial of God. There is no point in saying that this group do not free slaves or give food to the needy, and, moreover, they deny Our revelations. For such a denial renders worthless any action they may do. They dwell on the left hand, which indicates their degradation and disgrace. These people cannot scale the ascent.

"*With fire closing in upon them.*" (Verse 20) That is, they are encircled by it either in the sense that they are locked within it, or in the sense that it is their eternal abode. Its being close above them gives them no chance of breaking away from it. The two meanings are quite interesting.

These are then the fundamental facts concerning human life laid down from the point of view of faith, in a limited space but with great power and clarity. This remains the distinctive characteristic of Qur'ānic style.

SŪRAH 91

Al-Shams

(The Sun)

Al-Shams (The Sun)

سُورَةُ الشَّمْسِ

In the name of God, the Beneficent, the Merciful.

بِسْمِ ٱللَّهِ ٱلرَّحْمَٰنِ ٱلرَّحِيمِ

By the sun and his morning brightness, (1)

وَٱلشَّمْسِ وَضُحَىٰهَا ١

by the moon as she follows him, (2)

وَٱلْقَمَرِ إِذَا تَلَىٰهَا ٢

by the day, which reveals his splendour, (3)

وَٱلنَّهَارِ إِذَا جَلَّىٰهَا ٣

by the night, which veils him. (4)

وَٱلَّيْلِ إِذَا يَغْشَىٰهَا ٤

By the heaven and its construction, (5)

وَٱلسَّمَآءِ وَمَا بَنَىٰهَا ٥

by the earth and its spreading, (6)

وَٱلۡأَرۡضِ وَمَا طَحَىٰهَا ٦

by the soul and its moulding (7)

وَنَفۡسٖ وَمَا سَوَّىٰهَا ٧

and inspiration with knowledge of wickedness and righteousness. (8)

فَأَلۡهَمَهَا فُجُورَهَا وَتَقۡوَىٰهَا ٨

Successful is the one who keeps it pure, (9)

قَدۡ أَفۡلَحَ مَن زَكَّىٰهَا ٩

and ruined is the one who corrupts it. (10)

وَقَدۡ خَابَ مَن دَسَّىٰهَا ١٠

In their overweening arrogance the people of Thamūd denied the truth, (11)

كَذَّبَتۡ ثَمُودُ بِطَغۡوَىٰهَآ ١١

when their most hapless wretch broke forth. (12)

إِذِ ٱنۢبَعَثَ أَشۡقَىٰهَا ١٢

God's Messenger said to them: 'It is a she-camel belonging to God, so let her have her drink.' (13)

فَقَالَ لَهُمۡ رَسُولُ ٱللَّهِ نَاقَةَ ٱللَّهِ
وَسُقۡيَٰهَا ١٣

But they rejected him, and cruelly slaughtered her. For this their sin their Lord let loose His scourge upon them, and razed their city to the ground. (14)

فَكَذَّبُوهُ فَعَقَرُوهَا فَدَمۡدَمَ عَلَيۡهِمۡ
رَبُّهُم بِذَنۢبِهِمۡ فَسَوَّىٰهَا ١٤

He does not fear what may follow. (15)	وَلَا يَخَافُ عُقْبَٰهَا ۝١٥

Overview

This *sūrah*, which maintains the same rhyme in all its verses and keeps the same musical beat throughout, starts with several aesthetic touches which seem to spring out from the surrounding universe and its phenomena. These phenomena form the framework which encompasses the great truth which is the subject matter of the *sūrah*, namely, the nature of man, his inherent abilities, choice of action, and responsibility in determining his own fate.

This *sūrah* also refers to the story of the Thamūd and their negative attitude to the warnings they received from God's messenger, to their killing of the she-camel, and finally their complete annihilation. This provides an example of the unpromising prospects which await those who corrupt their souls instead of keeping them pure and who do not confine themselves within the limits of piety. "*Successful is the one who keeps it pure, and ruined is the one who corrupts it.*" (Verses 9–10)

God's Solemn Oath

> *By the sun and his morning brightness, by the moon as she follows him, by the day, which reveals his splendour, by the night, which veils him. By the heaven and its construction, by the earth and its spreading, by the soul and its moulding and inspiration with knowledge of wickedness and righteousness. Successful is the one who keeps it pure, and ruined is the one who corrupts it.* (Verses 1–10)

God swears by these objects and universal phenomena as He swears by the human soul, how it is fashioned and the inspiration it receives. The oath gives these creatures an added significance and draws man's attention to them. Man ought to contemplate these phenomena and try to appreciate their value and the purpose of their creation.

There exists in fact, some kind of a special language through which the human heart communicates with the universe. This language is part of human nature. It is a language which does not use sounds and articulation. It is a communication to hearts and an inspiration to souls which come alive whenever man looks up to the universe for an inspiring or cheerful sight. Hence, the Qur'ān frequently urges man to reflect upon his surroundings. It does this in various ways, sometimes directly and sometimes with hints, incidental touches and stimuli. In this case, for example, some phenomena of the universe are made the subject of God's oath, in order to serve as a framework for what follows in the *sūrah*. These explicit directives and indirect hints are very frequent in the *sūrahs* of the present volume. There is hardly any *sūrah* which does not encourage man, in one way or another, to communicate with the universe, in secret language, so that he may appreciate its signs and understand its address.

Here we have an inspiring oath by the sun and the mid-morning. The oath also specifies the time when the sun rises above the horizon, when it is indeed at its most beautiful. Indeed, mid-morning is, in winter, a time of refreshing warmth. In summer, it is a time when the atmosphere is just mild and fresh before the blazing heat of midday sets in, and the sun is at its clearest.

The oath is also by the moon as she follows the sun and spreads her beautiful and clear light. Between the moon and the human heart there is an age-long fascination that is well established in men's inmost souls. It is a fascination that is born anew every time the two meet. The moon issues her own special whispers and inspirations to the human heart, and she sings her songs of praise of God, the Creator. On a clear night, one can almost feel oneself sailing through the moonlight, clearing one's worries and enjoying perfect bliss as one feels the hand of the Maker beyond this perfect creation.

God also swears by the day as it reveals the sun. The Arabic wording of this verse, *wan-nahāri idhā jallāhā*, makes the possessive pronoun attached to 'splendour' ambiguous. Initially, one tends to take it as if it refers to the sun. The general context, however, suggests that it refers to the earth as it is lit by the sun. This method of changing referents is widely employed in the Qur'ān when the change is easily noticed and the subject matter familiar. Here we have a discreet allusion to the fact that sunlight reveals the earth and has a great effect on human life. Our familiarity with the sun and its light makes us tend to overlook its beauty and function. This Qur'ānic hint alerts us anew to this magnificent daily spectacle.

The same applies to the next verse, "*by the night, which veils him.*" (Verse 4) This is the opposite of what happens during the day. Night time is like a screen that covers and hides everything. It also leaves its own impressions on everyone, and its impact on human life is no less important than that of the day time.

God then swears "*by the heaven and its construction.*" (Verse 5) When heaven is mentioned, our immediate thoughts go to the huge dome-like sky above us in which we see the stars and the planets moving, each in its orbit. But we are in fact uncertain of the exact nature of heaven. However, what we see above us does bear the idea of building and construction because it looks to us a firm and solid whole. As to how it is built and what keeps it together as it floats in infinite space, we have no answer. All that has been advanced in this field is only theory that is liable to be invalidated or modified. We are certain, however, that God's hand is the one which holds this structure together, as emphasized elsewhere in the Qur'ān: "*It is God who upholds the heavens and the earth lest they collapse. Should they collapse none could uphold them after He will have ceased to do so.*" (35: 41) This is the only definite and absolute truth about the matter.

The oath then includes the earth and its spreading as preparatory to the emergence of life. Indeed, human and animal life would not have been possible had the earth not been spread out. It is indeed the special characteristics and the natural laws which God has incorporated in the making of this earth that make life on it possible, according to His will and plan. It appears that if any of these laws were violated or upset, life on earth would become impossible or change its course. The most important of these is perhaps the spreading out of the earth which is also mentioned in *Sūrah* 79, The Pluckers: "*After that He spread out the earth. He brought out water from it, and brought forth its pastures.*" (79: 30–31) When the *sūrah* mentions the spreading out of the earth, it actually reminds us of God's hand which brought this about.

A Look into the Human Soul

The *sūrah* moves on to state the basic truth about man, and relates this truth to the various phenomena of the universe, for man is one of the most remarkable wonders in this harmonious creation: "*By the soul and its moulding and inspiration with knowledge of wickedness and righteousness. Successful is the one who keeps it pure, and ruined is the one who corrupts it.*" (Verses 7–10)

The basis of the Islamic concept of human psychology is outlined in these four verses, along with verse 10 of the preceding *sūrah*, The City, "*And [We have] shown him the two paths,*" and verse 3 in *Sūrah* 76, Man, which says: "*We have shown him the right path, be he grateful or ungrateful.*" They supplement the verses which point out the duality in man's make-up in *Sūrah* 38, Ṣād, which says: "*Your Lord said to the angels, 'I am creating man from clay. When I have fashioned him, and breathed of My spirit into him, kneel down and prostrate yourselves before him.'*" (38: 71–72) These verses also supplement and relate to the verses which define man's responsibility and accountability for his actions, such as the one in *Sūrah* 74, The Cloaked One, which reads: "*Everyone is held in pledge for whatever he has wrought,*" and the verse in *Sūrah* 13, Thunder, which states that God's attitude to man is directly related to man's own behaviour: "*God does not change a people's lot until they change what is in their hearts.*" (13: 11) These and similar verses define the Islamic view of man with perfect clarity.

God has created man with a duality of nature and ability. What we mean by duality is that the two ingredients in his make-up, i.e. earth's clay and God' spirit, form within him two equal tendencies to good or evil, to either follow divine guidance or go astray. Man is just as capable of recognizing the good as he is of recognizing the evil in everything he encounters, and he is equally capable of directing himself one way or the other. This dual ability is deeply ingrained within him. All external factors, like divine messages, only serve to awaken his ability and help it take its chosen way. In other words, these factors do not create this innate ability; they only help it to develop.

In addition to his innate ability, man is equipped with a conscious faculty which determines his line of action. Hence, he is responsible for his actions and decisions. He who uses this faculty to strengthen his inclinations to what is good and to purify himself and to weaken his evil drive will be prosperous and successful. By contrast, a person who uses this faculty to suppress the good in him will ruin himself: "*Successful is the one who keeps it pure, and ruined is the one who corrupts it.*" (Verses 9–10)

There must be, then, an element of responsibility attached to man's conscious faculty and freedom of choice. Since he is free to choose between his tendencies, his freedom must be coupled with responsibility. He is assigned a definite task related to the power given to him. But God, the Compassionate, does not leave man with no guidance other than his natural impulses or his conscious, decision-making faculty. God helps him by sending him messages which lay down accurate and permanent criteria, and points out to him the signs, within him and in the world at large, which should help him choose the right path and clear his way of any obstructions so that he can see the truth. Thus, he recognizes his way easily and clearly and his conscious decision-making faculty functions in full knowledge of the nature of the direction it chooses and the implications of that choice.

This is what God has willed for man and whatever takes place within this framework is a direct fulfilment of His will.

From this very general outline of the Islamic concept of man emerge a number of vital and valuable facts: firstly, that this concept elevates man to the high position of being responsible for his actions and allows him freedom of choice, within the confines of God's will that has granted him this freedom. Responsibility and freedom of choice, therefore, make man the honoured creature of this world, a position worthy of the creature in whom God has blown something of His own spirit and whom He has made with His own hand and raised above most of His creation.

Secondly, it puts man's fate in his own hands – according to God's will as already explained – and makes him responsible for it. This stimulates caution in him as well as a positive sense of fear of God. For he knows then that God's will is fulfilled through his own actions and decisions: "*God does not change a people's lot until they change what is in their hearts.*" (13: 11) This is in itself a great responsibility which demands that one should always be alert.

Thirdly, it reminds man of his permanent need to refer to the criteria fixed by God in order to ensure that his desires do not get the better of him. Thus man stays near to God, follows His guidance and illuminates his way by divine light. Indeed, the standard of purity man can achieve is limitless.

Historical Example

The *sūrah* then gives an example of the failure which befalls those who corrupt themselves, and erect a barrier between themselves and divine guidance: "*In their overweening arrogance the people of Thamūd denied the truth, when their most hapless wretch broke forth. God's Messenger said to them: 'It is a she-camel belonging to God, so let her have her drink.' But they rejected him, and cruelly slaughtered her. For this their sin their Lord let loose His scourge upon them, and razed their city to the ground. He does not fear what may follow.*" (Verses 11–15)

The story of the Thamūd and their messenger, Ṣāliḥ, is mentioned several times in the Qur'ān. A discussion of it is given every time it occurs. The reader may refer for further details to the commentary on *Sūrah* 89, The Dawn, in this volume. The present *sūrah*, however, states that the people of Thamūd rejected their prophet and accused him of lying simply because they were arrogant and insolent. Their transgression is represented here by the most hapless wretch among them rushing to slaughter the she-camel. He is the most wretched as a result of his crime. Their messenger had warned them in advance, saying, "*It is a she-camel belonging to God, so let her have her drink.*" This was his condition when they asked him for a sign. The sign was that the she-camel had the water for herself one day and left it for the rest of the cattle the next day. The she-camel must have had something else peculiar to her, but we shall not go into detail because God has not told us about it. The Thamūd, however, did not heed their messenger's warnings but killed the she-camel. The person who perpetrated the crime, the arch sinner, is the most-wretched, but they were all held responsible because they did not take him to task. On the contrary, they applauded what he did. A basic principle of Islam is that society bears a collective responsibility in this life. This does not conflict with the principle of individual responsibility in the hereafter when everyone is answerable for his own deeds. It is a sin, however, not to counsel and urge one another to adhere to what is good and not to punish evil and transgression.

As a result of the Thamūd's arrogance and their outrageous crime, a calamity befell them: "*For this their sin their Lord let loose His scourge upon them, and razed their city to the ground.*" (Verse 14) The Arabic verse uses the verb *damdama* for '*let loose His scourge*', which creates, by its repetitiveness, an added feeling of horror, as we learn that the city was completely razed to the ground.

"*He does not fear what may follow.*" (Verse 15) All praises and glorification be to Him. Whom, what and why should He fear? The meaning aimed at here is what the statement entails: he who does not fear the consequences punishes most severely. This is true of God's punishment.

In conclusion, we say the *sūrah* provides a link between the human soul, the basic facts of the universe, its constant and repetitive scenes and God's unfailing law of punishing tyrant transgressors. This He does according to His own wise planning which sets a time for everything and a purpose for every action. He is the Lord of man, the universe and fate.

SŪRAH 92

Al-Layl

(The Night)

Al-Layl (The Night)

سُورَةُ اللَّيۡلِ

In the name of God, the Beneficent, the Merciful.

بِسۡمِ ٱللَّهِ ٱلرَّحۡمَٰنِ ٱلرَّحِيمِ

By the night when she lets fall her darkness, (1)

وَٱلَّيۡلِ إِذَا يَغۡشَىٰ ١

by the day in full splendour, (2)

وَٱلنَّهَارِ إِذَا تَجَلَّىٰ ٢

by Him who created the male and the female: (3)

وَمَا خَلَقَ ٱلذَّكَرَ وَٱلۡأُنثَىٰٓ ٣

surely your endeavours have divergent ends. (4)

إِنَّ سَعۡيَكُمۡ لَشَتَّىٰ ٤

As for him who gives and is God-fearing (5)

فَأَمَّا مَنۡ أَعۡطَىٰ وَٱتَّقَىٰ ٥

and believes in the truth of the ultimate good, (6)

وَصَدَّقَ بِٱلْحُسْنَىٰ ﴿٦﴾

We shall smooth the way to perfect ease. (7)

فَسَنُيَسِّرُهُۥ لِلْيُسْرَىٰ ﴿٧﴾

But as for him who is a miser and deems himself self-sufficient, (8)

وَأَمَّا مَنۢ بَخِلَ وَٱسْتَغْنَىٰ ﴿٨﴾

and rejects the truth of the ultimate good, (9)

وَكَذَّبَ بِٱلْحُسْنَىٰ ﴿٩﴾

We shall smooth the way to affliction. (10)

فَسَنُيَسِّرُهُۥ لِلْعُسْرَىٰ ﴿١٠﴾

What will his wealth avail him when he goes down [to his grave]. (11)

وَمَا يُغْنِى عَنْهُ مَالُهُۥٓ إِذَا تَرَدَّىٰٓ ﴿١١﴾

It is for Us to give guidance, (12)

إِنَّ عَلَيْنَا لَلْهُدَىٰ ﴿١٢﴾

and Ours is the life to come, and this first life. (13)

وَإِنَّ لَنَا لَلْءَاخِرَةَ وَٱلْأُولَىٰ ﴿١٣﴾

I warn you, therefore, of the raging fire, (14)

فَأَنذَرْتُكُمْ نَارًا تَلَظَّىٰ ﴿١٤﴾

which none shall have to endure but the most hapless wretch, (15)

لَا يَصْلَىٰهَآ إِلَّا ٱلْأَشْقَى ﴿١٥﴾

who denies the truth and turns away. (16)

ٱلَّذِى كَذَّبَ وَتَوَلَّىٰ ﴿١٦﴾

Kept away from it will be him who is God-fearing, (17)	وَسَيُجَنَّبُهَا ٱلْأَتْقَى ﴿١٧﴾
who gives away his money to purify himself, (18)	ٱلَّذِى يُؤْتِى مَالَهُۥ يَتَزَكَّىٰ ﴿١٨﴾
not in recompense of any favours done him by anyone. (19)	وَمَا لِأَحَدٍ عِندَهُۥ مِن نِّعْمَةٍ تُجْزَىٰٓ ﴿١٩﴾
but only out of a longing for the countenance of his Lord, the Most High. (20)	إِلَّا ٱبْتِغَآءَ وَجْهِ رَبِّهِ ٱلْأَعْلَىٰ ﴿٢٠﴾
He shall indeed be well pleased. (21)	وَلَسَوْفَ يَرْضَىٰ ﴿٢١﴾

Overview

Within a framework of scenes taken from the universe and human nature, this *sūrah* states emphatically the basic facts of action and reward. This issue has diverse aspects: "*Surely your endeavours have divergent ends. As for him who gives and is God-fearing and believes in the truth of the ultimate good, We shall smooth the way to perfect ease. But as for him who is a miser and deems himself self-sufficient, and rejects the truth of the ultimate good, We shall smooth the way to affliction.*" (Verses 4–10)

The end in the hereafter is also varied, according to the type of action and the direction taken in this life: "*I warn you, therefore, of the raging fire, which none shall have to endure but the most hapless wretch, who denies the truth and turns away. Kept away from it will be him who is God-fearing, who gives away his money to purify himself.*" (Verses 14–18)

The subject matter of the *sūrah*, i.e. action and reward, is by nature double directional, so the framework chosen for it at the beginning of the *sūrah* is of dual colouring. It is based on contrasting aspects in the creation of man and the universe: "*By the night when she lets fall her darkness, by the day in full splendour, by Him who created the male and the female.*" (Verses 1–3) This is one form of artistic harmony used extensively in the Qur'ān.

An Oath by Universal Phenomena

"*By the night when she lets fall her darkness, by the day in full splendour, by Him who created the male and the female.*" (Verses 1–3) God swears by these two of His signs, namely, the night and the day, and describes them by the scene each produces on the horizon: the night as she enshrouds everything with her veil of darkness, and the day as it attains its full splendour. The night covers and conceals the land and all there is on it, and the day brightens up and makes every object apparent and visible. These times contrast in the astrological cycle and in their respective scenes, qualities and effects. God also swears by His creation of all species in two contrasting sexes: "*By Him who created the male and the female.*" (Verse 3) This completes the contrast both in the general atmosphere of the *sūrah* and in the facts it emphasizes.

The night and the day are two general phenomena which carry a certain message with which they inspire human hearts. The human soul is automatically affected by the cycle of the night and its curtain and the day and its splendid brightness. This continuous succession of night and day speaks about the universe, its mysterious secrets and phenomena over which man has no control. It suggests that there is a power which controls time in the universe as if it was a simple wheel. It also tells of never-ending change in the universe.

As one contemplates and meditates upon these phenomena one is bound to conclude that there is an able hand which controls the universe and alternates the night and day in that perfect, unfailing accuracy. One is also bound to conclude that the hand of God also controls the lives of men. He has not created them in vain, and He does not abandon them to lead a life without purpose.

However unbelievers try to drown this reality and divert attention away from it, our hearts remain responsive to this universe. We receive its intimations and ponder over its changes and phenomena. Contemplation and meditation endorse our innate feeling that there is a Controller whose presence is bound to be felt and recognized in spite of all conceited denials.

The same applies to the creation of male and female. In man and mammals it all starts with a living germ settling in a womb, a sperm which unites with a cell. What is the reason then for this difference in outcome? What is it that tells one germ to be a male, and instructs another to be a female? Discovery of the operative factors does not make the matter any different. How do the male factors exist in one case and the female in another? What makes the end product, i.e. division of the species into two sexes, so fitting with the course of life as a whole and a guarantee of its continuity through procreation?

Is it all a coincidence? Even coincidence has a rule which deems it impossible for all those elements to come together accidentally. The only explanation is that there is a Controller in charge who creates the male and the female according to a carefully worked out plan which has a definite objective. There is no room for chance in the order of this universe.

Moreover, the male and female division is not limited to mammalia alone: it is applicable to all animate species, including plants. Singularity and oneness belong only to the Creator who has no parallel whatever.

A Journey with Divergent Ends

God swears by these contrasting aspects of the universe and of man's creation and constitution that the striving of human beings is diverse. Since the roads they follow lead to different ends, their rewards are also diverse. Good is not the same as evil; following right guidance is unlike wrong-doing; and righteousness is different from corruption. Generosity and God-consciousness are unlike hoarding and conceit. The faithful are totally different from those devoid of faith. Variance of ways necessitates variance of destinations: "*Surely your endeavours have divergent ends. As for him who gives and is God-fearing and believes in the truth of the ultimate good, We shall smooth the way to perfect ease. But as for him who is a miser and deems himself self-sufficient, and rejects the truth of the ultimate good, We shall smooth the way to affliction. What will his wealth avail him when he goes down [to his grave].*" (Verses 4–11)

"*Your endeavours have divergent ends.*" (Verse 4) These endeavours vary in essence, motives, directions and results. Men have diverse temperaments, environments, concepts and concerns, so much so that every man seems to be a distinct world unto himself living in his own, special planet.

This is a fact, but along with it there is another general fact which applies to all beings and their different worlds. It groups them into two distinct classes and two contrasting positions. It assigns to each its distinctive label: one "*who gives and is God-fearing and believes in the truth of the ultimate good;*" and another "*who is a miser and deems himself self-sufficient, and rejects the truth of the ultimate good.*"

These are the two positions at which disparate souls line up where all diverse striving and divergent ways of life end. Each group has its way in this life smoothed, with all obstructions removed: "*As for him who gives and is God-fearing and believes in the truth of the ultimate good, We shall smooth the way to perfect ease.*" (Verses 5–7) He who is charitable, God-fearing and believes in an ideology which is synonymous with ultimate good has indeed done his best to purify himself, seeking right guidance. Hence, he deserves the help and grace which God has, by His own will, committed Himself to provide. For without this grace man finds himself absolutely helpless. He whose path to perfect ease and comfort is made smooth by God achieves something great. What is more, such a person achieves this great goal in this life without difficulty. He lives in ease. Indeed, ease flows from him to all around him. Ease becomes characteristic of his movement, action and handling of all things and situations. Success and quiet contentedness become the distinctive mark of his life in all its details and general aspects. He attains the highest grade of all, in the sense that he joins the Prophet as a recipient of God's promise to His Messenger: "*We shall smooth your way to perfect ease.*" (87: 8)

> *But as for him who is a miser and deems himself self-sufficient, and rejects the truth of the ultimate good, We shall smooth the way to affliction. What will his wealth avail him when he goes down [to his grave].* (Verses 8–11)

He who sacrifices nothing of himself or his wealth, professes that he is in no need of His Lord or His guidance and disbelieves in His message and religion, makes himself vulnerable to evil. For so doing he deserves that everything should be made hard for him. Hence, God makes easy his path to affliction, and withholds from him all kinds of help. God makes every stride he takes really hard, drives him away from the path of right guidance, and leaves him to traverse the valleys of misery, although he may imagine himself to be taking the road to success. How greatly mistaken he is! He loses balance: thus he tries to avoid falling only to go down heavily, and finds himself further away from the path set by God, deprived of His pleasure. When he eventually goes down to his grave, he can make no use of the wealth he has hoarded. It is that very wealth that has caused him to imagine himself in no need of God or His guidance. "*What will his wealth avail him when he goes down [to his grave].*" (Verse 11) Facilitating evil and sin is the same as facilitating the way to affliction, even though the sinful may be successful and prosperous in this life. For is there any affliction worse than hell? Indeed, hell is affliction itself!

Thus the first part of the *sūrah* ends having made clear that there are only two ways for all mankind at all times and in all places. All humanity forms into two parties, under two headings, however numerous their colours and forms may be.

And Different Ends

The second part states the fate of each group. It emphasizes firstly that the end and reward of each group is fair and inevitable, for guidance has been provided and warnings have been issued: "*It is for Us to give guidance, and Ours is the life to come, and this first life. I warn you, therefore, of the raging fire, which none shall have to endure but the most hapless wretch, who denies the truth and turns away. Kept away from it will be him who is God-fearing, who gives away his money to purify himself, not in recompense of any favours done him by anyone but only out of a longing for the countenance of his Lord, the Most High. He shall indeed be well pleased.*" (Verses 12–21)

One aspect of God's grace and mercy to His servants is that He has taken it upon Himself to provide clear guidance that is readily acceptable to human nature, and to explain it as well through His messages and messengers, and by means of the signs He has provided. Thus, no one has a valid argument for deviation, and no one will suffer injustice: "*It is for Us to give guidance.*" (Verse 12) Then follows a straightforward statement of the essence of power which has control over man and everything around him, from which he can have no shelter: "*and Ours is the life to come, and this first life.*" (Verse 13)

By way of elaboration on the two facts just mentioned, namely, God's provision of guidance and that to Him belongs this life and the hereafter, i.e. the realms of action and reward, there is a reminder to us that He has given clear warning to us all: "*I warn you, therefore, of the raging fire.*" (Verse 14) It is only the most wretched of mankind who are thrown in this fire. Indeed there is no wretchedness worse than suffering in hell: "*None shall have to endure [it] but the most hapless wretch.*" (Verse 15) We then have a definition of such a wretched person. It is he "*who denies the truth and turns away.*" (Verse 16) He denies this message and turns away from divine guidance. He does not answer his Lord's beckoning so that He may guide him as He has promised any who come towards Him with an open mind.

"*Kept away from it will be him who is God-fearing.*" (Verse 17) A person who fears God will be the happiest, in contrast to the most hapless wretch. The *sūrah* similarly gives a definition of such a person. He is the one "*who gives away his money to purify himself.*" (Verse 18) He has no vain motive or need to satisfy any snobbery. He spends it voluntarily not out of any indebtedness, seeking gratitude from no one. His only objective is the pleasure of his Lord, the Most Exalted: "*Not in recompense of any favours done him by anyone but only out of a longing for the countenance of his Lord, the Most High.*" (Verses 19–20)

What can the righteous person expect in return for spending his money in self-purification, and for seeking the pleasure of his Lord? The reward which the Qur'ān states is indeed surprising, and very unfamiliar: "*He shall indeed be well pleased.*" (Verse 21) It is the pleasure that fills the believer's heart and soul, animates everything in his life, and radiates to all around him. What a reward, and what grace! "*He shall indeed be well pleased.*" He will be satisfied with his religion, his Lord and his destiny. He will be content with whatever befalls him of comfort or discomfort, and whether he is poor or wealthy. He will be free of anxiety and hard feelings. He does not worry about his burden being too heavy or his goal being too far. This satisfaction is in itself a reward, great beyond description. Only the person who sacrifices himself and his wealth for it and who seeks to purify himself and to win God's pleasure deserves this reward. It is God alone who can pour such a reward into those hearts which submit to Him with all sincerity and pure devotion. Having paid the price, the believer "*shall indeed be well pleased.*" At this point, the reward comes as a surprise, but it is a surprise awaited by the one who attains the standard of the righteous, whose main qualifications are spending for self-purification and seeking God's pleasure. Such a person will be well pleased and well satisfied.

SŪRAH 93

Al-Ḍuḥā

(The Morning Hours)

Al-Ḍuḥā (The Morning Hours)

سُورَةُ الضُّحَىٰ

In the name of God, the Beneficent, the Merciful.

بِسْمِ اللَّهِ الرَّحْمَٰنِ الرَّحِيمِ

By the bright morning hours, (1)

وَالضُّحَىٰ ١

and the night when it grows still and dark, (2)

وَاللَّيْلِ إِذَا سَجَىٰ ٢

your Lord has neither forsaken you, nor does He hate you. (3)

مَا وَدَّعَكَ رَبُّكَ وَمَا قَلَىٰ ٣

Surely the life to come will be better for you than this present life. (4)

وَلَلْآخِرَةُ خَيْرٌ لَّكَ مِنَ الْأُولَىٰ ٤

And, certainly, in time your Lord will be bounteous to you and you will be well pleased. (5)

وَلَسَوْفَ يُعْطِيكَ رَبُّكَ فَتَرْضَىٰ ٥

Has He not found you an orphan and given you a shelter? (6)	أَلَمْ يَجِدْكَ يَتِيمًا فَـَٔاوَىٰ ﴿٦﴾
And found you in error, and guided you? (7)	وَوَجَدَكَ ضَآلًّا فَهَدَىٰ ﴿٧﴾
And found you poor and enriched you? (8)	وَوَجَدَكَ عَآئِلًا فَأَغْنَىٰ ﴿٨﴾
Therefore do not wrong the orphan, (9)	فَأَمَّا ٱلْيَتِيمَ فَلَا تَقْهَرْ ﴿٩﴾
nor chide away the beggar, (10)	وَأَمَّا ٱلسَّآئِلَ فَلَا تَنْهَرْ ﴿١٠﴾
but speak of your Lord's favours. (11)	وَأَمَّا بِنِعْمَةِ رَبِّكَ فَحَدِّثْ ﴿١١﴾

Overview

This *sūrah*, in subject matter, expression, images, connotations and rhythm provides a touch of tenderness and mercy. It is a message of affection, the touch of a benevolent hand to soothe pain and remove hardship. At the same time, it generates an air of contentment and confident hope.

The *sūrah* is dedicated in its entirety to the Prophet (peace be upon him). It is a message from his Lord which touches his heart with pleasure, joy, tranquillity and contentment. All-in-all, it proffers mercy and compassion to his restless soul and suffering heart.

Several accounts mention that the revelation of the Qur'ān to the Prophet came, at one stage, to a halt and that the angel Gabriel stopped coming to him for a while. The unbelievers therefore said, "Muḥammad's Lord has bidden him farewell!" God therefore revealed this *sūrah*.

Revelation, Gabriel's visits and the link with God were the Prophet's whole equipment along his precarious path. They were his only solace in the face of hard rejection and his sole comfort against outright repudiation. They were the source from which he derived his strength to stand steadfast against the unbelievers who were intent on rebuff and refusal, and on directing a wicked, vile attack against the Prophet's message and the faith he preached.

So when the revelation was withheld, the source of strength for the Prophet was cut off. His life spring was sapped and he longed for his heart's friend. Alone he was left in the wilderness, without sustenance, water, or the accustomed companionship of his beloved friend. It was a situation which heavily taxed human endurance.

Then this *sūrah* was revealed and it came as a river of compassion, mercy, hope, comfort and reassurance. "*Your Lord has neither forsaken you, nor does He hate you. Surely the life to come will be better for you than this present life. And, certainly, in time your Lord will be bounteous to you and you will be well pleased.*" (Verses 3–5) Your Lord has never before left you or rejected you, or even denied you His mercy or protection. "*Has He not found you an orphan and given you a shelter? And found you in error, and guided you? And found you poor and enriched you?*" (Verses 6–8)

Do you not see the proof of all this in your own life? Do you not feel it in your heart? Do you not observe it in your world? Most certainly, "*your Lord has neither forsaken you, nor does He hate you.*" (Verse 3) Never was His mercy taken away from you and nor will it be. "*Surely the life to come will be better for you than this present life.*" (Verse 4) And there will be much more: "*And, certainly, in time your Lord will be bounteous to you and you will be well pleased.*" (Verse 5)

This statement is given in the framework of a universal phenomenon: "*By the bright morning hours, and the night when it grows still and dark.*" (Verses 1–2) The expression spreads an air of affection, kindliness and complete satisfaction. "*Your Lord has neither forsaken you, nor does He hate you. Surely the life to come will be better for you than this present life. And, certainly, in time your Lord will be bounteous to you and you will be well pleased. Has He not found you an orphan and given you a shelter? And found you in error, and guided you? And found you poor and enriched you?"* (Verses 3–8) Such tenderness, mercy, satisfaction and solace are all felt in the sweet and soothing words which softly thread along the *sūrah* echoing the morning hours and still night, the times most conducive to clarity. During these periods one's reflections flow like a stream, and the human soul is best able to communicate with the universe and its Creator. It feels the universe worshipping its Lord and turning towards Him in praise with joy and happiness. In addition, the night is described as growing still and dark. It is not the dark gloomy night as such but the still, clear and tranquil night, covered with a light cloud of sweet longing and kind reflection. It is a picture similar to that of the orphan's life. More still, the night is cleared away by the crossing morning and thus the colours of the picture beautifully match those of the framework, making for perfect harmony.

The scene drawn here is one of perfect beauty. Such perfection is divine, unparalleled and inimitable.

Unfailing Favours

> *By the bright morning hours, and the night when it grows still and dark, your Lord has neither forsaken you, nor does He hate you. Surely the life to come will be better for you than this present life. And, certainly, in time your Lord will be bounteous to you and you will be well pleased.* (Verses 1–5)

God vows by these two calm and inspiring periods of time and establishes a relationship between natural phenomena and human feelings. Thus, mutual response is encouraged between human hearts and the universe, which is beautiful, alive and sympathetic to all living beings. Hence, hearts live in peace with the world, relaxed and happy.

This mode of expression is particularly appropriate in this *sūrah* as the feeling of fellowship is stressed here. It is as if the Prophet is being told straightaway that his Lord had already blessed him with the fellowship of the world around him and that he was by no means forsaken or left alone.

Then follows a clear and emphatic assertion: "*Your Lord has neither forsaken you, nor does He hate you.*" (Verse 3) He has not left you, nor has He been harsh to you as is alleged by those who want to afflict your heart and soul. For He is your Lord and you belong to Him. He is your sustainer and protector. God's favours on you have neither run out nor have they been stopped. You, Muḥammad, are to get much more and better favours in the hereafter than you are getting in this life. "*Surely the life to come will be better for you than this present life.*" (Verse 4)

God is saving for you, Muḥammad, what will satisfy you in your mission and ease your hard path and bring about the victory of your message, vindicating the truth you advocate. These thoughts were in fact preoccupying the Prophet's mind as he encountered his people's adamant rejection, ill-treatment, and malice. "*In time, your Lord will be bounteous to you and you will be well pleased.*" (Verse 5)

The *sūrah* then goes on to remind the Prophet of his Lord's attitude towards him from the very beginning of his mission so that he can reflect on how favourably God treats him. This to make him recall the happy memories of divine kindness: "*Has He not found you an orphan and given you a shelter? And found you in error, and guided you? And found you poor and enriched you?*" (Verses 6–8) Reflect on your present life and on your past. Has He ever forsaken you or hated you even before He charged you with prophethood?

You were born an orphan but God protected you. He made so many people kind to you, especially your uncle Abū Ṭālib, though he followed a religion different from yours. You were poor and He made your heart rich with contentment, and made you rich through your business gains and wife's wealth, so that you would not suffer from poverty or yearn for the riches that abound all around you.

You were also brought up in an ignorant society, full of confused beliefs and concepts, where erring ways and practices abounded. You did not like those beliefs, concepts and practices but you could not find a clear and suitable way out. You could find your way neither in the world of *jāhiliyyah*, nor with the followers of Moses and Jesus who adulterated their beliefs, distorted their original form and went astray. But God has guided you through His revelations and the way of life He has laid down, establishing a firm bond between Him and you.

This guidance in the wilderness of disbelief and confusion is the greatest favour of them all. The happiness and reassurance it brings about cannot be matched. The Prophet had been greatly perturbed and afflicted because of the cessation of revelation, and the malicious attitude of the unbelievers during the period of its cessation. Hence comes this reminder to put his heart at ease and to reassure him of his Lord's promise that he will never be abandoned.

God takes the opportunity of mentioning the Prophet's earlier orphanhood, error and poverty in order to instruct him, and all Muslims, to protect every orphan, be charitable to every beggar, and to speak of the great favours God has bestowed on them. The first and most important of these is having been guided to Islam. "*Therefore do not wrong the orphan, nor chide away the beggar, but speak of your Lord's favours.*" (Verses 9–11)

As we have frequently mentioned, these instructions reflect the needs of the day, in that greedy and materialistic society in which the weak, who could not defend their own rights, were not catered for. Islam came to reform that society with God's laws which establish equity, justice and goodwill. Speaking of God's bounties, especially those of guidance and faith, expresses gratitude to Him who has given us all that we have. It is the recipient's practical manifestation of thanks.

SŪRAH 94

Al-Sharḥ

(Solace)

Al-Sharḥ (Solace)

سُورَةُ الشَّرْحِ

In the name of God, the Beneficent, the Merciful.

بِسْمِ ٱللَّهِ ٱلرَّحْمَٰنِ ٱلرَّحِيمِ

Have We not opened up your heart, (1)

أَلَمْ نَشْرَحْ لَكَ صَدْرَكَ ١

and relieved you of your burden, (2)

وَوَضَعْنَا عَنكَ وِزْرَكَ ٢

which weighed heavily on your back? (3)

ٱلَّذِىٓ أَنقَضَ ظَهْرَكَ ٣

And have We not given you high renown? (4)

وَرَفَعْنَا لَكَ ذِكْرَكَ ٤

With every hardship comes ease. (5)

فَإِنَّ مَعَ ٱلْعُسْرِ يُسْرًا ٥

Indeed, with every hardship comes ease. (6)	إِنَّ مَعَ ٱلْعُسْرِ يُسْرًا ﴿٦﴾
When you have completed your task resume your toil, (7)	فَإِذَا فَرَغْتَ فَٱنصَبْ ﴿٧﴾
and to your Lord turn with love. (8)	وَإِلَىٰ رَبِّكَ فَٱرْغَب ﴿٨﴾

This *sūrah* was revealed soon after the preceding one, *Sūrah* 93, The Morning Hours, as if it were a continuation of it. Here, also, the feelings of sympathy and an atmosphere of delightful, friendly discourse abound. It portrays the divine care the Prophet enjoys and explains the measures taken out of concern for him. The *sūrah* also gives the good news of forthcoming relief, points out to the Prophet the secret of ease, and emphasizes his strong ties with God.

"*Have We not opened up your heart, and relieved you of your burden, which weighed heavily on your back? And have We not given you high renown?*" (Verses 1–4) This suggests that the Prophet was troubled for some reason concerning the message he was entrusted with, and the obstacles in its way. These verses also suggest that the difficulties facing his mission weighed heavily on his heart, making him feel the need for urgent help and backing. Hence this comforting address.

"*Have We not opened up your heart,*" so that it may warm to this message? Have We not facilitated it for you, endeared it to you, defined its path and illuminated it for you to see its happy end? Look into your heart! Do you not see it to be full of light, happiness and solace? Reflect on the effects brought about by all the favours bestowed on you! Do you not feel comfort with every difficulty, and find contentment with every kind of deprivation you suffer?

"*And relieved you of your burden, which weighed heavily on your back?*" (Verses 2–3) Your burden was so heavy that it almost broke your back, but We relieved you of that. Relief took the form of giving your heart a lift so that you might feel your mission easier and your burden not so hard to shoulder. Another aspect of the relief was the guidance you received on how to discharge your mission and how to appeal to people's hearts. Furthermore, there is relief for you in the revelation of the Qur'ān which explains the truth and helps you to drive it home to people easily and gently. Do you not feel all this when you think of how heavy your burden was? Do you not feel it to be lighter after We opened up your heart?

"*And have We not given you high renown?*" (Verse 4) We exalted you among those on high, on earth and in the whole universe. We raised your fame high indeed as we associated your name with that of God's whenever it is pronounced. "No Deity but God, Muḥammad is God's Messenger." Indeed, this is the highest degree of praise. It is a position granted only to Muḥammad, with no share of it to anyone else. God has willed that one century should turn after another and generations succeed generations with millions and millions of people in all corners of the world honouring the blessed name of Muḥammad with prayers for peace and blessings to be granted him, and with his profound love entrenched in their hearts. Your fame spread far and wide when your name became associated with this divine way of life.

Certainly the mere fact that you were chosen for this task is an exaltation to which no one else in this universe can ever aspire. How can there remain any feeling of affliction or hardship after this favour which heals all such difficulties?

God, nevertheless, addresses His beloved messenger kindly. He comforts and reassures him, explaining to him how He has given him unceasing ease. "*With hardship comes ease. Indeed, with every hardship comes ease.*" (Verses 5–6) Hardship is never absolute, for ease always accompanies it. When your burden became too heavy, We lifted up your heart and relieved you.

This is strongly emphasized by a literal repetition of the statement: "*With hardship comes ease.*" The repetition suggests that the Prophet had endured serious hardship and much affliction. This reminder recalls the various aspects of care and concern shown to the Prophet and then reassures him emphatically. A matter which afflicts Muḥammad's soul so much must be very serious indeed.

Then follows a statement pointing out the aspects of comfort and the factors contributing to the lifting up of hearts and spirits, which is of great help to Muslims as they travel along their hard and long way: "*When you have completed your task resume your toil, and to your Lord turn with love.*" (Verses 7–8)

With hardship goes ease, so seek relief and solace. When you have finished whatever you may have to do, be it a matter relating to the delivery of your message or an affair of this life, then turn with all your heart to what deserves your toil and striving, namely devotion and dedication in worship. "*And to your Lord turn with love.*" (Verse 8) Seek Him alone and let nothing whatsoever distract you. Do not ever think of the people you call on to believe in Him. A traveller must have his food with him, and this is the real food for your journey. A fighter for a cause needs to have his equipment, and this is the equipment necessary for you. This will provide you with ease in every difficulty you may encounter, and with comfort against every kind of affliction you may suffer.

The *sūrah* ends on the same note as the preceding *sūrah,* The Morning Hours. It leaves us with two intertwined feelings. The first is a realization of the great affection shown to the Prophet, which overwhelmed him because it was the love of his Lord, the Compassionate, the Merciful. The other feeling is one of sympathy shown to his noble self. We can almost feel what was going on in his blessed heart at that time which required this reminder of delightful affection.

It is this mission of Islam: a grave trust and a burden which weighs him down. It is nevertheless the rising of the divine light, the link between mortality and eternity, existence and non-existence.

SŪRAH 95

Al-Tīn

(The Fig)

Al-Tīn (The Fig)

سُورَةُ التِّينِ

In the name of God, the Beneficent, the Merciful.

بِسْمِ اللَّهِ الرَّحْمَٰنِ الرَّحِيمِ

By the fig and the olive, (1)

وَالتِّينِ وَالزَّيْتُونِ ١

and by Mount Sinai, (2)

وَطُورِ سِينِينَ ٢

and by this secure city, (3)

وَهَٰذَا الْبَلَدِ الْأَمِينِ ٣

We indeed have created man in the finest form, (4)

لَقَدْ خَلَقْنَا الْإِنسَانَ فِي أَحْسَنِ تَقْوِيمٍ ٤

then We brought him down to the lowest of the low, (5)

ثُمَّ رَدَدْنَاهُ أَسْفَلَ سَافِلِينَ ٥

except for those who believe and do good deeds; for theirs shall be an unfailing recompense. (6)	إِلَّا ٱلَّذِينَ ءَامَنُوا۟ وَعَمِلُوا۟ ٱلصَّٰلِحَٰتِ فَلَهُمْ أَجْرٌ غَيْرُ مَمْنُونٍ ۝٦
Who, then, can henceforth cause you to deny the Last Judgement? (7)	فَمَا يُكَذِّبُكَ بَعْدُ بِٱلدِّينِ ۝٧
Is not God the most just of judges? (8)	أَلَيْسَ ٱللَّهُ بِأَحْكَمِ ٱلْحَٰكِمِينَ ۝٨

Overview

The basic fact outlined in this *sūrah* is that God has given man an upright nature. This is essentially in perfect harmony with the nature of faith. With faith it attains its ultimate perfection. But when man deviates from this upright nature and from the straight path of faith he sinks into the lowest abyss.

God swears to the validity of this by the fig, *tīn*, the olive, *zaytūn*, Mount Sinai, *Ṭūr Sīnīn* and the secure city of Makkah, *al-balad al-amīn*. As we have already seen in many *sūrahs* in this part of the Qur'ān, this oath is the framework which perfectly fits the essential facts presented within it.

The Ṭūr in Sinai is the mountain on which Moses received his divine summons. The secure city is Makkah, which houses the Ka'bah, God's inviolable house. The relationship between the two on the one hand and religion and faith on the other is obvious. But a similar relationship is not readily clear with regard to the figs and olives. Suggestions as to the significance of these are numerous. It is said that the fig refers to the fig tree in heaven, with the leaves of which Adam and his wife, Eve, tried to cover their private parts. Another suggestion is that it refers to the place where the fig tree appeared on the mountain where Noah's ark landed.

As for the olive, it is suggested that it refers to the Mount of Ṭūr Zaitā in Jerusalem. It is also said that it refers to Jerusalem itself. Another suggestion is that it refers to the olive branch brought back by the pigeon which Noah released from the ship to examine the state of the floods. When the pigeon brought back an olive branch, he knew that the land had reappeared and that vegetation was growing.

A different opinion posits that the fig and olive mentioned in the *sūrah* are simply those two kinds of food with which we are familiar. Alternatively, it is claimed, they are symbols of growth out of land.

There is another reference in the Qur'ān to the olive tree in association with Mount Sinai. The verse there reads as follows: "*And a tree issuing from Mount Sinai which bears oil and seasoning for all to eat.*" (23: 20) This, however, is the only case where reference to the fig tree is made in the Qur'ān.

Hence, we cannot say anything definite on this matter. However, on the basis of parallel frameworks in other *sūrahs*, the most likely explanation of the fig and olive mentioned here is that they refer to certain places or events which have some relevance to religion and faith or to man as the creature fairest in shape and form. This may have been established in heaven where man's life began. The harmony between this detail and the main fact outlined in the *sūrah* is yet another example of the unique method of the Qur'ān whereby the framework fits perfectly with the facts contained within it.

Man's Fair Shape

The essential fact of the *sūrah* is embodied in the verses: "*We indeed have created man in the finest form, then We brought him down to the lowest of the low, except for those who believe and do good deeds; for theirs shall be an unfailing recompense.*" (Verses 4–6)

God has perfected all His creation; and the special emphasis laid here and elsewhere in the Qur'ān on man's being endowed with perfect form shows clearly that man has enjoyed extra divine care. Moreover, God's care for man, despite his distortion of his upright nature and the corruption he indulges in, suggests that God has given him special rank and special weight in the universe. God's care is most clearly apparent in the moulding of man's highly complicated physical structure and his unique spiritual and mental make-up.

The emphasis here is on man's spiritual qualities since these are the ones which drag man down to the most ignoble state when he deviates from his upright nature and turns away from belief in God. Needless to say, man's physical structure does not sink to such a low level. Moreover, the superiority of man's creation is most clearly apparent in his spiritual qualities. He is made in such a way as to be able to attain a sublime standard, superior to that of the highest ranking angels. This is illustrated in the story of the Prophet's ascension to heaven. Then, Gabriel stopped at a certain level and Muḥammad, human as he was, was elevated much higher.

At the same time, man is given the dubious ability to sink down to levels unreached by any other creature: "*Then We brought him down to the lowest of the low.*" (Verse 5) In this case, the animals are superior to him and more upright, since they do not violate their nature. They praise the Lord and fulfil their function on earth as they are guided to do. But man who has been given the fairest form and abilities denies his Lord and so sinks right down.

"*We have created man in the finest form.*" (Verse 4). This is a reference to his nature and abilities. "*Then We brought him down to the lowest of the low.*" (Verse 5) That is, when he forces his nature away from the line God has defined for him. Having laid down the way, God left man to choose whether to follow it or not.

"*Except for those who believe and do good deeds.*" (Verse 6) For these are the ones who stick to their upright nature, consolidate it with faith and righteous deeds, and who elevate it to the highest level it can attain in this world so they can finally attain a life of perfection in the world of perfection: "*For theirs shall be an unfailing recompense.*" (Verse 6) But those who cause their nature to sink to the lowest of the low go down along their slippery road until they reach the lowest level, that is, in hell where their humanity is shed and they are completely debased. Both ends are natural results of two widely different starts and lines of action.

Thus, the importance of faith in human life becomes clear. Faith is the elevating path through which upright human nature ascends to its ultimate perfection. It is the rope stretched between man and his Maker. It is the light showing him where to step along the elevating path. When the rope is cut and the light put out, the inevitable result is the fall down the steep path into the lowest of the low. The clay element in man's make-up separates from the spiritual element and man, along with stones, becomes the fuel for hell-fire.

In light of this fact, the Prophet is addressed in this manner: "*Who, then, can henceforth cause you to deny the Last Judgement? Is not God the most just of judges?*" (Verses 7–8) What makes you, man, deny this religion after you have known this fact, realized the importance of faith in the life of humanity, and become aware of the destiny awaiting those who disbelieve? Why do you turn away from this light and refuse to follow the straight path laid down by God?

"*Is not God the most just of judges*?" (Verse 8) Is not He the most just when He gives this ruling concerning the destiny of creation? Is not God's wisdom clearest and most reassuring as He rules between believers and unbelievers? Justice is certainly clear and wisdom is manifest. Hence, we are taught in a *ḥadīth* related by Abū Hurayrah that when one reads this *sūrah* one should answer the rhetorical question, "*Is not God the most just of judges?*" by saying: "Indeed, and I am a witness to that."

SŪRAH 96

Al- 'Alaq

(The Germ-Cell)

Al- 'Alaq (The Germ-Cell)

سُورَةُ العَلَق

In the name of God, the Beneficent, the Merciful.

بِسْمِ ٱللَّهِ ٱلرَّحْمَٰنِ ٱلرَّحِيمِ

Read in the name of your Lord who has created (1)

ٱقْرَأْ بِٱسْمِ رَبِّكَ ٱلَّذِى خَلَقَ ﴿١﴾

– created man out of a germ-cell. (2)

خَلَقَ ٱلْإِنسَٰنَ مِنْ عَلَقٍ ﴿٢﴾

Read – for your Lord is the most Bountiful One, (3)

ٱقْرَأْ وَرَبُّكَ ٱلْأَكْرَمُ ﴿٣﴾

who has taught the use of the pen, (4)

ٱلَّذِى عَلَّمَ بِٱلْقَلَمِ ﴿٤﴾

taught man what he did not know. (5)

عَلَّمَ ٱلْإِنسَٰنَ مَا لَمْ يَعْلَمْ ﴿٥﴾

Indeed, man becomes grossly overweening, (6)

كَلَّآ إِنَّ ٱلْإِنسَٰنَ لَيَطْغَىٰٓ ﴿٦﴾

once he thinks himself self-sufficient. (7)

أَن رَّءَاهُ ٱسْتَغْنَىٰٓ ﴿٧﴾

Surely to your Lord all must return. (8)

إِنَّ إِلَىٰ رَبِّكَ ٱلرُّجْعَىٰٓ ﴿٨﴾

Look at the one who tries to prevent (9)

أَرَءَيْتَ ٱلَّذِى يَنْهَىٰ ﴿٩﴾

a servant of God from praying! (10)

عَبْدًا إِذَا صَلَّىٰٓ ﴿١٠﴾

Think: does he follow the right guidance (11)

أَرَءَيْتَ إِن كَانَ عَلَى ٱلْهُدَىٰٓ ﴿١١﴾

and enjoin [others to be] God-fearing? (12)

أَوْ أَمَرَ بِٱلتَّقْوَىٰٓ ﴿١٢﴾

Think: if he denies the truth and turns his back, (13)

أَرَءَيْتَ إِن كَذَّبَ وَتَوَلَّىٰٓ ﴿١٣﴾

does he not realize that God sees all? (14)

أَلَمْ يَعْلَم بِأَنَّ ٱللَّهَ يَرَىٰ ﴿١٤﴾

Nay, if he does not desist, We will most certainly drag him by his forelock, (15)

كَلَّا لَئِن لَّمْ يَنتَهِ لَنَسْفَعًۢا بِٱلنَّاصِيَةِ ﴿١٥﴾

his lying, sinful forelock. (16)

نَاصِيَةٍ كَٰذِبَةٍ خَاطِئَةٍ ﴿١٦﴾

Then let him call his henchmen. (17)

فَلْيَدْعُ نَادِيَهُۥ ﴿١٧﴾

We will call the guards of hell. (18)	سَنَدۡعُ ٱلزَّبَانِيَةَ ١٨
No, pay no heed to him, but prostrate yourself and draw closer to God. (19)	كَلَّا لَا تُطِعۡهُ وَٱسۡجُدۡ وَٱقۡتَرِب ۩ ١٩

The First Revelation

It is universally agreed that the opening of this *sūrah* was the first Qur'ānic revelation. The accounts stating that other verses were revealed first are not authentic. Imām Aḥmad transmits the following *ḥadīth* on the authority of 'Ā'ishah, the Prophet's wife:

> The first aspect of revelation to God's Messenger was that his dreams came true. Whatever vision he might have in his sleep would occur exactly as he had seen. Then, he began to enjoy seclusion. He used to retreat alone into the cave of Ḥirā' where he would spend several days in devotion before going back to his family. He used to take some food with him, and when he came back, he would take a fresh supply for another period. He continued to do so until he received the truth while in the cave of Ḥirā'. The angel came to him and said, 'Read.' He replied, 'I am not a reader.' The Prophet says, 'He held me and pressed hard until I was exhausted, then he released me and said, 'Read,' and I replied, 'I am not a reader.' So, he held me and pressed me hard a second time until I was exhausted, then he released me and said, 'Read.' I replied, 'I am not a reader.' He then held me and pressed me hard for the third time. Then he said, 'Read in the name of your Lord who has created – created man out of a germ-cell. Read – for your Lord is the most Bountiful One, who has taught the use of the pen, taught man what he did not know.' The Prophet returned home to Khadījah trembling and said, 'Wrap me! Wrap me!' They wrapped him and his fear subsided. He turned to Khadījah and exclaimed, 'What has

> happened to me?' and related to her what had happened and said, 'I fear for myself.' And Khadījah replied, 'Fear not, be calm and relax. God will not let you suffer any humiliation, because you are kind to your relatives, you speak the truth, you assist anyone in need, you are hospitable to your guests and you help in every just cause.' Then she took him to Waraqah ibn Nawfal, her paternal cousin who was a Christian convert and a scholar with a good knowledge of Arabic, Hebrew and the Bible. He had lost his eyesight and had grown very old. Khadījah said to Waraqah, 'Cousin, would you like to hear what your nephew has to say?' Waraqah said, 'Well, nephew, what have you seen?' The Prophet related to him what he had seen. When he finished, Waraqah said, 'It is the same revelation as was sent down to Moses. I wish I was a young man so that I might be alive when your people turn you away from this city.' The Prophet exclaimed, 'Would they turn me away?' Waraqah answered 'Yes! No man has ever preached a message like yours but was met with enmity. If I live till that day, I will certainly give you all my support.' But Waraqah died soon after that ...

This *ḥadīth* is related by al-Bukhārī and Muslim in both of the most authentic books of the Prophet's traditions. Al-Ṭabarī also relates the following *ḥadīth* on the authority of 'Abdullāh ibn al-Zubayr:

> The Prophet said, 'While I was asleep he came to me carrying a case made of very rich material in which there was a book. He said, 'Read.' I replied, 'I am not a reader.' He pressed me so hard that I felt I was about to die. Then he released me and said, 'Read.' I asked 'What shall I read?' (I said this only out of fear that he might repeat what he had already done to me.) He said, 'Read in the name of your Lord who has created – created man out of a germ-cell. Read – for your Lord is the most Bountiful One, who has taught the use of the pen, taught man what he did not know.' I read it. He stopped, then left me and went away. I woke up feeling that it was actually written in my heart.' The Prophet went on to say, 'No man was ever more loathsome to me than poets

> or the deranged. I could not bear even looking at either. I thought, 'The man (meaning himself) is undoubtedly a poet or deranged. This shall not be said about me among the Quraysh. Let me climb high up in the mountain and throw myself down and get rid of it all.' I went to carry out this intention. When I was half way up in the mountain I heard a voice coming from the heavens saying, 'Muḥammad, you are God's Messenger and I am Gabriel.' I raised my head up to the sky and I saw Gabriel in the image of a man with his feet one next to the other, up on the horizon. He said again, 'Muḥammad, you are God's Messenger and I am Gabriel.' I stood in my place looking up at him. This distracted me from my intention. I was standing there unable to move. I tried to turn my face away from him and to look up at the sky, but wherever I looked, I saw him in front of me. I stood still, moving neither forward nor backward. Khadījah sent her messengers looking for me and I remained standing in my place all the while until they went back to her. He then left me and I went back to my family.

This tradition is related in these details by Ibn Isḥāq, on the authority of Wahb ibn Kaysān.[1]

A Momentous Event

I reflected for a while upon this event. We have all read it many times in books; either those of the Prophet's biography or those explaining the meaning of the Qur'ān. But we either read it casually or give it little thought and go on with our reading.

Yet this is an event which has immense significance. It is an event which has an important bearing on the life of humanity; but much as we try today to perceive its great value, many of its aspects remain beyond our perception. It is no exaggeration to describe this event as the greatest in the long history of human existence.

1. Ibn Hishām, *Al-Sīrah al-Nabawiyyah*, Dār al-Qalam, Beirut, Vol. 1, n.d., pp. 252–3.

The true nature of this event is that God, the Great, the Compeller, the Almighty, the Supreme, the Sovereign of the whole universe, out of His benevolence, has turned to that creation of His which is called man, and which takes its abode in a hardly visible corner of the universe, the name of which is the earth. He has honoured this species of His creation by choosing one of its number to be the recipient of His divine light and the guardian of His wisdom.

This is something infinitely great. Some aspects of its greatness become apparent when man tries, as best as he can, to perceive the essential qualities of God: absolute power, freedom from all limitations and everlastingness; and when he reflects, in comparison, on the basic qualities of God's servants who are subject to certain limitations of power and life duration. One may then perceive the significance of this divine care for man. He may realize the sweetness of this feeling and manifest his appreciation with thanksgiving, prayer and devotion. He feels that the whole universe shares in the general happiness spread by the revelation of divine words to man in his obscure corner of the universe.

What is the significance of this event? With reference to God, it signifies that He is the source of all great bounties and unfailing compassion. He is the Benevolent, the Loving, who bestows His mercy and benefactions for no reason except that benevolence is one of His divine attributes. As for man, this event signifies that God has bestowed on him an honour the greatness of which he can hardly ever appreciate and for which he can never show enough gratitude, not even if he spends all his life in devotion and prostration. This honour is that God has taken notice and care of him, established contact with him and chosen one of the human race as His Messenger to reveal to him His words; that the earth, man's abode, has become the recipient of these divine words, which the whole universe echoes with submission and devotion.

This great event began to bear on the life of humanity as a whole right from the first moment. It marked a change in the course of history, following the change it brought about in the course followed by human conscience. It specified the source man should look up to in order to derive his ideals, values and criteria. The source is heaven and divine revelations, not this world and man's own desires. When this great event took place, the people who recognized its true nature and adapted their lives accordingly enjoyed God's protection and manifest care. They looked up to Him directly for guidance in all their affairs, large and small. They lived and moved under His supervision. They expected that He would guide them along the road, step by step, stopping them from error and leading them to the right way. Every night they expected to receive some divine revelation concerning what they had on their minds, providing solutions for their problems and saying to them, 'Do this and leave that.'

The period which followed the event was certainly remarkable: 23 years of direct contact between the human race and Supreme Society. The true nature of this cannot be recognized except by those who lived during this period and experienced it: witnessed its start and end, relished the sweet flavour of that contact and felt the divine hand guiding them along the road. The distance which separates us from that reality is too great to be defined by any measure of length this world has known. It is a distance in the world of conscience incomparable to any distance in the material world, not even when we think of the gaps separating stars and galaxies. It is a gap that separates the earth and heaven; a gap between human desires and Divine revelation as sources from which concepts and values are derived; a gap between *jāhiliyyah* and Islam, the human and the divine.

The people who lived at the time were fully aware of its uniqueness, recognized its special place in history and felt a huge loss when the Prophet passed away to be in God's company. This marked the end of that unique period.

Anas related that Abū Bakr said to 'Umar after the Prophet had passed away: 'Let us go to visit Umm Ayman as the Prophet used to do.'[2] When they went to her she burst into tears. They said, 'What are you crying for? Don't you realize that God's company is far better for the Prophet?' She replied, 'That is true, I am sure. I am only crying

2. Umm Ayman was the nurse who took care of the Prophet during his childhood. He remained grateful to her throughout his life. – Editor's note.

because revelation has ceased with his death.' This made tears spring to their eyes and the three of them cried together. [Related by Muslim.]

The impact of that period has been in evidence in the life of humanity ever since its beginning up to this moment, and it will remain in evidence until the day when God inherits the earth and all that walks on it. Man was reborn when he started to derive his values from heaven rather than earth and his laws from divine revelation instead of his own desires. The course of history underwent a change the like of which has never been experienced before or since. That event, the commencement of revelation, was the point at which the roads crossed. Clear and permanent guidelines were established which cannot be changed by the passage of time or effaced by events. Human conscience developed a concept of existence, and human life and its values became unsurpassed in comprehensiveness, clarity and purity of all worldly considerations. The foundations of this divine code were firmly established in the world and its various aspects and essential standards were made clear, '*so that anyone who was destined to perish might perish in clear evidence of the truth and anyone destined to live might live in clear evidence of the truth.*' (8: 42) There would no longer be any excuse of lack of clarity. Error and deviation would be upheld deliberately, in the face of clear guidance.

The beginning of revelation was a unique event at a unique moment marking the end of one era and the start of another. It was the demarcation line in the history of mankind, not merely in the history of a certain nation or a particular generation. It was recorded by the universe and echoed in all its corners. It was also recorded in man's conscience which today needs to be guided by what God has revealed and never lose sight of it. Man needs to remember that this event was a rebirth of humanity which can take place only once in history.

A Special Type of Education

It is self evident that the rest of the *sūrah* was not revealed at the same time as its opening but at a later date. It refers to a certain situation and later events in the Prophet's life, after he was instructed to convey his message and offer his worship in public, and after he was met with opposition by the unbelievers. This is indicated in the part of the *sūrah* which begins: "*Look at the one who tries to prevent a servant of God from praying!*" (Verses 9–10) Yet there is perfect harmony between all parts of the *sūrah*. The facts it relates after the opening part are also arranged in a perfect order. These two factors make the *sūrah* one perfectly harmonious unit.

> *Read in the name of your Lord who has created – created man out of a germ-cell. Read – for your Lord is the most Bountiful One, who has taught the use of the pen, taught man what he did not know.* (Verses 1–5)

This is the first *sūrah* of the Qur'ān, so it starts with the name of God. It instructs God's Messenger right at the very first moment of his blessed contact with the Supreme Society and before taking his very first step along the way of the message he was chosen to deliver, to read in the name of God, '*Read in the name of your Lord.*' The first attribute of God's it mentions is that of creation and initiation: '*... your Lord who has created.*' Then it speaks in particular of the creation of man and his origin: '*created man out of a germ-cell.*' He is created from a dried drop of blood which is implanted in the womb: a humble and unsophisticated substance. This reflects the grace and mercy of the Creator as much as it reflects His power. It is out of His grace that He has elevated this germ-cell to the rank of man who can be taught and who can learn: '*Read! For your Lord is the most Bountiful One, who has taught the use of the pen, taught man what he did not know.*' The gulf between the origin and the outcome is very wide indeed. But God is limitless in His ability and generosity; hence this extremely wonderful change.

Here also emerges the fact of man's teaching by the Creator. The pen has always been the most widespread means of learning and it has always had the most far-reaching impact on man's life. This fact was not as clear at the time of revelation as it is now. But God knows the value of the pen; hence, this reference to the pen at the beginning of this His final message to humanity, in the first *sūrah* of the Qur'ān. Yet God's Messenger charged with the delivery of this message could not write. Had the Qur'ān been his own composition, he would not have stressed this fact at the first moment. But the Qur'ān is a message God has revealed.

The *sūrah* then states the source of learning, which is God. From Him man receives all his knowledge, past, present and future. From Him man learns any secret revealed to him about this universe, life and himself.

This single paragraph revealed at the very first moment of the Islamic message states the comprehensive basis of faith and its concepts. Everything starts, works and moves in His name. He is the One who creates, originates and teaches. Whatever man learns and whatever experience and knowledge he acquires come originally from God. He has taught man what he did not know. The Prophet recognized this basic Qur'ānic fact. It governed his feelings, teachings and practices for the rest of his life because it is the principal fact of faith.

Imām Ibn Qayyim al-Jawziyyah summarizes the Prophet's teaching concerning remembrance of God:

> The Prophet was the most perfect man with regard to his remembrance of God. Indeed whatever he spoke was in the line of such remembrance. His commands, prohibitions, legislation, what he taught about the Lord and His attributes, judgements, actions, promises and threats were all part of this remembrance. So were his praise and glorification of God, prayers, his feelings of fear and hope and even his silence. He was conscious of God at all times and in every state. His praise of God was part of his very nature as if he praised Him with every breath. Indeed he praised Him as he stood up, sat or reclined and when walking, riding, moving, at home or travelling.
>
> When he woke up he used to say, 'Praise be to God who has given us life after He had caused us to die. To Him we shall be resurrected.' [Related by al-Bukhārī.]

'Ā'ishah said that the Prophet used to say when he woke up at night, 'God is Supreme,' and would repeat it ten times. Then he would repeat ten times the statement, 'There is no deity but God,' and pray, 'My Lord, I seek refuge with You against constraint in this life and on the Day of Resurrection,' repeating it also ten times. Then he would start his formal prayers. 'Ā'ishah also said that when the Prophet woke up at night for his devotion he would say, 'There is no God but You, my Lord. Praise be to You. I beseech You to forgive my sins and appeal to You for mercy. My Lord, enrich my knowledge and cause not my heart to go astray after You have granted me Your guidance. Grant me Your mercy, for You are the most Bountiful One.' [Both *aḥādīth* are related by Abū Dāwūd.]

The Prophet has also taught us that whoever gets up at night and says, 'There is no deity other than God alone; He has no partner; to Him belongs all dominion and to Him is due all praise; He is able to do everything; praised is God who is limitless in His glory; there is no deity but God; God is great; no power can operate without His permission; He is the Great, the Supreme,' and after this says, 'My Lord, forgive me,' or any other prayer, his prayers will be answered. Should he make ablution and offer prayers, these will be accepted. [Related by al-Bukhārī.]

God's Messenger once stayed overnight at Ibn 'Abbās's home, who later reported that when the Prophet woke up he raised his hands to the sky and read the last ten verses of *sūrah* Āl 'Imrān before going on to say, 'My Lord, to You belongs all praise; You are the light of heaven and earth and all therein; praise be to You, the true Lord; Your promise is true; whatever You say is true; the meeting with You is true; heaven is true; hell is true; the Prophets are true; and the Hour is true. I submit myself to You, I believe in You and depend on You. To You I shall return. Any dispute I may enter into is for You. To You I turn for judgement. Forgive me all my sins, past and future, public and secret. You are my Lord and there is no God but You. No power can operate without God's permission; He is the Great, the Supreme.' [Related by al-Bukhārī, Muslim and Aḥmad.]

'Ā'ishah related that when the Prophet woke up at night to worship he used to say, 'My God, the Lord of Gabriel, Mikā'īl and Isrāfīl, the Creator of heaven and earth, who knows what is concealed and what is made public. You judge between Your servants in their disputes. Guide me, with Your own will, to the truth over which people argue and dispute, for You guide whom You will to the straight path.' She might have also said that he used to say this at the start of his prayers. [Related by Muslim, al-Tirmidhī and Ibn Mājah.]

After offering the *witr* prayer, the Prophet used to repeat three times, 'Glorified be God, the Holy One.' [Related by Abū Dāwūd, al-Nasā'ī and Aḥmad.]. When he went out of his house he would say, 'In the name of God. I place my trust in God. My Lord, I appeal to You to guard me against going astray or causing anyone to go astray, and against making a slip or causing anyone to slip, and being unjust to anyone or being victim to any injustice by others, and against acting ignorantly, or being ignorantly done by.' [Related by al-Tirmidhī, Abū Dāwūd and Aḥmad.]

The Prophet said, "Whoever says as he leaves his home: 'In the name of God. I place my trust in God. No power is operative without God's leave,' will be answered: 'You are rightly guided and well protected,' and the devil will be made to turn away from him." [Related by al-Tirmidhī and Abū Dāwūd.]

Referring to the night when he was host to God's Messenger, Ibn 'Abbās said that when the Prophet left for the dawn prayers at the mosque he said, 'My Lord, give me light in my heart, tongue, ears and eyes: give me light in front of me, over me and below me, and make the light You give me abundant.' [Related by al-Bukhārī and Muslim.]

Abū Sa'īd al-Khudrī relates that the Prophet said: "When a man goes out to the mosque for prayers and says, 'My Lord, I appeal to You by the right of those who pray to You, and the right of my journey to You. I have not come out with any feeling of self-sufficiency, nor in hypocrisy or conceit, nor to seek reputation. I have come out with the hope of avoiding Your anger and earning Your pleasure. I pray to You to save me from hell and to forgive me my sins; You are the only One who forgives sins;' seventy thousand angels will be charged with praying for his forgiveness and God will receive and welcome him until he finishes his prayers.' [Related by Aḥmad and Ibn Mājah.]

Abū Dāwūd related that the Prophet used to say when he entered the mosque, 'I seek refuge with God, the Great, and His Holy face, and His old power against Satan, the outcast.' When a man says this, the Devil says, 'He is now protected against me for the rest of the day.'

The Prophet said: "Whenever any of you comes to the mosque, let him pray and ask peace for the Prophet and say, 'My Lord, open to me the doors of Your mercy.' When he leaves the mosque, let him say, 'My Lord, I pray to You to give me out of Your grace.'" [Related by Muslim, Abū Dāwūd and Ibn Mājah.]

It is also related that when the Prophet entered the mosque, he would ask peace for Muḥammad (himself) and his household, then he would say, 'My Lord, forgive me my sins and open the doors of Your mercy to me.' When he left, he would again ask peace for Muḥammad and his household, and say, 'My Lord, forgive me my sins and lay open to me the doors of Your grace.' [Related by Aḥmad and al-Tirmidhī.]

After offering the dawn prayers, God's Messenger used to stay in his praying place until sunrise, utilizing his time in remembrance of God.

In the morning, he would say, 'Our Lord, we have lived till this morning by Your will, and we also live till evening by Your will. We live and die by Your will. To You we will return.' [Related by al-Tirmidhī, Abū Dāwūd and Ibn Mājah.]

He also used to say, 'The morning has appeared. This morning all dominion belongs to God, praised be He. There is no deity but God alone. He has no partner; to Him belongs all the universe and to Him is all praise due. He is able to do what He wills. My Lord, I pray to You to give me of the best of this day and the best of the days to follow. I seek refuge with You against the evil of this day and the days to follow. My Lord, I seek Your refuge against laziness and the evils of old age, against suffering in hell and suffering in the grave.' In the evening he would repeat the same prayer substituting evening for morning. [Related by Muslim.]

Abū Bakr, the Prophet's Companion said once to him: "Teach me some prayers to say in the morning and in the evening." God's Messenger taught him the following prayer, 'My Lord, the Creator of heaven and earth, who knows the visible and the unseen, the perceptible and the imperceptible, the Lord and Possessor of all, I declare that there is no deity but You. I appeal to You to protect me against my own evil and the evil of Satan; I seek Your refuge against doing myself any harm or causing harm to any Muslim.' The Prophet told Abū Bakr to say this prayer in the morning, evening and before going to bed. [Related by al-Tirmidhī and Abū Dāwūd.][3]

When God's Messenger had a new garment, he would mention it by name (for example, a shirt, gown or turban) and say, 'My Lord, praise be to You. You have given me this. I pray to You to give me its goodness and the goodness for which it was made; and to guard me against its evil and the evil for which it was made.' [Related by al-Tirmidhī, Abū Dāwūd, Aḥmad and al-Nasā'ī.][4]

The Prophet was in the habit of saying the following prayer when he returned home, 'Praise be to God who has given me

---

3. Ibn al-Qayyim, *Zād al-Ma'ād*, Beirut and Kuwait, 1994, Vol. 2, pp. 365–371. Many more *aḥādīth* are also included under the same chapter.

4. Ibid., Vol. 2, p. 379.

this shelter and what is sufficient for me; and praise be to God who has given me food and drink, and praise be to God who has given me abundance out of His generosity. I pray to You to extend Your protection to me against hell.' [Related by Abū Dāwūd.]

It is confirmed in the two most authentic *Ḥadīth* anthologies by al-Bukhārī and Muslim that, as the Prophet was about to enter the toilet, he used to say, 'My Lord, I pray to You to rid me of evil things.'[5]

When he finished his toilet, he used to say, 'I seek Your forgiveness, my Lord.' [Related by al-Tirmidhī.]. It is also reported that he would say, 'Praise be to God who has ridden me of harm and given me good health.' [Related by Ibn Mājah.][6]

It is also confirmed that he once put his hand in a water container and said to his Companions, 'Make ablutions in the name of God.' [Related by al-Nasā'ī.][7]

When he saw the new moon, he used to say, 'My Lord, let it come to us with security, faith, safety and submission to You. New moon, God is my Lord and Your Lord.' [Related by al-Tirmidhī, Aḥmad and al-Dārimī.][8]

When he started eating, he used to say, 'In the name of God.' He also said, 'When any of you eats, let him mention the name of God. If he forgets to do so, let him say [when he remembers], in the name of God at the beginning and at the end.' [Related by al-Tirmidhī.][9]

Thus was the life of God's Messenger. It was conditioned, down to every single detail, by the divine instruction which he received at

5. Ibid., Vol. 2, p. 383.
6. Ibid., Vol. 2, pp. 386–387.
7. Ibid., Vol. 2, p. 387.
8. Ibid., Vol. 2, p. 396.
9. Ibid., Vol. 2, p. 397.

the very first moment of his message. This instruction helped his faith to be established on a genuine basis.

Arrogance and Ingratitude

It is God, then, who creates, teaches and bestows His abundant bounties on man. This implies that man should acknowledge God's benevolence and be grateful for it. But what actually happens is something different.

The second part of the *sūrah* deals with man's transgression. "*Indeed, man becomes grossly overweening, once he thinks himself self-sufficient. Surely to your Lord all must return.*" (Verses 6–8) It is God who gives to man in abundance and makes him independent. He also creates and teaches him and extends to him His generous treatment. But men in general – except for those guarded by faith – are not thankful for their independence which is made possible by what they are given. They do not recognize the source of this grace, which is the same as the source of their creation, knowledge and livelihood. They behave arrogantly and transgress all limits instead of being dutiful and thankful.

The image of the transgressing, conceited person who has forgotten his origin is followed by a comment charged with an implicit warning: "*Surely to your Lord all must return.*" (Verse 8) Where can this proud and overweening person then turn?

At the same time a fundamental rule of the Islamic faith is emphasized. That is, all must refer to God in every matter, thought or action. He is the only resort and refuge. The good and the bad, the obedient and the sinner, the righteous and the wrongdoer, the rich and the poor, will all return to Him. Even the man who tyrannizes when he thinks himself independent will come to Him eventually.

Thus, the first two sections of the *sūrah* lay down the essential components of the Islamic ideological concept: creation, education and honour come from God alone, and to Him all will return: "*Surely to your Lord all must return.*" (Verse 8)

The third section of this short *sūrah* tackles a particularly appalling form of tyranny. Its description in the inimitable Qur'ānic style fills us with wonder and dismay that it should take place at all. "*Look at the one who tries to prevent a servant of God from praying! Think: does he follow the right guidance and enjoin [others to be] God-fearing? Think: if he denies the truth and turns his back, does he not realize that God sees all?*" (Verses 9–14)

Our dismay is enhanced by the manner of expression which takes the form of address and conversation, using short sentences that follow in rapid succession. The effect can hardly ever be produced by ordinary written language. 'Look at' this ghastly business actually taking place! "*Look at the one who tries to prevent a servant of God from praying.*" (Verses 9–10) Have you seen this repulsive sight? Have you realized how repugnance is doubled by the fact that the person being prevented from his prayers is in fact following divine guidance. He merely enjoins righteousness and piety, yet he is discouraged and told to desist!

Yet the transgressor outdoes himself by taking a still more abhorrent stand, "*Think: if he denies the truth and turns his back.*" (Verse 13) The closing note is one of implicit warning, similar to that of the previous paragraph, "*Does he not realize that God sees all?*" (Verse 14) He sees everything: the denial of truth, the turning away from it, as well as the prevention of believers from offering their prayers. Since God sees all, something must be done on the basis of what He sees. This is the implicit warning.

Thus, we have a scene of tyranny trying to suppress the call of faith and obedience to God. This is followed immediately by a stern warning stated explicitly this time: "*Nay, if he does not desist, We will most certainly drag him by his forelock, his lying, sinful forelock. Then let him call his henchmen. We will call the guards of hell.*" (Verses 15–18) The Arabic term, *lanasfa'n*, used for 'drag' has a marked violence about it. The dragging is by the forelock, the part of the head raised high by every conceited tyrant. It undoubtedly deserves to be hit violently: "*His lying, sinful forelock!*" The tyrant may think of calling his clan and supporters to come to his aid: "*Then let him call his henchmen.*" On the other side, "*We will call the guards of hell,*" and they are powerful and ruthless. The outcome of the battle is never in doubt.

In the light of this frightening destiny for the unbelievers, the *sūrah* concludes with an instruction to God's obedient servants to persevere and follow the path of faith: "*No, pay no heed to him, but prostrate yourself and draw closer to God.*" (Verse 19) Do not obey this tyrant who tries to stop you from offering your devotion and conveying your message. Prostrate yourself before your Lord and bring yourself closer to Him through worship and obedience. As for the tyrant, leave him to the guards of hell who are sure to mete out to him what he deserves.

Some authentic reports say that the *sūrah*, with the exception of the first part, refers to Abū Jahl who once passed by the Prophet while he was praying at *Maqām Ibrahīm*, close to the Ka'bah. He turned to him and said, 'Muḥammad, have I not ordered you to stop these practices?' He also added some warning to the Prophet who gave him a stern reply. This was possibly the time when the Prophet seized Abū Jahl by the collar and warned him of his impending doom. Abū Jahl said, 'Muḥammad, what do you threaten me with? I am sure I have the largest following in this valley.' Hence, the revelation, '*Let him call his henchmen.*' Ibn 'Abbās, the Prophet's learned Companion, said in comment: "Had he called them, the angels charged with meting out punishment would have taken him away there and then."

The *sūrah*, however, is general in its significance. It refers to every obedient believer calling men to follow the path of God and to every tyrant who forbids prayer, threatens the believers and acts arrogantly. The concluding divine instruction is therefore: "*No, pay no heed to him, but prostrate yourself and draw closer to God.*" (Verse 19)

SŪRAH 97

Al-Qadr

(Power)

Al-Qadr (Power)	سُورَةُ ٱلْقَدْرِ
In the name of God, the Beneficent, the Merciful.	بِسْمِ ٱللَّهِ ٱلرَّحْمَٰنِ ٱلرَّحِيمِ
From on high have We bestowed it [i.e. the Qur'ān] on the Night of Power. (1)	إِنَّآ أَنزَلْنَٰهُ فِى لَيْلَةِ ٱلْقَدْرِ ١
Would that you knew what the Night of Power is! (2)	وَمَآ أَدْرَىٰكَ مَا لَيْلَةُ ٱلْقَدْرِ ٢
The Night of Power is better than a thousand months. (3)	لَيْلَةُ ٱلْقَدْرِ خَيْرٌ مِّنْ أَلْفِ شَهْرٍ ٣
On that night the angels and the Spirit by their Lord's leave descend with all His decrees. (4)	تَنَزَّلُ ٱلْمَلَٰٓئِكَةُ وَٱلرُّوحُ فِيهَا بِإِذْنِ رَبِّهِم مِّن كُلِّ أَمْرٍ ٤
That night is peace, till the break of dawn. (5)	سَلَٰمٌ هِىَ حَتَّىٰ مَطْلَعِ ٱلْفَجْرِ ٥

A Most Distinguished Night

This *sūrah* speaks about the promised great night which the whole universe marks with joy and prayer. It is the night of perfect communion between this world and the Supreme Society. That night marked the beginning of the revelation of the Qur'ān to Muḥammad (peace be upon him), an event unparalleled in the history of mankind for its splendour and the significance it has for the life of mankind as a whole. Its greatness is far beyond human perception. "*From on high have We bestowed it [i.e. the Qur'ān] on the Night of Power. Would that you knew what the Night of Power is! The Night of Power is better than a thousand months.*" (Verses 1–3)

The Qur'ānic statements which relate this great event radiate with God's clear and shining light: "*From on high We bestowed it on the Night of Power.*" (Verse 1) There is also the light of the angels and the Spirit moving between the earth and the Supreme Society. "*On that night the angels and the Spirit by their Lord's leave descend with all His decrees.*" (Verse 4) In addition, there is also the light of dawn which the *sūrah* represents as perfectly harmonious with the light of the Qur'ān and the angels as well as with their spirit of peace: "*That night is peace, till the break of dawn.*" (Verse 5)

The night in question here is the same night referred to in *Sūrah* 44, Smoke: "*From on high We bestowed it [i.e. the Qur'ān] on a blessed night, for We would warn [mankind]; on a night when every precept was made plain as a commandment from Us. We have ever sent forth messengers as a blessing from your Lord. It is He alone who hears all and knows all.*" (44: 3–6) It is clearly established that it is a night during the month of Ramaḍān, as stated in *Sūrah* 2, The Cow: "*It was in the month of Ramaḍān that the Qur'ān was revealed: a guidance for mankind and a self-evident proof of that guidance and a standard to distinguish right from wrong.*" (2: 185) This means that the Night of Power marked the beginning of the revelation of the Qur'ān to the Prophet and his mission of delivering it to mankind.

Ibn Isḥāq related that the first revelation, consisting of the opening of *Sūrah* 96, The Germ-Cell, took place during the month of Ramaḍān, when God's Messenger was at his devotion in the Cave of Ḥirā'.

A number of *aḥādīth* specifying this night have come down to us: some stress that it is on 27 Ramaḍān, others on 21; a few others say it is one of the last ten days and still some others do not go beyond saying that it is in Ramaḍān.

Its name, *Layalt al-Qadr*, or the Night of Power, may be taken to mean deliberate planning, management and organization, or it may mean value, position and rank. Both meanings are relevant to the great, universal event of the revelation of the Qur'ān and the assigning of the message to the Prophet. It is indeed the greatest and most significant event the universe has ever witnessed. It is the event which explains most clearly how human life benefits by God's planning, management and organization. This night is better than a thousand months. The figure here and elsewhere in the Qur'ān does not signify a precise number. It simply denotes something very high. Many thousands of months and many thousands of years have passed without leaving behind a fraction of the changes and results brought about during that blessed and happy night.

This night is too sublime for proper human perception: "*Would that you knew what the Night of Power is!*" (Verse 2) There is no reason to attach any value to the legends circulated concerning this night. It is great because God chose it for the revelation of the Qur'ān, so that its light may spread throughout the universe, and divine peace may spread in human life and conscience. That night is great because of what the Qur'ān includes: an ideology, a basis for values and standards and a comprehensive code of moral and social behaviour, all of which promote peace within the human soul and in the world at large. It is great because of the descent of the angels, and Gabriel in particular, by their Lord's leave, carrying the Qur'ān. They fill all the space between heaven and earth in such a splendid, universal celebration, vividly portrayed in this *sūrah*.

When we look today in retrospect, after the lapse of numerous generations, at that glorious and happy night, imagine the fascinating celebration the world then witnessed, and ponder over the essence of revelation and its far-reaching effects on human life and values, we appreciate how great this event was. We can then understand, to some extent, why the Qur'ānic reference to that night is made in such an equivocal way: "*Would that you knew what the Night of Power is!*" (Verse 2)

On that night every matter of significance was made plain and distinct; new values and standards were established; the fortunes of nations were determined; and values and standards were sorted out.

Humanity, out of ignorance and to its misfortune, may overlook the value and importance of the Night of Power. When humanity does so ignore it, it loses the happiest and most beautiful sign of grace which God bestowed on it. It also suffers the loss of the real happiness and peace gifted to it by Islam, namely, the peace of conscience, family and society. What it has otherwise gained of material civilization is inadequate compensation for its loss. Humanity is miserable in spite of higher production levels and better means of existence. The splendid light which once illuminated its soul has been put out; the happiness which carried it high up to the Supreme Society has been destroyed; the peace which overflowed in people's hearts and minds has disappeared. Nothing can compensate for the happiness of the human soul, the heavenly light and elevation to the loftiest ranks.

We, the believers in Islam, are commanded not to forget or neglect this event. The Prophet has taught us an easy and enjoyable way to commemorate it, so that our souls may always be in close communion with it and with the universal event which it witnessed. He has urged us to spend this night of each year in devotion. He said: "Seek the Night of Power in the last ten nights of Ramaḍān." [Related by al-Bukhārī and Muslim.] He also said: "Whoever spends the Night of Power in worship, with a pure motive of faith and devotion, will have all his past sins forgiven." [Related by al-Bukhārī and Muslim.]

Islam is not mere formalities. Hence, the Prophet specifies that the consecration of that night must be motivated by faith and devotion. This would make its consecration by any individual an indication of his or her full awareness of the far-reaching effects of what took place on that night.

The Islamic method of education and character building links worship with faith and establishes truth in our hearts and consciences. By this method, worship is considered a means for maintaining full awareness of this truth, its clarification and firm establishment in our minds, hearts and souls. This method has been proved to be the best for the revival of this truth so that it has an unfailing influence on people's behaviour. The theoretical understanding of this truth cannot, on its own and without worship, establish it or give it the necessary impetus for its operation in the life of the individual or society. This link between the anniversary of the Night of Power and its consecration in faith and devotion is a part of the successful and straightforward method of Islam.

SŪRAH 98

Al-Bayyinah

(The Clear Proof)

Al-Bayyinah (The Clear Proof)

سُورَةُ البَيِّنَةِ

In the name of God, the Beneficent, the Merciful.

بِسْمِ ٱللَّهِ ٱلرَّحْمَـٰنِ ٱلرَّحِيمِ

It is inconceivable that the unbelievers among the people of the earlier revelations and the idolaters could have ever changed their ways until there had come to them the clear evidence of the truth: (1)

لَمْ يَكُنِ ٱلَّذِينَ كَفَرُوا۟ مِنْ أَهْلِ
ٱلْكِتَـٰبِ وَٱلْمُشْرِكِينَ مُنفَكِّينَ
حَتَّىٰ تَأْتِيَهُمُ ٱلْبَيِّنَةُ ١

a Messenger from God reciting revelations blest with purity, (2)

رَسُولٌ مِّنَ ٱللَّهِ يَتْلُوا۟ صُحُفًا مُّطَهَّرَةً ٢

wherein are sound decrees of high value. (3)

فِيهَا كُتُبٌ قَيِّمَةٌ ٣

Nor did the people given revelations in the past break up their unity until after such clear evidence of the truth had been given to them. (4)

وَمَا تَفَرَّقَ ٱلَّذِينَ أُوتُوا۟ ٱلْكِتَٰبَ إِلَّا مِنۢ بَعْدِ مَا جَآءَتْهُمُ ٱلْبَيِّنَةُ ﴿٤﴾

Yet they were ordered to do nothing more than to serve God, to worship Him alone with sincere dedication and purity of faith, to attend to their prayers and to pay their *zakāt*. That is surely the right religion, pure and straight. (5)

وَمَآ أُمِرُوٓا۟ إِلَّا لِيَعْبُدُوا۟ ٱللَّهَ مُخْلِصِينَ لَهُ ٱلدِّينَ حُنَفَآءَ وَيُقِيمُوا۟ ٱلصَّلَوٰةَ وَيُؤْتُوا۟ ٱلزَّكَوٰةَ ۚ وَذَٰلِكَ دِينُ ٱلْقَيِّمَةِ ﴿٥﴾

The unbelievers among the people of the earlier revelations and the idolaters will be in the fire of hell, where they will abide. They are the worst of all creatures. (6)

إِنَّ ٱلَّذِينَ كَفَرُوا۟ مِنْ أَهْلِ ٱلْكِتَٰبِ وَٱلْمُشْرِكِينَ فِى نَارِ جَهَنَّمَ خَٰلِدِينَ فِيهَآ ۚ أُو۟لَٰٓئِكَ هُمْ شَرُّ ٱلْبَرِيَّةِ ﴿٦﴾

But those who believe and do righteous deeds are the best of all creatures. (7)

إِنَّ ٱلَّذِينَ ءَامَنُوا۟ وَعَمِلُوا۟ ٱلصَّٰلِحَٰتِ أُو۟لَٰٓئِكَ هُمْ خَيْرُ ٱلْبَرِيَّةِ ﴿٧﴾

Their reward [awaits them] with their Lord: the gardens of Eden through which running waters flow, in which they will abide forever. God is well pleased with them and they with Him. This is for him who is God-fearing. (8)

جَزَآؤُهُمْ عِندَ رَبِّهِمْ جَنَّٰتُ عَدْنٍ تَجْرِى مِن تَحْتِهَا ٱلْأَنْهَٰرُ خَٰلِدِينَ فِيهَآ أَبَدًا ۖ رَّضِىَ ٱللَّهُ عَنْهُمْ وَرَضُوا۟ عَنْهُ ۚ ذَٰلِكَ لِمَنْ خَشِىَ رَبَّهُۥ ﴿٨﴾

Overview

As stated in our copies of the Qur'ān and according to the greater number of reports, this *sūrah* is a Madinan revelation. There are, however, some reports which classify it as Makkan. Although its classification as a Madinan revelation carries more weight in view of these reports and its mode of expression and style, yet the possibility of its being Makkan cannot be ruled out. The fact that it mentions *zakāt*, i.e. the obligatory charity, and the people of earlier revelations is not a clear-cut argument against the Makkan possibility. Some *sūrahs* which are indisputably Makkan mention the people of earlier revelations. Furthermore, there were some Makkans, a few, who followed earlier divine religions. Some of these adopted Islam but others did not. Moreover the Christians from Najran came to the Prophet when he was still in Makkah, and they accepted the Islamic faith, as it is well-known. Moreover, *zakāt* is mentioned in some *sūrahs* that were indisputably revealed in Makkah.

This *sūrah* deals in a positive manner with a number of facts relating to history and faith. The first fact is that the sending of God's Messenger, Muḥammad (peace be upon him), was essential to the transformation of people of earlier revelations and idolaters, who had found their way into disbelief. They could not leave their erring ways behind without the Prophet's mission: "*It is inconceivable that the unbelievers among the people of the earlier revelations and the idolaters could have ever changed their ways until there had come to them the clear evidence of the truth: a Messenger from God reciting revelations blest with purity, wherein are sound decrees of high value.*" (Verses 1–3)

Secondly, religious discord and conflict among the people of earlier revelations did not arise out of ignorance of their own religion, or from any obscurity or ambiguity in it. On the contrary, they ran into discord after they had received true knowledge and clear proof: "*Nor did the people given revelations in the past break up their unity until after such clear evidence of the truth had been given to them.*" (Verse 4)

Thirdly, with regard to its origin, divine faith is one. Its fundamentals are simple and clear and do not, by themselves and by their plain and easy nature, make for division or conflict: "*Yet they were ordered to do nothing more than to serve God, to worship Him alone with sincere dedication and purity of faith, to attend to their prayers and to pay their* zakāt. *That is surely the right religion, pure and straight.*" (Verse 5)

Fourthly, those who disbelieved after receiving clear proof are the worst creatures of all, while those who believe and do good deeds are the best. Hence the two receive totally different rewards: "*The unbelievers among the people of the earlier revelations and the idolaters will be in the fire of hell, where they will abide. They are the worst of all creatures. But those who believe and do righteous deeds are the best of all creatures. Their reward [awaits them] with their Lord: the gardens of Eden through which running waters flow, in which they will abide forever. God is well pleased with them and they with Him. This is for him who is God-fearing.*" (Verses 6–8)

Need for a Divine Message

> *It is inconceivable that the unbelievers among the people of the earlier revelations and the idolaters could have ever changed their ways until there had come to them the clear evidence of the truth: a Messenger from God reciting revelations blest with purity, wherein are sound decrees of high value.* (Verses 1–3)

The world was desperately in need of a new message. Corruption was so widespread that reform could not come about except by means of a new message, a new method of orientation and a new movement. Disbelief had become the characteristic of the followers of all creeds and doctrines, whether pagan or earlier divine revelations [i.e. the Jews and the Christians]. They could only turn away from disbelief by means of this new message and at the hands of a messenger who would himself be the proof, clear, unmistakable and specific. "*A Messenger from God reciting revelations blest with purity*;" that is, purified of all idolatry and disbelief, "*wherein are sound decrees of high value.*" The Arabic term *kutub*, which in modern usage means 'books', is given in our translation as 'sound decrees'. In the past, it was normally used in reference to the subject under discussion and its instructions or obligations. These pure revelations are indeed the Qur'ān which contains valuable and important directives.

Hence the message delivered by the Prophet came at a most suitable time. The new revelations, with all that they included of themes and decrees, were vouchsafed so that they could bring about a far-reaching reform of this world. As to how badly the world needed this message, let us content ourselves with some inspiring remarks from Sayyid Abu'l Ḥasan 'Alī Nadwī:

> The sixth century of the Christian era, it is generally agreed, represented the darkest phase in the history of our race. Humanity had reached the edge of the precipice, towards which it had been tragically proceeding for centuries, and there appeared to be no agency or power in the whole world which could come to its rescue and save it from crashing into the abyss of destruction.
>
> In his melancholy progress from God-forgetfulness to self-forgetting, man had lost his moorings. He had grown indifferent to his destiny. The teachings of the prophets had been forgotten: the lamps that they had kindled either had been put out by the storms of moral anarchy or the light they shed had become so feeble that it could illumine the hearts of but a few men, most of whom had sought refuge in passivity and resignation. Having been vanquished in the battle between spiritualism and materialism, they had shut themselves up in monasteries or gone into the wilderness. Such of them as were still left in the whirlpool of life had aligned themselves with the ruling classes of their lands. They helped them in the satisfaction of their sensual desires and in the maintenance of unjust political and economic systems and co-operated with them in reaping unlawful benefits out of the wealth of the people...
>
> Great religions became playthings in the hands of debased ecclesiastics who corrupted and twisted them beyond recognition, so much so that if it were possible for their founders to return to the physical life, they could not have recognized them. In

> consequence of the moral debasement of the great centres of civilization and general disorder and unrest, people everywhere got entangled in their internal problems. They had no message to offer to the world. The world had become hollow from within; its life-springs had dried up. It possessed neither the light of religious guidance for their personal conduct nor any abiding and rational principles for running a state.[1]

This outlines briefly the condition of mankind and religions just before the advent of the Prophet Muḥammad (peace be upon him). The Qur'ān refers in various parts to the aspects of disbelief which spread among the people of the earlier revelations as well as the idolaters. Among these references to the Jews and Christians are: "*The Jews say: 'Ezra is the son of God,' while the Christians say: 'The Christ is the son of God.'*" (9: 30) "*The Jews say the Christians have no basis for their faith and the Christians say the Jews have no basis for their faith.*" (2: 113) The Qur'ān also refers to the Jews as follows: "*The Jews say, 'God's hand is shackled!' It is their own hands that are shackled. Rejected [by God] are they for what they say. Indeed, both His hands are outstretched. He bestows [His bounty] as He wills.*" (5: 64) It says about the Christians: "*Unbelievers indeed are those who say: 'God is the Christ, son of Mary.'*" (5: 72) And: "*Unbelievers indeed are those who say: 'God is the third of a trinity.'*" (5: 73) The Qur'ān also speaks about the idolaters: *"Say: 'Unbelievers! I do not worship what you worship, nor do you worship what I worship. I shall never worship what you worship, nor will you ever worship what I worship. You have your own religion and I have mine.'"* (109: 1–6) There are many other statements in the Qur'ān which support this view.

In addition to such disbelief, there were backwardness, division, ruin as well as other evil spread throughout the world.

> There was, briefly, not a single nation in the whole world of the sixth century of the Christian era that could be called healthy

1. Abu'l Ḥasan 'Alī Nadwī, *Islam and the World*, Academy of Islamic Research Publications, Lucknow, 1980, pp. 13–14.

> in temperament, not a single society that was imbued with high ethical ideas, nor a single State that was based on principles of justice, equity and fairness, nor yet a leadership that possessed knowledge and wisdom, nor a religion that represented the pure teachings of the Prophets of God.[2]

Hence, the divine grace extended to mankind required that a messenger be sent by God to recite purified scriptures containing valuable and important themes. There was no other way of putting an end to such widespread corruption except by sending a messenger, who would deliver mankind from their misery and provide them with divine guidance.

Internal Division and Hostility

Having made this fact clear at the outset, the *sūrah* goes on to state that the people of earlier revelations in particular did not experience religious conflict and division as a result of ignorance, on their part, or confusion or complication on the part of their religion. Instead, their divisions occurred after true knowledge and clear signs were delivered to them through God's messengers: *"Nor did the people given revelations in the past break up their unity until after such clear evidence of the truth had been given to them."* (Verse 4)

The first division occurred among the Jews who split into sects and groups before the advent of the Prophet Jesus. Although their prophet was Moses and the Torah was their book, they divided into five main sects, namely, the Sadducees, the Pharisees, the Asians, the Extremists and the Samaritans. Each had their own characteristics and their own ways. Later on a division between the Jews and Christians took place in spite of the fact that Jesus was the last prophet sent to the Children of Israel. He came to endorse the Torah and confirm it. Nevertheless, the quarrel between the Jews and Christians reached a high level of violent enmity and hatred. History

2. Ibid., pp. 43–44.

tells us about the horrifying massacres that took place between the two parties.

> The mutual jealousy and hatred between Christians and Jews, which did not permit them to forego any opportunity of settling an old score, was brought to its climax towards the close of the sixth century. In 610 A.D. the Jews of Antioch rebelled against the Christians, and the Emperor Phocas sent his famous general, Bonosus, to put down the uprising. It was he who set about his business with such enthusiasm that the whole of the Jewish population was wiped out. Thousands of Jews perished by the sword, while hundreds more were either drowned, burnt alive or thrown to the wild beasts.[3]
>
> Such atrocities were repeated again and again between the Jews and Christians. Al-Maqrīzī says in his book *Al-Khiṭaṭ*, "During the reign of the Byzantine Emperor Phocas, Chosroes, the Shah of Persia, dispatched his armies to Syria and Egypt. They destroyed the churches of Jerusalem, Palestine and the rest of the Syrian land. They wiped out all the Christians and pursued them to Egypt, where they slaughtered them in large numbers and enslaved an unimaginable number. The Jews helped them in fighting the Christians and destroying their churches. They poured from all directions to help the Persians and came from Tiberia, the Mount of Galilee, Nazareth village and the City of Tyre and all around Jerusalem. They committed all sorts of atrocities against the Christians, organized ghastly massacres, destroyed two Christian churches in Jerusalem, burnt their places, stole a piece of the pillar of the Cross and captured the Patriarch of Jerusalem and a great many of his friends and companions..." Al-Maqrīzī goes on to relate the Persian conquest of Egypt; then he writes: "At that time, the Jews in the City of Tyre rebelled and sent messengers from among themselves to other cities and towns and all agreed to lay a trap for the Christians and kill them. A war broke out between the Jews and Christians in which the number of the Jews was

3. Ibid., pp. 17–18.

around 20,000. They destroyed the Christian churches around Tyre. But the Christians surrounded them and raised much greater numbers, so the Jews suffered a ghastly defeat and a great number were killed. At the time Heraclius ascended to power in Constantinople. He defeated the Persians by setting a trap for the Shah, who left him eventually and went away. Then he marched from Constantinople to re-establish his authority over Syria and Egypt and to renew what the Persians had destroyed. The Jews from Tiberia and other places went out to meet him. They presented him with precious gifts and begged him to guarantee their security and to take an oath to this effect. He granted their request. He went on to Jerusalem where he was received by the Christian population holding up their Bibles, crosses, and incense, and burning candles. He was very much displeased at seeing the city and its churches destroyed. He expressed his sorrow to the local Christians who told him about the uprising by the Jews and their siding with the Persians, the massacre of the Christians and the destruction of their churches. They told Heraclius to level a blow to the Jews but he protested that he had already guaranteed their security and had taken an oath to that effect. Their monks, cardinals and priests gave their judgement that the killing of the Jews was justifiable on the grounds that they had played a trick in order to win that assurance from him before he knew what they had done. The clergy also pledged to atone for Heraclius' oath by committing themselves and all Christians to fast a certain Friday every year for the rest of time. Thus he leaned to their argument and wreaked such a savage vengeance upon the Jews that in the Byzantine provinces of Syria and Egypt those alone could save themselves who could take to flight or go into hiding.

These reports give us an idea about the degree of savagery the two parties had reached, their watching for every chance to strike their enemy and heeding no rules in the process.[4]

4. Abu'l Ḥasan ʿAlī Nadwī, *Mādhā Khasir al-ʿĀlam binḥiṭāṭ al-Muslimīn*, which is the Arabic edition of *Islam and the World*, n.d., pp. 9–11.

Then divisions and differences broke out among the Christians themselves in spite of the fact that their book is one and their messenger is one. They were divided first in matters of faith; then they split up into hostile and warring factions. Their differences concerned the nature of Jesus and whether he had a divine or human nature, the nature of Mary, his mother, and also the nature of the Trinity which they claim constitutes God. The Qur'ān relates two or three of their sayings on these issues: *"Unbelievers indeed are those who say: 'God is the Christ, son of Mary.'"* (5: 72) And: "*Unbelievers indeed are those who say: 'God is the third of a trinity.'*" (5: 73) And, "*God will say: Jesus, son of Mary! Did you say to people, 'Worship me and my mother as deities beside God?' [Jesus] answered: 'Limitless are You in Your glory! I could never have claimed what I have no right to [say].'*" (5: 116)

> The most violent of doctrinal divisions was that which erupted between the Byzantine State and the Christians of Syria and the Christians of Egypt, or, in a more accurate definition, the Melkites and the Monophysites. The main dispute centred around the alleged combination of the divine and human natures in Jesus. The Melkite Christians of Syria held that he was both divine and human, while the Monophysites of Egypt insisted upon his being truly divine, the human part of his nature having lost itself in the divine as a drop of vinegar loses its identity in an ocean. The dispute between the two parties became so strong during the sixth and seventh centuries that it looked as if it were a ceaseless war between two rival religions, or a dispute between Jews and Christians. Each faction saying to the other that its stand was without foundation.
>
> Emperor Heraclius (610–641) tried after his victory over the Persians in 638 to reconcile the contending creeds in his state and to unite them by compromise. This compromise took the shape of a general ban on indulging in any argument on the nature of Jesus Christ, the Messiah, and whether he had a single

or dual nature. But everyone had to accept the doctrine of a single energy in Christ.[5] Agreement on this was established at the beginning of 631, and thus the Menothelian creed was declared the official creed of the state and all those of its populations who belonged to the Christian Church. Heraclius was determined to give the new creed overall supremacy, and he utilized all means to this end. But the Copts disputed his authority and declared their total rejection of this innovation and deviation. They took the opposing stand and sacrificed their all for the old faith. The Emperor tried once again to unite all the creeds and settle the differences. He was content that people should accept that there is a single will for Christ.[6] As for the other issue, namely, the realization of that will by action, he deferred taking a stand on it altogether. He also banned all parties from indulging in arguments and debates on these issues. He included all this in an official message which he delivered to all parts of the Eastern world. But the message failed to end the storm. Instead, brutal persecution of a sort that would send a shiver through any mortal, was administered by the Emperor in Egypt for ten years. Men were savagely tortured before being drowned. Huge torches were lit and directed onto the miserable prisoners until the fat ran from both sides of their bodies to the floor. Prisoners were put in sacks which were then filled with sand and thrown into the sea.[7]

All these disputes among the people of earlier revelations took place after "*clear evidence of the truth had been given to them.*" (Verse 4) They were not lacking in knowledge and proof, but they were blindly driven by their desires into deviation.

---

5. The doctrine of a single energy in Christ was that the allegedly divine and human natures in Jesus had one active force.

6. The doctrine of a single energy was repudiated, and the doctrine of a single will (the Monothelete formula) was propounded in 638.

7. Nadwī, *Mādhā Khasir al-'Ālam*, pp. 3–5. This is summarized in the English edition, *Islam and the World*, p. 15.

Clear and Simple

Yet religion is clear in its original form and the faith is simple in its essence: "*Yet they were ordered to do nothing more than to serve God, to worship Him alone with sincere dedication and purity of faith, to attend to their prayers and to pay their* zakāt. *That is surely the right religion, pure and straight.*" (Verse 5)

This is the basis of divine religion throughout history and in all its forms. It is simply the worship of God alone. A sincere and pure submission to Him, a detachment from polytheism in all its shapes and forms, the establishment of regular worship and the payment of the regular obligatory charity, or *zakāt*: "*That is surely the right religion, pure and straight.*" (Verse 5) It is a pure and sincere faith that is firmly established in the heart, the worship of God alone which is a translation of this faith, and spending money for God's cause as He has stated. He who fulfils these injunctions has met the requirements of faith, as the people of earlier revelations were commanded to do, and as these requirements are outlined in all forms of divine faith. It is one religion, the same faith in all the successive messages, as preached by the messengers of God. It is a religion free from all ambiguity and complication; a faith which gives no reason for division and dispute. It is very clear and very simple. How completely different this religion is from those complicated and confusing concepts and from those lengthy polemics.

Since clear evidence was given to them formerly in their own religions through their own prophets, and since clear evidence was given to them again, full of life, in the form of a messenger from God reciting pure revelations, and offering them a clear and simple faith, then the true path becomes very clear. So does the destiny of unbelievers, as also that of believers: "*The unbelievers among the people of the earlier revelations and the idolaters will be in the fire of hell, where they will abide. They are the worst of all creatures. But those who believe and do righteous deeds are the best of all creatures. Their reward [awaits them] with their Lord: the gardens of Eden through which running waters flow, in which they will abide forever. God is well pleased with them and they with Him. This is for him who is God-fearing.*" (Verses 6–8)

Muḥammad (peace be upon him) was the last messenger, and Islam, which he preached, the final message. Messengers from God came successively every time corruption spread in human life. Their objective was to make mankind return to righteousness. Those who deviated from the right path had one chance after another to correct their behaviour. But now that God had willed to close His messages to earth by this final, comprehensive, perfect and accomplished message, then the last chance was also given. This entailed either the adoption of faith leading to salvation, or the denial of faith ending in destruction. For disbelief now is an established evidence of unlimited evil, while accepting the faith is proof of goodness which goes to its absolute end.

"*The unbelievers among the people of the earlier revelations and the idolaters will be in the fire of hell, where they will abide. They are the worst of all creatures.*" (Verse 6) It is a clear and absolute verdict which leaves no room for argument or dispute. It is applicable even if some of their actions, values or systems were good, since these were not based on believing in this final message and messenger. No appearance of goodness makes us entertain even the slightest doubt in this judgement, since apparent goodness is detached from the upright method of living laid down by God.

"*But those who believe and do righteous deeds are the best of all creatures.*" (Verse 7) This is also an absolute verdict that makes for no dispute or argument. Its condition is also clear, free from any ambiguity or deception. The condition is faith, not merely being born in a land which claims to be Islamic, or in a family which claims to belong to Islam. Nor is it a few words which one repeats again and again. It is the acceptance of faith which establishes its effects on actual life, "*and do righteous deeds.*" It is entirely different from the words that go no further than the lips. As for righteous deeds, these are everything God has commanded to be done in matters of worship, behaviour, action and day-to-day dealings. The first and most important of these righteous deeds is the establishment of God's law on this planet, and the government of people according to what God has legislated. Those who act accordingly are the best creatures of all.

"*Their reward [awaits them] with their Lord: the gardens of Eden through which running waters flow, in which they will abide forever.*" (Verse 8) These gardens are a specially prepared, permanent and happy dwelling. Happiness is symbolized here by security against death and by a prevalent feeling of contentment as against anxiety which mars and disrupts all earthly comforts. It is also symbolized by the running waters flowing through these gardens; a picture which adds a sense of ease, life and beauty.

The *sūrah* then adds some refined touches to the picture it portrays of their perpetual happiness: "*God is well pleased with them and they with Him.*" (Verse 8) God's pleasure with them is much more exalted and far more enjoyable than any happiness. Moreover, in their inmost souls they feel happy with their Lord. They are well pleased with the destiny He has set for them, delighted with the grace He has granted them, and enchanted by this relationship with their Lord: "*God is well pleased with them and they with Him.*"

"*This is for him who is God-fearing.*" (Verse 8) This is the final assertion. It stresses that all that has been said is dependent on the nature of the relationship between man's heart and God. It also depends on man having a feeling of God which urges him to all sorts of good deeds and militates against all sorts of deviation. It is a feeling which removes barriers, lifts curtains and makes man's heart stand bare before God, the One, the All-Powerful. Such a feeling helps make worship and submission to God pure and purges human actions from all elements of hypocrisy and idolatry. So he who truly fears his Lord cannot allow his heart to entertain the slightest shred of influence by any being other than God, the Creator of all. Such a person knows that God rejects any deed done for the sake of anyone other than Him. For God is in no need of partners. Every action must be purely for Him or else He rejects it.

SŪRAH 99

Al-Zalzalah

(The Earthquake)

Al-Zalzalah (The Earthquake)

سُورَةُ الزَّلْزَلَةِ

In the name of God, the Beneficent, the Merciful.

بِسْمِ ٱللَّهِ ٱلرَّحْمَٰنِ ٱلرَّحِيمِ

When the earth is rocked by her [final] earthquake, (1)

إِذَا زُلْزِلَتِ ٱلْأَرْضُ زِلْزَالَهَا ١

when the earth shakes off her burdens, (2)

وَأَخْرَجَتِ ٱلْأَرْضُ أَثْقَالَهَا ٢

and man asks: ‘What is the matter with her?’ (3)

وَقَالَ ٱلْإِنسَٰنُ مَا لَهَا ٣

On that day she will tell her news, (4)

يَوْمَئِذٍ تُحَدِّثُ أَخْبَارَهَا ٤

for your Lord will have inspired her. (5)

بِأَنَّ رَبَّكَ أَوْحَىٰ لَهَا ٥

On that day people will come forward, separated from one another, to be shown their deeds. (6)	يَوْمَئِذٍ يَصْدُرُ ٱلنَّاسُ أَشْتَاتًا لِّيُرَوْا۟ أَعْمَٰلَهُمْ ﴿٦﴾
Whoever does an atom's weight of good shall see it then, (7)	فَمَن يَعْمَلْ مِثْقَالَ ذَرَّةٍ خَيْرًا يَرَهُۥ ﴿٧﴾
and whoever does an atom's weight of evil shall see it then also. (8)	وَمَن يَعْمَلْ مِثْقَالَ ذَرَّةٍ شَرًّا يَرَهُۥ ﴿٨﴾

Overview

According to some reports, this *sūrah* is a Madinan revelation, but other reports suggest that it was revealed in Makkah. The latter reports seem to be more valid, because the *sūrah*'s mode of expression and subject matter are more in line with the style and subjects of Makkan *sūrahs*.

The *sūrah* makes a violent wake-up call to drowsy hearts; the subject matter, scene drawn and rhythm all contributing to the effect of this jolt. It is a powerful blast that makes the earth and all that is on it quake and tremble. Men hardly recover their senses when they find themselves confronted with the reckoning, weighing and evaluating of actions and deeds. They immediately receive their recompense. All this is expressed in just a few short phrases, which is characteristic of this part of the Qur'ān as a whole and forcefully portrayed in this particular *sūrah*.

The Results of a Life's Work

When the earth is rocked by her [final] earthquake, when the earth shakes off her burdens, and man asks: 'What is the matter with her?' On that day she will tell her news, for your Lord will have inspired her. (Verses 1–5)

It is the Day of Judgement when the firm earth trembles and quakes violently and yields up her long-carried loads of bodies and metals and other matters which have weighed heavily on her. It is a scene that makes every firm and solid object under the feet of the listeners shake and totter. They think themselves to be staggering and toddling along and the earth beneath them shuddering and quaking. It is a scene which separates one's heart from everything on earth it clings to, assuming it to be firm and everlasting. The Qur'ān imparts to these scenes a kind of movement which is transmitted almost to the very sinews of the listener. Such immediate impact is all the more forceful because man is portrayed as confronting and reacting to it all: "*And man asks: 'What is the matter with her?'*" (Verse 3)

It is the question advanced by one who is bewildered, astonished, surprised and puzzled, who sees something unfamiliar, encounters what is imperceptible, and beholds what makes him impatient and agitated. So he blurts out: What is the matter with her? What is quaking and shaking her so violently? He cries as he reels and staggers, trying to hold on to anything which may support or keep him upright. But all around him waver and totter violently.

Man has experienced earthquakes and volcanoes which have filled him with awe and terror, and have brought to him ruin and destruction. But when man witnesses the quake of the Day of Resurrection he will see no similarity between it and the earthquakes and volcanoes of this world. He neither knows its secrets, nor does he remember anything similar to it. It is something dreadful, taking place for the very first time.

"*On that day*", when this quake occurs, leaving man entirely shaken, "*she will tell her news, for your Lord will have inspired her.*" (Verses 4–5) This earth will then tell her news, describe her condition and what has happened to her. It will all have been brought about simply because 'your Lord has inspired her,' ordered her to shake and quake so fiercely and shake off her burdens. She obeys only the Lord's orders *'in true submission!'* (84: 5) She will relate her news because what will take place is a simple and clear account of what lies behind it of God's orders and inspiration to the earth.

At this point when man is astonished, puzzled and crying out, and as the rhythm gasps with dread and terror, surprise and wonder, tottering and shuddering, crying out: What is the matter with her? What has happened to her? – at this point he encounters the scene of resurrection, reckoning, weighing and recompense. "*On that day people will come forward, separated from one another, to be shown their deeds. Whoever does an atom's weight of good shall see it then, and whoever does an atom's weight of evil shall see it then also.*" (Verses 6–8)

In the twinkling of an eye we behold people rising from their graves. "*On that day people will come forward, separated from one another.*" (Verse 6) We behold them issuing forth from all over the globe: "*as if they were swarming locusts.*" (54: 7) This scene is also unknown to man, it is something unprecedented, unique in nature. "*On that day, the Earth will split asunder and they will come out in haste.*" (50: 44) Wherever you look you behold a ghost hurrying away, caring for nothing and never looking back or turning his head left or right. They all are "*rushing to the summoner,*" (54: 8), with their heads down and their eyes staring forward, "*for each one of them will on that day have enough preoccupations of his own.*" (80: 37) It is a scene indescribable in human language. It is both ghastly and astonishing. All these adjectives and all their synonymous and analogous terms cannot describe it. It would be better conceived with a stretch of imagination and contemplation within the limits and capacity of our minds.

"*On that day people will come forward, separated from one another, to be shown their deeds.*" (Verse 6) This is far more terrible and dreadful. People go to where they will be shown their deeds. They have to face their deeds and their rewards or punishments.

Encountering one's own deeds may, sometimes, be far more severe than any other punishment. Man sometimes does things which he avoids even thinking about when he is alone.

In a spell of repentance and remorse, man may even turn his face from some of his deeds because they are so ghastly. So, in what condition will he be on that day when he faces his deeds in front of all mankind and in the presence of God Almighty? It is a terrible and frightful punishment, although it is only that they are shown their deeds and have to confront their labours. However, following this confrontation comes the accurate reckoning which does not leave out an atom's weight of good or evil. "*Whoever does an atom's weight of good shall see it then, and whoever does an atom's weight of evil shall see it then also.*" (Verses 7–8)

"*An atom's weight!*" Early commentators on the Qur'ān explain this phrase as "a mosquito" or "a particle of dust" which can only be seen when exposed to sunlight. These were the smallest things they could think of, and which may be referred to as an atom. But now we know that the word 'atom' refers to a definite thing which is much smaller than a particle of dust seen in sunlight. For the particle of dust can be seen by the human eye while it is impossible to see the atom, even with the help of the most powerful microscopes in modern laboratories. It is only conceived by scientists. None of them has seen it either with his own eyes or with his microscope. All that they have seen is its effects.

This atom, or what is similar to it in weight, whether good or bad, will be brought forth and shown to its doer, who will then receive its reward. At that time man does not undervalue any of his actions and deeds, whether good or bad. He does not say, "Oh, this is a trivial thing which has no weight or consideration." On the contrary, his conscience will be as sensitive to everything he has done as an accurate scale registering even the weight of an atom favourably or unfavourably. There is nothing parallel or similar to this measure in this world, except the heart of a believer. Such a heart is sensitive to even an atom's weight of either good or evil.

But there are some hearts in this world which are unmoved even by mountains of sin and crime. They remain unaffected while suppressing fountains of goodness which are far firmer than mountains. These hearts are conceited on this earth but on the Day of Judgement they are crushed under their own burdens.

SŪRAH 100

Al- ʿĀdiyāt

(The Coursers)

Al- ʿĀdiyāt (The Coursers)	سُورَةُ العَادِيَاتِ
In the name of God, the Beneficent, the Merciful.	بِسْمِ ٱللَّهِ ٱلرَّحْمَٰنِ ٱلرَّحِيمِ
By the snorting coursers, (1)	وَٱلْعَـٰدِيَـٰتِ ضَبْحًا ١
striking sparks of fire, (2)	فَٱلْمُورِيَـٰتِ قَدْحًا ٢
rushing to assault at dawn, (3)	فَٱلْمُغِيرَٰتِ صُبْحًا ٣
raising a trail of dust, (4)	فَأَثَرْنَ بِهِۦ نَقْعًا ٤
storming into any army: (5)	فَوَسَطْنَ بِهِۦ جَمْعًا ٥
man is surely ungrateful to his Lord, (6)	إِنَّ ٱلْإِنسَـٰنَ لِرَبِّهِۦ لَكَنُودٌ ٦

وَإِنَّهُۥ عَلَىٰ ذَٰلِكَ لَشَهِيدٌ ﴿٧﴾	and to this he himself bears witness; (7)
وَإِنَّهُۥ لِحُبِّ ٱلْخَيْرِ لَشَدِيدٌ ﴿٨﴾	and truly, he is passionate in his love of wealth. (8)
أَفَلَا يَعْلَمُ إِذَا بُعْثِرَ مَا فِى ٱلْقُبُورِ ﴿٩﴾	Does he not know that when the contents of the graves are scattered about, (9)
وَحُصِّلَ مَا فِى ٱلصُّدُورِ ﴿١٠﴾	and what is in the breasts is brought out – (10)
إِنَّ رَبَّهُم بِهِمْ يَوْمَئِذٍ لَّخَبِيرٌۢ ﴿١١﴾	that on that day their Lord [will show that He] is fully aware of them? (11)

Overview

This *sūrah* is presented in rapid and violent strokes. The text moves swiftly from one scene to another. As we come to the last verse, everything – the verbal expressions, connotations, subject matter and rhythm – settle down in a manner similar to that of a courser reaching the finishing line.

The *sūrah* starts with a scene of war steeds running, snorting, striking sparks of fire with their hoofs, launching a raid at dawn and blazing a trail of dust, cleaving suddenly into the centre of the enemies' camp, taking them by surprise and striking terror and fear in their hearts.

Then follows a picture of the human soul: a scene of ingratitude, ignobleness, greed and extreme miserliness. Immediately after that there is a description of graves laid open and their contents scattered, and the secrets of hearts poured out. Finally the trail of dust, ingratitude and miserliness, the contents of graves and dragged out secrets all come to the same terminus. They come to God and settle down: "*On that day their Lord [will show that He] is fully aware of them?*" (Verse 11)

The rhythm of the *sūrah* is robust and thunderous, and thus fits well with the dusty and clamorous atmosphere generated by the upturned graves and the secrets violently pulled out of people's breasts. These characteristics of the rhythm are also appropriate to the picture of ingratitude, thanklessness and extreme miserliness. The framework for this picture is provided by a dusty and tumultuous stampede of horses racing and thundering. Thus the frame and the picture are in perfect harmony with each other.

Witness to His Shortcomings

> *By the snorting coursers, striking sparks of fire, rushing to assault at dawn, raising a trail of dust, storming into any army: man is surely ungrateful to his Lord, and to this he himself bears witness; and truly, he is passionate in his love of wealth.* (Verses 1–8)

God swears by the war horses and describes their movements one after the other: running, snorting and neighing. They strike their hoofs against rocks, producing sparks of fire. They wage their attack early at dawn in order to take the enemy by surprise, producing a trail of dust during the unexpected battle. They swiftly pierce the enemy ranks creating disorder and confusion amongst them. These successive stages were well known to those who were first addressed by the Qur'ān. The fact that God swears by the horses provides an emphatic suggestion that the movement portrayed is a lovable one and that people should respond to it actively. This they do only after realizing how precious it is in God's measure, which is reflected in His paying attention to it. Added to all this is the harmony between this scene and the scenes which are the subject of the divine oath, namely the state of the human soul when it is devoid of faith and its impetus. The Qur'ān draws our attention to this state in order that we may gather all our will-power to combat it. For God is perfectly aware of how deeply it is ingrained in man and what great pressure it exercises on him.

"*Man is surely ungrateful to his Lord, and to this he himself bears witness; and truly, he is passionate in his love of wealth.*" (Verses 6–8) It is a fact that man reacts with ingratitude to all the bounties of his Lord. He denies the favours which God confers on him. His thanklessness and ingratitude is reflected in a host of actions and verbal statements which will serve as witness against him. Or perhaps, on the Day of Judgement, he may testify against himself, admitting his ingratitude: "*and to this he himself bears witness.*" (Verse 7) For on the Day of Judgement he will speak the plain truth even against himself, without contention or excuse. "*And truly, he is passionate in his love of wealth.*" (Verse 8)

Man is a passionate self-lover. But he loves only what he imagines to be good for himself: wealth, power and the pleasures of this world. This is his nature unless he has faith which changes his concepts, values and even his concerns. Faith changes his ingratitude to humble thankfulness. It changes his greed and miserliness to benevolence and compassion. It makes him aware of the proper values which are worthy of being the object of ambition and hard competition. Indeed these are much more exalted than money, power and mundane pleasures.

Man without faith is an ignoble creature, having only trivial ambitions and petty concerns. However large his desires, however strong his ambitions and high his objectives may seem, he remains sunk in the cesspool of this earth, confined within the limits of this life, imprisoned in self. He cannot be freed or elevated except by an attachment to a world superior to this earth, extending beyond this life; a world which originates from God who is the First Being and returning to God the Eternal; a world into which this life and the life hereafter converge and which has no end.

Hence, the final touch in the *sūrah* provides the cure for ingratitude, greed and miserliness. It portrays the scene of resurrection in a way that makes man shudder, and puts his love for wealth and indulgence in worldly riches out of his mind, unshackling his soul and setting it free from earthly attachments: "*Does he not know that when the contents of the graves are scattered about, and what is in the breasts is brought out – that on that day their Lord [will show that He] is fully aware of them?*" (Verses 9–11)

It is a violent and frightening scene in which we witness the 'scattering about' of the contents of the graves and the bringing out of closely-guarded secrets. The Arabic terms, *buʿthira* and *ḥuṣṣila*, used here for scattering and pulling are very forceful, suggesting an atmosphere of violence and force.

Does he not know what happens when this will take place? Mere awareness of all this is enough to inspire man to seek an answer and explore every avenue in search of it. For it finally rests where every matter and destiny is settled: "*on that day their Lord [will show that He] is fully aware of them?*" (Verse 11)

So to their Lord is their end. On that day He shows that He knows them and all their affairs and secrets. God certainly knows everything at all times and in all conditions, but knowledge of "that day" has the effect of drawing their attention. It is a knowledge which necessitates reckoning and reward. This implicit meaning is the one underlined here.

All in all this *sūrah* is a swift, vehement and breathless piece, with a sudden terminus of meaning, expression and rhythm all at the same time.

SŪRAH 101

Al-Qāri ʿah

(The Striker)

Al-Qāri ʿah (The Striker)	سُورَةُ القَارِعَةِ
In the name of God, the Beneficent, the Merciful.	بِسْمِ ٱللَّهِ ٱلرَّحْمَٰنِ ٱلرَّحِيمِ
The Striker! (1)	ٱلْقَارِعَةُ ﴿١﴾
What is the Striker? (2)	مَا ٱلْقَارِعَةُ ﴿٢﴾
Would that you knew what the Striker is! (3)	وَمَآ أَدْرَىٰكَ مَا ٱلْقَارِعَةُ ﴿٣﴾
The day when people will be scattered moths, (4)	يَوْمَ يَكُونُ ٱلنَّاسُ كَٱلْفَرَاشِ ٱلْمَبْثُوثِ ﴿٤﴾
and the mountains like tufts of carded wool. (5)	وَتَكُونُ ٱلْجِبَالُ كَٱلْعِهْنِ ٱلْمَنفُوشِ ﴿٥﴾

Then he whose weight [of good deeds] is heavy in the balance, (6)	فَأَمَّا مَن ثَقُلَتْ مَوَٰزِينُهُۥ ﴿٦﴾
shall enjoy a happy life. (7)	فَهُوَ فِى عِيشَةٍ رَّاضِيَةٍ ﴿٧﴾
But he whose weight is light in the balance, (8)	وَأَمَّا مَنْ خَفَّتْ مَوَٰزِينُهُۥ ﴿٨﴾
shall have the abyss for his home. (9)	فَأُمُّهُۥ هَاوِيَةٌ ﴿٩﴾
Would that you knew what this is like! (10)	وَمَآ أَدْرَىٰكَ مَا هِيَهْ ﴿١٠﴾
It is a scorching fire. (11)	نَارٌ حَامِيَةٌۢ ﴿١١﴾

Overview

Al-Qāriʿah, or the Striker, means the resurrection. Elsewhere in the Qur'ān it is given names such as the Overwhelming One, the Deafening Shout, the Stunning Blast and the Enveloper. The term *al-Qāriʿah* also connotes hitting and knocking hard. It knocks people's hearts with its engulfing horror.

The *sūrah* as a whole deals with the Striker, its essence, what takes place in it and what it eventually leads to. Thus the *sūrah* portrays one of the scenes of the Day of Resurrection.

The scene portrayed here is one of horror directly affecting man and mountains. In this scene people look dwarfish in spite of their great number. For they are like scattered moths. They fly here and there having no power or weight, going through the dilemma of moths which rush to destruction, having no aim or purpose.

On the other hand, the mountains, which used to be firm and solidly based, seem to be like carded wool carried away by winds, and even by a light breeze. Thus, it is in harmony with this image that the Day of Resurrection is described as the one that strikes or knocks out. The connotations used and the rhythm are in consonance with the effects of the Striker on both people and mountains. The *sūrah* spreads an air of awe and expectation about the outcome of reckoning.

Determination of People's Fates

"*The Striker! What is the Striker! Would that you knew what the Striker is!*" (Verses 1–3) This *sūrah* starts with the single word, *al-Qāriʿah*, rendered in English as the Striker. It is thrown like a shot, without any further information, predicate or adjective. As such it creates through its sound and connotations an ambiance of awe and apprehension.

The word is immediately followed by a question suggesting alarm: "*What is the Striker?*" (Verse 2) It is that dreadful and formidable thing which arouses curiosity and questioning. Then comes the answer in the form of a cryptic exclamation: "*Would that you knew what the Striker is!*" It is too great to be comprehended or imagined. Then follows the answer which states what takes place in it but refrains from stating its exact nature: "*The day when people will be scattered moths, and the mountains like tufts of carded wool.*" (Verses 4–5)

This is the first scene of the Striker, a scene that leaves people's hearts in panic and makes limbs tremble with fear. The listener feels that everything he clings to in this world is flying all around him like dust. Then comes the end of all mankind. "*Then he whose weight [of good deeds] is heavy in the balance, shall enjoy a happy life. But he whose weight is light in the balance, shall have the abyss for his home. Would that you knew what this is like! It is a scorching fire.*" (Verses 6–11)

It is useful for us to consider the weights, whether heavy or light. This means that there are standards which God credits with being valuable and others that are valueless. This is the general meaning of the statement which the *sūrah* wants to convey. However, God knows best the exact nature of the balance determining such weights. To indulge in a sophisticated, logical and linguistic argument about the meaning of the Qur'ānic term, *mawazīn*, used here is in itself a departure from the Qur'ānic spirit and indicates that the reader is not interested in the Qur'ān or in Islam.

"*Then he whose weight* [*of good deeds*] *is heavy in the balance*, according to God's measures and evaluation, "*shall enjoy a happy life.*" God makes this statement general without any detailed information. Thus, the statement imparts to man the connotations of content and satisfaction or, indeed, pure happiness.

"*But he whose weight is light in the balance*," according to God's same measure and evaluation, "*shall have the abyss for his home.*" The Arabic text uses the term, *umm*, 'mother', for what is rendered here as 'home'. It is to his mother that a child turns for help and protection as he seeks shelter and security at home. But such people with light measure can only turn and resort to the abyss! The expression is a fine one, beautifully ordered. It also has a shade of obscurity preparing the way for subsequent clarification which adds to the depth of the intended effect: "*Would that you knew what this is like!*" (Verse 10) It is again the cryptic exclamation used often in the Qur'ān which emphasizes that it is beyond comprehension and vision. Then comes the answer in the closing note: "*It is a scorching fire.*" (Verse 11)

Such is the mother of any person whose weight of good deeds is light. This is his mother to whom he turns for help and protection and for security and comfort. But what does he find with such a mother? He finds nothing but the abyss and a scorching fire. The expression here makes a sudden jolt to represent the hard reality.

SŪRAH 102

Al-Takāthur

(Rivalry for Worldly Gain)

سُورَةُ التَّكَاثُرِ

Al-Takāthur (Rivalry for Worldly Gain)

بِسْمِ ٱللَّهِ ٱلرَّحْمَٰنِ ٱلرَّحِيمِ

In the name of God, the Beneficent, the Merciful.

أَلْهَىٰكُمُ ٱلتَّكَاثُرُ ١

You are preoccupied by greed for more and more, (1)

حَتَّىٰ زُرْتُمُ ٱلْمَقَابِرَ ٢

until you go down to your graves. (2)

كَلَّا سَوْفَ تَعْلَمُونَ ٣

Nay, in time you will come to know! (3)

ثُمَّ كَلَّا سَوْفَ تَعْلَمُونَ ٤

Again, in time you will come to know! (4)

كَلَّا لَوْ تَعْلَمُونَ عِلْمَ ٱلْيَقِينِ ٥

Indeed, were you to know [the truth] with certainty... (5)

You would, most certainly, see the fire of hell. (6)	لَتَرَوُنَّ ٱلۡجَحِيمَ ﴿٦﴾
Again, you will, most certainly, see it with your very eyes. (7)	ثُمَّ لَتَرَوُنَّهَا عَيۡنَ ٱلۡيَقِينِ ﴿٧﴾
Then on that day you will certainly be questioned about your joys and comforts. (8)	ثُمَّ لَتُسۡـَٔلُنَّ يَوۡمَئِذٍ عَنِ ٱلنَّعِيمِ ﴿٨﴾

Greedy Preoccupations

This *sūrah* has a rhythm that is both majestic and awe-inspiring; as if it were the voice of a warner standing on a high place, projecting his voice as it rings out in weighty emphasis. He calls out to people who are drowsy, drunken, confused. They approach a precipice with their eyes closed and their feelings numbed. So the warner increases the volume of his voice to the limit: "*You are preoccupied by greed for more and more, until you go down to your graves.*" (Verses 1–2)

You drunken and confused lot! You who take delight and indulge in rivalry for wealth, children and the pleasures of this life, from which you are sure to depart! You who are absorbed with what you have, unaware of what comes afterwards! You who will leave the object of this rivalry, and what you seek pride in, and go to a narrow hole where there is no rivalry or pride! Wake up and look around, all of you! For indeed, "*you are preoccupied by greed for more and more, until you go down to your graves.*" (Verses 1–2)

With a deep and grave rhythm the *sūrah* then strikes their hearts with the terror awaiting them after they are left in their graves: "*Nay, in time you will come to know!*" (Verse 3) Then it repeats the same note, employing the same words and the same firm and terrifying rhythm: "*Again, in time you will come to know!*" (Verse 4) Then it adds to the depth and awe of this assurance, and hints at the grave prospect that lies beyond, the terrifying essence of which they do not recognize in their flush of intoxication and rivalry for worldly riches: "*Indeed, were you to know [the truth] with certainty...*" (Verse 5)

The conditional sentence is not completed in the text. This is acceptable as a refined form of Arabic. It adds to the feeling of awe generated by the *sūrah*. The inference here is that had they known what they should know for certain, they would not have indulged in such rivalry for petty gain. The *sūrah* then discloses the fearful fact which has been withheld: "*You would, most certainly, see the fire of hell.*" (Verse 6)

It then emphasizes this fact and enhances its impact on people's hearts: "*Again, you will, most certainly, see it with your very eyes.*" (Verse 7)

Finally, it puts the last statement which makes the drunkard sober, the lethargic conscious, the confused attentive and the self-indulgent tremble and feel apprehension at his indulgence in comfort and pleasure: "*Then on that day you will certainly be questioned about your joys and comforts.*" (Verse 8) You will be questioned concerning all this: How did you get it? How did you dispense with it? Was it obtained from a lawful source and dispensed with lawfully? Or was it gained unlawfully and used in a sinful manner? Have you praised and thanked God for it? Have you given the poor their due? Have you spent some of it on others? Or monopolized it all for your selves? "*You will be questioned*" about your rivalry in gathering and amassing wealth and about what you take pride in. It is a burden which you, in your preoccupation and enjoyment, think little of. But beyond it lie heavy responsibilities.

This is a self-expressing *sūrah*. It leaves its impact on us by its meaning and rhythm. It leaves the heart occupied, burdened with the problem of the hereafter, inattentive to the trivialities of this worldly life and its petty concerns.

It portrays the life of this world as a fleeting wink in the long span of existence: "*You are preoccupied by greed for more and more, until you go down to your graves.*" (Verses 1–2) The wink of this life is over and its small leaf is turned. Thereafter time stretches on and the burdens become heavier. The style of the *sūrah* presents this inference, achieving harmony between the actual reality and its manner of expression.

Whenever we read this awe-inspiring and majestic *sūrah*, we feel its rhythm travelling upwards in space at the beginning and downwards to the deep, deep level at the end. We feel the burden of this wink of a life on our shoulders as we walk heavily along the road. Then we start questioning ourselves about the smallest and most trivial of our deeds.

SŪRAH 103

Al-ʿAṣr

(The Declining Day)

Al-ʿAṣr (The Declining Day)

سُورَةُ العَصْرِ

In the name of God, the Beneficent, the Merciful.

بِسْمِ ٱللَّهِ ٱلرَّحْمَٰنِ ٱلرَّحِيمِ

I swear by the declining day, (1)

وَٱلْعَصْرِ ١

that man is a certain loser, (2)

إِنَّ ٱلْإِنسَٰنَ لَفِى خُسْرٍ ٢

except for those who have faith and do righteous deeds and counsel one another to follow the truth and counsel one another to be patient in adversity. (3)

إِلَّا ٱلَّذِينَ ءَامَنُوا۟ وَعَمِلُوا۟ ٱلصَّٰلِحَٰتِ
وَتَوَاصَوْا۟ بِٱلْحَقِّ وَتَوَاصَوْا۟ بِٱلصَّبْرِ ٣

Overview

This very short *sūrah* outlines a complete system for human life based on the Islamic viewpoint. It defines, in the clearest and most concise form, the basic concept of faith in the context of its comprehensive reality. In a few words the whole Islamic constitution is covered and in fact, the Muslim community is described in its essential qualities and message in one verse only, the last. Such is the clear and most expressive style of which only God is capable.

The great fact which this *sūrah* affirms is simply that throughout the history of mankind there has been one worthwhile and trustworthy path, which is, specifically, the one the *sūrah* describes. All other ways lead only to loss and ruin. As it says in outline, this way means first the adoption of faith, followed by good deeds and exhortation to follow the truth and to persevere in the face of adversity.

Faith and Its Significance

What does the adoption of faith then mean? We shall not give here its juristic definition. Instead, we shall describe its nature and importance in human life.

Faith is the characteristic by which man, a small creature with a life of short duration in a limited world, attains closeness to the Absolute and Everlasting Originator of the universe and all that exists in it. He thus establishes a link with the whole universe, which springs from that One Origin, with the laws governing it and the powers and potentialities it provides. As a result, he breaks away from the narrow boundaries of his trivial self to the broadness of the universe, from his inadequate power to the great unknown universal energies, and from the limits of his short life to the eternity that God alone comprehends.

This bond with God grants man assured power, limitless scope and freedom. It endows him with great enjoyment of this beautiful life and enriches his life with a mutual friendship with other creatures. Thus life becomes a pleasant journey for man everywhere and at all times. From this an everlasting happiness and intimate understanding of life and creation are derived. This is the invaluable gain, to lack which is an immeasurable loss.

The qualities of faith are also precisely those of sublime and dignified humanity, such as the worship of one God which elevates man above servitude to others and establishes within him the truth of all mankind's equality so that he neither yields nor bows down his head to anyone other than God, the One, the Absolute. The result is that man enjoys true liberty, which radiates from within his conscience following his realization that there is only one power and one Lord in this world. This liberation is spontaneously developed from such an awareness, for it is the only logical sequence.

Godliness is the second quality of dignified humanity. This quality determines for man the source from which he derives his concepts, values, criteria, considerations, doctrines, laws and whatever brings him into relation with God, the world at large and with his fellow human beings. Thus, equity and justice replace personal desires and self-interest. This strengthens the believer's realization of the value of his way of life and keeps him above all *jāhiliyyah* concepts, interests and mundane values. This is so even when a believer finds himself alone, with no one else of his kind. For he counters all these features with values he derives directly from God. As such, they are the highest in value, most sound and most deserving of devotion and esteem.

A third quality of faith and dignified humanity is the clarity of the relationship between the Creator and His creatures. Thus, man, who is a creature restricted by his own world, is connected with the Everlasting Truth without any mediator. It supplies his heart and soul with light and contentment; and it gives him confidence and purpose. It eliminates from his mind perplexity, fear and anxiety, as well as any inclination towards arrogance and tyranny over others.

Following the path ordained by God, with steadfastness and clarity of vision, is the next quality of the community of believers. This must be maintained so that goodness does not come about casually, incidentally or without deliberation but rather springs from definite motives and heads towards certain aims. People united for God's cause collaborate. Thus, with a single definite purpose and a single distinguished banner, the Muslim community is raised. This is true for all generations that are similarly welded together.

Another quality is belief in the dignity of man in God's sight. This heightens man's regard for himself and restrains him from aspiring to a position higher than that which the Creator has defined for him. For man to feel that he is dignified in God's sight is the loftiest concept he may attain of himself. Any ideology or philosophy that abases this valuation and ascribes a dishonourable origin to man, separating him from the Supreme Society of God is, in effect, nothing but a position of ignominy and degradation, even though it may not say so openly. Hence, the effects of Darwinism, Freudianism and Marxism are among the most horrid disasters human nature has encountered. For they teach mankind that all abasement and downright animalism are natural phenomena with which we should be familiar and of which we need not be ashamed.

Purity of motivation is yet another quality of the dignified humanity established by faith. This directly follows the realization of man's dignity in God's sight, His supervision over human conscience and His knowledge of what man harbours in his innermost soul. A normal human being, whom the theories of Freud, Karl Marx and their type have not deformed, feels ashamed should another person come to know what unhealthy feelings he may incidentally experience. The believer feels the awesome presence of God in his innermost consciousness and his awareness makes him tremble. He, therefore, resorts to self-purification and spiritual cleansing. A refined moral sense is the natural fruit of faith in God who is just, kind, compassionate, generous and forbearing and who abhors evil, loves goodness, knows every furtive look and every secret thought. From this follows the believer's responsibility, which is the direct result of his free-will and the fact that God is aware of all that he does and feels. It stimulates within him healthy awareness, sensitivity, serenity and foresight. His is a communal, rather than an individual responsibility. What is more is that it is a responsibility towards all humanity, pure and simple. A believer feels all this in every action. He achieves a higher degree of self-respect and calculates results before taking any step. He is of value in the world and the whole realm of existence and has a role in its smooth running.

The final quality is man's elevation above greed for worldly gains, preferring instead God's richer, everlasting reward for which all people should strive, as the Qur'ān directs them to do. Such striving for all that is good results in spiritual elevation, purification and cleansing. Of immense help in this regard is the fact that a believer has a broad scope for action: between this life and the next and between the heavens and the earth. Man's elevation lessens his anxiety about the results and fruits of his actions. He does what is good only because it is good and because God requires it. It is never his concern whether it leads to further goodness in his own short life. God, for whom he performs the good, neither dies, forgets nor ignores anyone's deeds. The reward is not to be received here, for this life is not the last. Thus, a believer acquires the power to continue to perform good deeds without waiting for immediate results. He is sustained in his determination to do good deeds by his unshakable belief in God. This is what guarantees that doing good becomes a carefully chosen way of life, not a casual incident or motiveless event. It is this belief that supplies believers with the power and fortitude to face evil, whether manifested in the despotism of a tyrant, the pressures of *jāhiliyyah*, or the frailty of their will-power to control their passions. All these represent pressures which arise primarily from a sense that this life is too short for us to achieve our aims and pleasures and from our inability to comprehend the deeper results of doing good or to see the ultimate victory of right over evil. Faith provides a radical and perfect way of dealing with such feelings.

Faith in Human Life

Faith is the foundation of all goodness in human life. It is from faith that all forms of goodness spring and to which all its fruits are due. What does not spring from faith is a branch cut from its tree: it is bound to fade and perish; or else, it is a stray shoot, limited and temporary! Faith is the axis to which all the fine fabric of life's networks is connected. Without it life is a loose event, wasted through the pursuit of yearnings and fantasies. It is the ideology which brings together diversified deeds under a consistent system, following the same route and geared to the same mechanism, possessing a definite motive and a well-defined goal.

Hence, all deeds not stemming from this origin and not related to that way are completely disregarded by the Qur'ān. Islam is invariably candid over this. In *Sūrah* 14, Abraham, we read: "*The works of those who disbelieve in their Lord are like ashes which the wind blows about fiercely on a stormy day. They cannot achieve any benefit from all that they might have earned.*" (14: 18) In *Sūrah* 24, Light, we read: "*As for the unbelievers, their deeds are like a mirage in the desert, which the thirsty traveller supposes to be water, but when he comes near to it, he finds that it is nothing.*" (24: 39) These are clear statements discrediting every deed not related to faith. The fact is that faith gives a person's deed a motive that is connected with the origin of existence and an aim compatible with the purpose of all creation. This is a logical view of an ideology that attributes all events to God. Whoever dissociates himself from Him, vanishes and loses the reality of his existence.

Faith is a sign of health in a person's nature and soundness in his disposition. It also indicates man's harmony with the nature of the whole universe, and the presence of mutual effect between man and the world around him. His life, as long as his behaviour is straightforward, must bring about an orientation which ends up in his adoption of faith because of what this universe itself possesses of signs and testimonies about the absolute power that created it. Were the contrary the case, something must then be wrong or lacking in the state of the recipient, i.e. man, which would be a sign of corruption that only leads to loss and nullifies any deed which might somehow give an appearance of righteousness. So extensive and comprehensive, so sublime and beautiful, so happy is the believers' world that the world of unbelievers appears, by comparison, minute, trivial, low, feeble, ugly and miserable.

Need for Righteous Deeds

Doing what is righteous is the natural fruit of faith. It is a spontaneous interaction generated once the reality of faith settles inside the human heart and mind. For faith is a positive and active concept which, once it has pervaded the human conscience, hastens to reflect itself to the outside world in good deeds. This is the Islamic view of faith. It must be dynamic. If it is not, then it is either phoney or non-existent, just as a flower cannot withhold its fragrance which naturally spreads. Otherwise, it is not in the flower at all.

From all this we recognize the value of faith: it is dynamic, active, creative, productive and totally devoted to God's pleasure. It is the opposite of narrowness, negativity or introversion. It is not just sincere and innocent intentions that never develop into actions. This is the distinguishing characteristic of Islam that makes it a creative power in practical life.

All this is logical only as long as faith remains the link with the way of life God has outlined. This way of life is characterized by perpetual dynamism in the world and among people. It is founded according to a specific plan and orientated towards a definite goal. Moreover, faith propels humanity towards implementing what is good, pure, constructive and utilitarian.

Counselling one another to follow the truth and to persevere in the face of adversity reveals a picture of Islamic society which has its own very special entity, a unique inter-relationship between its individual members and a single objective. It fully understands its position, role and duties. It realizes the essence of its faith and what it has to do of good deeds which include, among other tasks, the leadership of humanity along its own way. To execute this tremendous duty, mutual counselling and exhortation become a necessity.

From the meaning and nature of the very word 'counsel' appears a most magnificent picture of a united, co-ordinated, righteous and enlightened community or society which pursues right, justice and goodness on this earth. This is exactly how Islam wants the Muslim community to be.

Mutual counsel aimed at that which is right is a necessity because it is hard always to maintain what is right, bearing in mind that the obstacles in its way are innumerable: egoistic passions and predilections, false concepts in the social environment, and the tyranny, inequity and despotism of some. Hence the mutual exhortation urged here means reminding, encouraging and expressing the unity of aim and destination and equality in duty and responsibility. It also collects individual efforts into a unified whole and thus increases feelings of brotherhood in every guardian of truth, in so far as there are others with him to exhort, encourage, support and love him. This is precisely the case with Islam, the righteous way of life whose establishment requires a co-ordinated, interdependent, self-sufficient and self-supporting community.

Counsel and exhortation to persevere in the face of adversity are also a necessity because the sustenance of faith and good deeds and catering for right and equity are the hardest tasks to carry out. This makes endurance utterly indispensable. Endurance is also necessary when adapting oneself to the Islamic way of life, confronting others, and when afflicted with ill-treatment and hardship. Perseverance is necessary when evil and falsehood triumph. It is necessary for traversing the length of the route, putting up with the slowness of the process of reform, the obscurity of the road-posts and the lengthy road leading to the destination.

Exhortation to endure hardship and persevere against adverse conditions broadens man's capacities by inspiring unity of aim and direction as well as feelings of togetherness in everyone, equipping them with love, fortitude and determination. It generates vitality in the community where the truth of Islam can survive and through which it is implemented.

Judging by the doctrine which the Qur'ān outlines for the life of the successful group which attains salvation, we are gravely shocked to see the loss and the ruin in which humanity today finds itself everywhere. We are amazed at the frustrations humanity suffers in this present world and at how humanity turns away from the goodness God has bestowed upon it. We are the more distressed by the absence of a righteous and faithful authority to stand up for the truth. Moreover, the Muslims, or rather people claiming to be Muslims, are the farthest of all from what is good and the most averse to the ideology God ordained for their community and the one route He pointed out for their deliverance from loss and ruin. People, in the very realm where this righteousness took its roots, have deserted the banner God raised for them, that is the banner of faith. They have raised instead banners of race which have never done them any good throughout their history or given them a respectable position either on earth or in the heavens. For it was Islam that raised for them the banner totally conforming to God's will, hoisted in His name only and identified with Him alone. Under this banner the Arabs triumphed, were predominant and gave humanity a righteous, strong, enlightened and successful leadership for the first time in human history. Shaikh Abu'l al-Ḥasan 'Alī Nadwī outlines the characteristics of this unique leadership:

> Once the Muslims were aroused, they quickly burst the bounds of Arabia and threw themselves zealously into the task of the fuller working out of human destiny. Their leadership held the guarantee of light and happiness for the world; it gave the promise of turning humanity into a single divinely-guided society. Some of the characteristics of Muslim leadership were:
>
> The Muslims had the unique advantage of being in possession of the divine book (the Qur'ān) and the sacred law (the Shariah). They did not have to fall back on their own judgement on the vital questions of life, and were thus saved from the manifold difficulties and perils that are attendant upon such a course. The divine word had illumined all the avenues of life for them and had enabled them to progress towards a destination which they clearly envisaged. With them it was not to be a case of trial and error. Says the Holy Qur'ān: "*Can he who is dead, to whom We give life and a light whereby he can walk amongst men, be like him who is in the depths of darkness from which he can never come out?*" (6: 122)

They were to judge among men on the basis of the revealed word; they were not to diverge from the dictates of justice and equity; their view was not to be blurred by enmity, hatred or desire for revenge. "*O you who believe, stand out firmly for God as witnesses to fair dealing, and let not the hatred of others to you make you swerve to wrong and depart from justice. Be just; that is nearer to piety; and fear God, for God is well acquainted with all that ye do.*" (5: 8)

They had not by themselves leapt into power all of a sudden from the abysmal depth of degradation. The Qur'ān had already beaten them into shape. They had been brought to a high level of nobility and purity by the Prophet through long years of unremitting care. The Prophet had conditioned them to a life of austerity and righteousness; he had instilled into their hearts the virtues of humility and courageous self-denial; he had purged them clean of greed and of striving after power, renown or wealth. It was laid down by him as a fundamental principle of Islamic polity that "We shall not assign an office under the government to anyone who makes a request for it, or shows his longing for it in any other way." [Related by al-Bukhārī and Muslim.]

The Muslims were as far removed from falsehood, haughtiness and mischief as white is from black. The following words of the Qur'ān had not in vain been grounded into them night and day: "*That home of the hereafter We shall give to those who intend not high-handedness or mischief on earth; and the end is (best) for the righteous.*" (28: 37)

Instead of aspiring for positions of authority and trust, they accepted them with great reluctance and when they did accept an official position they accepted it as a trust from God, to whom they would have to render full account of their sins of omission and commission on the Day of Judgement. Says the Holy Qur'ān: "*God commands you to render back your trusts to those to whom they are due; and when you judge between man and man, that you judge with justice.*" (4: 58) "*It is He Who has made you (His) vicegerents on the earth. He has raised you in ranks, some above others, that He might try you in the gifts you receive; for your Lord is quick in punishment, yet He is indeed Oft-Forgiving, Most Merciful.*" (6: 165)

Further, the Muslims were not the agents of any particular race or country; nor were they out to establish Arab imperialism. Their mission was a universal mission of faith and freedom. They were happily free from all the sickly obsessions of colour and territorial nationality. All men were equal before them. The Qur'ān had pointedly said: "*O mankind, We created you from (a single pair of) a male and a female; and made you into nations and tribes, that you may know each other [not that you may despise each other]. Verily the most honoured of you in the sight of God is [he who is] the most righteous of you. And God has full knowledge and is well acquainted [with all things].*" (49: 13)

Once the son of ʿAmr ibn al-ʿĀṣ, the Governor of Egypt, struck an Egyptian commoner with a whip. The matter was brought to the notice of Caliph ʿUmar. The Caliph did not show the least regard for the high status of the offender's father, and ordered the Egyptian straightaway to avenge himself for harm done to him. To the offender's father he administered this telling rebuke, "Why have you made them slaves when they were born free?"

The Arabs were not stingy in making the benefits of faith, culture and learning available to the non-Arabs. They did not care for the nationality or the family connections of the recipients when it came to the conferment of high honours and positions in the State. They were, as it were, a cloud of bliss that rained ungrudgingly over the entire world, and from which all peoples, everywhere freely profited according to their own capacity.

The Arabs allowed a free and equal partnership to all nations in the establishment of a new socio-political structure and in the advancement of mankind towards a fuller and richer moral ideal. There were no national divisions, no colour bars, no vested interests, no priesthood and no hereditary nobility in the Islamic

Commonwealth. No special benefits were reserved for anyone. There was nothing to prevent the non-Arabs from surpassing the Arabs in the various fields of life. Even as Doctors of *Fiqh* and Ḥadīth a number of non-Arabs attained to distinction for which the Muslims in general and the Arabs in particular feel proud. Ibn Khaldūn writes: "It is an amazing fact of history that though their religion is of Arabian origin and the Law that the Prophet had brought had an Arab complexion, with a few exceptions, all eminent men of learning in the Muslim *Millat* [i.e. faith], in the field of theological as well as secular sciences, are non-Arabs. Even those who are Arabs by birth are non-Arabs by education, language and scholarship. During the later centuries, too, the non-Arab Muslims continued to produce leaders, statesmen, saints and savants of exceptional merit. This would obviously not have been possible, had the Arabs been mean or prejudiced in sharing their opportunities with the people of other nationalities in the Islamic world. Humanity has many sides – physical, emotional, social, moral, mental and spiritual. We cannot neglect any one of them for the benefit of another. Humanity cannot progress to its highest level unless every human instinct is brought into proper play. It would be futile to hope for the establishment of a healthy human society till an intellectual, material, moral and spiritual environment is created in which a man is enabled to develop his latent potentialities in harmony with God's plan of creation. We learn from experience that this goal must remain a dream so long as the reins of civilization are not held by those who attach due importance to both the material and the spiritual yearnings of life, and can, together with having a high moral and spiritual sense, fitly appreciate the claims of flesh and blood upon man and the interrelationship between the individual and the society.[1]

Shaikh Nadwī then speaks of the reign of the first four Caliphs who ruled after the Prophet:

1. Abu'l al-Ḥasan 'Alī Nadwī, *Islam and the World*, pp. 75–78.

> We, consequently, find that no period in the recorded history of the human race has been more auspicious for it in the true sense of the term than what is known among the Muslims as *Khilāfat-i-Rāshidah*. During this epoch, all the material, moral and spiritual resources of man were brought into use to make him an ideal citizen of an ideal State. The Government was judged by the yard-stick of morality, and the morals were judged by their utility to lift humanity in permanent values and establishing justice in human society. Though the Islamic Commonwealth was the richest and the most powerful State of its time, the popular heroes and ideal personalities in it used to be drawn from among those who possessed, not earthly glory, but purity and nobleness of character. There was no disparity between power and morality. Material advancement was not allowed to outrun moral progress. That is why in the Islamic world the incidence of crime was very low in spite of the abundance of wealth and the great heterogeneity of its population. To put it in a nutshell, this epoch was the most beautiful springtime mankind has to this day experienced.[2]

We know some features of that glorious period of human history whose generation lived under the Islamic constitution, the pillars of which this particular *sūrah* erects. That happy period of history was made possible under the banner of faith carried by a group of believers who performed righteous deeds and encouraged each other to follow the truth and to persevere in adversity.

Profit and Loss

Now what, in the light of all this, is the loss humanity is suffering everywhere? How great is its failure in the battle between good and evil as a result of turning a blind eye to the great message the Arabs delivered to it when they raised the banner of Islam and thus assumed

2. Ibid., p. 80.

the leadership of mankind? Having abandoned Islam, the Arab nation is in the forefront of the caravan which is heading towards loss and ruin. Since then, the banners of mankind have been for Satan, falsehood, error, darkness and loss. No banner has been raised for God, truth, guidance, light or success. God's banner, however, is still there awaiting the arms that will raise it and the nation which under it will advance towards righteousness, guidance and success.

All that has been said so far concerned gain and loss in this life which, though of great importance, is very trivial in comparison with the hereafter. There is an everlasting life and a world of reality where real profit is made or real loss is suffered; that is, either the attainment of, or deprivation from, paradise and the pleasure of God. There man either accomplishes the highest of perfection allowed for him or completely collapses so that his humanity is crushed and ends up as worthless as pebbles or even worse: "*On the day when man will look on what his hands have forwarded and the unbeliever will cry: 'Would that I were dust.*'" (78: 40)

This *sūrah* is unequivocal in indicating the path leading humanity away from loss: "*except for those who have faith and do righteous deeds and counsel one another to follow the truth and counsel one another to be patient in adversity.*" (Verse 3) There is only one right path – that of faith, good deeds and the existence of a Muslim community whose members counsel one another to follow the truth and to show endurance and perseverance.

Consequently, whenever two Companions of God's Messenger were about to depart from each other, they would read this *sūrah*, after which they would shake hands. This was indicative of a pledge to accept this doctrine fully, to preserve this faith, piety and a willingness to counsel each other to follow the truth and to persevere in the face of adversity. It was a mutual compact to remain good elements in an Islamic society established according to that doctrine and to preserve the foundation of this society.

SŪRAH 104

Al-Humazah

(The Slanderer)

Al-Humazah (The Slanderer)

سُورَةُ الهُمَزَة

In the name of God, the Beneficent, the Merciful.

بِسْمِ اللَّهِ الرَّحْمَٰنِ الرَّحِيمِ

Woe to every taunting, slandering backbiter, (1)

وَيْلٌ لِّكُلِّ هُمَزَةٍ لُّمَزَةٍ ١

who amasses wealth and keeps counting it again and again, (2)

ٱلَّذِى جَمَعَ مَالًا وَعَدَّدَهُۥ ٢

thinking that his wealth will make him immortal. (3)

يَحْسَبُ أَنَّ مَالَهُۥٓ أَخْلَدَهُۥ ٣

By no means! He will indeed be flung into the crushing one. (4)

كَلَّا ۖ لَيُنۢبَذَنَّ فِى ٱلْحُطَمَةِ ٤

Would that you know what the crushing one is! (5)

وَمَآ أَدْرَىٰكَ مَا ٱلْحُطَمَةُ ٥

It is God's own kindled fire, (6)	نَارُ ٱللَّهِ ٱلْمُوقَدَةُ ﴿٦﴾
which will rise over people's hearts. (7)	ٱلَّتِى تَطَّلِعُ عَلَى ٱلْأَفْـِٔدَةِ ﴿٧﴾
It will close in upon them, (8)	إِنَّهَا عَلَيْهِم مُّؤْصَدَةٌ ﴿٨﴾
in towering columns. (9)	فِى عَمَدٍ مُّمَدَّدَةٍۭ ﴿٩﴾

Despicable Character

This *sūrah* portrays a real scene from the early days of the Islamic message, yet the same scene is repeated in every environment and society. It shows a vile, mean person who is given wealth and who uses it to tyrannize others, until he begins to feel himself almost unbearable. He thinks that wealth is the supreme value in life, before which all other values and standards come toppling down. He feels that since he possesses wealth, he controls other people's destiny without being accountable for his own deeds. He imagines that his money and his wealth is a god, capable of everything without exception, even of resisting death, making him immortal and stopping God's judgement and His retribution.

Deluded as he is by the power of wealth, he counts it and takes pleasure in counting it again and again. A wicked vanity is let loose within him driving him to mock other people's positions and dignity, to taunt and slander them. He criticizes others verbally, mocks them with his gestures, either by imitating their movements and voices or by ridiculing their looks and features, by words and mimicry, by taunt and slander.

It is a vile and debased picture of someone devoid of human ideals and generosity and stripped of faith. Islam despises this type of person whose characteristics are diametrically opposed to its own high standards of morality. Islam emphatically forbids mockery and ridicule of other people as well as deliberate fault-finding. But in this case the Qur'ān describes these actions as sordid and ugly, delivering a stern warning to anyone who indulges in them. This suggests that the *sūrah* is referring to an actual case of some unbelievers subjecting the Prophet and the believers to their taunts and slander. The reply to these actions comes in the form of a strong prohibition and awesome warning. There are some reports which name specific individuals as being the slanderers meant here, but these are not authentic, so we will not discuss them, but instead content ourselves with general observations.

The warning comes in the form of a picture of the hereafter portraying the mental and physical suffering there and drawing an image of hell which is both palpable and telling. It takes care to relate the crime to the punishment inflicted and to its effect on the culprit. On the one side there is the image of the taunting, slandering backbiter who mocks and ridicules others while he gathers wealth thinking that he is guaranteed immortality in this way. This image of a cynical calumniator seeking power through wealth is contrasted with the slighted, ignored person flung into a crushing instrument which destroys all that comes in its way. It soon crushes his structure and his pride.

The crushing instrument is "*God's own kindled fire.*" (Verse 6) Its identification as the fire of God suggests that it is an exceptional, unfamiliar sort of fire, full of terror. This fire 'rises' over the person who mocks and ridicules others. To complete the image of the slighted, ignored and crushed person, the fire closes in on him from all directions and locks him in. None can save him and none asks about him. Inside he is tied to a column, as animals are tied, without respect.

The tone of the vocabulary used in this *sūrah* is very strong '*Keeps counting it again and again; by no means! He will indeed be flung; rises, towering.*' By such expressions, forcefulness is emphatically conveyed: "*He will indeed be flung into the crushing one. Would that you know what the crushing one is! It is God's own kindled fire.*" (Verses 4–6) First comes the generalization and cryptic expression, then the exclamation suggesting great horror, and then the clear answer – all are forms of forceful expression. The style also conveys warnings: '*Woe to...; He will be flung into...; The crushing one...; God's kindled fire; which will rise over people's hearts, it will close in upon them; in towering columns.*' In all this there is a kind of harmony between imagery and feelings and the actions of the '*taunting, slandering backbiter.*'

At the time of its revelation, the Qur'ān followed up the incidents faced by the Islamic message whilst also leading it along its way. The Qur'ān is the infallible weapon which destroys the cunning of conspirators, shakes the hearts of enemies, and fills the believers with courage and determination to persevere. Indeed we recognize two significant facts in God's care here as He denounces this sordid type of people: firstly, we are shown the ugliness of moral decline and how people are rendered so abject. Secondly, we realize that He defends the believers, preserves their souls against their enemies' insults, shows them that God knows and hates what is inflicted on them, and that He will punish the wrongdoers. This is enough to elevate their souls and to make them feel their position high above the wicked designs of others.

SŪRAH 105

Al-Fīl

(The Elephant)

Al-Fīl (The Elephant)

سُورَةُ الفِيلِ

In the name of God, the Beneficent, the Merciful.

بِسۡمِ ٱللَّهِ ٱلرَّحۡمَٰنِ ٱلرَّحِيمِ

Are you not aware how your Lord dealt with the people of the Elephant? (1)

أَلَمۡ تَرَ كَيۡفَ فَعَلَ رَبُّكَ بِأَصۡحَٰبِ
ٱلۡفِيلِ ﴿١﴾

Did He not utterly confound their treacherous plan, (2)

أَلَمۡ يَجۡعَلۡ كَيۡدَهُمۡ فِي تَضۡلِيلٖ ﴿٢﴾

and send against them flocks of birds, (3)

وَأَرۡسَلَ عَلَيۡهِمۡ طَيۡرًا أَبَابِيلَ ﴿٣﴾

which pelted them with stones of sand and clay? (4)

تَرۡمِيهِم بِحِجَارَةٖ مِّن سِجِّيلٖ ﴿٤﴾

Thus He made them like stalks of devoured leaves. (5)

فَجَعَلَهُمۡ كَعَصۡفٖ مَّأۡكُولِۭ ﴿٥﴾

Historical Background

This *sūrah* refers to a widely famous incident in the Arabian Peninsula which took place before the commencement of the Islamic message. The incident shows very clearly how God protected the sacred area, which He willed to be the focal point of the last enlightenment, the cradle of the new faith, from where it was to begin its blessed march to exterminate *jāhiliyyah* from all corners of the world and to establish in its place God's infallible guidance.

The various reports about this incident relate that after the Abyssinians had expelled the Persians from Yemen and established their rule there, the Abyssinian governor of Yemen, Abrahah, built a superbly luxurious church giving it the name of the then Abyssinian Emperor. He did this after he had observed the love and enthusiasm of Yemeni Arabs – the same as those felt all over the Arab land – for the Ka'bah, the Sacred Mosque at Makkah. His purpose behind building the church was to make the Arabs forsake their attachment to the Mosque at Makkah and turn instead to his new luxurious church.

But the Arabs did not turn away from their historical shrine. They believed themselves to be the descendants of Abraham and Ishmael who built the House, which is the name they often used for the Ka'bah. For them, this fact was a source of pride in line with their tradition of honouring their forefathers. Vain and hollow as they were, their beliefs were, in their eyes, better and more profound than those of the people of earlier revelations [i.e. the Jews and Christians]. They viewed these religions as contradictory and futile.

As a result, Abrahah decided to pull the Ka'bah down in order to achieve his objective of turning the Arabs away from it. He therefore marched at the head of a great army equipped with elephants. At the front was a huge elephant which enjoyed special fame among Abrahah's men. News of Abrahah's march and his objective travelled throughout Arab lands giving rise to very strong feelings amongst the Arabs about the destruction of their sacred House. A nobleman of the royal family of Yemen, called Dhū Nafar, tried to stop the Abyssinian governor, calling on his people and other Arabs to fight

Abrahah and defend the House. Some Arab tribes joined him in a battle against Abrahah which Dhū Nafar lost before he was taken prisoner. Later, while Abrahah was on his way, he was intercepted by Nafīl ibn Ḥabīb al-Khath'amī, who had mobilized two Arab tribes as well as other Bedouin volunteers, but Abrahah again won the battle and captured Nafīl. Nafīl then agreed to act as a guide for Abrahah showing him the way. When the Abyssinian governor approached Ṭā'if, a number of its leaders went to him to say that the House he wanted to pull down was in Makkah and not at Ṭā'if. They did this in order to prevent him from destroying the house they had built for their idol, al-Lāt. They also provided him with a guide to show him the way to the Ka'bah.

Then, on his arrival at al-Mughammas, a valley *en route* from Ṭā'if to Makkah, Abrahah despatched one of his commanders to Makkah where he looted some belongings of the Quraysh and other Arabs, including 200 camels which belonged to 'Abd al-Muṭṭalib ibn Hāshim, the chief of Makkah and the Prophet's grandfather. Quraysh, Kinānah, Hudhayl and neighbouring Arab tribes then gathered together to fight Abrahah, but realized that they stood no chance of winning, so did not proceed any further. Then Abrahah sent a messenger to Makkah to meet its chief and convey to him that the governor of Yemen did not come to fight the people of Makkah, but just to pull the House down. If they left him to accomplish his objective, he would be pleased not to cause any further bloodshed. Abrahah also ordered his messenger to bring with him the Makkan chief, if the latter did not propose to fight. When the messenger communicated his master's message to 'Abd al-Muṭṭalib, the latter said: "By God, we do not want to fight him and we have no power to resist him. This is God's sacred House, built by His chosen friend, Abraham. If He protects it against Abrahah, it is because the House is His, and if He leaves it to him to destroy, we cannot defend it." 'Abd al-Muṭṭalib then went with the messenger to meet Abrahah.

Ibn Isḥāq said that 'Abd al-Muṭṭalib was a most handsome, charming and venerable-looking person. When Abrahah saw him he felt much respect for him. He felt that 'Abd al-Muṭṭalib was too noble to sit beneath his royal bed, but at the same time he did not wish his officers and troops to see him elevate his guest and sit him on his own couch, so instead he sat with 'Abd al-Muṭṭalib on the carpet. Then Abrahah ordered his interpreter to ask his guest what he wanted. 'Abd al-Muṭṭalib said he wanted to request the king to give him back his 200 camels which had been looted by his commander. Abrahah ordered his interpreter to tell 'Abd al-Muṭṭalib on his behalf: "I admired you when I first saw you but when I spoke to you I was disappointed. Do you come to talk to me about 200 looted camels and forget about the House which is an embodiment of your and your forefathers' religion and which I have come to destroy? You did not even say a word to persuade me to spare it."

'Abd al-Muṭṭalib said: "I am only the master of my camels, but the House has its own Lord who is sure to protect it." Abrahah snapped: "It cannot be defended against me." The Makkan chief said: "You take your chance!" Abrahah returned his camels to him.

'Abd al-Muṭṭalib went back to the Quraysh and told them of his encounter with the Abyssinian commander. He ordered them to leave Makkah and seek shelter in the surrounding mountains. Then he accompanied a few Quraysh dignitaries to the Ka'bah where he held the ring on its door in his hand. They all prayed hard to God for His help and protection of the House. 'Abd al-Muṭṭalib is reported to have recited the following lines of poetry in his prayer:

> Our Lord, a creature protects his property, so protect Yours.
> Let not their cross and their might ever overcome Your might.
> If You are leaving them to destroy our House of worship, then You surely have something in mind.

Abrahah, on the other hand, ordered his army to march with the elephants to complete their mission, but at a short distance from Makkah, their famous, huge elephant sat down and refused to go any further. The soldiers exerted all efforts to persuade the elephant to enter the city, but their attempts were in vain. This incident is a fact acknowledged by the Prophet. When his she-camel, al-Qaṣwā', sat down some distance from Makkah, on the day the Ḥudaybiyah peace agreement was concluded, the Prophet said to those of his Companions who claimed she had become mulish, that she had not and that mulishness was not part of her nature. "But," the Prophet added, "she has been prevented by the same will which debarred the elephant from entering Makkah." On the day of the conquest of Makkah, the Prophet said: "God protected Makkah against the elephant but He allowed His Messenger and the believers to take it under their control. Its sanctity today is the same as yesterday. Let those who hear this convey it to those who are absent."

Then God's will to destroy the Abyssinian army and its commander was fulfilled. He sent groups of birds to stone the attackers with pebbles of sand and clay, leaving them like dry and torn leaves, as the Qur'ān describes. Abrahah suffered physical injuries. The remainder of his army carried him back to Yemen, but his limbs began to separate from the rest of his body and he started losing one finger after another, until they arrived at Ṣana'ā'. According to various reports, Abrahah died after his chest was cleaved apart.

A Rationalist View

Versions of this event vary with regard to the description of the bird flocks, their size, the nature of the stones and the manner of their effect. Some accounts add that smallpox and measles broke out in Makkah that year. Those who are inclined to limit the scale of miracles and unfamiliar phenomena, seeking to explain all events as resulting from the operation of natural phenomena that are familiar to us, prefer to explain this event as an actual outbreak of smallpox and measles that afflicted the army. They further explain that the 'birds' could have been flies or mosquitoes carrying germs. The word 'bird' in Arabic refers to all that flies. Explaining this *sūrah* in his own commentary on this part of the Qur'ān, Imām Muḥammad 'Abduh says:

On the second day, a smallpox and measles epidemic broke out among Abrahah's soldiers. 'Ikrimah says: "It was the first time smallpox had appeared in the Arabia." Ya'qūb ibn 'Utbah says: "That was the year when measles and smallpox appeared in Arabia. The diseases had an almost unparalleled effect on their bodies: their flesh began to fall apart. The soldiers and their commander were horror-stricken and ran away. Abrahah was also hit. His flesh continued falling off his body, finger by finger, until eventually his chest broke up and he died at Ṣana'ā'."

This is what different reports have mentioned and what is logically acceptable. This *sūrah* shows us that the smallpox and measles were produced by solid stones carried and thrown on the soldiers by colossal flocks of birds that are helped on their way by winds.

It is in line with these reports to believe that those birds mentioned in the *sūrah* refer to a kind of fly or mosquito which carries the germs of some diseases, and that the stones were of dried and poisonous clay which the wind carried and which might have stuck to the birds' legs. When this clay touched any organism, it penetrated deep into it and then caused complications in wounds and injuries which upset the whole body, leading to the dropping off of flesh. Many kinds of these powerless birds are, as a matter of fact, among the most efficient of God's troops, which He uses for the destruction of whomsoever He wills. That little organism, called nowadays 'germ', is within this classification. It gathers in large groups, the number of which is unknown except to the Creator. It is not essential for the manifestation of God's might that the birds should be as large as mountain tops, or of a certain shape or colour, and it is not essential for this manifestation that we should know the size of those stones and the way they work. For God has troops of all kinds: "In everything He has a sign attesting to His oneness," as the saying goes.

There is no force in the universe but is subject to God's power. To that tyrant, Abrahah, who wanted to destroy the Ka'bah, God sent birds carrying smallpox and measles. Both he and his people were destroyed before entering Makkah. That was an act of grace and a blessing from God bestowed on the neighbours of His sanctuary in spite of the fact that they were idolaters. God wished to protect His House until He sent His Messenger, Muḥammad, to protect it with the force of faith and ideology. At the same time, it was a punishment from God inflicted on His enemies, the people of the Elephant, who wanted to destroy the House without reasonable justification.

This can be taken as a basis for understanding this sūrah. Nothing else can be accepted without logical explanation, even if it is authentically reported. Divine power is exhibited more strikingly when those who manifested their might by recruiting elephants, the largest quadruped animals, were destroyed and crushed by a tiny animal, invisible to human eyes. A wise person finds this certainly greater, more fascinating and miraculous.

Natural Phenomena and God's Power

This assumption [of smallpox or measles resulting from clay infected with the germs of those diseases] advanced by the well-versed Imam is contrasted with one included in some narratives, describing the stones thrown by the birds as causing the heads and bodies of the Abyssinians to split. They speak of the stones boring through their bodies, leaving them like remnants of dry leaves. To us, neither of the two explanations outweighs the other in manifesting God's might, or provides a better explanation of the event. Both are the same with regard to their possibility and the demonstration of God's power. Whether the natural phenomena known and familiar to man operated to destroy the people God willed to be destroyed, or His purpose was accomplished through some divine rule and phenomena of which man has no knowledge, are in our view exactly the same.

The divine rules of nature are not circumscribed by the boundaries of man's knowledge or what is familiar to him. For man knows only the fraction which God puts before him, and only that which suits his understanding and thought. Hence, so-called miracles are part of the rules of nature laid down by God, but they are miracles only when measured by human knowledge and experience.

Hence, there is no need for unease or doubt when faced with a supernatural event. Nor is there any need to seek an explanation for it, if the reports mentioning it are authentic, or there are enough reasons, based on what is in the texts, to suggest that it was supernatural, going beyond known natural laws. That a certain event should run according to familiar natural laws is no less significant or less effective than its following supernatural laws. Natural rules familiar to men are in fact miraculous when measured against human power and ability. Sunrise is a miracle, though it occurs every day, and the birth of every child is superhuman in spite of its happening every minute. If anyone wants to challenge this, let him try to devise a birth! The employment of birds of any kind to carry crushed stones infected with germs, and cast them at the raiding army the moment it was about to overwhelm the city and destroy the House, is indeed a great miracle. That God's will should have been realized in that way would comprise several miracles, with each regarded as a clear and spectacular manifestation of His might and will. Had this course been followed, it would not have been less significant or less striking than sending a certain kind of bird, carrying unfamiliar kinds of stones, to afflict human bodies with a peculiar sort of affliction at that particular time. The two courses are the same; both are miraculous and superhuman.

As for the event in question, the opinion advocating an unfamiliar, preternatural course carries more weight. This opinion visualizes that God sent groups of unfamiliar birds, carrying strange stones which caused extraordinary affliction to human bodies. To accept this opinion does not necessitate the acceptance of those narratives which describe the birds in most fascinating terms, similar to descriptions of legendary incidents that betray exaggeration.

God had a scheme for the House: He wanted to preserve it as a refuge for mankind where everyone finds peace, and to make it a gathering point for the followers of the new faith to march out in security in a free land, not subject to any external force or to any tyrannical government which might try to smother the new message in its cradle. God also wanted to make this event a permanent lesson, clear to everyone in all ages, so much so that in this *sūrah* He reminds the Quraysh, even after Muḥammad (peace be upon him) is given his message, of this grace He bestowed on them, making it an example of how He protects His sanctuaries and preserves them. There is no need for any attempt to impart a familiar image to this event, exceptional as it is in essence and circumstances. This is all the more so when we take into consideration the fact that what we know of smallpox and measles and their effects on man does not fit with what was reported of the effects of the incident on the soldiers' and their commander's bodies. Neither of the two diseases causes man's limbs to fall off, finger by finger and organ by organ. Nor does either disease cause the cleaving of one's chest. The Qur'ānic narrative suggests very clearly that this is what happened: "*Thus He made them like stalks of devoured leaves.*" (Verse 5)

Moreover, the reports of ʿIkrimah and Yaʿkūb ibn ʿUtbah do not state that smallpox hit the army. Neither report says anything more than that smallpox broke out that year for the first time in the Arabian Peninsula. Neither of the two men suggests that Abrahah and his army in particular fell victim to this epidemic. Besides, if only the army was affected by the diseases while the Arabs around remained safe – that is, if the birds were meant to strike only the army – then this is again preternatural. Since the event is in any case supernatural, why trouble ourselves in limiting it to a certain explanation only because this explanation is based on what is familiar to us?

The motives of the Rationalist School, of which Imām Muḥammad ʿAbduh was the leading figure, to limit the field of the supernatural and the imperceptible to our senses when explaining the Qur'ān, are both understandable and commendable. This school tried to explain such events within the bounds of the known and familiar natural laws. It was confronted with a superstitious trend which tightened its grip on the minds of the masses at that time. Moreover, it faced a flood of legends and Talmudic narratives which books explaining the Qur'ān were overburdened with, while fascination with modern technology and science on the one hand, and doubt in the principles of religion on the other, were reaching their zenith. The Rationalist School tried, therefore, to preserve the place of religion taking the standpoint that whatever it says is compatible with reason. Hence, this school strived to keep religion pure from any association with any kind of legend and superstition. It also tried to establish a religious mentality which understood natural laws and recognized that they were constant and infallible, and which attributed all human and universal functions and operations to these natural laws. This mentality is, in essence, the Qur'ānic mentality. For the Qur'ān refers people to natural laws as they constitute the permanent and infallible rule which organizes individual operations and diverse phenomena.

Yet resisting the pressures of superstition on the one hand and fascination with technology on the other left their stamps on the school. It became extra cautious, tending to make familiar natural laws the only basis for the divine laws of nature. Hence the Qur'ānic explanations of Shaikh Muḥammad 'Abduh and his two disciples Shaikh Rashid Rida and Shaikh 'Abd al-Qādir al-Maghribī clearly show a strong desire to reduce the greater number of miracles to only the more familiar of God's natural laws rather than the preternatural. They explain some of these miracles in a way that would be in line with what is called 'rational', and they are excessively cautious in accepting what is imperceptible to human senses.

With this understanding of the environmental factors behind the Rationalist School's trend, it should be noted that it has gone too far in overlooking the other side of the comprehensive concept which the Qur'ān aims to implant in Muslim minds. This is that

God's will and power are absolute, limitless and go far beyond the universal rules and laws He ordained, whether familiar to man or not. This absoluteness does not accept the human mind as a final arbiter. Neither does it accept the limits of the human mind as binding in such a way as to classify as probable only that which may be acceptable to human reason, and to demand 'rational' explanations for all that is unacceptable to it. This demand is frequently stated by advocates of this school.

Moreover, the divine laws of the universe are not only those familiar to man. Indeed, what is familiar to man is only a fraction of these laws. Both these and the unfamiliar laws are the same in manifesting the greatness of divine power and the exactness and precision of God's designs.

Nevertheless, we must be well guarded against superstition and at the same time reject any unfounded legend with conscious moderation, so that we neither succumb to the influence of particular environments nor feel urged by a need to resist a common tradition of a certain age.

There is a safe rule for approaching Qur'ānic texts, which may be appropriately stated here. We cannot approach what the Qur'ān states with prejudiced minds and preconceived ideas, whether generally or in relation to the subject matter of the statements under study. The opposite is the correct way: we must approach Qur'ānic statements in such a way that helps us to derive our concepts from them and formulate our ideas on their basis. What the Qur'ān states is final as it is. For what we call 'reason' and its adjudication on what the Qur'ān relates of events in the universe or of history, in our own world or in the realm of the imperceptible, is no more than the net result of our finite human existence and experience.

Although human reason is, in essence an absolute force, not subject to, or limited by, individual experiences or events, it is, after all, confined to human existence. This existence does not reflect the absolute, as this belongs to God. The Qur'ān comes from God, the Absolute. Hence, it is binding on us in the sense that whatever it states is the basis of our very 'rational' concepts. Then, no one can say of a certain Qur'ānic statement: 'It is unacceptable to reason, so a logical explanation must be sought for it,' as advocates of the Rationalist School frequently say. This does not mean that we should accept superstitions, it only stresses that human reason is not the arbiter of what the Qur'ān states. When the expressions of a Qur'ānic text are clear and straightforward, they determine how our reason should approach that text in order to formulate our views concerning its subject matter as well as regarding other universal facts.

A Momentous Event

Let us now examine the text of the *sūrah* itself and try to understand the significance of the story.

"*Are you not aware how your Lord dealt with the people of the Elephant*?" (Verse 1) It is a question that draws attention to the wonders involved in the incident itself and stresses its great significance. The incident was so well known to the Arabs that they used to consider it a sort of beginning of history. They would say, 'This incident happened in the year of the Elephant', and, 'That event took place two years before the year of the Elephant', or, 'This dates to ten years after the year of the Elephant'. It is well known that the Prophet was born in the year of the Elephant itself. This is perhaps one of the fascinatingly perfect arrangements of divine will.

The *sūrah* then is not relating to the Arabs something they did not know. It is a reminder of an event well known to them, aiming at achieving something beyond actual remembrance of it.

After this opening note, the *sūrah* tells the rest of the story in the form of a rhetorical question: "*Did He not utterly confound their treacherous plan?*" (Verse 2) This means that the designs of the people of the Elephant were useless, incapable of achieving anything at all. They were like someone who had lost his way and thus could not arrive at his destination. Perhaps this is a reminder to the Quraysh of the grace God bestowed on them when He protected and preserved the House at a time when they felt too weak to face the mighty aggressors, the people of the Elephant. Such remembrance was perhaps intentionally meant to make them feel their disgrace when they persistently denied God after He had helped them out of their weakness. It may also curb their conceit and heavy-handedness in their treatment of Muḥammad and the few believers who supported him. God destroyed the powerful aggressors who wanted to pull down His House, which serves as a sanctuary for all people. God, then, may destroy the new aggressors who try to persecute His Messenger and suppress His message.

The Qur'ān portrays superbly how the aggressors' defeat was brought about: "*Did He not... send against them flocks of birds, which pelted them with stones of sand and clay? Thus He made them like stalks of devoured leaves.*" (Verses 3–5) The birds flew in flocks. The Qur'ān uses a Persian term, *sijjīl*, which denotes 'stone and clay' to describe the substance with which the birds struck the aggressors. The dry leaves are described as "devoured" to denote that insects or other animals had eaten them. It is a vivid image of the physical shattering of the Abyssinian army as they were stricken with these muddy stones. There is no need to go into such explanations as that it was an allegorical description of their destruction by smallpox or measles.

The Arabs and Islam

The significance of this event is far reaching and the lessons deduced from its mention in the Qur'ān are numerous. It first suggests that God did not want the idolaters to take responsibility for protecting His House, in spite of the fact that they held it in deep respect and sought its security. When He willed to preserve the House and made it clear that He Himself was its protector, He left the idolaters to their defeat by the Abyssinians. Divine will then directly intervened to repel the aggression and preserve His sacred House. Thus the idolaters did not have a chance to hold the protection of the House as a 'favour they did to God' or as 'an act of honour'. If they had done so, they would have been prompted by fanatic *jāhiliyyah* impulses. This point gives considerable weight to the argument that the divine will of destroying the aggressors was accomplished through preternatural rules.

This direct intervention by God to protect the House should have prompted the Quraysh and the rest of the Arabian tribes to embrace Islam, the divine religion, when it was conveyed to them by the Prophet. Surely, their respect and guardianship of the House, and the paganism they spread around it, should not have been their reason for rejecting Islam! God's reminder to them of this event is a part of the Qur'ānic criticism of their stand, drawing attention to their amazing stubbornness.

The event also suggests that God did not allow the people of earlier revelations, represented in this case by Abrahah and his army, to destroy the sacred House or to impose their authority over the holy land, even when it was surrounded by the impurity of idolatry and idolaters were its custodians. Thus the House remained free from any human authority, safe against all wicked designs. God preserved the freedom of the land in order that the new faith would develop there completely free, not subjected to the authority of any despot. God revealed this religion as the force which supersedes all other religions. He wanted it to take over the leadership of humanity. God's will concerning His House and religion was accomplished long before any human being knew that the Prophet, who was to convey the new message, was born in the same year. We are reassured when we realize this aspect of the significance of the event. We know the wicked ambitions of international imperialist forces and world Zionism concerning the holy lands. We realize that these forces spare no effort to achieve their wicked ambitions. But we are not worried. For God who protected His House against the aggression of the people of earlier revelations when its custodians were idolaters will protect it again, if He wills, just as He will protect Madinah, His Messenger's city, against the wicked designs of evildoers.

Moreover, the event refers to the reality of the Arabian situation at that time. The Arabs did not have any role to play on the face of the earth. They did not even have an identity of their own before Islam. In the Yemen they were subjugated by either Persians or Abyssinians. If they had any government of their own, it was under the protection of the Persians. In the north, Syria was subject to Byzantine rule which was either direct or in the shape of an Arab government under Byzantine protection. Only the heartland of the Arabian Peninsula escaped foreign rule. But this was in a state of tribalism and division which deprived it of any weight in world politics. Tribal warfare could drag on for 40 years or longer, but neither individually nor as a group did these tribes count as a power in the eyes of the mighty empires neighbouring them. What happened with regard to the Abyssinian aggression was a correct assessment of these tribes' real strength when faced with a foreign aggressor.

Under Islam the Arabs had, for the first time in history, an international role to play. They also had a powerful state to be taken into consideration by world powers. They possessed a sweeping force that destroyed thrones, conquered empires, and brought down false, deviating and ignorant leaderships in order to take over the leadership of mankind. But what facilitated these achievements for the Arabs for the first time in their history was that they forgot their Arabism. They forgot racial urges and fanaticism. They remembered that they were Muslims, and Muslims only. They carried the message of a forceful and all-comprehensive faith, which they delivered to humanity with mercy and compassion. They did not uphold any sort of nationalism or factionalism. They were the exponents of a divine idea which gave mankind a divine, not earthly, doctrine to be applied as a way of life. They left their homes to struggle for the cause of God alone. They were not after the establishment of an Arab empire under which they might live in luxury and conceit. Their aim was not to subjugate other nations to their own rule after freeing them from the rule of the Byzantines or Persians. It was an aim clearly defined by Rib'iy ibn 'Āmir, the Muslims' messenger to the Persian commander, when he said in the latter's headquarters: "God ordered us to set out in order to save humanity from the worship of creatures and to bring it to the worship of God alone, to save it from the narrowness of this life so that it may look forward to the broadness of the life hereafter, and from the oppression of other religions so that it may enjoy the justice of Islam."

Then, and only then, did the Arabs have an identity, a power and a leadership. But all of these were devoted to God alone. They possessed their power and leadership as long as they followed the right path. But when they deviated and followed their narrow nationalistic ideas, and when they substituted for the banner of Islam that of factional bonds, they came under subjugation by other nations. For God deserted them whenever they deserted Him; He neglected them as they neglected Him.

What are the Arabs without Islam? What is the ideology that they hold, or they can give to humanity if they abandon Islam? What value can a nation have without an ideology which it presents to the world? Every nation which assumed the leadership of humanity in any period of history advanced an ideology. Nations which did not, such as the Tartars who swept over the east, or the Berbers who crushed the Roman Empire in the west, could not survive for long. They were assimilated by the nations they conquered. The only ideology the Arabs advanced for mankind was the Islamic faith which raised them to the position of human leadership. If they forsake it they will no longer have any function or role to play in human history. The Arabs should remember this well if they want to live and be powerful and assume the leadership of mankind. It is God who provides guidance for us lest we go astray.

SŪRAH 106

The Quraysh

The Quraysh

سُورَةُ قُرَيْشٍ

In the name of God, the Beneficent, the Merciful.

بِسۡمِ ٱللَّهِ ٱلرَّحۡمَٰنِ ٱلرَّحِيمِ

For the tradition of the Quraysh, (1)

لِإِيلَٰفِ قُرَيۡشٍ ١

their tradition of travelling in winter and summer. (2)

إِۦلَٰفِهِمۡ رِحۡلَةَ ٱلشِّتَآءِ وَٱلصَّيۡفِ ٢

Let them worship the Lord of this House, (3)

فَلۡيَعۡبُدُواْ رَبَّ هَٰذَا ٱلۡبَيۡتِ ٣

who provided them with food against hunger, and with security against fear. (4)

ٱلَّذِيٓ أَطۡعَمَهُم مِّن جُوعٖ وَءَامَنَهُم
مِّنۡ خَوۡفِۭ ٤

Lest They Forget

When Abraham, God's friend, or *khalīl* as he is called in Arabic, completed the building of the House of worship, the Ka'bah, and had purified it he turned to God with the following prayer: "*Lord, make this a land of security and make provisions of fruits for those of its people who believe in God and the Last Day.*" (2: 126) So God made that House one of peace; free from all human authority and from all tyranny. He granted security and peace to anyone seeking shelter in that House, while fear was all around it. Even when the people transgressed, ascribed divinity to beings other than God and worshipped idols, there was peace and security in it; for God had designed a purpose for this sacred House.

When the people of the Elephant marched to destroy the House, there happened to them what is described in the preceding *sūrah*, The Elephant. God preserved for the House its peace, security and sacredness. Of those who lived around it, God said: "*Do they not see that We have made a secure Sanctuary, and that men are being snatched away from all around them?*" (29: 67)

The Elephant incident had an added effect in greatly enhancing the sanctity of the House amongst the Arabs all over the Peninsula. It also strengthened the position of the Quraysh, the custodians of the House, in all Arabia. They were thus able to travel far and wide in peace and security. Wherever they went they met with generosity and high esteem. This encouraged them to establish two great routes for their commercial caravans, to the Yemen in the south and to Syria in the north. They organized two enormous trading expeditions; one to the Yemen in winter and the other to Syria in summer.

In spite of very poor conditions of security in all parts of the Arabian Peninsula at that time, and in spite of all the looting and plundering raids that were common in that land, the sanctity of the House in the eyes of all Arabs guaranteed security and peace in their flourishing business to those who lived near it and were its custodians. It created for the Quraysh a distinct and exclusive position and opened up for them an extensive and guaranteed means of sustenance in peace, security and contentment. The Quraysh became accustomed to these two profitable and peaceful trips, which were soon established among their traditional habits.

This is the specific grace of which God reminds the Quraysh, as He reminded them of the Elephant incident in the previous *sūrah*. It is the grace of their being accustomed to the winter and summer trips, and the abundance with which He endowed them by means of these two fruitful journeys. It is by the grace of God that while their land is desolate and dry, they still live a comfortable life. Out of His grace He secures them from fear whether in their hearths and homes, next to God's House, or on their journeys. Their security is the result of their being the custodians of the House, the sanctity of which is ordained and preserved by God against any violation.

God reminds them of these graces in order that they may be ashamed of their submission to other beings, while He is the Lord of the House. God says to them in effect: for this tradition of the Quraysh, namely their winter and summer trips, let them submit to the Lord of this House who guaranteed their security and so encouraged them to take such beneficial journeys. "*Let them worship the Lord of this House, who provided them with food against hunger, and with security against fear.*" (Verses 3–4) As their land was infertile, they would have starved had it not been for the sustenance supplied by God. "*And with security against fear.*" Poor as they were, and living in an insecure surroundings, their life would have been one of fear and apprehension. But God granted them security and allayed their fear.

This is a reminder which should have left a profound sense of shame in the hearts of the Quraysh, who were not unaware of the great value of the House and the effect of its sanctity on their lives. At the moment of danger and difficulty, the Quraysh used to appeal only to the Lord of that House and seek only His help. This was the case with 'Abd al-Muṭṭalib, who did not confront Abrahah with any army or physical strength. Instead 'Abd al-Muṭṭalib addressed himself only to the Lord of the House, because He was the only One who could protect His House. 'Abd al-Muṭṭalib did not appeal to any of the idols or craven images for help. He did not even say to Abrahah that these deities would protect their House. He only said to him, "I am only the master of the camels, but the House has its own Lord who is sure to protect it." But ignorance does not listen to any logic, or acknowledge what is right, or accept any reasonable argument.

This *sūrah* seems to be an extension of the preceding one, The Elephant, with regard to its subject matter and general tone. Nevertheless, it is an independent *sūrah* with the usual beginning of the Qur'ānic *sūrahs*, namely, "*In the name of God, the Beneficent, the Merciful.*" Qur'ānic commentators state that nine *sūrahs* were revealed between the revelation of this and the preceding *sūrah*, but that they were placed next to each other in the Qur'ān because of their close similarity of subject.

SŪRAH 107

Al-Mā ʿūn

(Small Kindness)

Al-Mā ʿūn (Small Kindness)

سورة الماعون

In the name of God, the Beneficent, the Merciful.

بسم الله الرحمن الرحيم

Have you seen him who denies religion? (1)

أرءيت الذي يكذب بالدين ١

It is he who thrusts the orphan away (2)

فذلك الذي يدع اليتيم ٢

and does not urge others to feed the needy. (3)

ولا يحض على طعام المسكين ٣

Woe, then, to those who pray (4)

فويل للمصلين ٤

but are heedless of their prayers; (5)

الذين هم عن صلاتهم ساهون ٥

who put on a show of piety (6)	ٱلَّذِينَ هُمْ يُرَآءُونَ ﴿٦﴾
but refuse to give even the smallest help to others. (7)	وَيَمْنَعُونَ ٱلْمَاعُونَ ﴿٧﴾

Overview

This *sūrah* is a Makkan revelation according to some authorities and a Makkan-Madinan one according to others, with the first three verses said to have been revealed in Makkah and the rest in Madinah. The latter view is perhaps weightier. Yet the *sūrah* is one interwoven entity, aiming at the establishment of one of the most fundamental aspects of faith. Hence we are more inclined to take it as being an entirely Madinan revelation. Its subject matter is more in line with the topics of the part of the Qur'ān revealed in Madinah. It relates to the phenomena of hypocrisy and false pretences which were unheard of among the Muslim community in Makkah. But there is no need to reject the assertion that the *sūrah* is a Makkan-Madinan one, because it is possible that the last four verses were revealed in Madinah and integrated with the first three on the grounds of similarity of subject matter. Having said that, let us now consider the *sūrah* and its theme.

Belief and Practice

This *sūrah* of seven short verses tackles an important and vital issue which could very well change the common meanings normally assigned to the terms 'faith', or *īmān*, and 'disbelief', or *kufr*. Moreover, it brings out the fundamental truth intrinsic in the nature of the Islamic faith, the enormous benefit it offers to all humanity and the abundant blessings with which God favoured mankind when He sent them His last message.

As a way of life, Islam is not built on ostentation and superficiality. The apparent aspects of the different acts of worship are, according to Islam, meaningless unless they are motivated by sincerity and devotion to God. Worship sincerely motivated produces effects within a person's heart, and these cause him to act righteously. The effects of worship are reflected in a type of social behaviour which elevates man's life on this earth.

No less true is the fact that Islam is not a loose, fragmentary, disjointed system from which one can pick and choose at leisure. On the contrary, it is a complete way of life with acts of worship and rites, as well as individual and collective obligations that are mutually complementary. Together they lead to a goal of which mankind is the sole beneficiary; a goal which ensures that hearts are purified, life is ennobled, and men co-operate for the common good and progress; a goal wherein abound God's blessings.

A person may profess to be a Muslim, that is, he accepts this religion and all its principles, offers prayers regularly and observes other acts of worship, and yet is lacking in the essence of faith and sincerity of belief. In fact, he may be very far from these. For there are signs which indicate the firm establishment of these qualities in people's hearts.

As explained in the commentary on *Sūrah* 103, The Declining Day, the essence of faith once firmly rooted in people's hearts and minds, immediately begins to operate and manifest itself in their behaviour. The *sūrah* stresses unequivocally that, if this is not the case, there is no faith.

"*Have you seen him who denies religion? It is he who thrusts the orphan away and does not urge others to feed the needy.*" (Verses 1–3) The *sūrah* starts with a question addressed to all who can see, generating suspense and holding their attention in order to make them discover the target and subject of the *sūrah*. Who is this creature identified by the Qur'ān as the one who denies the religion of Islam? The answer is given immediately: "*It is he who thrusts the orphan away and does not urge others to feed the needy.*" (Verses 2–3)

This definition of unbelievers may sound surprising when compared with a traditional definition of faith, but this is the crux of the matter. Indeed the one who denies the faith is he who harshly pushes away the orphan, humiliating him and hurting his feelings, and who does not care for the needy or their welfare. For if the truth of Islam has touched his heart in any degree, he would not commit such acts. True belief in Islam is not a verbal statement, but an overall change of the individual's heart, motivating him to benevolence and goodwill for all his fellow beings that are in need of his care and protection. God does not want mere words from His servants but demands deeds to support the spoken words which, otherwise, are as weightless and valueless as blown ash. Nothing can be more forceful than these three verses in affirming this fact which represents the nature of faith.

We do not intend here to indulge in a juristic discussion on the boundaries of faith and Islam. These are required in legal affairs, whereas this *sūrah* states the facts from God's point of view and judgement, which is quite different from the legal aspect.

Next, God offers a practical illustration of what is meant above: "*Woe, then, to those who pray but are heedless of their prayers.*" (Verses 4–5) These verses contain God's invocation against, or a threat of destruction to, those who offer prayers but are careless about them. Who exactly are such people? They are those "*who put on a show of piety but refuse to give even the smallest help to others.*" (Verses 6–7) Those who perform prayers but who do not aptly meet their requirements. They execute the mechanical aspects and pronounce the verbal formulae of prayers but their hearts are never alive to them, nor do they benefit by the spiritual nourishment prayers give. The essence and purpose of prayer and its component parts, such as Qur'ānic recitation, supplication and glorification of God, are never present in their souls. They offer prayers only to deceive others and not out of devotion to God. Hence, they are inattentive when they pray. They only outwardly perform their prayers. Muslims are required to offer their prayers regularly, having in mind that their prayers are a manifestation of their servitude to God alone. Thus, prayer leaves no result in those who are neglectful and inattentive to it. Consequently they refuse to give any kindness or help to their fellow beings and deny the slightest charity to any of God's servants.

Once again, we find ourselves presented with the fundamental truth and nature of this religion. A Qur'ānic verse threatens with destruction those who offer prayers precisely because they carry out meaningless movements devoid of any spirit or sense of purpose, intended for deceit and pretence, and not devoted to God. Since their prayers have not affected their hearts and behaviour, they are not merely useless but rather a sin for which they will be punished.

We thus gather the purpose behind what God demands of His servants when He instructs them to believe in, and worship Him. He seeks no benefit thereof for Himself, as He is in no need of anyone or anything. All He cares for is their own welfare and prosperity, purification of their hearts and happiness in their lives. God wishes human life to be elevated, happy, based on pure motives and characterized by mutual compassion, brotherhood and purity of hearts and behaviour.

To where then is humanity driving itself, moving away from this abundance of mercy; away from this wonderful and sublime path? How can mankind debase itself to living in the wilderness of a wretched and gloomy *jāhiliyyah* when it beholds the splendid light of faith before its very eyes at the cross-roads where it now stands?

SŪRAH 108

Al-Kawthar

(Abundance)

Al-Kawthar (Abundance)	سُورَةُ الكَوْثَرِ
In the name of God, the Beneficent, the Merciful.	بِسْمِ اللَّهِ الرَّحْمَٰنِ الرَّحِيمِ
We have certainly given you abundance. (1)	إِنَّآ أَعْطَيْنَٰكَ ٱلْكَوْثَرَ ١
So pray to your Lord and sacrifice to Him. (2)	فَصَلِّ لِرَبِّكَ وَٱنْحَرْ ٢
Surely, he who hates you is the one cut off. (3)	إِنَّ شَانِئَكَ هُوَ ٱلْأَبْتَرُ ٣

Overview

Similar to *Sūrahs* 93 and 94, The Morning Hours and Solace, this *sūrah* exclusively concerns the Prophet, seeking to cheer him up and assure him of happier prospects in his struggle. In it God threatens his enemies with destruction while directing the Prophet to the path of thanksgiving.

The *sūrah* represents a glimpse of the Prophet's life and the course of his mission in the early period at Makkah. It deals with the plots and insults directed against the Prophet and the divine message he conveys. The *sūrah* is an example of God's protection of His servant, the Prophet Muḥammad, and the few who followed him and believed in God. It is an instance of God's direct support to the believers in their struggle, supplying them with fortitude, restraint and promise, while threatening a terrible fate on their antagonists.

In this way, the *sūrah* symbolizes the reality of guidance, goodness and faith on the one hand and that of error, evil and disbelief on the other; the former category is one of abundance, profusion and expansive goodness, the latter one of scantiness, shrinking resources and annihilation.

Background

Among the people of the Quraysh, the Arab tribe which controlled Makkah, there were some impudent folk who viewed the Prophet and his mission with no small degree of antagonism. They would resort to machinations and taunts against him to deter the people from listening to the truth which he conveyed to them in the form of a divine message. Among them were people like Al-ʿĀṣ ibn Wā'il, ʿUqbah ibn Abī Muʿayṭ, Abū Lahab, Abū Jahl and others. They said about the Prophet that he was a man with no posterity, referring to the early death of his sons. One of them once remarked, "Do not be bothered with him; he will die without descendants and that will be the end of his mission."

Such a trivial and cunning taunt had a wide impact on the Arab society of the time, which set great store by sons. Such taunting delighted the Prophet's enemies and undoubtedly this was a source of depression and irritation to his noble heart. This *sūrah* was therefore revealed to comfort the Prophet and assure him of the abiding and profuse goodness which God had chosen for him and of the deprivation and loss awaiting his persecutors.

Blessings in Abundance

"*We have certainly given you abundance.*" (Verse 1) The word used in the *sūrah* and rendered here as 'abundance' is *kawthar*, derived from the stem word *kathrah* which signifies 'abundance' or 'a multitude'. This *kawthar* is unrestricted and unlimited. It indicates the opposite meaning to the one the impudent Quraysh tried to attach to the Prophet. We have given you that which is plentiful, overflowing and rich, unstinting and unending.

If anyone wishes to pursue and observe this abundance which God has given to His Prophet, he will find it wherever he looks and reflects. He will find it in Muḥammad's prophethood itself, which gave him a link with the great reality and the Supreme Being, who has no parallel and no partner. What indeed can the one who has found God be said to have lost?

He will also find it in this Qur'ān which was revealed to Muḥammad, every chapter of which is a fountain of richness that flows incessantly.

Moreover, he will find this *kawthar*, or abundance, manifest in Muslims' following of the Prophet's *sunnah*, i.e. way of life, throughout the centuries, in the far-flung corners of the earth, in the millions upon millions who follow in his footsteps and pronounce his name with respectful affection. He will see it in the millions upon millions of hearts that cherish his example and memory even to the Day of Resurrection.

He will also find this *kawthar*, or abundance, manifest in the goodness and prosperity which have accrued to the human race as a result of his message, and which reach those who know and believe in him as well as those who do not. He will also discern this abundance in various and manifold phenomena, attempting to enumerate which give, at best, only a passing feeling of a great reality.

This indeed is abundance in its absolute and unlimited sense. The *sūrah*, therefore, does not give it a specific definition. Several accounts relate that '*al-kawthar*' is a river in heaven granted to the Prophet. However, Ibn 'Abbās, the Prophet's learned cousin, contends that the river is but one part of the abundance which God has furnished for His Messenger. Keeping the circumstances and the whole context in mind, Ibn Abbās's view is the more valid.

"*So pray to your Lord and sacrifice to Him.*" (Verse 2) Having assured the Prophet of this munificent gift, which disproves what the calumniators and wicked schemers say, God directs the Prophet to be completely and sincerely thankful to Him for His bounty. He is to devote himself to Him alone in worship and ritual slaughter, taking no heed whatsoever of any form of idolatry and refusing to participate in the worship rituals offered by idolaters, especially when they invoke anyone other than God in their offerings.

Islam frequently lays emphasis on the pronouncing of God's name when slaughtering animals. It prohibits anything that is consecrated to any other being, which indicates the importance Islam attaches to the purification of human life from all forms of idolatry and all that leads to it. Because it is based on the principle of God's oneness in its purest sense, Islam does not aim merely at purifying human imagination and conscience. It pursues idolatry in all its manifestations, striving to eliminate its marks in man's consciousness, worship rituals and general behaviour. Life, Islam says, is one indivisible entity and must be treated as such. It must be cleansed inside out and completely oriented towards God, in all its aspects: worship, tradition and social behaviour.

"*Surely, he who hates you is the one cut off.*" (Verse 3) In the first verse, God specified that Muḥammad was not the one who had no posterity but, on the contrary, was the one endowed with abundance. In this verse, God throws back the taunt on those who hated and reviled the Prophet. Indeed, God's promise has come true. For, the influence and legacy of Muḥammad's enemies were short-lived, while his impact on human life and history has grown and deepened. Today we are witnessing the truth of this divine pronouncement as clearly as no one among those addressed by the Qur'ān for the first time ever did or imagined.

Faith and goodness cannot be barren. Their influence is both profound and deep-rooted. By contrast, falsehood, error and evil may grow and spread quickly, but they ultimately come to nothing.

God's criteria are different from the criteria laid down by man. Men are often deceived when they vainly believe their sense of judgement to be the criterion. Before us is the eloquent and enduring example of the Prophet. Of what value or interest to humanity have Muḥammad's slanderers and foes been to anyone?

On the other hand, calling others to the religion of God, to truth and goodness, can never be called futile. Neither can the righteous and the true be called deprived or cut off. How can it be, when this message itself comes from, and is supported by, God, the Immortal, the Eternal? But deprived and sterile indeed are disbelief, error and evil as are their votaries, however strong and widespread they may appear to be at any moment.

God affirms the truth; wily opponents are but liars!

SŪRAH 109

Al-Kāfirūn

(The Unbelievers)

Al-Kāfirūn (The Unbelievers)

سُورَةُ الكَافِرُونَ

In the name of God, the Beneficent, the Merciful.

بِسْمِ ٱللَّهِ ٱلرَّحْمَٰنِ ٱلرَّحِيمِ

Say: 'Unbelievers! (1)

قُلْ يَٰٓأَيُّهَا ٱلْكَٰفِرُونَ ١

I do not worship what you worship, (2)

لَآ أَعْبُدُ مَا تَعْبُدُونَ ٢

nor do you worship what I worship. (3)

وَلَآ أَنتُمْ عَٰبِدُونَ مَآ أَعْبُدُ ٣

I shall never worship what you worship, (4)

وَلَآ أَنَا۠ عَابِدٌ مَّا عَبَدتُّمْ ٤

nor will you ever worship what I worship. (5)

وَلَآ أَنتُمْ عَٰبِدُونَ مَآ أَعْبُدُ ٥

You have your own religion and I have mine.' (6)	لَكُمْ دِينُكُمْ وَلِىَ دِينِ ﴿٦﴾

No Meeting of the Ways

Although the Arabs before Islam did not deny God altogether, they did not know Him by His true identity as the One and the Eternal. They neither showed any true understanding of God, nor worshipped Him properly. On the contrary, they ascribed to Him, as partners, idols that were supposed to represent their great and pious ancestors or, in some cases, the angels whom they claimed to be God's daughters. Moreover, they alleged a kinship between Him and the *jinn*. They often ignored all these qualifications, however, and worshipped those idols themselves. But in all cases they claimed, as the Qur'ān quotes them, that they "*only worship them [i.e. their various deities] so that they may bring us near to God.*" (39: 3)

The Qur'ān also states: "*If you ask them who it is that has created the heavens and the earth, and subjected the sun and the moon (to fixed laws) they will say: God.*" (29: 61) And again: "*If you ask them who it is that sends down water from the sky, and thereby revives the earth after it has died, they will say: God.*" (29: 63) Moreover, God superseded their deities in their oaths and supplications.

But in spite of their belief in God, the polytheism they entertained fouled their concepts, traditions and rites to the extent that they assigned to their alleged deities a portion of their earnings and possessions, and even their offspring. In fact, they were at times forced to sacrifice their children. Concerning this, the Qur'ān has the following to say:

> *Out of the produce and the cattle He has created, they assign a portion to God, saying: 'This is for God' – or so they pretend – 'and this is for the partners we associate [with Him].' Whatever they assign to their partners never reaches God, but that which is assigned to God does reach their partners. How ill they judge!*

Thus have the partners they associate [with God] made the killing of their own children seem goodly to many idolaters, seeking to bring them to ruin and to confuse them in their faith. Had God willed otherwise, they would not have done so. Leave them, then, to their false inventions. They say: 'Such cattle and crops are forbidden. None may eat of them save those whom we permit' – so they falsely claim. Other cattle they declare to be forbidden to burden their backs; and there are cattle over which they do not pronounce God's name, inventing [in all this] a lie against Him. He will surely requite them for their inventions. They also say: 'That which is in the wombs of these cattle is reserved to our males and forbidden to our women.' But if it be stillborn, they all partake of it. He will requite them for all their false assertions. He is Wise, All-Knowing. Losers indeed are those who, in their ignorance, foolishly kill their children and declare as forbidden what God has provided for them as sustenance, falsely attributing such prohibitions to God. They have gone astray and they have no guidance. (6: 136–140)

The Arabs were also convinced that they were the followers of the religion of Abraham and that they were better guided than the people of earlier revelations [i.e. the Jews and Christians] inhabiting the Arabian Peninsula at the time: the Jews and Christians preached respectively that Ezra and Jesus were the sons of God whereas they, the Arabs, worshipped angels and *jinn* – the true offspring of God according to them. Their belief, they maintained, was more logical and more conceivable than that of the Christians and Jews. Nonetheless, all were forms of idolatry.

When Muḥammad (peace be upon him) declared his religion to be that of Abraham, they argued that there was no reason for them to forsake their beliefs and follow Muḥammad's instead, since they too were of the same religion. In the meantime, they sought a sort of compromise with him proposing that he should prostrate himself before their deities in return for their prostration to his God, and that he should cease denouncing their deities and their manner of worship in reciprocation for whatever he demanded of them! This confusion in their concepts, vividly illustrated by their worship of various deities while acknowledging God, was perhaps what led them to believe that the gulf between them and Muḥammad was not unbridgeable. They thought an agreement was somehow possible by allowing the two camps to co-exist in the region and by granting him some personal concessions!

To clear up this muddle, to cut all arguments short and to firmly distinguish between one form of worship and the other, and indeed between one faith and the other, this *sūrah* was revealed in such a decisive, assertive tone. It was revealed in this manner to demarcate monotheism, i.e. *tawḥīd*, from polytheism, i.e. *shirk*, and to establish a true criterion, allowing no further wrangling or vain argument.

"*Say: 'Unbelievers! I do not worship what you worship, nor do you worship what I worship. I shall never worship what you worship, nor will you ever worship what I worship. You have your own religion and I have mine.*'" (Verses 1–6) Following one form of negation, assertion and emphasis after another, the *sūrah* sets its message in absolute clarity. It starts with the word, '*Say*,' which denotes a clear divine order stressing the fact that the whole affair of religion belongs exclusively to God. Nothing of it belongs to Muḥammad himself. Moreover, it implies that God is the only One to order and decide. Address them, Muḥammad, by their actual and true identity: "*Say: Unbelievers!*" (Verse 1) They follow no prescribed religion, nor do they believe in you. No meeting point exists between you and them anywhere. Thus the beginning of the *sūrah* brings to mind the reality of difference which cannot be ignored or overlooked.

"*I do not worship what you worship*," is a statement affirmed by "*I shall never worship what you worship*." Similarly, "*nor do you worship what I worship*," is repeated for added emphasis and in order to eliminate all doubt or misinterpretation.

Finally, the whole argument is summed up in the last verse: "*You have your own religion, and I have mine*," meaning that you, unbelievers, and I, Muḥammad, are very far apart, without any bridge to connect us. This is a complete distinction and a precise, intelligible demarcation.

Such an attitude was essential then in order to expose the fundamental discrepancies in the essence, source and concepts of the two beliefs, i.e. between monotheism and polytheism, faith and unbelief. Faith is the way of life which directs man and the whole world towards God alone and determines for him the source of his religion, laws, values, criteria, ethics and morality. That source is God. Thus life proceeds for the believer, devoid of any form of idolatry. Idolatry on the other hand is the opposite of faith. The two never meet.

On the whole, the distinction we are dealing with here is indispensable both for those who call on people to accept Islam and the people themselves, because *jāhiliyyah* concepts are often mixed with those of Islam in those societies which previously followed the Islamic way of life, but have later deviated from it. Of all communities, they are certainly the most rigid and hostile to the idea of regaining faith in its healthy, clear and straightforward form, certainly more so than those who have not known Islam originally. They take it for granted that they are righteous while they grow more and more perverse!

The existence of noble beliefs and thoughts in those societies, albeit mixed with base ones, may tempt the advocate of the Islamic system to hope for their quick return, thinking he may be able to strengthen such good aspects and rightly correct undesirable features! Such temptation is, however, dangerously misleading.

Jāhiliyyah and Islam are two totally different entities, separated by a wide gulf. The only way to bridge that gulf is for *jāhiliyyah* to liquidate itself completely and substitute for all its laws, values, standards and concepts their Islamic counterparts. The first step that should be taken in this respect by the person calling on people to embrace Islam is to segregate himself from *jāhiliyyah*. He must be separated to the extent that any agreement or intercourse between him and *jāhiliyyah* is absolutely impossible unless and until the people of *jāhiliyyah* embrace Islam completely: no intermingling, no half measures or conciliation is permissible, however clever *jāhiliyyah* may be in usurping or reflecting the role of Islam. The chief characteristic of a person who calls on others to adopt Islam is the clarity of this fact within himself and his solemn conviction of being radically different from those who do not share his outlook. They have their own religion, and he has his. His task is to change their standing point so that they may follow his path without false pretence or compromise. Failing this, he must withdraw completely, detach himself from their life and openly declare to them: "*You have your own religion, and I have mine.*" (Verse 6)

This is a *sine qua non* for contemporary advocates of Islam. They badly need to realize that they are calling for Islam today in entirely neo-*jāhiliyyah* surroundings, amongst ex-Muslim people whose hearts have grown harder and whose beliefs have deteriorated considerably. They need to understand that there is no room for short-term or half-baked solutions, compromises, or partial redemption or adjustment, and that their call is for a uniquely distinguished Islam, in contrast to such people's conception. They must face these people bravely and put it to them explicitly: you have your own religion, and we have ours. Our religion is based on absolute monotheism whose concepts, values, beliefs and laws cover all aspects of human life and are all received from God and no one else.

Without this basic separation confusion, double-dealing, doubt and distortion will certainly persist. And let it be clear in our minds here that the movement advocating Islam can never be constructed on any ambiguous or feeble foundations, but has to be built upon firmness, explicitness, frankness and fortitude as embodied in God's instruction to us to declare: "*You have your own religion, and I have mine.*" (Verse 6) Such was the way adopted by the Islamic message in its early days.

SŪRAH 110

Al-Naṣr

(Divine Help)

Al-Naṣr (Divine Help)

سُورَةُ النَّصْرِ

In the name of God, the Beneficent, the Merciful.

بِسْمِ ٱللَّهِ ٱلرَّحْمَٰنِ ٱلرَّحِيمِ

When God's help and victory come, (1)

إِذَا جَآءَ نَصْرُ ٱللَّهِ وَٱلْفَتْحُ ١

and you see people embracing God's religion in large numbers (2)

وَرَأَيْتَ ٱلنَّاسَ يَدْخُلُونَ فِى
دِينِ ٱللَّهِ أَفْوَاجًا ٢

then extol your Lord's limitless glory, and praise Him, and seek His forgiveness. He is the One who accepts repentance. (3)

فَسَبِّحْ بِحَمْدِ رَبِّكَ وَٱسْتَغْفِرْهُ إِنَّهُۥ
كَانَ تَوَّابًۢا ٣

Overview

This short *sūrah* brings the good news to Muḥammad, God's Messenger, that God's help will be forthcoming, as will victory and peoples' collective acceptance of His religion. It instructs him to turn towards his Lord in devoted adoration coupled with a humble request for His forgiveness. The *sūrah* also presents the nature and the righteousness of this faith and its ideology, which elevates humanity to a standard of dignity, dedication and freedom that it can never attain except through responding to the call of Islam and implementing the Islamic message.

Of the several traditions regarding the revelation of this *sūrah*, we quote the one related by Imām Aḥmad which runs as follows: "'Ā'ishah said that God's Messenger used to repeat very frequently, towards the end of his life: 'All glorification and praises are due to God. I seek His forgiveness; and I repent of my sins.' He also said: 'My Lord told me I would see a sign in my community. He ordered me to glorify and praise Him, the Forgiving, and ask His pardon when I see this sign. Indeed, I have. *When God's help and victory come, and you see people embracing God's religion in large numbers then extol your Lord's limitless glory, and praise Him, and seek His forgiveness. He is the One who accepts repentance.*'" [Related also by Muslim with a different chain of transmission.]

Ibn Kathīr says in his commentary on the Qur'ān: "The victory mentioned in this *sūrah* refers, as unanimously agreed, to the conquest of Makkah. The Arab tribes were awaiting the settlement of the conflict between the Quraysh and the Muslims, before making a decision about their acceptance of Islam, saying that if Muḥammad were to prevail over his people, he would indeed be a prophet. Consequently, when that was accomplished they accepted Islam in large numbers. Within two years of the conquest of Makkah, the whole Arabian Peninsula was dominated by Islam, and, all thanks to God, every Arab tribe declared its belief in Islam."

In his *Ṣaḥīḥ* al-Bukhārī quotes 'Amr ibn Salamah as saying: "When Makkah fell to Islam, every tribe hastened to declare to God's

Messenger its acceptance of Islam. They were waiting for it to take place, saying, 'Leave him alone with his people. He would indeed be a prophet if he prevailed over them…'"

These reports are chronologically in line with the wording of the *sūrah*, in the sense that its revelation was a sign of something to follow, with some instructions to the Prophet on what he should do when this event would take place.

There is, nevertheless, a different report which is not difficult to reconcile with the one we have already discussed. 'Abdullāh ibn 'Abbās, the Prophet's cousin and learned Companion, reports: "'Umar used to let me join the company of elders who were present at Badr, but some of them felt uneasy and asked why I should be allowed with them when I was of the same age as their own children. But 'Umar said to them, 'You know to what family he belongs.' One day 'Umar invited them all and invited me as well. I felt that he wanted to show them why he gave me such a privilege. He asked them, 'What do you make of God's saying: *When God's help and victory come*?' Some of them replied, 'It is an order that we must praise Him and seek His forgiveness when He helps us to triumph and bestows His favours on us.' Others remained silent. Then 'Umar asked me, 'Do you agree with this view, Ibn 'Abbās?' I answered in the negative. 'Umar asked me again, 'What, then, do you say?' I replied, 'It was a sign from God to His Messenger indicating the approach of the end of his life. It means: *when God's help and victory come*, you should know that your end is near, *then extol your Lord's limitless glory, and praise Him, and seek His forgiveness. He is the One who accepts repentance*.'" 'Umar commented, 'To my knowledge, it only means what you have just said.'" [Related by al-Bukhārī.]

So it is possible that God's Messenger, having witnessed his Lord's sign, realized that he had fulfilled his mission in this life, and that it was time for him to depart, which was what Ibn 'Abbās actually meant.

A different report related by al-Bayhaqī, also on Ibn 'Abbās's authority, mentions that when this *sūrah* was first revealed, the

Prophet asked his daughter, Fāṭimah, to come over and told her, 'My death has been announced to me.' She was seen to start crying. But a little later she smiled. Some time later she explained, "I cried when he told me of his approaching death. But he then said to me, 'Be patient, because you will be the first of my household to join me', so I smiled."

According to this last *ḥadīth*, the time of the revelation of the *sūrah* is actually fixed as coming later than the sign. That is, the victory and the people's collective acceptance of Islam. When events took place in this fashion the Prophet knew that his life would soon come to a close. But again the first account is more authentic and fits in more suitably with the import of the *sūrah*, especially as the incident concerning Fāṭimah and her crying and smiling is related in a different context which agrees with the version we prefer. This other report goes as follows: "Umm Salamah, the Prophet's wife, said: 'The Prophet invited Fāṭimah one day during the year of the victory and spoke to her in private. She cried. Then he spoke to her again and she was smiling. After he died, I asked her about the incident and she explained, God's Messenger told me he was soon to die, so I cried. Then he told me that I would be the next most celebrated woman in heaven, next to Maryam bint 'Imrān, so I smiled.'" [Related by al-Tirmidhī.]

This report agrees with the general meaning of the Qur'ānic text and with what Imām Aḥmad related, which also appears in Muslim's *Ṣaḥīḥ*. That is, there was a sign between God and His Messenger, which the *sūrah* specifies. Hence, when the victory that secured Makkah to Islam was accomplished, the Prophet knew that he was soon to meet his Lord. Hence he spoke to Fāṭimah in the manner described by Umm Salamah.

An Awaited Event

We will now consider the permanent import and instructions outlined in this short *sūrah*: "*When God's help and victory come, and you see people embracing God's religion in large numbers, then extol your Lord's limitless glory, and praise Him, and seek His forgiveness. He is the One who accepts repentance.*" (Verses 1–3)

The beginning of the first verse implicitly presents a concept of what goes on in this universe and the events that take place in this life. It also covers the actual role of the Prophet and his followers in the progress of Islam, and to what extent it depends on their efforts. '*When God's help and victory...*', denotes that it is help granted by God, and it is He who brings about victory in His own good time, in the form He decides and for the purpose He determines. The Prophet and his Companions have nothing to do with it at all, and they obtain no personal gain from it. It suffices for them that He does it through them, appoints them as its guards and entrusts it to them. This is all they acquire from God's help, the victory and people's acceptance *en masse* of His religion.

According to this concept, the duty of the Prophet and his Companions whom God chose and gave the privilege of being the instruments of victory for His cause, was to turn to Him at the climax of victory in praise, expressing gratitude and seeking forgiveness. Gratitude and praise are for His being so generous as to have chosen them to be the standard-bearers of His religion; for the mercy and favour He did to all humanity by making His religion victorious; and for the conquest of Makkah and people's collective acceptance of Islam.

His forgiveness is sought for any defective feeling, privately entertained, such as vanity, which sometimes creep into one's heart when victory is attained after a long struggle. It is almost impossible for human beings to prevent this happening and therefore God's forgiveness is to be sought. Forgiveness also has to be sought for what might have been insinuated within one's heart during the long and cruel struggle and for petulance resulting from a conceived delay of victory, or the effects of convulsive despair, as the Qur'ān mentions elsewhere: "*Do you reckon that you will enter paradise while you have not suffered like those [believers] who passed away before you? Affliction and adversity befell them, and so terribly shaken were they that the Messenger and the believers with him would exclaim, 'When will God's help come?' Surely, God's help is close at hand.*" (2: 214)

It is also necessary to seek God's forgiveness for one's shortcomings in praising God and thanking Him for His infinite favours which are granted at all times. "*If you were to count God's favours, never will you be able to number them.*" (16: 18) However great one's efforts in this respect are, they are never adequate.

Seeking forgiveness at a moment of triumph also arouses feelings of weakness and imperfection at a time when an attitude of pride and conceit seems natural. All these factors guarantee that no tyranny will afflict the vanquished. The victorious leader is made to realize that it is God who has appointed him, a man who has no power of his own and who is devoid of any strength, for a predetermined purpose; consequently the triumph and the conquest as well as the religion are all His, and to Him all things ultimately return.

This is the lofty, dignified ideal the Qur'ān exhorts people to toil towards, an ideal in which man's exaltation is in neglecting his own pride and where his soul's freedom is in his subservience to God. The goal set is the total release of human souls from their egoistic shackles, their only ambition being to attain God's pleasure. Along with this release there must be exerted effort which helps man flourish in the world, promotes human civilization and provides a rightly-guided, unblemished, constructive, just leadership devoted to God.

By contrast, man's efforts to liberate himself while in the grip of egoism, shackled by his zest for worldly things, or overpowered by his cravings, turn out to be absolutely useless unless he frees himself from personal desires and ambitions. His loyalty to God must be made to override everything else, particularly at the moment of triumph and the collection of booty. Such behaviour, which God wants humanity to attain, was the characteristic feature of all the Prophets.

Such was the case with the Prophet Joseph, when all he wanted was achieved and his dream came true: "*And he raised his parents to the highest place of honour, and they fell down on their knees, prostrating themselves before him. He said: 'Father, this is the real meaning of my dream of long ago. My Lord has made it come true. He has been gracious to me, releasing me from prison, and bringing you all from the desert after Satan had sown discord between me and my brothers. My Lord is gracious in whatever way He wishes. He is All-Knowing, truly Wise.'*" (12: 100)

Then, at that moment of climax, Joseph took himself away from the jubilations and embracing arms to turn towards his Lord, praising Him with a pure sense of gratitude: "*My Lord, You have given me power and imparted to me some understanding of the real meaning of statements. Originator of the heavens and the earth! You are my guardian in this world and in the life to come. Let me die as one who has surrendered himself to You, and admit me among the righteous.*" (12: 101)

Thus any sense of his own egotism and happiness brought about by his reunion with his family vanished, and the picture we are left with is that of an individual, Joseph, praying to God to help him remain submissive to Him until he dies and to let him, out of His mercy and grace, join His righteous servants.

So, it was also with the Prophet Solomon, when he saw the Queen of Sheba's throne brought into his very reach: "*When he saw it set in his presence he said: 'This is of the bounty of my Lord, that He may try me whether I give thanks or remain ungrateful. He who gives thanks does so for his own good, and he who is ungrateful, well, my Lord is all sufficient and bountiful.'*" (27: 40)

And so indeed it was with Muḥammad throughout his life. In the moment of triumph, as the conquest of Makkah was accomplished, he entered the city on the back of his camel with his head bowed low. He forgot the joy of victory and thankfully bowed his head seeking his Lord's forgiveness, even though he had just conquered Makkah, whose people had openly and unashamedly persecuted and expelled him. This also was the practice of his Companions after him.

Thus, upon belief in God, was that great generation of humanity raised very high, reaching an unparalleled standard of greatness, power and freedom.

SŪRAH 111

Al-Masad

(Fire Flames)

Al-Masad (Fire Flames)	سُورَةُ المَسَدِ
In the name of God, the Beneficent, the Merciful.	بِسْمِ ٱللَّهِ ٱلرَّحْمَٰنِ ٱلرَّحِيمِ
Doomed are the hands of Abū Lahab; doomed is he. (1)	تَبَّتْ يَدَآ أَبِي لَهَبٍ وَتَبَّ ١
His wealth and his gains shall avail him nothing. (2)	مَآ أَغْنَىٰ عَنْهُ مَالُهُۥ وَمَا كَسَبَ ٢
He shall have to endure a flaming fire, (3)	سَيَصْلَىٰ نَارًا ذَاتَ لَهَبٍ ٣
and his wife, the carrier of firewood, (4)	وَٱمْرَأَتُهُۥ حَمَّالَةَ ٱلْحَطَبِ ٤
shall have a rope of palm fibre round her neck. (5)	فِي جِيدِهَا حَبْلٌ مِّن مَّسَدٍۭ ٥

Background

Abū Lahab, whose real name was 'Abd al-'Uzzā ibn 'Abd al-Muṭṭalib, was the Prophet's uncle. He was so nicknamed because of the radiant look on his face. Together with his wife, Abū Lahab was one of the most hostile opponents of God's Messenger and the ideas he propagated.

Ibn Isḥāq related the following report by Rabī'ah ibn 'Abbād al-Daylī: "When I was young I once watched, with my father, God's Messenger preaching Islam to the Arab tribes, saying 'O sons of... (calling their respective tribal names), I am God's Messenger sent to order you to submit to, and worship Him alone, invoking nothing else beside Him, and to believe in me and protect me until I carry out what God has entrusted to me.' A cross-eyed, bright-faced man was behind him, who used to say, after he had finished, 'O sons of... This man wants you to forsake al-Lāt and al-'Uzzā [two prominent idols worshipped by the pagan Arabs] and your allies of the *jinn*, the children of Mālik ibn Aqmas and to substitute for them these innovations and nonsense he has come up with. Do not listen to him, nor follow what he preaches.' I asked my father who that man was and he told me that it was Abū Lahab, the Prophet's uncle." [Related by Aḥmad and al-Ṭabarānī.]

This is but one incident of Abū Lahab's intimidation and ill-will towards the Prophet and his message. His wife, Arwā bint Ḥarb ibn Umayyah, Abū Sufyān's sister, gave him unfailing support in his virulent, relentless campaign.

Such was Abū Lahab's attitude towards the Prophet from the very start of his divine mission. Al-Bukhārī relates, on Ibn 'Abbās's authority, that "one day the Prophet went out to al-Baṭḥā', a large square in Makkah, climbed a hill and summoned the people of the Quraysh. When they came to him, he addressed them, saying, 'Were I to tell you that an enemy is drawing near and will attack you tomorrow morning or evening, would you believe me?' 'Yes,' they replied. 'So listen to me,' he went on, 'I am warning you of [God's] gruesome torment.' Abū Lahab was there and snapped at him, 'Damn you! For this have you called us?'" [Another version says: Abū Lahab stood up shaking the dust off his hands and saying, 'Damn you all day long...'] Then this *sūrah* was revealed.

Another instance was when the Hāshimite clan [i.e. the Prophet's own clan], under Abū Ṭālib's leadership, decided on grounds of tribal loyalty to protect the Prophet despite their rejection of the religion he preached. Abū Lahab was the only one to take a different stand. He joined with the Quraysh instead, and was with them in signing the document imposing a complete social and business boycott on the Hashimites so as to starve them out unless they delivered the Prophet to them.

Abū Lahab also ordered his two sons to renounce Muḥammad's two daughters to whom they had been engaged before Muḥammad's prophetic assignment. His aim was to burden the Prophet with their living and welfare expenses.

Thus, Abū Lahab and his wife, Arwā, who was also called Umm Jamīl, continued with their persistent onslaught against the Prophet and his message. The fact that they were close neighbours of the Prophet made the situation even worse. We are told that Umm Jamīl used to carry thorns and sharp wood and place them along the Prophet's path [although it is thought that the phrase *'the carrier of firewood'* in the *sūrah* is used only metaphorically to indicate her lies and malice about him].

The Final Word

This *sūrah* was revealed as a counterattack against Abū Lahab's and his wife's hostile campaign. God took it upon Himself to say the final word on behalf of His Messenger.

"*Doomed are the hands of Abū Lahab; doomed is he.*" (Verse 1) The Arabic term, *tabba*, rendered here as 'doomed' also signifies failure and cutting off. The term is used twice in two different senses. It is used first as a prayer, while in the second instance it implies that the prayer has been already answered. So, in one short verse, an action is realized which draws the curtains upon a battle scene. What later follows is merely a description of what took place with the remark that "*his wealth and his gains shall avail him nothing.*" (Verse 2) He can have no escape. He is defeated, vanquished and damned.

This was his fate in this world, but in the hereafter "*he shall have to endure a flaming fire.*" (Verse 3) The fire is described as having flames in order to emphasize that it is raging.

"*And his wife, the carrier of firewood,*" will reside there with him having "*a rope of palm-fibre round her neck,*" with which, as it were, she is being dragged into hell, or which she used for fastening wood bundles together, according to whether a literal or metaphorical interpretation of the text is adopted.

The language of this *sūrah* achieves remarkable harmony between the subject matter and the atmosphere built around it. Abū Lahab will be plunged into a fire with *lahab*, which is the Arabic for flames; and his wife who carries the wood, a fuel, will be met with the same fire with a palm-fibre rope around her neck. Hell, with its fiercely burning *lahab*, or flames, will be inhabited by Abū Lahab. At the same time his wife, who collects thorns and sharp woods, materials which can significantly increase the blaze of a fire, puts them all in the Prophet's way. Hence, she will, in time, be dragged into hell with a rope tied round her neck, bundled like firewood. How perfectly matched are the words and the pictures portrayed: the punishment is presented as being of the same nature as the deed: wood, ropes, fire and *lahab*!

Phonetically, the words are arranged in a way which provides wonderful harmony between the sounds made by the tying of wood into bundles and pulling the neck by ropes. Read in Arabic the opening verse, "*Tabbat yadā abī Lahabin wa tabb.*" You will not fail to note that it sounds like a hard sharp tug, analogous to that of bundles of wood or an unwilling person being dragged by the neck into a wild fire; all is in phase with the fury and violent, bellicose tone that goes with the theme of the *sūrah*. Thus, in five short verses making up one of the shortest *sūrahs* in the Qur'ān, the vocal melodies click neatly with the actual movement of the scene portrayed.

This extremely rich and powerful style led Umm Jamīl to claim that the Prophet was in fact satirizing her and her husband. This arrogant and vain woman could not get over being referred to by such a humiliating phrase as '*the carrier of firewood,*' who '*shall have a rope of palm fibre round her neck.*' Her rage grew wilder when the *sūrah* became popular among the Arab tribes who greatly appreciated such fine literary style!

Ibn Isḥāq relates: "Umm Jamīl, I was told, having heard what the Qur'ān said about her and her husband, came to the Prophet who was with Abū Bakr at the Ka'bah. She was carrying a handful of stones. God took her sight away from the Prophet and she saw only Abū Bakr to whom she said, 'Where is your comrade? I have heard that he has been satirizing me. Were I to find him, I would throw these stones right into his face. I, too, am gifted in poetry.' Then she chanted before leaving:

> The contemptible we obey not!
> Nor what he says shall we accept!

"Abū Bakr turned around to the Prophet and said, 'Do you think that she saw you?' 'No,' replied the Prophet, 'God made her unable to see me.'"

Al-Bazzār relates on Ibn 'Abbās's authority that "when this *sūrah* was revealed Abū Lahab's wife sought the Prophet. While he was with Abū Bakr she appeared. Abū Bakr suggested to the Prophet: 'She will not harm you if you move out of her sight.' 'Do not worry,' said the Prophet in a soothing manner. 'She will not see me.' She came to Abū Bakr and said: 'Your friend has lampooned us!' 'By the Lord of this Ka'bah, he has not,' Abū Bakr assured her. 'He is no poet and what he says is not poetry,' he added. She said, 'I believe you,' and then left. Abū Bakr then enquired from the Prophet whether she had seen him and he said, 'No, an angel was shielding me all the time she was here.' So much was her fury and her indignation at what she thought was poetry and which Abū Bakr rightly refuted.

Thus, the humiliating picture of Abū Lahab and his wife has been recorded to last forever in this eternal book, the Qur'ān, to show God's anger with them for their animosity towards His Messenger and message. All those who choose to take a similar attitude towards Islam, therefore, will meet with the same disgrace, humiliation and frustration, both in this life and in the life to come.

SŪRAH 112

Al-Ikhlāṣ

(Purity of Faith)

Al-Ikhlāṣ (Purity of Faith)

In the name of God, the Beneficent, the Merciful.

Say: He is God, the One and only God (1)

the Eternal, the Absolute. (2)

He begets none, nor is He begotten, (3)

and there is nothing that could be compared to Him. (4)

سُورَةُ الإخلاص

بِسْمِ ٱللَّهِ ٱلرَّحْمَٰنِ ٱلرَّحِيمِ

قُلْ هُوَ ٱللَّهُ أَحَدٌ ١

ٱللَّهُ ٱلصَّمَدُ ٢

لَمْ يَلِدْ وَلَمْ يُولَدْ ٣

وَلَمْ يَكُن لَّهُۥ كُفُوًا أَحَدٌۢ ٤

God's Absolute Oneness

This short *sūrah* is equivalent to one-third of the Qur'ān, as authentic *aḥādīth* confirm. Al-Bukhārī, the leading *Ḥadīth* scholar, relates a ḥadīth which mentions the case of one who had heard another man reciting this *sūrah* repeatedly. He went to the Prophet the following morning and told him disapprovingly about what he had heard, as though he felt that it was too little. The Prophet commented, "I swear by Him who holds my soul in His hand that it [i.e. this *sūrah*] is equivalent to one third of the Qur'ān."

And, indeed, there is nothing surprising in that. For God's oneness which the Prophet was ordered to declare to the whole world is a belief to be ingrained in our minds, an explanation of human existence and a way of life in itself. From this standpoint, the *sūrah* can be said to have embraced, in the clearest of terms, the principal and most fundamental ideas of the great truth of Islam.

The Arabic term, *aḥad*, used here to refer to God's oneness is much more precise than the more frequently used term, *wāḥid*, which means 'one'. *Aḥad* has the added connotations of absolute and continuous unity and an absence of equals.

God's oneness is such that there is no reality and no true and permanent existence except His. Moreover, every other being acquires whatever power it may possess from God who rules over this world. Nothing else whatsoever plans anything for the world nor, for that matter, decides anything in it.

This is the belief that should be entrenched in us. It gives us a full explanation of human existence. Once this belief is clear and the explanation has established itself in our minds, our hearts are purified of all falsities and impurities. They are thus released from all bonds except their bond with the Unique Being to whom alone the reality of existence belongs and who is the only effective power in this world. Thus, the human heart is released from bondage to anything in this world, even if it cannot shirk the notion that other beings exist. Indeed, why should our hearts aspire to anything that has neither a permanent reality, nor any independent power to function in this world? The only real existence is that of the Divine Being and the truly effective power is Divine Will.

When a human heart releases itself from believing in anything but the one truth of God, and upholds this everlasting truth, it begins to enjoy its freedom from all shackles, false ideas, evil desires, fears and confusions of any sort. Indeed, when a human heart finds God, it benefits much and loses nothing. So why should it desire anything but God's pleasure? Why should it fear anything, since there is no absolutely effective power but that of God?

When a concept that sees nothing in the world but the reality of God establishes itself in our hearts and minds, we begin to see this genuine and permanent reality in everything He has made. This is when our hearts feel the hand of God in everything. There is only one level beyond this and that is when our hearts feel nothing but God's reality in the whole universe.

Thus, every event and every movement in this life and in the universe is attributed to the first and only cause; that is, God who brings other causes into play and influences their effectiveness. The Qur'ān takes great care to establish this truth. It has always put aside apparent causes, associating events directly with God's will. It says: "*When you threw [a handful of dust] it was not your act, but God's.*" (8: 17) "*For victory comes only from God.*" (8: 10 and 3: 126) "*You have no will except as God wills.*" (76: 30)

By disregarding all apparent causes and connecting matters directly with God's will, a feeling of relief gently penetrates our hearts so that we recognize the only Saviour from whom we can ask whatever we may wish, and by whom we are rescued from all fear. We are no longer impressed by apparent influences, reasons and causes that bear no reality or true existence in themselves.

These are the steps of the way some mystics, or Sufis, tried to climb, but they deviated too far from it. For Islam wants people to follow this route struggling with the realities of life, and leading a human life in which they exercise the role God has assigned to human beings on earth, using all their resources and fulfilling all the obligations laid upon them.

From this concept of God's oneness stems a perfect way of life based on an explanation of human existence and whatever outlooks, feelings, and traits it stimulates. This way of life is based on the worship of God alone whose will is the only effective power in the world. Thus, people seek refuge with Him in times of need and fear, happiness and discomfort, ease and hardship. For what is the use of turning towards a non-existent or powerless being? This way of life looks to God alone as its benefactor. From Him we receive our beliefs, outlooks, values, criteria, legislation, institutions, systems, ethics and traditions.

A Complete Way of Life

On this basis a complete way of life is formulated, in which people perform all their activities and make sacrifices absolutely and only for God, hoping always to be nearer the truth. This way of life strengthens bonds of love, brotherhood, mutual sympathy and care between all beings and human hearts. For when we speak of liberation from complete submission to these feelings we are by no means suggesting that people should despise or hate them or escape from practising them. Instead they arise from the creative hand of God and they all owe their existence to Him. They are a gift to us from God who loves us and whom we love. Therefore, they deserve our love.

It is a sublime and lofty way of life that looks at this earth as small, life as short, its enjoyments and luxuries as worth little; and the breaking away from hindrances as humanity's great aim. In Islam, however, this release does not mean seclusion, isolation and neglect, nor does it mean contempt for, or escape from life. Instead it simply means a continuous and sincere endeavour and an everlasting struggle to lead humanity towards submission of everything in human life to God alone. Consequently, it is the fulfilment of man's role as God's vicegerent on earth with all its obligations, as we have already explained.

Liberation of the soul through a life of isolation and extreme spiritualism is easy to achieve but Islam does not approve of it, because it wants its followers to fulfil man's role assigned to him by God who placed him in charge of the earth and to provide the leadership humanity needs. This is the harder way that guarantees man's elevation and achieves the victory of divine will within him. This is real liberation, for it urges the human soul to fly to its divine source and achieve its sublime status within the scope God, the wise Creator, has defined for it.

For the sake of all this, the first address the Islamic message made was devoted to the establishment of the reality of God's oneness in people's hearts and minds. In this form, the Islamic message is seen by the soul, heart and mind, as a full explanation of human existence, a way of life and not merely a spoken word or an inert belief. It is life in its entirety and religion in its totality. Whatever details are later put in place are no more than the natural fruits of its establishment in people's hearts and minds.

All the deviations that afflicted the followers of earlier divine religions, and which corrupted their beliefs, ideas and lives arose, in the first place, from a deterioration of the concept of God's absolute oneness in their minds. But what distinguishes this concept in the Islamic faith is the fact that it is deeply rooted throughout human life. Indeed, it forms the foundation of a realistic and practical system for human life, clearly reflected in both legislation and belief.

To say, "*He is God, the One and only God,*" (Verse 1) means that "*He is the Eternal, the Absolute,*" (Verse 2) and that "*He begets none, nor is He begotten, and there is nothing that could be compared to Him.*" (Verses 3–4) But the Qur'ān states it all in detail for added emphasis and clarification.

"*The Eternal, the Absolute*" also means the Lord to whom all creation turns for help, and without whose permission nothing is decided. God is the One and only Lord. He is the One God and Master while all other beings are but His servants. To Him and Him alone are addressed all prayers and supplications. He and only He decides everything independently. No one shares His authority.

"*He begets none, nor is He begotten,*" means that the reality of God is deep-rooted, permanent and everlasting. No changeable circumstances ever affect it. Its quality is absolute perfection at all times. Birth is descent and multiplication and implies a developed being after incompleteness or nothingness. It requires espousal which is based on similarity of being and structure. All this is utterly impossible in God's case. So the quality of 'One' includes the renouncement of a father and a son.

"*There is nothing that could be compared to Him,*" means that no one resembles Him in anything or is equivalent to Him in any respect, either in their reality of being, in the fact that He is the only effective power, or in any of His qualities or attributes. This is implied in the statement of his being 'One' made in the first verse, but it is repeated so as to confirm and elaborate upon that fact. It is a renunciation of the two-god belief which implies that God is the God of Good while Evil has its own lord who, as the belief goes – is in opposition to God, spoils His good deeds and propagates evil on earth. The most well-known two-god belief was that of the Persians, who believed in a god of light and a god of darkness. This belief was known to the people in the south of the Arabian Peninsula, where the Persians once had a state and exercised sovereignty.

This *sūrah* firmly establishes and confirms the Islamic belief in God's oneness just as *Sūrah* 109, The Unbelievers, is a denunciation of any similarity or meeting point between the Islamic concept of God's oneness and any belief that ascribes human form, attributes, or personality to God. Each *sūrah* deals with God's oneness from a different angle. The Prophet used to start off his day reciting these two *sūrahs* in the *sunnah,* or voluntary prayer before the obligatory dawn or *fajr* prayer. This, surely, was immensely significant.

SŪRAH 113

Al-Falaq

(The Daybreak)

Al-Falaq (The Daybreak)

سُورَةُ الفَلَقِ

In the name of God, the Beneficent, the Merciful.

بِسْمِ ٱللَّهِ ٱلرَّحْمَٰنِ ٱلرَّحِيمِ

Say: I seek refuge in the Lord of the Daybreak, (1)

قُلْ أَعُوذُ بِرَبِّ ٱلْفَلَقِ ١

from the evil of anything that He has created; (2)

مِن شَرِّ مَا خَلَقَ ٢

from the evil of darkness when it gathers; (3)

وَمِن شَرِّ غَاسِقٍ إِذَا وَقَبَ ٣

from the evil of the conjuring witches; (4)

وَمِن شَرِّ ٱلنَّفَّٰثَٰتِ فِى ٱلْعُقَدِ ٤

from the evil of the envious when he envies. (5)

وَمِن شَرِّ حَاسِدٍ إِذَا حَسَدَ ٥

Overview

This *sūrah*, along with the following one, Mankind, contains a directive from God primarily to His Prophet and secondly to the believers at large, to take refuge in Him and seek His protection in the face of any source of fear, subtle or apparent, known or unknown. It is as if God – limitless is He in His glory – is unfolding His world of care, and embracing the believers in His guard. He is kindly and affectionately calling on them to resort to His care through which they will feel safe and at peace. It is as if He is saying to them: I know that you are helpless and surrounded by foes and fears. Come to Me for safety, contentment and peace. Hence, the two *sūrahs* start with, "*Say: I seek refuge in the Lord of the Daybreak,*" and, "*Say: I seek refuge in the Lord of mankind.*"

Several accounts have been handed down concerning the revelation and popularity of these two *sūrahs*. They all fit in neatly with the above interpretation that God, the Most Merciful, offers His care and shelter to His faithful servants. God's Messenger loved these two *sūrahs* profoundly, as is clearly apparent in his traditions.

'Uqba ibn 'Āmir, a Companion of the Prophet, reports that the Prophet said to him: "Have you not heard the unique verses that were revealed last night, '*Say: I seek refuge in the Lord of the Daybreak,*' and '*Say: I seek refuge in the Lord of mankind.*'" [Related by Mālik, Muslim, al-Tirmidhī, Abū Dāwūd and al-Nasā'ī.]

Jābir, the Prophet's Companion, said: "God's Messenger said to me once, 'Jābir! Recite!' and I asked, 'What shall I recite?' He replied, 'Recite, '*Say: I seek refuge in the Lord of the Daybreak,*' and ' *Say: I seek refuge in the Lord of mankind.*' So I recited them and he commented, 'Recite them [as often as you can] for you shall never recite anything equivalent to them.'" [Related by al-Nasā'ī.]

Dharr ibn Ḥubaysh said that he had inquired from Ubayy ibn Ka'b, the Prophet's Companion, about *al-Mu'awwadhatayn*, a name that refers to these two *sūrahs* together, saying, "Abū al-Mundhir! Your brother, Ibn Mas'ūd says so and so. (For some time Ibn Mas'ūd was under the false impression that these two *sūrahs* were not part of the Qur'ān, but he later admitted his mistake.) What do you think of that?" He replied, "I asked God's Messenger about this and he told me that he had been instructed to say the text of these *sūrahs* and he had carried out the instruction. We surely say the same as God's Messenger had said." [Related by al-Bukhārī.] All these reports throw powerful light on that underlying factor of God's kindness and love to which the two *sūrahs* draw attention.

Protection against Evil

God – limitless is He in His glory – refers to Himself in this *sūrah* as the Lord of the daybreak. The Arabic term, *falaq*, simply means 'daybreak', but it could be taken to mean 'the whole phenomenon of creation,' with reference to everything springing forth into life. This interpretation is supported by God's saying in *Sūrah* 6, Cattle: "*It is God who splits (fāliq) the grain and the fruit-stone. He brings forth the living out of that which is dead ... He is the One who causes the day to break (fāliq). He has made the night to be [a source of] stillness, and the sun and the moon for reckoning.*" (6: 95–96) If the meaning 'daybreak' is adopted, refuge is being sought from the unseen and the mysterious with the Lord of the daybreak, who bestows safety as He kindles the light of day. If, however, *fāliq* is taken to mean 'creation', then refuge from the evil of some creature is being sought with the Lord of all creation. In both cases, harmony with the theme of the *sūrah* is maintained.

"*From the evil of anything that He has created.*" (Verse 2) The phrase contains no exceptions or specifications. Mutual contact between various creatures, though no doubt advantageous, brings about some evil. Refuge from it is sought with God by the believers in order to encourage the goodness such a contact produces. For He who created those creatures is surely able to provide the right circumstances that lead them on a course where only the bright side of their contact prevails.

"*From the evil of darkness* [*i.e. ghāsiq*] *when it gathers [i.e. waqab].*" (Verse 3) From a linguistic point of view, *ghāsiq*, means 'substantially pouring out' and *waqb* is the name given to a little hole in a mountain through which water issues forth, while *waqab* is the verb denoting such an action. What is probably meant here is the night, with all that accompanies it when it rapidly engulfs the world. This is terrifying in itself. In addition it fills our hearts with the possibility of an unknown, unexpected discomfort caused by a savage beast, an unscrupulous villain, a striking enemy or a hissing poisonous creature, as well as anxieties and worries [which may lead to depression and uneasiness], evil thoughts and passions that are liable to revive in the dark, during one's state of solitude at night. This is the evil against which the believer needs God's protection.

"*From the evil of conjuring witches,*" (Verse 4) refers to various types of magic, whether by deceiving people's physical senses or by influencing their will-power and projecting ideas onto their emotions and minds. The verse specially refers to a form of witchcraft carried out by women in Arabia at the time who tied knots in cords and blew upon them with an imprecation.

Magic is the production of illusions, subject to a magician's designs, and it does not offer any kind of new facts or alter the nature of things. This is how the Qur'ān describes magic when relating the story of Moses in *Sūrah* 20, Ṭā Hā: "*They [Pharaoh's magicians] said, 'Moses, Will you throw down your gear first or shall we be the first to throw?' He said: 'Throw down yours.' And by the power of their magic, their cords and staffs appeared to him as though they were running. Moses conceived a secret fear within him. But We said: 'Fear not! You shall have the upper hand. Throw that which is in your right hand! It will swallow up that which they have made. That which they have made is but the deceitful show of witchcraft. Come where he may, a magician shall never be successful.'*" (20: 65–69). Thus, their cords and staffs did not actually turn into snakes but it seemed so to the onlookers, Moses included, to the point where he felt uneasy inside. He was restrained by the transformation of his own stick into a real snake, by God's doing, to destroy the phoney ones.

This is the nature of magic as we ought to conceive it. Through it a magician is capable of influencing other people's minds, causing them to think and act according to his own suggestions. We refrain from going any further with this. It is indeed an evil from which God's protection needs to be sought.

A few unsupported reports, some of which have been quoted by authentic sources, allege that after the Prophet had settled in Madinah, Labīd ibn al-Aʿṣam, a Jew, put a magic spell on him that affected the Prophet for several days or months so that, according to some versions, he felt he was having marital relations with his wives when he was not; or, according to others, thought of having done something when he had not. According to these reports, by reciting this *sūrah* and the next one, Mankind, he was released from such a state.

But surely these stories contradict the very idea of the Prophet's infallibility in word and deed and do not agree with the belief that all his actions are indicative of the Islamic way of life for all Muslims. Above all, they conflict with the Qur'ānic statements emphatically denying his being influenced by any kind of magic whatsoever, as claimed by some opponents of Islam. Hence, we dismiss such stories, on the grounds that the Qur'ān is the ultimate arbiter, and that singularly narrated traditions are left out in matters concerning faith. These stories have not had proper backing, which is an essential qualification for a tradition to be accepted as authentic. What weakens such stories even further is that the two *sūrahs* were revealed in Makkah while these stories relate the incident as having occurred some years later, in Madinah!

"*And from the evil of the envious when he envies.*" (Verse 5) Envy is the evil, begrudging reaction one feels towards another who has received some favour from God. It is also accompanied by a very strong desire for the end to such favours. It is also possible that some harm to the envied may result from such a baseless grudge. This may either be the outcome of direct physical action by the envier, or from suppressed feelings alone.

We should not be uneasy to learn that there are countless inexplicable mysteries in life. There are several phenomena for which no account has been offered up till now. Telepathy and hypnosis are two such examples.

We should not try to deny the psychological effects of envy on the envied person just because we cannot ascertain how this takes place by scientific means and methods. Very little is known about the mysteries of envy and the little that is known has often been uncovered by chance and coincidence. In any case, there is in envy an evil from which the refuge and protection of God must be sought. For He, the Most Generous, Most Merciful, who knows all things, has directed the Prophet and his followers to seek His refuge from such evil. It is unanimously agreed by all Islamic schools of thought that God will always protect His servants from such evils, should they seek His protection as He has directed them to do.

Al-Bukhārī relates that 'Ā'ishah said: "The Prophet would blow into both hands when getting into bed to sleep, and recite: '*Say: He is God, the One...*' and, '*Say: I seek refuge in the Lord of the Daybreak...*' and, '*Say: I seek refuge in the Lord of mankind*', and, starting with his head, he would run his palms over his face and the front part of his body, before running them over the rest of his body. He did this three times." [Also related by Abū Dāwūd, al-Tirmidhī and al-Nasā'ī.]

SŪRAH 114

Al-Nās

(Mankind)

Al-Nās (Mankind)

سُورَةُ ٱلنَّاسِ

In the name of God, the Beneficent, the Merciful.

بِسْمِ ٱللَّهِ ٱلرَّحْمَٰنِ ٱلرَّحِيمِ

Say: I seek refuge in the Lord of mankind, (1)

قُلْ أَعُوذُ بِرَبِّ ٱلنَّاسِ ﴿١﴾

the King of mankind, (2)

مَلِكِ ٱلنَّاسِ ﴿٢﴾

the God of mankind, (3)

إِلَٰهِ ٱلنَّاسِ ﴿٣﴾

from the mischief of the slinking prompter, (4)

مِن شَرِّ ٱلْوَسْوَاسِ ٱلْخَنَّاسِ ﴿٤﴾

who whispers in the hearts of mankind, (5)

ٱلَّذِى يُوَسْوِسُ فِى صُدُورِ
ٱلنَّاسِ ﴿٥﴾

from among *jinn* and mankind. (6)	مِنَ ٱلۡجِنَّةِ وَٱلنَّاسِ ۝٦

The Lord of Mankind

In this *sūrah* refuge is sought in the Lord, Sovereign and God of mankind from the insidious whisperer, *jinn* or human, who prompts evil ideas in people's minds. The *sūrah* presents God's relevant attributes to keep away this invisible evil which the mind on its own cannot shut out. For the Lord is He who preserves, directs, cherishes and protects mankind; the Sovereign is He who owns, governs and independently runs the world; and God is the One who supersedes all other beings and supervises over all their affairs. The particular mention of mankind here brings man closer to God's protection and care.

God, in His grace, instructs His Messenger and his community of followers to recognize these of His attributes, and to seek His protection against this sneaking evil which locates itself within their hearts. For they cannot rid themselves of such an evil which surreptitiously and imperceptibly creeps into their hearts, unless they are helped by God, the Lord, the Sovereign.

The nature of this evil-importing medium is identified in the text first as '*the slinking prompter.*' Its function is outlined as to '*whisper in the hearts of mankind.*' Then its origin is specified as '*from among* jinn *and mankind.*'

The style adopted here is quite significant because it draws our attention fully to the identity of this sneaking whisperer after describing its nature in order to show the process by which such evil is insinuated. This enables us to be alert and able to confront it. When we are given the full picture we know that this sneaking whisperer operates secretly. We also realize that it can be either *jinn* or human, for human beings can easily spread their evil stealthily.

We do not know how the *jinn* perform this whispering, but we certainly find its repercussions in the behaviour of individuals as well as in human life generally. We know for sure that the battle between Adam (man) and Iblīs (Satan) is a very old one. War between the two was declared by Satan out of the evil inherent in him, his conceit, envy and resentment of man. He was given God's permission to carry out this battle for some purpose which only God knows. But, significantly, man has not been left alone, dispossessed of the necessary means of protection. He has been provided with the power of faith, [that is, conscious belief in, and knowledge of, God and His attributes through conviction and sincere devotion]. Meditation and seeking refuge in God are among the most effective weapons. When man neglects these means of security and defence, he indeed has only himself to blame.

Ibn ʿAbbās quotes the Prophet as saying: "Satan besieges a person's heart, but he subsides whenever that person conscientiously remembers God. He only insinuates his evil when a person is heedless of Him."

As for humans, we know a great deal of their curious ways of whispering and prompting. Some types are more devilish than the Devil, such as: 1) a bad companion who injects evil into his comrade's heart and mind while he is unaware, thinking his friend to be trustworthy; 2) a ruler's counsellor or advisor who 'whispers' all sorts of evil thoughts to him, trying to turn him into a tyrant; 3) an unscrupulous slanderer who fabricates and decorates tales to make them sound factual and convincing; 4) a hustler of immoral business dealings who tries to get through to people by exploiting their sensual, carnal desires. There are scores of other 'whisperers' who inconspicuously lay their traps, utilizing different weak points which they deliberately look for. These are more devilish than even the *jinn* themselves. Faced with evil in this guise, man is incapable of ensuring his own safety. God therefore points out to him the means he can employ in this fierce battle.

There is also a very direct significance in describing the '*prompter*' as '*slinking*'. While this description indicates the secretiveness of the whisperer on the one hand, it is, on the other, an illusion to its intrinsic feebleness whenever it is discovered or resisted. It subsides and meekly withdraws when met in the open; or, as the Messenger said in his accurate illustration: "He (Satan) subsides whenever one conscientiously remembers God, but insinuates his evil whenever one is heedless of Him." This fortifies any believer's heart against this timid, subsiding whisperer.

Nevertheless, the battle is everlasting since this '*prompter*' is always watchful for the right moment, when one neglects remembrance of God, to implant its evils. For a believer to be conscious of God once in a while is not sufficient, as the war continues till the end of time. The Qur'ān vividly states this in a scene that is full of life:

> *When We said to the angels, 'Prostrate yourselves before Adam,' they all prostrated themselves; but not so Iblīs [Satan]. He said, 'Am I to bow down before one whom You have created out of clay?' [And] he added: 'Do You see this being whom You have exalted above me? Indeed, if You will give me respite until the Day of Resurrection, I shall bring his descendants, all but a few, under my sway.' [God] said: "Begone! As for those of them who follow you, hell will be the recompense of you all, a most ample recompense. Entice with your voice such of them as you can. Muster against them all your cavalry and your infantry, and share with them wealth and offspring, and promise them [what you will] – indeed, whatever Satan promises them is nothing but a means of deception. But over My servants you shall have no power. Your Lord is sufficient as a Guardian.* (17: 61–65)

This concept of the battle and the source of evil in it, whether provoked by Satan himself or by his human agent, inspires man to feel that he is not helpless in it; since God, his Lord and Sovereign of the universe controls all creations and events. Though He has permitted Satan to attack, He has supreme power over him and He has also provided guidance for mankind. God leaves to Satan only those who neglect Him. By contrast, those who live in consciousness of Him are safe and protected against his intimidation and incitements. Thus, righteousness is supported by the only true power, God's, whereas evil is backed by a '*slinking prompter*', a sneaky whisperer, cowardly in the open field, quick to retreat in war, and easily defeated when we seek refuge with God.

This is the most perfect concept of the battle between good and evil. It is a concept which protects human beings against defeat and provides them with strength, confidence and contentment.

Praise be to God at the beginning and at the end. From Him we derive confidence and success. To Him we turn for unfailing support.

Index

H

I

N

O

P